Conrad Weiser
Pennsylvania Peacemaker

Arthur D. Graeff

an imprint of Sunbury Press, Inc.
Mechanicsburg, PA USA

an imprint of Sunbury Press, Inc.
Mechanicsburg, PA USA

First Edition Copyright © 1945 by Arthur D. Graeff.
Second Edition Copyright © 2019 by Lawrence Knorr.
Cover Copyright © 2019 by Sunbury Press, Inc.
All photographs Copyright © 2014–2019 by
Lawrence Knorr. All rights reserved.

Sunbury Press supports copyright. Copyright fuels creativity, encourages diverse voices, promotes free speech, and creates a vibrant culture. Thank you for buying an authorized edition of this book and for complying with copyright laws. Except for the quotation of short passages for the purpose of criticism and review, no part of this publication may be reproduced, scanned, or distributed in any form without permission. You are supporting writers and allowing Sunbury Press to continue to publish books for every reader. For information contact Sunbury Press, Inc., Subsidiary Rights Dept., PO Box 548, Boiling Springs, PA 17007 USA or legal@sunburypress.com.

For information about special discounts for bulk purchases, please contact Sunbury Press Orders Dept. at (855) 338-8359 or orders@sunburypress.com.

To request one of our authors for speaking engagements or book signings, please contact Sunbury Press Publicity Dept. at publicity@sunburypress.com.

ISBN: 978-1-62006-194-7 (Trade paperback)

Library of Congress Control Number: Application in Process

FIRST DISTELFINK PRESS EDITION: August 2019

Product of the United States of America
0 1 1 2 3 5 8 13 21 34 55

Set in Bookman Old Style
Designed by Crystal Devine
Cover design (2nd edition): Lawrence Knorr
Editor (1st edition): Marie Knorr Graeff
Editor (2nd edition) and index: Lawrence Knorr

Continue the Enlightenment!

𝔅𝔩𝔢𝔰𝔰𝔢𝔡 are the peacemakers, for they shall be called the children of God.

—Matthew 5:9

CONTENTS

Preface		vii
I.	The Exodus to Canaan	1
II.	Clearing the Path of Friendship	16
III.	Mid-Winter Journey to Onondaga	41
IV.	Expanding Indian Affairs	59
V.	A Perplexed Christian	74
VI.	A Man of Affairs	99
VII.	A Diversity of Duties	112
VIII.	The Treaty of Lancaster	138
IX.	Two Missions to New York	165
X.	Standing "Newter"	188
XI.	To the Ohio Country	206
XII.	Rival Claims	228
XIII.	Building Bridgeheads for Peace	245
XIV.	Inter-Colony Quarrels	271
XV.	The Founder of Institutions	301
XVI.	The Storm	320
XVII.	Treaties of Easton	357
XVIII.	Posterity Will Not Forget	378
Epilogue	The Legacy of Conrad Weiser *by Lawrence Knorr*	386
Afterword	My Friend Arthur Graeff *by George M. Meiser, IX*	392
Index		395

Preface

In presenting Conrad Weiser to the reading public, the author makes no claims to have written a definitive biography of the man. The fabric of this account is woven from the threads of Weiser's eventful life. There is, however, no attempt to reconstruct a fully-rounded picture of the man who moved through these scenes. The student of genealogy will be obliged to look elsewhere for the details of Weiser's ancestry and the extent and relationship of his offspring.

The writer has deliberately confined his account to recorded and documented facts, reluctantly omitting legends and traditions which surround the memory of his subject. Some of the legends commonly associated with him are attributed to more than one person amid these colonial scenes. Such we leave to the story-teller.

The one objective held constantly in view throughout the progress of this study has been to set forth the services rendered by this remarkable man against the backdrop of colonial history. For we believe that our generation can profit by the examples set by men who met and solved the problems of their own day and age. Thus, biography can be made functional in our own time and the printed page does more than merely rattle the bones of history. With this objective in view, there was no room for mere hero-worship or for sensational revelations tending merely to discredit earlier contributions.

The author wishes to have his work considered as the narrative of Conrad Weiser, rather than an attempt to interpret the character of the man. To achieve this aim it has been necessary to go far afield, across the colonies north of the Potomac, into Ohio, and into French Canada. It has been necessary to construct and organize into one continuous story a segment of history for which there were but few guideposts and historically accepted channels.

If in his efforts to bring together the many factors which enter into this narrative, the author has failed to present a coherent picture at all times, he has tried at least to present a correct one thoroughly documented and derived almost entirely from original sources.

Arthur Dundore Graeff
Robesonia, Pennsylvania

CHAPTER I

The Exodus to Canaan

"In the year 1696, on the 2nd of November, I, Conrad Weiser, was born in Europe, in the land of Württemberg, in the county of Herrenberg, the village is called Astaet, and was christened at Kupingen, near by ---------." (From Conrad Weiser's autobiography written circa 1758.)

Devastating and cruel wars had ruined the farms and villages of German Protestants whose homes and farms lay in the path of contending armies. For thirty years, from 1618 to 1648, the southern portions of Germany had been ransacked and ravaged by one invader after another. The Treaty of Westphalia brought only temporary peace to the harassed population of the lower Rhine valley. The rapacity of the two French Louis, the Fourteenth and Fifteenth, combined with the outrages perpetrated in the name of Christianity by bigoted zealots within the afflicted areas, made life intolerable for the one-tenth of the native population which had survived all scourges prior to 1709. Then a new hope appeared on the northern horizons.

The Palatine exodus from the Lower Rhine valley took the form of mass migration during the spring and summer of 1709. Thousands of distressed farmers and tradesmen salvaged what they could from the wrecked homes and ravaged fields to follow the only prospect of rescue that was left to them. In far-away England a benevolent queen had been touched by the reports of their miseries and her generous heart had prompted her to offer sanctuary to her fellow Protestants. It was no mere perfunctory gesture by which the early Germans spoke of her as "Good Queen Anne." Her generosity did not end with an invitation or with an assurance of hospitality. It was a continuing factor in all her dealings with the Palatine refugees who became wards of her kingdom. Certainly, she must have known sorrow in her own life, for this fecund queen was the mother of seventeen children, not one of whom lived beyond the age of ten years. She was an ardent Protestant and in her mother's heart found compassion for others of that faith who were suffering religious persecution.

The vanguard of the emigrants from the war-torn and bigotry-blighted Rhine areas came to London, by way of Holland, during the summer of 1709. Conrad Weiser, aged twelve, together with his father, Johann Conrad Weiser, three brothers, and four sisters, left their home in Gross Aspach, Württemberg. "In this place (Gross Aspach)," writes Conrad Weiser in his diary, "my ancestors, from time immemorial, were born and buried—as well on my father's as on my mother's side."[1] On June 24, 1709, the Weisers joined the throng of expatriates moving northward along the Rhine river to Rotterdam.

Johan Conrad Weiser, Senior, had laid aside his uniform of the Württemberg Blue Dragoons in 1700, four years after the birth of his son, John Conrad, to assume the duties of a burgher in Gross Aspach, Württemberg. There he followed his trade as a baker and served his community as a local magistrate, just as his father and grandfather and his brother Hans Michael had served before him.[2]

The year 1709 brought tragedy to the Weiser home, when Johann Conrad Weiser's wife, Anna Magdalene (née Uebele), aged

---

[1]. Conrad Weiser's Autobiography; Rupp Collection, Library of Congress, Washington, D. C. This brief account of Weiser's life, written by himself in German, when he neared the close of his life, is a curious document. It is written in a pocket-sized notebook and only the right-hand page is devoted to the life account. The left page always bears a quotation from scriptures. But this is not the only unique feature. The first line of each page of text is written in some hand other than Weiser's as if someone were suggesting the theme or story that was to follow. The main text is Weiser's, beyond a doubt. There have been several translations of the autobiography, the best of which was made by Dr. H. H. Muhlenberg and published in the Collections of the Historical Society of Pennsylvania, Philadelphia (1853), 1:1. It is the leading article of the first publication of the Society.
[2]. Schopf, Eugen, *J. K. Weiser, Vater und Sohn*, Stuttgart, Germany, 1938, 17. Schopf denotes Conrad Weiser's birthplace as Affstaett. Both autobiography and tombstone have the erroneous form "Astaet."

forty-three, mother of sixteen children, passed to her reward. Conrad Weiser, writing in his diary, said of his mother: "She was a God-fearing woman and much beloved by her neighbors." Her motto was: "Jesus I live for Thee; I die for Thee, Thine am I in life and death."

The eldest of these children, Catharine, had been married to one Konrad Boss and the growing family taxed the capacity of the house of Weiser. Seeking a way out of his difficulties the elder Weiser sold his house, gardens, meadows, and vineyards to his son-in-law, Boss. Taking eight of his children, including John Conrad, Jr. with him, he joined the trek of the Palatine refugees, traveling to Holland.

Holland sympathized with the plight of the wanderers, but could not provide permanent shelter. The inpouring of thousands of Huguenots from France, after the Revocation of the Edict of Nantes (1685) had taxed Dutch resources to the limit. The burgomaster of Rotterdam refused to permit the itinerant refugees to enter the city and forced them to seek shelter in temporary quarters on the outskirts of Rotterdam in a village named Groningen.[3] From this point the bedraggled victims of intolerance were taken overland, trudging over swamps and wading shallow canals, to the old channel-harbor of Hellefoetsluice,[4] there to await the arrival of British ships, which would convey them to Good Queen Anne's domain.

Thousands of destitute arrivals in London tried the long purse and patience of the British kingdom. Hurriedly quarters were provided for them in tents on the greensward of Blackheath Common,[5] a public park which adjoins Greenwich, where Queen Anne Stuart had her summer palace. It was as if she wished to have her charges where she could be near them. Other groups were placed in abandoned rope-yards, in over-age vessels which were rotting in the harbors, in barns in Surrey, in Walworth, Camberwell, and

---

3. From Contemporary (1709) Newspapers in the Archivbouw of Rotterdam, Netherlands.
4. Hellefoetsluice on the Herring River, Netherlands. Visited August 1939. The building known as the White Hostel was used to quarter Palatines awaiting transportation to England. In 1939 the same building provided shelter for more than 100 Jewish refugees awaiting ships that would take them to America.
5. Blackheath Common, a renowned spot in English history. There Wat Tyler assembled his rebellious men in 1381. The Danes, when invading England encamped there in 1011. The Londoners welcomed the return of Henry V after his glorious victory of Agincourt and there in 1660 Charles II was hailed by the populace at the time of the Restoration of the Stuarts.

in St. Katherine Docks. The Weisers were among those quartered in tents on Blackheath, as is shown by subsistence lists kept by Pastor John Tribekko. The Greenwich Observatory, by which international time is computed, was constructed several years before the Palatines set up their tents on Blackheath. In this setting Conrad Weiser and his brothers and sisters, together with thousands of their fellow countrymen, awaited their fate.

Throughout the summer the refugees continued to come, Pauper in London complained that these foreigners were receiving more gratuities from the crown than native Englishmen received. Hard pressed to find a solution to the problem of permanently settling her wards in peace and safety Queen Anne listened to many plans presented to her by her advisors, the Board of Trade. There were plans to send these unfortunate people into the Welsh mines. Anne refused to consider this, declaring that the Palatines were farmers and not miners. There was a plan to send many of them into the Sherwood Forest. No, said Anne, they were not foresters. Still, another plan was to send several thousands of the refugees to Jamaica, there to develop the sugar industry. To this plan, Anne agreed until she learned that Jamaica was subject to occasional earthquakes and to almost constant heat. She then rescinded her approval of the plan.[6]

One of the plans which gained royal approval was to send several thousand to the province of New York, there to engage in the manufacture of naval stores, such as tar, pitch, and resin. The Board of Trade hoped to make Britain economically independent of Sweden, the only source of supply for such naval stores. The directors of the Board entered into some agreements with Robert Livingston, owner of vast tracts of land known as Livingston Manor, located on the Hudson River. Weiser tells us that it was near Christmas Day in 1709 that he and his father, three brothers and four sisters, embarked for the New World. They sailed on the ship *Lyon* and arrived in New York harbor on June 13, 1710, nearly one year after they left their Palatinate home.

---

6. Series of Colonial Office Documents, Public Record Office, London; Vide 1939. Some of these have been published in the *Documentary History of New York*. Volume III; others in *papers relating to the Palatines and the first settlement of Newburgh, Orange County."* New York, n.d.; See also Walter Allen Knittle, *Early Eighteenth Century Platine Emigration*, Philadelphia, 1937.

Not far from the present city of Catskill, New York, on both east and west banks of the Hudson River, seven villages were built in which the immigrant families were settled. Of these villages, the largest was named Queensbury, a settlement of more than a hundred families. Johann Conrad Weiser was made the listmaster of the village. This meant that he was responsible for the distribution of subsistence allotments and the keeping of the records of the persons who were in his charge. In 1711 the elder Weiser led a company of Palatine volunteers from the village of Queensbury in an expedition against French Canada as one of the campaigns of the struggle which American history calls Queen Anne's War.[7]

The plan to produce naval stores, tar, resin, and pitch from the pine trees which lined the Hudson proved to be an ill-starred venture from every standpoint. After the Palatines had cut down thousands of trees and girdled many thousands more, it was learned that the species of pine would not yield the desired products. Because Livingston and New York's colonial Governor, Robert Hunter, had incurred a huge debt in provisioning the workers, both men looked to the British Board of Trade for payment, even though the venture was a failure. They never recovered the sums which they expended.

From the standpoint of the Palatine refugees, the whole undertaking resulted merely in plunging them more deeply into debt to their masters. When they entered the service of Livingston and Hunter they accepted the status as a mass indenture, agreeing that they would contribute their labor to the production of naval stores until the profits would show a sum large enough to repay all the expenses which their transportation and subsistence had caused. With the failure of the enterprise, they were no nearer freedom and more heavily in debt than before their labors in the pine woods began.[8]

Dissatisfaction with their lot manifested itself as early as 1711, when Jean Cast, Assistant Commissary to the Palatines,

---

7. Lists of volunteers published Volume IX, *Papers Relating to Palatines*. Supra.
8. See *The German Emigration to America*, 1700–1740, by H. E. Jacobs, Pennsylvania German Society Proceedings, 1897, 8:110–125.

overheard a group of them gathered around a fire discussing their prospects: "Shall we have only the land back of our villages?" asked one of them.

"We must be loyal to Queen Anne," urged another.

"Patience and Hope make fools of those who fill their heads with them," complained still others.[9]

The spirit of unrest grew as the year 1711 advanced. Early in May, the commissioners for the Palatines wrote to Colonel Sir Richard Ingoldsby, commander of British troops stationed at Albany, declaring "there is no good to be done with these people who will obey no orders without compulsion." They asked for a detachment of soldiers to guard the Palatines at the Manor. One week later thirty soldiers were sent to the Manor. On the day following the arrival of the troops, May 10, 1711, Governor Hunter wrote to the Board of Trade saying that the Germans complained that they must work "as the Israelites did of old, with a Sword in one Hand and an Axe in the other." Hunter had visited the Palatines in their villages; he had talked with their leaders and had departed, feeling that the grumbling had been quelled, when a messenger followed to inform the governor that the Palatines had mutinied. The governor returned to the Manor with the messenger and sent out word that the Germans should select a few deputies to state their complaints. Instead of a few deputies, a large mob appeared to shout their protests. Thereupon Hunter ordered that the terms of the indenture should be read to the mob in the German language. The Palatines were silenced.

Was this the freedom which they had sought? They had never understood the terms of the contract which they had signed until they heard its terms in their own language. Was this the "Verlangte Canaan"[10] that Pastor Tribekko had pictured to them in his sermon on Blackheath, London? When some of their leaders protested that they never understood that the terms of the original contract called for indentured service, Jean Cast, one of the commissioners, was vexed. He thundered that he would not only treat them as Redemptioners but would make slaves out of them. To give force to this threat seventy additional soldiers were

---
9. *Jean Cast to Governor Robert Hunter; Documentary History of New York*, 3:394.
10. Text of a sermon preached to Palatines in Savoy Chapel, near Blackheath, London, 1710.

sent from the fort at Albany on the next day. All Palatines were disarmed and all special commissioners granted to militia officers such as Weiser were revoked.

Added to these rebuffs of the spirit were the physical hardships which had to be endured because of the lack of food and the failure of the commissioners to supply the victuals needed to sustain life. In June 1711 the commissioners began to quarrel among themselves; a bitter feud raged between Governor Hunter and Livingston, while the hungry Palatines were forced to eat putrid beef or starve. Escape was hopeless because the bonds of their contract bound them to their villages.

Stout-hearted members of the group had not lost faith, however. The sojourn at Livingston Manor was merely the wandering in the wilderness before these 18th-century Israelites should see the Promised Land. Into the vocabulary of some of the leaders there had crept a magic word, Schoharie; somewhere to the north and west in the Indian country, where the Mohawks lived. In the old world, Queen Anne had been their benefactor; here the chiefs of the forest kingdoms would come to their rescue.

In a way, not quite clear to us now, some chiefs of the Mohawk tribe, probably of the clan of the Mohicans, had learned of the plight of the Palatines and taking pity on their distressed white brothers had invited them to settle on the Indian lands along the Schoharie Creek, west of Albany, in New York province. There is a record that some of the Palatines thought that such a promise was made to them before they left London. Conrad Weiser tells us in his diary that some American Indians had visited the encampment at Blackheath in 1709 and out of compassion for the misery of the poor refugees quartered there had offered to present them with good lands on the Schoharie Creek.[11]

---

11. See Conrad Weiser's Autobiography. The account of this pledge rests only on Weiser's testimony and of course it is possible, that as a boy on Blackheath, Weiser did meet and see and hear the Indian make such a promise. But it must be remembered that Weiser wrote his autobiography near the close of his life, circa 1738, and he may have accepted as fact what he had heard from his elders. In my study of contemporary documents and newspapers in London, 1939, I found no reference to any visits of Indian to the British Capital, nor was this claim advanced by Johann Conrad Weiser and the other emissaries who came to London in 1720 to establish the claim of the Palatines to the Schoharie lands, when the settlers were threatened with eviction by the Dutch patroons. See Knittle, Walter Allen: *The Early Palatine Immigration*, Philadelphia, Pa., 1937, 150–152; See also Cobb, S. H., *The Story of the Palatines*, New York, 1807, 107.

As time passed conditions grew no better among the settlers of Livingston Manor. One misfortune after another befell the lords of the manor until they were quite willing to accede to the plea that the Palatines should be allowed to go where and when they pleased, provided they remained in the province of New York. During the winter of 1712–1713, Johann Conrad Weiser and several other deputies visited the Mohawk chieftains and arranged with them to permit the settlement of lands along the Schoharie Creek. At last, the Palatines were free to go to Schoharie!

During the early spring of 1713, these German pioneers built their first settlement. Conrad Weiser describes that first year: "They broke ground to plant corn, though poorly. But this year our hunger was hardly endurable. Many of our feasts were of wild potatoes and ground beans, which grew in abundance. We cut mallow and pickled juniper berries. If we were in need of meal we were obliged to travel thirty-five to forty miles and beg it on trust. One bush was gotten here, and one more there, sometimes after an absence from one's starving family for two or three days. With sorrowful hearts and tearful eyes, the morsel was looked for—and often did not come at all." Just east of the Schoharie Creek there is a creek which to this day is known as Louse Creek. According to local tradition, it received its name from the Palatines who washed their foul clothing there. During the first year, they had no clothes but those which they had worn on their persons.[12]

The recurring misfortunes of the Palatine pioneers would have broken the spirits of less hardy people. Adversity haunted them at every turn and economic disasters followed in quick succession. Confronted by untoward fate, two outstanding virtues which characterized the group enabled them to survive, and eventually triumph, over the chain of untoward circumstances which threatened to overcome them. The first of these virtues was their knowledge of farming. The earliest English settlements in America—Jamestown and Plymouth, both had their "starving time" during their early years. One mysterious English settlement in North Carolina succumbed completely to the rigors of pioneering in a remote corner of the world, and another, in Newfoundland, was abandoned because it did not prosper. These

---

12. Information supplied, 1935, by Arthur Stevenson, historian of Schoharie County, New York.

English settlers were not farmers. They could not smite the earth and force it to feed them. In this regard, the Palatines, however, were well equipped. Many of them had been peasants, bred in the culture of intensive cultivation of the soil, familiar with nature's whims and conversant with her language. Lacking food, they could find it, above or under the soil, dangling from trees as fruit and nuts or ornamenting bushes as berries. Given sufficient growing time, they could bid nature serve up a bountiful harvest instead of being broken by her exactions. This was their first and most constant virtue.

Their second saving-grace grew out of their agrarian culture. Their partnership with nature helped them to establish a degree of friendship, even kinship, with nature's own children, the Indians. The early Germans, unlike most other settlers, did not exploit the furry treasures of the forest. Neither did they girdle and burn down the trees, destroying the habitat of wild animals and birds, nor did they defraud and demoralize the Indians with traffic in liquor and glittering valueless baubles. The relations between the German settlers and the Indians present a striking contrast to other phases of early colonial history which ring with the eerie sound of the war whoop and paint the color of crimson on many a page.

In the development of these splendid relationships between the dwellers on the frontier the Weisers, father and son, were important factors. With the consent of his father, Conrad, aged seventeen, left his Schenectady home to live with the Maqua (Iroquois) Indians for a period of eight months. This decision may have been influenced by the elder Weiser's second marriage, which brought a step-mother into the home and consequent domestic altercations between a grown son and a new parental authority.[13]

---

13. Of the eight children brought to America by the elder Weiser, only four lived at Schoharie. Two sons, both younger than Conrad, namely George Frederick and Christopher, were indentured in New York to pay for the passage of the Weiser's. George was indentured to a man named S. Smith in Smithtown, New York, and Christopher was indentured to a person in Long Island. The youngest son, John Frederick, aged only 3 when the family emigrated, survived the journey to America but died in Livingston Manor, 1711.

The three sisters of Conrad, Margareta, Magdalena and Sabina, all older than he, had left the Schoharie home before Conrad departed to live with the Indians.

Three children had already been born to John Conrad Weiser and his second wife before young Conrad left his father's roof. Their names were Jon Frederick, Jacob, and Rebecca.

The fact that the boy was the last to leave his father's house and live with his stepmother long enough to see three children added to the family, refutes statements by some writers which

During these formative months of his life, young Conrad lived the life of an Indian, absorbed much of their culture, learned their language and suffered the privations to which these improvident people were subjected, especially during the winter months.

In a very real sense, Weiser's sojourn with the Six Nations was a training school for the great work which later years demanded of him. There, under the guidance of the Mohawk chief, Quagnant, he learned the language of the Six Nations; he shared with the Indians the privations of forest homes and hand to mouth existence. In this formative stage of life, he absorbed much of the lore and the social customs of a people who remained a mystery to the great mass of settlers in America. His experience made him, almost at once, the interpreter between "the high-nettled Dutch [Germans?]" and the neighboring tribes. "On such occasions," says Weiser, "I was immediately sent for to interpret for both parties. I had a great deal of business, but no pay. None of my people understood their language, excepting myself, and by much exertion I became perfect, considering my age and circumstances."

After the first year, the Germans in the Schoharie community prospered. Seven villages, named after the deputies who had originally negotiated with the Indians for the land,[14] grew up in the valley of the Schoharie. Niederlandish (Dutch) patroons, casting their eyes westward from their Hudson plantations saw the wilderness melt away; saw fine bank-barns arise and fill with harvests; saw green, brown, and yellow fields dot the landscape like a patchwork quilt along the slopes of the Mohawk and Schoharie. Seeing these things, they consulted their original surveys and patents. These were subject to various interpretations. The patroons found in them clauses which could be interpreted to give them claims to the Schoharie lands. When the Dutch landlords asserted their claims, dispossession and eviction again threatened the Palatines who had already wandered so far and moved so often. There were numerous clashes between sheriff's deputies

---

would lead the reader to believe that the second marriage of his father was the cause of his leaving home. Weiser complains about his step-mother in his autobiography but there is no record of a family scene or overt act.

14. Weiserdorf; Ober Weiserdorf; Kniskerndorf; Gerlachsdorf; Hart-mannsdorf; Fuchsdorf; Schmidtsdorf and Brunnendorf.

and the farmers who regarded the lands as their own. In one of these clashes, one of the Weisers was arrested on the charge of being particularly active in resisting the authorities. The account of the arrest appears in the *Documentary History of New York, Volume III*, page 688, but it is not clear which of the Weisers, father or son, was made a prisoner. It must be noted that the elder Weiser was active in maintaining the claims of the original settlers. In 1720, in company with two other Palatine deputies, he made a sea voyage, fraught with many disasters, to lay the claims of his people before George I of England.[15] "When they reached England," Conrad writes, "they found times had changed and that there was no longer a Queen Anne on the throne." On the other hand, the father was no longer an impetuous young man when the arrest was made. The prisoner was probably the son.

Wearying of the protracted arguments concerning land patents a group of fifteen Palatine families left their Schoharie homes in 1723 to wander once more through the wilderness and settle eventually in the Tulpehocken region of Pennsylvania. A year prior to their exodus they had sent a delegation to Pennsylvania to examine the prospects of a settlement there.[16] The report of their deputies was very favorable. Accordingly, with the aid of some Indians, they cut their way through the forests to the upper reaches of the Susquehanna River and floated in canoes to the mouth of the Swatara Creek and from thence, up the Swatara to Tulpehocken.[17]

Conrad Weiser did not accompany the first group which made the long trek from Schoharie to Tulpehocken. "Afterwards," he writes, "namely in 1729, I removed to Pennsylvania, and settled in Tulpehocken . . ." Tulpehocken, the Land of Turtles! To the distressed victims of persecution and disaster, it was the Promised Land of Canaan. Benevolent Pennsylvania offered sanctuary. Her limestone soil, shaded by black walnut trees, watered by gurgling springs, grooved by pleasant valleys between majestic mountains, was indeed the Land of Milk and Honey where the Manna fell from

---
15. George I was the first ruler of the German House of Hanover. Queen Anne died in 1714.
16. Penn-Physick Papers, Historical Society of Pennsylvania.
17. Lichtenthaeler, Frank E., *They Drove Their Cattle Overland*, Historical Society of Berks County Review, July 1940.

heaven and a generous Penn spread his sheltering cloak over the oppressed and beleaguered of all lands.

Conrad Weiser listened to the beckoning call from Pennsylvania in 1729 when he followed his countrymen to the Tulpehocken region. In 1720, while his father was in England, he was married to "My Anne Eve," as he speaks of her. She was the daughter of his neighbor, Peter Feg, a fellow Palatine refugee. To this union, four children were born while they were still residents of Schoharie and nine others were born to them in Pennsylvania.

We have little direct testimony about Weiser's early manhood or his activities between the years from 1720 until his arrival in Pennsylvania.[18] But there are numerous references in later accounts of his journeys to New York on behalf of Pennsylvania and other colonies to lead us to believe that he must have been active in Indian affairs during those years. He knew many of the northern chieftains and had earned for himself the Mohawk name Ziguras before he came to Penn's colony. However, we do have significant evidence that the trials and tribulations which the youth shared with thousands of his own people left a deep impression upon his memory and prepared him for the great part he was to play in early American history. This evidence is drawn from a unique feature of his autobiography, written when he neared the close of his days on earth. Each new page of his life account is introduced by a biblical phrase drawn from the Psalms, Lamentations or the book of Job. These texts were obviously selected because they symbolized the experiences described in the account. After one bitter experience, he records: "Thou O Lord remainest forever; thy throne from generation to generation. Turn Thou us unto Thee, O Lord, and we shall be turned; renew our days as of old." Lamentations V: 19-22.

---

18. The author discounts as doubtful a letter published in Schopf's *Vater und Sohn*, 71, in which it is made to appear that the first settlers of Tulpehocken sent a message to Schoharie inviting Conrad Weiser to come to Pennsylvania.

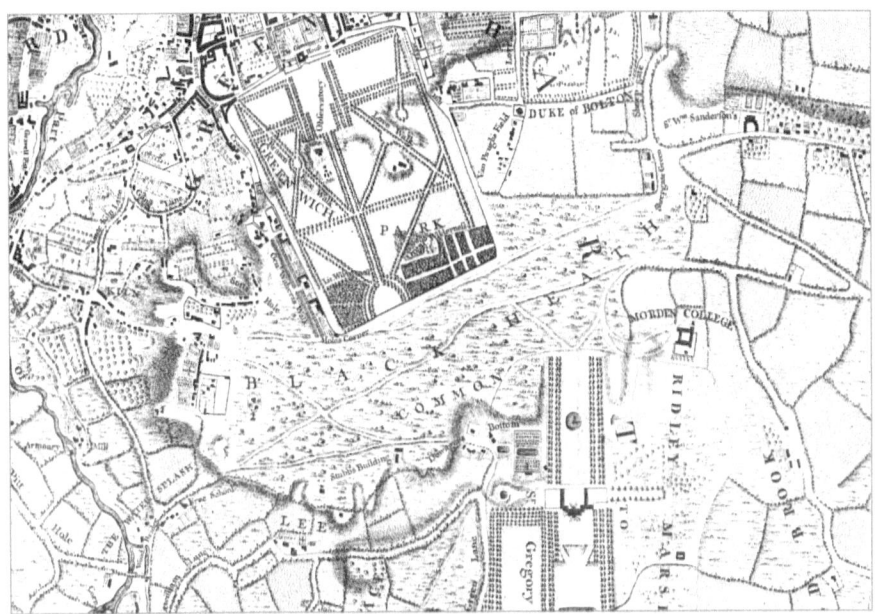
Early map of the Blackheath Common in England

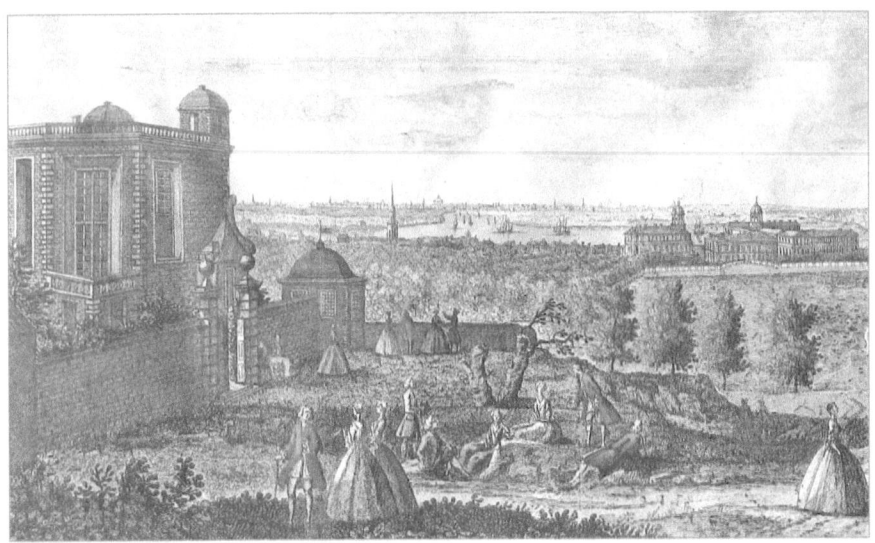
Early painting of the famous Greenwich Observatory. The Weisers were encamped near it while refugees.

Portrait of Queen Anne circa 1705

Robert Hunter, colonial governor of New York

The Exodus to Canaan

Sa Ga Yeath Qua Pieth Tow, king of the Maquas just prior to Weiser's arrival

CHAPTER II

Clearing the Path of Friendship

The Tulpehocken Creek weaves a serpentine course through the fertile valley which lies between the ridges of the Blue and South Mountains of eastern Pennsylvania. Tulpehocken is derived from *Tulpewaki*, an Indian word meaning the Land of Turtles. Here was the Canaan which the Palatine refugees found at the end of their journey in search of security and freedom. The vanguard of émigrés from Schoharie occupied the lands which today form the western limits of Berks County, extending into the eastern townships of present-day Lebanon County. In 1723 all of this area was included in Lancaster County.

When Conrad Weiser and his family arrived in Tulpehocken, six years after the first group had emigrated from Schoharie, he took up his land and built his cabin at the southeastern edge of the earlier settlements, just east of the present-day Womelsdorf and close to the trail which led from Philadelphia through Tulpehocken, across the Blue or Endless Mountains, to the Delaware Indian village of Shamokin (now Sunbury) on the Susquehanna River.

Shamokin was the capital of the Delaware Nation and occasionally there were Indian deputies traveling along the Indian path which led, southeastward, to the English capital at Philadelphia. At first Weiser's stone cabin probably indicated no more to the Delawares than an additional settler's homestead. But when Shikellamy, a sachem of the Oneidas, passed that way he recognized the tenant as his white friend, Ziguras, the former interpreter for the New York Maquas. Shikellamy, or Swatane, as he was sometimes known, was destined to pass through Tulpehocken frequently because he was vice-regent for the Six Nations who had established suzerainty over the Delawares and other Pennsylvania Indians.

The Iroquois or Five Nations, comprising the powerful Oneidas, Senecas, Onondagas, Mohawks, and Cayugas, became the Six Nations in 1714 when a tribe of southern Indians, the Tuscaroras, came north and were received into the Iroquois Confederacy. Because of superior political organization, these Six Nations became the most powerful group of Indians known to the settlers of the American colonial period. Through conquest and diplomacy, they had established a sort of sovereignty over the other tribes which shared the Atlantic seaboard with English and French settlers. Their authority extended southward into the Carolinas, west to the unexplored reaches of the Ohio, and east into New England.

Geographically the Six Nations held a strategic position. Wedged between the French possessions to the north and other French settlements to the southwest these powerful tribes held the balance of power in the struggle between European nations for domination of the American continent. They could afford to play English and French interests against each other and by maintaining neutrality, threaten to turn the balance on one side or the other. The young English settlements could hardly have survived the series of colonial wars (1740–1763) against the combined forces of French armies and hostile Iroquois on the warpath. In these contests, Conrad Weiser was the chief reliance of the British to hold the Six Nations fast in the English interest. He spoke their language, knew their mode of living, and held their supreme confidence throughout the trying period of colonial wars.

From 1731 until his death in 1760 this intrepid German immigrant labored in the English service, sometimes against superhuman odds. In bidding for Iroquois support many advantages were on the side of the French. Jesuit missionaries from French Canada had proselyted among many tribes, converting many Indians to the Catholic faith; Frenchmen, wanting only the pelts for trade, had not hewn down the trees in which furry creatures lived; they had not brought plows to break the soil in lowlands or wives to populate towns and villages in the backwoods; they were generous with their firewater and tolerant of most of the vices of the aborigines. In contrast, the pious Calvinists, the individualistic Scotch-Irishmen, and other homesteading English subjects threatened to eradicate the Indians' forest kingdom by building farms and villages. And yet, due largely to Weiser's unusual sagacity, his sincerity of purpose, and indefatigable services, the path of peace was kept open for a quarter of a century while Britain's mastery of a continent was made possible.

Shikellamy introduced Weiser to the Pennsylvania colonial authorities in 1731.[1] Up to this time the province had relied upon Indian traders to act as interpreters in the various conferences which were held with Delawares, Conoys, Nescopecks, and other tribes of Pennsylvania Indians. Formerly John Scull and Edmund Cartlidge, agents for the merchant Edward Shippen, performed these services.

This arrangement was not satisfactory to the authorities for several reasons. First, these agents were not always in, or near, Philadelphia. Their duties took them into the woods on trading expeditions and sometimes, when most needed, they were beyond summoning. Secondly, white traders were not persons likely to inspire a great degree of confidence among those whom they exploited with their wares in sharp trading practices.[2] Thirdly, while Scull and Cartlidge may have been proficient in the use of the tongue spoken by the Pennsylvania tribes, they had no knowledge of the Maqua language spoken by the deputies of the Six Nations. Weiser possessed all the qualifications needed and was burdened by none of these deterrents. Instead of seeking to make his fortune

---

1. James Logan to E. Shippen, August 18, 1731: "I fully expected to have seen John Scull here, this evening, and am unhappily disappointed . . . if still in town I beg him to hasten hither for I must have an interpreter...for the old man and Shikellimy will not be content to stay." Logan MSS, 2:8. While this does not state that Shikellimy secured the services of Weiser, the latter's appearance on the scene a few months later, in company with Cehachquey, a Cayuga, and Shikellimy, who had just returned from a journey to the Six Nations, would indicate that the red men realized the need of Weiser's services. In the conferences of December 10–11, at Philadelphia, Weiser and Scull acted as interpreters. Colonial Records, 3:442–443: "Allowance to be made to Shekallamy for his Journey to the Six Nations, and to Conrad Weyser, for coming hither with him from Tulpehocken."
2. The fact that the Pennsylvania Germans were not traders accounts, in part, for their success as peacemakers among the Indians. Note the services of Zeisberger, Post, Zinzendorf, Prylaeus, Spangenberg, and others.

by trading, Weiser built his future security upon the purchase of real estate. Surveys for purchases to add to his original tract were made as early as 1733.[3] He spoke the Six Nations language and his home was close enough to Philadelphia to be summoned by the governor and at the same time not far distant from the Indian capital at Shamokin. He could always be found by those who needed him. Once discovered, his services became indispensable to Governor Patrick Gordon and his successors.

Indian affairs in the American colonies reached their climax during the French and Indian War (1754–1763), when two European giants contended for the rich prize known, somewhat nebulously, as the Ohio country. The conflict between French and British interests in Ohio developed into open warfare when the youthful Washington led his expedition into the Ohio country which sent the world into the Seven Years' War. The embers of that conflict had been smoldering for a generation. In 1731 James Logan, a Pennsylvania merchant and president of the Provincial Council, dreamed dreams of the rich Ohio country. His agents, who had carried mirrors, trinkets, vermilion, and strouds across the mountains into the regions where only Indians dwelled, and eloquent in their descriptions of the great country which lay beyond the confines of mapped Pennsylvania. The "Ohio Country" was a geographical expression which embraced everything beyond the Eastern ridges of the Alleghenies. That vast domain must not be permitted to fall into Frenchy hands, reasoned Logan, and thus, later, reasoned the Crown of Great Britain.

In 1731 Logan found cause for alarm. The Shawnees, a tribe of Pennsylvania Indians, had permitted several of their braves to visit Canada during the summer of that year. When they returned from Canada, in company with a few Frenchmen, they had raised the French flag in an Indian village in the Ohio country. "We were troubled to hear this," confided Logan to his "Friend Conrad Weiser," as he customarily addressed the interpreter, "for the Shawanese Indians have been in league with our government above thirty years and the Land on the Ohio belongs to the Five Nations . . . We have sent to the Shawanese to come back and

---

3. James Steele's Letter Book (1730–1741), Historical Society of Pennsylvania, 54.

live with us as our friends."⁴ In this letter, Weiser was instructed to consult his friend Shikellamy at Shamokin and to plan to deal with the matter at the next Indian conference in Philadelphia.

Shrewdly Logan, as manager of Indian affairs for Pennsylvania, planned to enlist the aid of the Six Nations Confederacy in blocking French aggression. During the summer and autumn of 1731, Shikellamy had traveled to New York province, carrying a message from Pennsylvania to the Six Nations chieftains, inviting them to attend a conference in Philadelphia. In December Shikellamy made a report on his journey, stating that the chieftains had declined to make the journey during the winter months. They would come, however, "when the Days grow longer and the Sun gives more Heat." This was the promise of the chiefs at Tsanandowa, the capital of the Seneca nation. The Senecas were the westernmost tribe of the Six Nations and their interests were most directly concerned with the French usurpation of the Ohio region.

The northern snows do not melt until late in March or early April. The venerable sachems of the Six Nations took their own good time in setting out on their long journey from northern and western New York to Philadelphia. In March 1732 the Pennsylvania Assembly voted a sum of money to be paid out of the Public Treasury to defray the expenses of the "Chiefs of the Five Nations (who) are daily expected."⁵ But April, May, June, and July wore on without any news about the approach of Indian deputies from the north. It was August before the colonial officers were apprised that the motley assemblage of chieftains from the forest empire were nearing Philadelphia, escorted by their friend Conrad Weiser. On August 14, Governor Gordon issued a proclamation to all tavern keepers to "furnish what meat and drink the Six Nations need . . . the charge will be defrayed by the Government." The guests of the province arrived on August the 18th. After several days spent in exchanging courtesies, they assembled in Council on the 23rd. Conrad Weiser, born in German-speaking Württemberg, acted

---

4. James Logan to "Friend Conrad Weiser," December 15, 1731, Logan MSS, 2:14. Logan gives Weiser a lesson in tact: "Tell this to Shikellimy and Chehachque, that they may mention it after they have delivered their first Message, but not as a part of their Message, or as if they were sent back about it, but only occasionally as a Piece of News." Logan sometimes used the term Five Nations, forgetting the addition of the Tuscaroras.
5. March 19, 1732, Votes of the Assembly, 3:183.

as interpreter between English-speaking Pennsylvanians and Maqua-speaking chiefs of six nations.[6]

The conference continued through August until September 11th. Thomas Penn, a son of the founder, was in regular attendance. The addresses to the Indians were made on his behalf, because as proprietor, Penn personified his province. The Indians, in their turn, replied to Brother Onas, their name for Penn. The deputies were asked searching questions as to their relations with the French "to the Northward and Westward." To this they replied, through Weiser, that although they had "hung on the Kettle," (meaning prepared for war) they had listened to Onontijo, Governor of New France, plead for peace. The Indians had promised the French to "plant a Tree and make a deep Hole under it," in which to bury their hatchets. Onontijo then said he would "add a Top to the tree so that it should reach up to the Heavens, that no Wind or Storm should shake or hurt it."[7]

At one point in the conference, it was felt that the deputies might be inclined to speak more freely if the public were kept out of the council chambers. Weiser was asked to inquire of the Indians whether, or not, they preferred to carry on their discussion behind closed doors. The interpreter consulted with the chiefs and reported that the Indians were satisfied to conduct the discussions in the white man's way. This incident illustrates how the provincial authorities relied upon Weiser to deal tactfully with the Indians. It was his duty to acquaint them with the white man's laws regulating conduct in a city and to explain to them unfamiliar scenes and situations which confronted them. Among other trying situations which presented themselves, there was an earthquake in Philadelphia on September 5th, which was so severe that it was felt as far north as Boston and Montreal.[8]

Concerning the action of the Shawnees on the Ohio the deputies of the Six Nations expressed a willingness to cooperate with Pennsylvania in urging these people to return to Penn's domain. They blamed the disaffection of the tribe upon the machinations of a French interpreter, Cahichodo, who had built houses on lands

---
6. Colonial Records, supra, 464–465.
7. Ibid., 466.
8. Kalm, Peter, *Travels in North America*, London, 1771, 1:44.

which belonged to the Senecas in Ohio. They had "advised" him to leave, but, up to the time of their departure from New York he had not taken their "advice." They had carried their complaints to the French Governor in Canada.

After three weeks as guests of Philadelphia, a new treaty of amity was formed between Pennsylvania and the Six Nations. In their own words, the Indians had "brightened the chain of Friendship." During these negotiations, the deputies had proposed to the council that henceforth all conferences should be "managed by means of Shekallamy and Conrad Weiser." To which the provincial delegates made reply that they would "clear the Road from Philadelphia to the Six Nations . . . have our Eyes fixed upon that Road that no man may stop to encumber it" and "As to what you said about employing Shekallamy and Conrad Weiser, on which you gave the first Strings of Wampum, we are very glad you agree with us in the choice of so good Men to go between us. We believe them to be very honest, and will with Cheerfulness employ them, and to confirm this we give another Stroud Matchcoat."[9]

Gifts and belts of wampum were exchanged before the Indians set out upon their homeward journey. With grand ceremony the chief speaking of the Indians, Hetequantagechty, placed a finely painted mantle of dressed otter skins on the shoulders of Onas, Thomas Penn. Many a farewell cup was drunk before they mounted the horses which were provided by the province to carry them from Philadelphia to Tulpehocken and from there to Mahoni, now Penn's Creek, Snyder County. As a direct result of the treaty of 1732 Weiser had established himself as a successful Indian agent and the confidant of James Logan.

Pocketing his fee of twelve pounds[10] for his services, Weiser escorted his charges back to Tulpehocken and provided wagons for the continuance of their journey to the Susquehanna, where

---

9. All quotations from the conference and the figures of speech used in the text may be found in the Minutes of the Provincial Council which we designate as the Colonial Records, 3:462–483 passim.
10. "The Reward to Conrad Weyser, who had accompanied the Indians hither from Tulpehocken, had been very careful of them, and was very serviceable on this present Treaty." Further, Shikellamy and Weiser were "Men not only very acceptable to the Indians . . . but likewise seemed to be Persons of Truth and Honesty, on which Account it would be necessary to give them all due Encouragement. It is resolved that the Sum of Eight Pounds be paid to Shikellimy & Twelve Pounds to Conrad Weyser . . ." Colonial Records, 3:477.

they lingered through the winter months among their "cousins," the Delawares.

The winter of 1732-1733 was very severe. Contemporary newspapers record that ice covered the Delaware to a thickness of fifteen inches and horse-drawn sleighs crossed and re-crossed the river from the Pennsylvania to the New Jersey side at will. Most of the eastern settlements were snow-bound and no intercourse took place between the English and the sachems of the remote Indian nations. It was not until June 1733, that forest diplomacy again claimed the attention of Thomas Penn and his appointed deputies.

On Saturday, June 16, 1733, Shikellamy and Conrad Weiser, in company with three braves, arrived in Philadelphia and requested an audience. Two days later the Indian deputies were admitted to the council, where they delivered their messages through the interpreter, Conrad Weiser.

The Indians had "ill News" to make known to their white brothers. The terms of the Treaty of Friendship concluded with Pennsylvania during the previous year required that Onas (Penn) should be apprised of all news affecting relations between Indians and the English. The Ganawese Indians[11] living on the Conoy Creek between Paxtang and Conestoga, Lancaster County, feared reprisals from the government of Virginia for some murders which Sir William Gooch, governor of that province, alleged had been committed by Ganawese warriors against settlers on the "border of Virginia." Loathe to believe that an English governor would make war upon the friends of Onas without first consulting his white brother, these emissaries had come to Philadelphia to learn what Onas knew about the matter.

This was news to the Pennsylvania authorities, and, at first, they were disinclined to believe it, because the messengers could bring no confirmation of the report other than the alarm expressed by the Ganawese Indians themselves. Would Shikellamy investigate the matter further by visiting the Ganawese village

---

11. Ganawese Indians sometimes known as the Conoys. Conoy Township is in northwestern Lancaster County. Ganawese, translated means "cornshellers." Paxtang, or Paxton, is in Dauphin County. Conestoga near Safe Harbor, Lancaster County.

and make "the strictest enquiry possible" and send a full report? This the vice-regent of the Six Nations promised to do.

A few weeks later, August 6, the matter was brought forcibly to the attention of the Pennsylvania Council, when Ullaloes, a chief of the Ganawese Indians, appeared before that body bearing a letter from James Mitchell of Donegal, near Conoy. The letter, evidently written at the request of the Ganawese, expressed fears of attack from Virginia and protested that they were innocent of the murder charge. When interrogated, Ullaloes explained that some Ganawese warriors had set out on an expedition against a rival tribe to the south and had returned with two scalps. They reported that a third scalp was missing, the body of the victim having been removed by the enemy before the scalp could be taken. But, declared the Ganawese chieftain, they were the scalps of Indian enemies, the Tutelos, and not the scalps of English people. And now, lamented Ullaloes, one hundred white warriors were coming northward to punish the Ganawese for a crime which they had not committed. The scalps could be seen in their town and identified as the scalps of Indians, not white men.

Council dismissed the Ganawese with the admonition that they should not believe all rumors they heard and that if they had "not done amiss they have nothing to fear."

Ten days later Shikellamy and Weiser appeared before Council together with Hetequantagechty, who had been the chief spokesman for the Six Nations at the Treaty of 1732. Their errand concerned several matters of importance, but the Ganawese alarm was the first matter discussed.

According to instructions, Shikellamy had visited the Conoy village. There he had learned that roving Ganawese had killed three Tootelaes and secured two scalps near the borders of Virginia. While on their homeward journey the Conoy braves had joined company with a Delaware Indian to whom they had boasted of their valor. During a drunken brawl this Delaware was beaten by his companions and later, in a spirit of vengeful spite, had spread the falsehood that the victims of the raid were white people. Shikellamy had seen the tufts of hair which the Ganawese brought with them and gave it as his opinion that "from the Marks upon them, of their hair in some places being pulled out, of its being greased and tied up in a small bundle of the top of the head" he was positive that the scalps had belonged to Indians.

Council assured Shikellamy that they accepted his version of what had happened and stated that his account agreed with the story which the Ganawese had related ten days earlier. "We now think no more of it."

Council had hoped that the Ganawese matter was closed after Shikellamy made his report. But through the woodland defiles, fleet-footed messengers were relaying rumors of an impending crisis in Indian affairs. The Ganawese sent a message to the Iroquois capital at Onondaga, concerning a mysterious matter, the substance of which is not clear. In September 1734, several deputies came from the northern capital to Philadelphia, but they brought no important news and transacted no business beyond the usual deluge of compliments and exchange of dressed deerskins for far more valuable presents from the Penns.[12] The colonial authorities were puzzled to know what had occasioned this fruitless visit. Some inferences may be drawn from the fact that the Six Nations' deputies refused to talk until Conestoga and Ganawese Chiefs including Ullaloes, were present at the conference. We may assume Ullaloes dissuaded the northern sachems from discussing the real purpose of their visit.

On July 31, 1734, Governor Gordon of Pennsylvania had received a letter from Sir William Gooch, Governor of Virginia, charging that a group of Ganawese Indians had murdered settlers in his province and demanding that the "villains" be punished. Gooch's letter was dated July 13, 1735. Whether the date was in error or whether the letter was delayed one year in transit is not clear. Governor Gordon replied that "from many concurring Circumstances I concluded it to be the same fact which had been charged on them (Ganawese) about fourteen months since." New inquiries were made this time by the magistrates of Lancaster County. Their reports confirmed the suspicions of the Virginia authorities.[13]

---

12. John Penn, brother of Thomas and a joint proprietor of Pennsylvania, arrived in Pennsylvania in 1733 and was in attendance at most of the sessions of the Provincial Council.
13. Samuel Blunston to Patrick Gordon, August 13, 1734, Pennsylvania Archives, 1st ser., 1:437–438.

All of this was known to Gordon and the Penns when the abortive conference of September 1734 was held with Ganawese Indians present. But Conrad Weiser was not there at the time to give counsel or act as interpreter. How much he figured in the investigation we cannot say, except that in September 1733, Robert Charles, secretary of the Province, wrote Weiser, "I am sorry to hear you have been so much harassed by the visits of the Indians."[14]

It was not until August 1735, when Weiser and the Ganawese chief were both present, that Thomas Penn charged the Ganawese with responsibility for the murder of the Virginia settlers and demanded that the perpetrators of the crime be delivered for trial.

Confronted with this definite accusation Ullaloes pleaded that he had thought the whole affair, "long since at an End." But, declared he, the murderers could not be delivered because all of them had since been slain in another battle in the south lands.[15]

The account of the Ganawese murder has been presented here to show the difficulties which confronted officials in Philadelphia in dealing with their wayward wards and allies. Cloistered within the confines of a city they could not know what was transpiring in the leafy regions beyond the settlements. Wily natives, imposing upon the credulity of Quaker gentlemen, could fabricate all sorts of tales for the ears of their ever-generous hosts in the City of Brotherly Love. The Philadelphia people had learned that they could not rely upon reports made by Indians. Even Shikellamy had either falsified the true facts in the Ganawese matters or was, himself, grossly misinformed. The farther the settlements penetrated the interior of Penn's domain, the more complex became Indian problems and the more important became the services of the one white man who lived near the frontier and enjoyed the confidence of the powerful tribes. More and more the provincial authorities were to find that they would be forced to call upon Conrad Weiser.

In addition to the Ganawese matter which was first mentioned at the June 1733, conference, there arose complaints made by the Indians against the rum traffic, particularly against one trader, Peter Cheaver; complaints against John Harris, who had

---
14. Robert Charles to Conrad Weiser, September 13, 1733, Peters MSS, 1:18.
15. Colonial Records, 3:657. This statement was confirmed by the report of the magistrates of Lancaster County, Pennsylvania Archives, supra, 437–439.

built a house at the mouth of the Choniata (Juniata River) on unpurchased lands; fears that Onas was not true to his pledges of Friendship. Such ugly sounds had come to them "under the Ground," meaning secretly.

Another conference was held in August 1733. This time Hetaquantagechty, chief spokesman of the Six Nations, brought mournful news of a "very great Sickness" which had reduced the population among the Six Nations during the very severe winter Also, reported the sachem, the French were at war with some western Indians, who were vassals of the Iroquois. It was feared that the Six Nations might be drawn into the struggle. It was reported too that smallpox was taking a terrific toll of life among the tribes to the northward.

The Provincial authorities gave their condolences and then proceeded to charge that the warriors of the Six Nations who recently had passed through western settlements in Pennsylvania were "very disorderly; they killed several hogs, cut down corn and threatened to do further mischief." This charge Hetaquantagechty denied, blaming the misdeeds on the untrustworthy Shawnees, who had already incurred the displeasure of Pennsylvania ty raising the French flag in their villages.

In October 1734, Weiser, Shikellamy, and Hetaquantagechty came before Council.[16] The Indians denied that the group which had come so mysteriously a month earlier had any right to speak for the Six Nations. A complaint was made against Madame Montour,[17] a half-breed who was influential in Pennsylvania villages. She was charged with spreading false rumors. There was a repetition of appeals for better regulation of the rum trade.

---

16. The Provincial Council had expected a visit from a large delegation of chieftains. On Aug. 29, 1734. Robert Charles wrote to Weiser:
   My Friend Weiser:
       The Proprietors having received Information that the Chiefs of the Six Nations are on their Road hither, hath directed me to desire of you, that if they come by Tulpehocken, you will accompany them to this place (Philadelphia) and take Care that they are supplied with Provisions at their several Stages, the Charge whereof will be defrayed here.
       I have received 38 lbs. 6s., the amount of your account which you may have from me when you please.
       Your Friend and humble Servant
       Robt. Charles
   Peters MSS, 1:20.
17. Madame Montour, a daughter of a French army officer and a Huron woman. Born circa 1684. Captured by warriors of the Six Nations and reared by them. Married an Oneida, Carondawana. Mother of Andrew and Margaret Montour. Mother and son will play important parts as the life of Conrad Weiser unfolds.

This complaint was heard time and time again, during Indian conferences, but each time that the authorities tried to stop the trade in firewater the Indians themselves reversed their pleas and begged that it should not be interrupted.

The Council learned that the wayward Shawnees were trying to prevail upon the Delaware tribe, residing at Shamokin, to join them in moving outside the bounds of Pennsylvania, but, that Sassoonan, the Delaware king, had forbidden any of his subjects to leave their villages.

A conference in August 1735, dealt with land claims of the Susquehanna Indians. This was the first time that Weiser was called upon to serve as interpreter in a conference which did not include Six Nation chieftains. Ancient treaties were made between William Penn and sachems who had died long ago were reproduced by the Penn heirs and Weiser was called upon to explain the terms of the forgotten agreements.[18] It was necessary to instruct these forest children in the law of continuing through succeeding generations obligations inherited from signers of treaties. It was at this conference, too, that the denouement of the Ganawese was accomplished and the Indians departed for their homes, a penitent people, while Weiser pocketed his fee of twelve pounds for services "on the present Treaty and on the two late messages from the Six Nations."

One month later, September 1735, Weiser again accompanied a group of Six Nations messengers who brought word the Shawnees had refused the orders of their superiors to come eastward. They had murdered a Seneca chieftain who had "pressed them so closely" to heed the Iroquois demands. The Shawnees had fled to Virginia after perpetrating their crime. Might it not be proper, they asked to write to Governor Gooch[19] "who is a warlike man" and enlist his aid in punishing the culprits.

---

18. Referring to the "Dongon Deed" sale, recognition of which was given by the Susquehanna chiefs in the treaty of 1700. The Indians had agreed that the lands on the Susquehanna should belong to William Penn and his heirs "as long as the Sun and Moon shall endure, or Water flow to the Rivers." Colonia Records, supra, 650–655 passim.

19. Sir William Gooch, governor of Virginia, had served as an officer under the Duke of Marlborough during the War of the Spanish Succession. The Indians' reference to his warlike character probably grew out of the threatening language which Gooch had used in demanding punishment for the Ganawese murders. The phrase "warlike man" may have been used to impress Quakers, whose pacifism disturbed the Iroquois braves.

Council then urged that chiefs of all the nations should come to Philadelphia "next spring" to confer at length on weighty matters.

The Treaty of 1732 had "cleared the Path"; "brightened the Chain"; and "kindled the Fire" of friendship between Pennsylvania and the mighty Iroquois Confederacy. The concluding articles called for another conference in 1733 for ratifying the terms of the treaty, the Indian deputies having insisted upon submitting its terms to their own council fire at Onondaga for confirmation by all their chiefs. But four years passed before the irregular processes of forest diplomacy effected a second general conference in Philadelphia. The conferences referred to in the intervening years (1732-1736) were on a small scale and could not be regarded as treaty-making assemblages.

A series of excuses caused postponements during the three summers between 1732 and 1736. At the time of the audition given Hetaquantagechty in 1735 Council had urged that nothing should interfere with the visit of deputies "next spring." In August 1736, a group of Delaware and Susquehanna Indians led by the Delaware King, Allumpees, had imposed their presence upon the hospitality of Philadelphia. Ostensibly they had come to offer condolences to the Pennsylvania Council on the death of Governor Patrick Gordon who died August 1736, but his Excellency's passing had been too recent to permit news of it to reach the Susquehanna before the forty-odd mendicants had set out upon the gift-seeking journey.

Hiding their exasperation, Council members made perfunctory speeches of welcome, gave a meager present and told the Delawares that they should send for the Six Nations deputies. All business, henceforth, they were told would be conducted through Conrad Weiser.[20] In this way, the Delawares were informed that Pennsylvania recognized the sovereignty of the Six Nations over all Pennsylvania Indians.

Six weeks passed. On September 2, 1736, Henry Kobel, a Palatine neighbor of Weiser's in Tulpehocken, stopped at James Logan's palatial home, Stenton, in Germantown, to deliver a lengthy

---

20. Colonial Records, 4:53-56.

letter from Conrad Weiser.[21] Due to the death of Gordon, Logan as President of Council became the acting executive authority of the province. He found much food for thought in the letter which Weiser had written.

Two days before Weiser had penned his letter an Indian runner had come to Tulpehocken, bearing a message from Hotquantogechte" (Hetaquantagechty) announcing that two advance deputies of the Six Nations had arrived at Shamokin. They heralded the approach of the "Chiefs of every one of the Five Nations," en route to Philadelphia. However, to transact some business with their vassals the Delawares and Shawnees, all Indians in the Susquehanna region were to be assembled at Shamokin. The deputies would tarry nine or ten days in that village before continuing to Philadelphia. As to numbers in the party "what I can learn particular of them is 75 of them, but what Crew will follow them from everywhere is uncertain."

The Indian runner had brought word to Weiser of an invasion by the "flatheads,"[22] a nickname for the southern Indians. The Flatheads were inveterate enemies of all the Six Nations, and the subordinate tribes forming the Confederacy. The Flathead invasion was against the Shawnees village at "Alligeny"—but the "accidental" arrival of thirty Delaware warriors in the Shawnees village had frightened away the southern Indians. It was rumored that the invaders "went off towards the Great Island (near present-day Lock Haven). The Delawares went after them." In concluding his letter Weiser offered to perform any services which Logan would require of him.

On September 5 Logan replied to Weiser.[23] "I must communicate to thee what thou must keep entirely to thyself," began the letter. Troubles had been brewing with Maryland province. Thomas Penn's and Lord Baltimore's land claims had strained relations between the two proprietary neighbors and now Governor Samuel Ogle of Maryland was conniving with Civility and other Susquehanna Chieftains to negotiate a sale of Susquehanna lands "to

---

21. Weiser to Logan, Logan MSS, 10:59. Unpublished correspondence of James Logan, Historical Society of Pennsylvania.
22. Flatheads – a term applied to the Catawba and Cherokee Indians, age-old enemies of the Six Nations.
23. Logan MSS, 10:60.

wrench them out of our Proprietors' hands." By all means, Weiser should endeavor to prevent this matter from coming to the attention of the Six Nations during their stay at Shamokin. Thomas Penn was planning to use the forthcoming conference as a means of negotiating such a purchase from the Six Nations, overlords of the Susquehanna tribes, thus establishing more firmly his own land claims in that region.

Weiser was given orders to go, at once, to meet the deputies at Shamokin, "carefully to watch them, insinuating thyself as far as possible into their Counsels and hasten them down to my House." Stenton, Logan's own mansion, would be thrown open to house the assorted delegates. There Thomas Penn would broach to them the matter of a land sale. Weiser must point out to the chieftains that the center of the city would be too busy a place in which to kindle their fires. Also, if possible, Weiser should endeavor to keep down the number of guests; Allumpees and his people, the Delawares, should be discouraged from coming "since they have been here so lately at the Expense of the Government."

In a letter addressed to Logan, dated "Tulpyhocen, September 16," Weiser made a report on his visit to Shamokin.[24] He had reached the Indian capital two days before the deputies arrived. Eighteen canoes, the foremost displaying a white flag, glided down the east branch of the Susquehanna to the point where the two arms of that river meet. There on the eastern bank of the main Susquehanna, where the city of Sunbury stands today, were built the huts of the Delawares. One hundred and ten natives disembarked from the canoes and quartered themselves, "some in Houses and some outdoors." Some of the Chiefs and their retinues were aged and infirm; Weiser advised that wagons should be furnished to transport them to Philadelphia. A settler who had made the journey with them shook hands with each one as they left the water's edge. Weiser was puzzled to know the name of the man but only learned that he had acted as interpreter along the route of their journey.

Some of the older chiefs recognized Weiser as Ziguras, his Mohawk name. They invited him to join their councils. Weiser responded to their greeting by inviting them to Philadelphia in

---
24. Ibid., 62.

the name of "your Brother Pen (Onas)." After chatting with his old friends "an our" (sic) Weiser "took is leave," but the Indians urged him "not to go to sleep before Council broke up." He attended their council and received a pledge that they would accept "Brother Pen's" invitation. "I expect them at my house the 18th or 19th."

On September 13, Ziguras said his farewells at Shamokin and returned to Tulpehocken. His report told Logan "I could not perceive the least sign of their showing anything from Maryland, therefore I thought not feet [fit] to mention anything." The letter ended with a suggestion to Logan that belts of wampum be provided in advance of the conference in Philadelphia, "each about 1½-foot long."

Thomas Penn and James Logan sat in the library at Stenton on September 17, 1736, discussing the contents of Conrad Weiser's letter.[25] If we could conjecture at this point we would venture to suggest that the two men were greatly perplexed. Logan had warned Weiser against the issue with Maryland, but there was another delicate matter, closer to Philadelphia. Some land transactions had engendered bitterness in the Delaware nation and some New Jersey Indians were plotting trouble. Weiser's report of discussions at Shamokin made no mention of any issue concerning the New Jersey Indians; but, reasoned Logan it would be better for all concerned if the Delaware Chiefs should be absent from the forthcoming treaty purchase.

Together Logan and Penn framed a reply. They were "concerned to find the Company [of Indians] is so very numerous." It would be impossible to entertain so many guests at Stenton before the 26th of the month. Would Weiser detain them at his home in Tulpehocken long enough to delay their arrival in Philadelphia? Fifteen pounds were being sent by the messenger Henry Noble [Kobel] to reimburse Weiser for his expenses as host to more than a hundred Indians. It was to be spent "frugally as well as decently managed lest their expectations be too much raised." Wagons should be provided to carry the sick and lame from Tulpehocken, as requested of Weiser at Shamokin. "You are full furnished with them at Tulpehocken and you may doubtless get what is necessary for hire, but perhaps one may doe."

---

25. Ibid., 2:57.

Logan's invitation to Stenton was not accepted without some grumbling among the Indians. Not the least attractive feature about their excursion to the south was the opportunity to roam the streets of Philadelphia, peering into shop windows, pawing over wares exhibited for sale on the sidewalks; lolling about the tavern doors and dram shops and gazing contemptuously at the foibles which the Philadelphians paraded along High Street, or leering, vulgarly, as well-dressed Quaker ladies passed through the streets on their way to tea at some friend's house. Sensing that the bid of Logan's suburban home was an adroit subterfuge to keep them out of the city proper, they had urged Weiser, at Shamokin, to suggest that "Shop keepers keep their Goods in the House while we are there." Evidently, they were not to be denied their holiday.

While the Indians were detained at Weiser's home in Tulpehocken they received rural entertainment. The small one-room cabin could not house them. Weiser's large family taxed its guests who used the orchards and the lawns as couches—one hundred and ten guests of the province shuffling away their time in Tulpehocken and waiting until Logan and Penn could entertain them at Stenton.

"Pray dispose them" begged Logan in a letter to Weiser written when the company of deputies and their families neared the city, September 25,[26] "Pray dispose them beforehand to continue at my House for some Days . . . besides that, the Town has been very sickly of late, but mention no more of this than thou in thy own Judgment thinks." Logan stated that Philadelphia was "very sickly." After the Indians had spent several days as guests of Stenton, they were informed that smallpox was ravaging Philadelphia and that it "would be a great trouble to us to see any of them [the Indians] taken with that Distemper."

Grateful for the consideration of their welfare the Indians insisted, notwithstanding, that since the fires had been kindled in Philadelphia, they should be permitted to make their answer there. True, the fire was burning in the city, responded Council, metaphorically, but its embers could be carried to the outskirts and a continuous fire be maintained in this way.

---

26. Maria Dickinson, Logan MSS.

The public transactions between members of Council who moved to Stenton and the Six Nations envoys took the form of reaffirmed pledges to keep the chain bright, the path opened and the fire kindled. Weiser acted as interpreter at all meetings and as advisor to Council members on several delicate matters which arose. For two days and three nights the ragged, unwashed natives, chiefs, squaws, and children encamped at Stenton mansion. They stretched their length upon the well-kept lawns and dragged moccasined feet across the velvet carpets of the finest residence in the province. Their primitive way of life was out of keeping with the refined splendor of the wealthy Quaker domicile. The Indians soon wore out their welcome at Logan's home. On October 2 Logan and the Council acceded to the Indian demands for a meeting in the city. The entire company moved to Philadelphia and held their final conferences, extending to October 14th, in the great meeting house at the corner of Second and High (Market) Streets. Despite all the fanfare and elaborate preparations for the meeting very few matters were concluded. There was the familiar discussion of the rum traffic; the terms of the alliance between the contracting parties and the usual exchange of civilities.

One vital point of the treaty was a demand from the Six Nations that Pennsylvania support their claims to Susquehanna lands which lay within the borders of Maryland and Virginia. On this head Council refused to commit itself because "we ought to be better informed." Herein lay the seeds of further Indian problems. But the Indians did agree to sign a release to all Susquehanna lands which lay in the province of Pennsylvania.

On October 12, James Logan informed Council that at a meeting with Penn and himself, the Indians had paid high tribute to Conrad Weiser and Shikellamy, "whose Bodies the Indians said were to be equally divided between them and us, we to have one half and they the other; that they had found Conrad faithful and honest; that he is a true Man and had spoke their Words and our Words, and not his own." Logan went on to say that the Indians had presented Weiser with "Skin to make him Shoes and two deer Skins to keep him warm." Shikellamy, the Indians requested, should be rewarded by the province, and in this way, the exchange of tributes would be complete. Council ordered that six pounds be expended for such things as Shikellamy "may most want." Conrad Weiser, "who is extremely useful on all such occasions," was given an outright present of twelve pounds.[27]

On October 16, Philadelphians breathed a sigh of relief as their unwelcome Indian guests set "on the Departure homewards." Conrad Weiser was charged with conducting them safely as far as Shamokin. A sum, not exceeding twenty pounds, was supplied to defray the costs of the journey.

Two days later, after the Indians had reached Weiser's home in Tulpehocken, James Logan, contemplating the results of the conference, realized that the land purchases had not been completed.[28] He remembered many things "after the Indians are gone." Pleading that both he and Penn had been sick[29] during the time of the treaty, Logan wrote to Weiser, imploring him to conclude the terms of purchase. Weiser must take "great care to explain that his [Logan's] illness is the Cause for not taking up matters at Stenton—at one time I just died away for a minute."

Complications had arisen which called for the exercise of extreme tact, wrote Logan. Now the issue of the lands along the Delaware River was broached. It was Weiser's assignment to see to it that the Six Nations released their lands to the Penns. Nutimis, a Jersey Indian, had tried "to raise war between Indians and English." During the treaty discussions, he had come to Philadelphia, demanding that the Six Nations support his Jersey people in laying claims to the lands along the Delaware. Weiser was cautioned to prevail upon the Six Nations "not to dispose of any lands" in Pennsylvania province to any other white men or Indians. In this way, the Pennsylvania authorities sought to take the grounds for complaint from under the feet of both the Delaware and New Jersey Indians.

Two deeds were sent to Tulpehocken, properly executed, but unsigned. It was Weiser's duty to prevail upon a dozen chiefs to sign one or other of the deeds. Logan's advice was "to Flatter

---

27. The major portion of the Treaty of 1736 is published in Volume IV of the Colonial Records of Pennsylvania. The gift and tribute to Weiser do not appear in this source but are included in the complete treaty as published by Benjamin Franklin, reprinted in 1938, by the Historical Society of Pennsylvania, edited by Julian Boyd and Carl Van Doren.
28. Logan to Weiser, October 18, 1736, Logan MSS, 2:58.
29. The records show that Logan's illness (?) did not prevent him from presiding at each session of the Council during the treaty negotiations. Thomas Penn was 0resent most of the time.

the Six Nations—compare their virtues with vices of others who are weak and knavish, such as Civility [Conestoga], Pesquetomen [Delaware], Nutimis [Jersey] and the like." No details were omitted from the list of instructions. Weiser was to have several of his Tulpehocken neighbors present as witnesses; Indians were to make their marks as signatures, but Weiser was urged to write their names after their marks. A stick of sealing wax and the seal of the Province were despatched to Weiser's home and James Logan waited quietly at Stenton to receive word that Pennsylvania's boundaries had been extended westward of the Susquehanna "to the setting sun, and northward to the Endless [Blue] Mountains."

Meanwhile, Weiser led his undisciplined charges to his Tulpehocken home. A sad welcome greeted him there. During his absence his son, Benjamin, had died and other children were seriously ill.[30] One hundred and ten Indians fastened themselves upon his hospitality for one week to help share his grief. The Senecas became drunk and troublesome. Lazy natives littered the *Bauernhof* as they spread their filthy blankets on the lawns and under trees. Such was the setting for one of the most important land purchases in colonial history. Fifteen chieftains signed the complete deed, and four young braves were prevailed upon to affix their signatures lest time take its toll from the ranks of the sachems and none survived to be confronted with their mark a quarter of a century hence. "It went very hart about l[a]lying over their right upon the Delaware," wrote Weiser,[31] "because they said they had nothing to doe about the land, they were afaired they should doe anything a miss to their gosens [cousins], the delawares."

The Senecas were too drunk to join the homeward journey to Mahoni.[32] Weiser was forced to trust his property to others while he led the deputies north into the hills. "There is no help for it. They are disabled to Carry for sickness and Strong Liquors Sak[e]."

The Tulpehocken Treaty of 1736, negotiated and witnessed by Palatine immigrants with New York province Indians, gave to the

---
30. Weiser's Autobiography, Rupp Collection, Library of Congress, Washington, D.C.
31. Weiser to Logan, Logan MSS, 5:65.
32. Near Selinsgrove, Pa.

Quaker proprietors in Philadelphia claims to lands which trebled the deeded area of the province. The treaty made Pennsylvania an ally of the powerful Six Nations in their claims of suzerainty over local tribes and opened wide the door for the extension of Iroquois claims against Maryland and Virginia, whose shores were split by the Susquehanna, the "River of the winding shore." Although the goods which the Indians received for their lands were given to them before they left Philadelphia, the actual deed was signed in Tulpehocken.

Logan expressed his satisfaction with Weiser's diplomacy, but confessed "no small uneasiness both on Account of the loss of thy Child and the great Trouble those disorderly people have continued to give thee."[33] Thus very deftly, the shrewd Logan closed a chapter on Indian affairs.

Chief Shikellamy

---

33. Logan MSS, 2:59.

An old postcard depicting Conrad Weiser's homestead near Tulpehocken

Thomas Penn, the son of William Penn

Virginia colonial governor Sir William Gooch

Pennsylvania colonial governor Patrick Gordon

Madame Montour

James Logan

Logan's home Stenton in Germantown

CHAPTER III

Mid-Winter Journey to Onondaga

With lavish hands, Stuart monarchs in England could bestow vast tracts of land in North America upon their court favorites. Boundaries could be expressed in the nebulous terms of degrees of latitude and longitude, but actual surveys would have to wait until forests were penetrated, mountains crossed, and frontiers extended. But Indian sachems gathered about council fires deep in the American wilderness, knew nothing of cartographs or royal grants and patents. Lands which they had not themselves sold to white men were, to their manner of thinking, their own. True, they had relinquished their claims to narrow strips along the seaboard where white-winged ships could bring the European goods to be exchanged for pelts, but the forest empire extending to the Land of the Setting Sun was still their own. To the Indian, land ownership was tribal and not individual.

In these uncharted areas, tribal interests often conflicted. Age-old hatreds between these aboriginal people frequently flared into warfare. Squatting before the glowing council fires at Onondaga venerable chieftains dreamed of the glory of conquest and of extended empire. Already they had subdued all the northern tribes, but the sunny southland, where the Catawbas and Cherokees dwelled, offered new worlds for conquest to the young braves who were inspired by the tales of heroism they heard from their elders. They too would conquer and add to the domains of the Six Nations empire.

Pennsylvania tribes had been subjugated by the Iroquois Confederacy and, so long as they comported themselves before their masters, Indian wars would not trouble the land of the Penns. But the "Flatheads," as the southern Indians were designated, lived within the grants to Virginia and the Carolinas. To satisfy their desire for glory, young Senecas, Cayugas, Onondagas, or Oneidas were forced to traverse the valleys of Pennsylvania to reach their intended victims to the southward. Their war paths led through territories which English maps called Pennsylvania, even though the Indians still believed the land to be their own. Their destinations on such forays were the westward reaches of the Potomac River and the Shenandoah Valley in Virginia.

These sporadic Indian incursions were, to say the least, annoying to the Virginia authorities. Remote settlers suffered from the raids when hungry braves helped themselves to harvests and livestock while on the warpath. If a settler resisted the thieving ways of the Indians he stood in danger of losing his own scalp.

In 1736, Sir William Gooch, governor of Virginia, wrote to Colonel William Cosby, governor of New York Province, urging him to use his influence to keep the Six Nations warriors at home. Gooch proposed that Cosby should inaugurate a peace treaty which would put an end to the annual spring-time excursions which sent scalp-hunting Iroquois southward. Governor Cosby died while Gooch's letter was in transit; consequently, the appeal was never answered.

Early in 1737, Governor Gooch turned to James Logan, President of Pennsylvania Council, imploring that province to act as a mediator in bringing about a lasting peace between the northern Indians and the Cherokees.[1] The Cherokees had expressed their willingness to treat with Six Nations deputies at Williamsburg, the Virginia capital. Would Pennsylvania dispatch someone to the Six Nations Council at Onondaga to invite their representatives to such a conference? Such a messenger should be sent at once, in order that the message could reach Onondaga before melting snows opened the war paths to marauding braves.

---
1. James Logan to Sir William Gooch, Logan Papers, 2:87.

Peace-loving Quakers were pleased to accept Gooch's proposal. In 1732 they had entered into a Treaty of Friendship with the Iroquois, which the Indians regarded as an alliance. If roving bands of warriors could be kept at home, Pennsylvania would be spared the problem of providing for them as they crossed through the province. Moreover, the shrewd Logan saw that a difficult situation might arise someday if the Iroquois should demand that Pennsylvania, as an ally of the Six Nations, should join in a war against the royal colony of Virginia. Unthinkable that two of His Majesty's colonies should be at war with each other; even more distasteful to the Quaker mind! Far better to assist in negotiating a peace between the rival factions of Indians and thereby obviate the danger of being forced to fulfill the terms of Pennsylvania's alliance with the Six Nations!

On January 22, 1737 (February 2, 1737, in the new style calendar), James Logan wrote to Governor Gooch, stating "that our Interpreter, C. Wyser, in whom the chiefs of those Nations repose great Confidence and, who joined with one of themselves (Shikellamy) . . . should go directly from hence with the message."

In a letter written on the same day, Logan told Weiser, "Now as there is no person more proper to be sent to treat with those people on the subject than thyself . . . thou art thereby desired and hereby authorized to go to Onondaga."

Conrad Weiser happened to be in the city of Philadelphia on the day that Logan penned his instructions. He agreed to undertake the journey despite all the hazards it presented. His ready acceptance enabled Logan to assure Gooch "he (Weiser) proposes to set out in a few days." Little did Gooch or Logan know the nature of the errand on which they sent their agent. January 1737, was one of the coldest periods on record. Newspapers reported that "people die of the severe Cold. Ice on the River is so firm that Booths are erected and on it people pass, not only on foot but on Horseback and Sleighs." The river continued to be frozen beyond the middle of February. On February 19, it was recorded that the ice was still there. Thus, the icy fingers of winter gripped the settlements on the Delaware and Schuylkill.[2]

---

2. *Pennsylvania Gazette*, January 25, 1737, no. 423. Published by Franklin.

Onondaga, near Syracuse, New York, was two hundred and fifty miles north of Tulpehocken, more than 300 miles north of Philadelphia, as measured by the circuitous footpaths which led through mountain defiles and across rivers which could be forded only at shallow points along their curving courses. Indians never ventured upon such a journey unless all the natural elements favored them.[3] Conrad Weiser was ordered to undertake this mission in the middle of one of the severest of winters.

On February 27, 1737, Weiser, the ambassador extraordinary, set out from his Tulpehocken home, taking with him Christopher (Stoeffel) Stump,[4] a Palatine neighbor, and an Onondaga Indian named Owisgera. This Indian had come south in 1736 to the powwow at Stenton in Philadelphia and then had become too ill to return home with his companions. Throughout the winter Weiser had cared for him at Tulpehocken and nursed him back to health; now the Onondaga welcomed the chance to return home.

The first day's journey, on horseback, carried the party to Tolheo,[5] near present-day Rehrersburg in Berks County. This was the last outpost of the English settlements. Through snow, one foot deep, the three travelers climbed the Kittatinny (Blue) Mountain, following the Indian path which later was known as the Shamokin Trail.[6] More snow fell while they rested for their second night on the crest of the mountain. "On the 2nd and 3rd of March," wrote Weiser, "we found nothing but ice under the newly fallen snow on the north side of the mountain, which caused dangerous falls to ourselves and horses."[7]

3. In a letter to Christopher Sauer, Weiser described some of his experiences: "I was ordered to undertake a journey of 500 English miles through a Wilderness." From the collection of Abraham H. Cassel. Translated by Miss Helen Bell. Published in the *Pennsylvania Magazine of History and Biography*, Philadelphia, Pa., 1877, 1:163–164.
4. Hans Georg Stumpf, wife and two children, embarked from Holland for London, July 27, 1709. Also entered on the New York Subsistence List, London Public Record Office, C.O. 5-1230. Also microfilms by the author, 1939—Christopher Stumpf, called Stoffel by Weiser, probably was one of the two children referred to above.
5. See *Richard Penn's Manor of Andolhea* by George Wheeler, *Pennsylvania Magazine of History and Biography* (1934), 58:193–212. Earlier writers interpreted the term "Tolheo" as a point farther west along the Swatara Creek. See Rupp, I.D., *History of Berks and Lebanon Counties*, 1844, 44—Andolhea, an Indian name, was corrupted by the early Germans to "Tolheo," the syllable "an" being interpreted as "at" Tolheo.
6. The present mountain road leading from Bethel in Berks County to Pinegrove in Schuylkill County. The new highway, being constructed (1934) nearby, crosses the old path at several points.
7. The narrative of the journey has been compiled from several sources, chief among which is "A Journey made in 1737," Weiser's own day by day account of his experiences. It was translated by Hiester H. Muhlenberg, M.D., and published in the Collections of the Historical Society of

After wading through snows, waist-deep, as they plodded their way through the gap in Second Mountain (near Pine Grove), they crossed the plateau of Broad Mountain which opens into the broad Lykens Valley in Schuylkill County. From there the three men wended their way through "Klinger's Gap" in Mahantango Mountain[8] and on the fourth of March, reached the Delaware Indian village of Shamokin (Sunbury).

At Shamokin, they were forced to linger for several days while they awaited an opportunity to cross the Susquehanna River. Their route lay along the eastern bank of the West Branch (Otzinachson) of the Susquehanna. Their immediate destination was the home of Shikellamy, near present-day Milton, Pennsylvania. The commission which Weiser held stipulated that the vice-regent of the Six Nations should accompany him on the journey. Although Weiser had provided himself with food for the journey he saw most of his stores disappear into the mouths of hungry Indians while he tarried in Shamokin. In vain he tried to replenish his stock. The Indians at Shamokin were on the verge of famine.

Several days passed before a canoe could be obtained in which to effect a crossing of the river. On March sixth an Indian trader rowed the three men to the opposite shore, "but not without great danger . . . the river being full of floating ice. We were obliged to leave our horses behind, as it was impossible to get them across." On the seventh day, they reached the "Zilly Aqauche" (Chillisquaque Creek in Northumberland County). The creek was swollen and treacherous, but "an old Shawno, by name Jenoniowana, took the party across in his canoe." As a reward, Weiser gave the man "some needles and a pair of shoestrings."

On the next day, the travelers reached Shikellamy's village only to find that the sachem had gone to Paxtang (Lancaster County) on a hunting trip. No Indian could be induced to go in search of the chieftain because the elements were too angry. Torrents of

---

Pennsylvania (1853), 6–22. Another account appears in English in a manuscript collection of the above society. The latter is obviously a copy of Weiser's report to the Pennsylvania Council. Also, an article entitled "Notes on the Iroquois and Delaware Indians," published in the *Pennsylvania Magazine of History and Biography*. See letter of Christopher Sauer, supra. Other references to this journey appear in Weiser's papers, the Logan papers, and the Penn manuscripts.

8. Mahantango, an Indian term meaning "the place where we had much venison." The location was later surveyed and named "Spread Eagle Manor," the present site of Klingerstown, Pa., in the northwest corner of Schuylkill County.

water had spilled into the rivers; rain, snow, and sleet fell relentlessly for four days. After a delay of one week, Shikellamy arrived in the village accompanied by Tawagaret, a Six Nations warrior, returning belatedly from the wars in Virginia.

Three more days were consumed in preparing for the extended journey northward. Tawagaret decided to avail himself of the opportunity to return to his own people. Now there were five men in the party. It was March 21, but reports from the north said that the snows were still waist-deep in the woods and "it was not possible to proceed without snowshoes."

Shikellamy's village could not furnish supplies to the travelers. "It was with great difficulty," wrote Weiser, "that I procured a small quantity of corn meal and a few beans. We had already begun to feel the pangs of hunger." Almost two hundred snow-covered miles lay between them and their destination.

On the morning of March 21, the five travelers reached the Canusorago or the Muncy Creek, which was crossed in a canoe "not without a great danger." Weiser records that two English traders attempted to cross the swollen creek later, only to have their boat capsize, resulting in the drowning of one of the men.

The Weiser party passed a place "where the Indians in former times had a great fortification on a height; it was surrounded by a deep ditch, the earth was thrown up in the form of a wall, about nine or ten feet high and as many broad. But it is now in decay, as from appearance it had been deserted beyond the memory of man." That which Weiser observed was probably a vestige of the ancient Andastes civilization of prehistoric Pennsylvania. Judging from his description, the "fortifications" resembled the mounds found in Ohio and other mid-western states, built as elaborate tombs to the memory of braves who lay buried there.

Two days of travel brought the party to Olstuago,[9] where Madame Montour, a daughter of a French army officer, "but now in mode of life a complete Indian," ruled as queen over the Indians who lived in the village. The Madame welcomed Weiser and

---

9. Olstuago, west of Muncy Creek, near Montoursville, Pa. Two Indian trails from the north converged at Muncy Creek. The Weiser Party followed the trail which led to the western branch of the Susquehanna. The Montour hut was located opposite a point known today as Sand Hill on the outskirts of Montoursville. From information supplied by Mr. Charles Loose, local historian of Montoursville and by W. C. Champion, Esq., Williamsport, Pa.

his companions, permitting the two Pennsylvanians to quarter themselves in her hut. The Olstuago Indians were suffering from famine, but from a secreted hoard, the queen provided generous portions of food for Weiser and Stump. For the first time in ten days, said Weiser, their hunger was sated. Their benefactor warned them, however, that the Indians to the northward had no food, "which my fellow travelers refused to believe until we found it true by experience."

They tarried in these hospitable surroundings for two days and on March 24 set out once more through snow "two feet deep . . . but frozen so hard that we could walk over the surface." Soon the snow became deeper. The weary travelers waded through a valley which was walled by "frightful high mountains and rocks." Here Weiser was tempted to abandon the trip and turn back. But the Indians "encouraged me to persevere."

Conrad Weiser, the European, was on trial. He had proven his skill in counsel; he had been tried in the balance and Indians found him not wanting in integrity; his native companions knew that he was held in high regard by the English authorities and they marveled at his use of a quill dipped in paint to record thoughts and send a message. But here in the forests, when all the elements were hostile and nature's children were forced to wrestle with their mother and no quarter given, how could Ziguras endure these tests? No, he dared not quail. He must force every sinew and summon every ounce of courage to plod on; the body might be forced to surrender, but the spirit, never!

The Indians took the lead in trying to find a path along the side of the mountain.[10] They "clambered with hands and feet . . . we followed after . . . there was considerable danger of freezing our feet, as we were often obliged to cross the stream (Loyalsock). In three hours of travel, they had not covered more than one mile when they halted to pitch camp for the night. Owisgera, the sickly

---

10. In reconstructing the route followed by Weiser it appears that after leaving Olstuago the party followed the Loyalsock Creek northward to a point beyond the Loyalsock Mountain and then by a northwesterly route reached the Lycoming Creek near present-day Trout Run, Lycoming County. From Trout Run, the route passed through Ralston to the point where Lycoming, Tioga and Bradford Counties meet. Weiser describes the point where Lycoming and Towanda Creeks divide, the former flowing westward to enter the west branch of the Susquehanna and the Towanda flowing eastward to enter the east branch of the same river. The waters of these two creeks are reunited again at Shamokin, which was the colonial name of the present Sunbury.

Onondaga, had not been able to keep up the pace and the other four members of the party were forced to halt to give him a chance to rejoin the party. Boughs of spruce trees were cut and placed on the snow so that the weary men could lie down to sleep under a roof of snow-covered trees. The next morning, they "were all stiff from the cold, which during the night had been excessive."

They had reached the valley of the Diadachton (Lycoming) or the Lost and Bewildered Creek. To avoid crossing and re-crossing this stream time and again as it meandered from side to side through the narrow valley, the five men crept along the sides of the mountain, "we clung on to bushes with our hands; and thus, we climbed on." Every step was perilous. Shikellamy narrowly escaped death when his foot slipped and a branch of a fir tree snapped in his hands.

The Oneida sachem slipped along the icy incline for three rods, approaching a precipice which would have tumbled him down one hundred feet upon rocky crags to certain death. By a stroke of good fortune, the pack which Shikellamy carried swung loose from his body and wound itself around a tree, thus holding the chieftain hanging by a strap until Weiser and Stoffel could descend and rescue him. When all danger had passed Shikellamy looked at the steep cliff which had yawned beneath him and declared: "I thank the Great Lord and Creator of the World that he had mercy on me, and wished me to continue to live longer."

At one point they were forced to wade the Lycoming, waist deep in a rushing torrent. Its icy water froze their clothes to their bodies after they reached the opposite shore. "The wood(s) was so thick that, for a mile at a time, we could not find a place the size of a hand where the sun could penetrate, even in the clearest weather."

"During the night it began to storm and the wind blew terribly . . . It is such a desolate region that I often thought I must perish in this frightful wilderness." They had reached the valley of *Otkon*. Otkon, the Evil Spirit, said the Indians, ruled the valley. He wreaked calamity upon all who incurred his displeasure. Misfortune crowded their day. Tawaragret fell and rolled down a cliff side. For hours he lay unconscious. Hunger pangs began to gnaw at their vitals. "It stormed again (next day) terribly and snowed at times as if it wished to bury us." Could Otkon be appeased, asked Weiser of his native companions. Yes, but it called for sacrifice and they had nothing to give, and it called for magic and none of the Indians were magicians.

On the 27th, a gruesome sight greeted the weary travelers; they saw two human skulls nailed upon poles. The Indians explained that they were the skulls of two of their comrades who were returning from the wars in South Carolina, bringing Flathead prisoners with them. One stormy night Otkon, the evil one, had untied the prisoners, who then turned upon their captors, killed them and fixed their skulls on poles.

Here was a grim reminder of the purpose of their mission. It was to prevent such murderous sorties that Weiser and his companions were suffering the hardships which they were encountering. Could they reach the Onondaga "Long House" before the braves set out for Virginia again? It was March 28th, old style, which would be April 8th in modern calendars. Fourteen days of travel still lay ahead of them. After mid-April, the snows would be gone and bloodthirsty natives would be on the warpath.

On the same day, Weiser prepared the last meal which the common stock of supply would furnish. Tawagaret assured his friends that his neighbors at Owego would be able to supply provisions, but his village was still a few days journey to the northeastward. Before reaching Owego, the party would pass through the village of the Sugar Indians on Sugar Creek. Perhaps they would have food.

The spirit of Otkon still pursued them. Although they found less snow after they left the Lycoming regions they encountered "impetuous" streams. Rebellion raised its ugly head when the Indians refused to follow Weiser's orders on devising methods for crossing Oscohu (Sugar Creek). They were "irritable from hunger, the Indians fell to abusing Stoeffel (Stump) who they said was to blame that I had not followed their advice. When I took his part, they treated me in the same way, called me a coward who loved his life, but must die of hunger on this spot." Shikellamy joined in the abuse. He belittled Weiser's woodsmanship, threatening to report his incapacities to the governor and to Thomas Penn. Tawagaret declared that he was "too proud to follow a European."

To this charge Weiser replied that it was a European characteristic to love one's life, also to love one's fellow men; while Indians loving their own lives were cruel to others. Then he took matters into his own hands, declaring that "I had so far followed their advice, but now I required them to follow mine."

The point at issue was how to cross the Oscohu, the fierce, Sugar Creek. The Indians wanted to build a raft, which Weiser disapproved, because of the velocity of the current and the submerged rocks on which the craft might snag. Instead, urged Conrad, the party should follow downstream to find a shallow place that could be forded, even if it meant going all the way to the Susquehanna River. Shikellamy scoffed at this plan; Weiser did not know how far it was to the Susquehanna, and even if he did, he could not find it. Now came the German's chance to triumph. In his pocket, Weiser carried a compass which his Indian companions regarded as a curious toy. He knew the direction they were traveling and by observing the height of the mountain peaks upstream and downstream he could reason that the land became more level and the current of the river less ferocious, and therefore the attempt to cross should be made further downstream.

Shikellamy insisted that his plan should prevail; that after all he had been appointed as the guide. Weiser replied that while his friend might be the guide, Logan had appointed him commander; therefore, Shikellamy would have to choose which course to follow. At one last request before parting company Conrad asked his friend to obey him in this instance.

Weiser set out to follow his own plans, announcing that those who wished might fall into line. Stump followed promptly and Owisgera did likewise. After sulking for a few moments Shikellamy joined the Weiser train, but Tawagaret remained obstinate. According to Weiser's testimony, his own plan for crossing the stream proved to be the better and later the Indians thanked him "for my good council, and for resisting their wishes so boldly." Meanwhile, Tawagaret had built a raft and attempted a crossing according to the Indians' plan. After a series of humiliating spills into icy waters the warrior succeeded in making a landing and rejoined the main party, humbly admitting that he had acted foolishly.

That evening the hungry travelers reached Oscohu, the village of the Sugar Indians. But they found no food. "We found nothing but hungry people who sustained life with the juice of the sugar trees." Even though Weiser had his pockets filled with Indian trinkets he could not exchange any of the baubles for food. "My only comfort this evening was, that whoever labors or is tired will find sweet sleep."

On March 29th, Weiser and his followers left the village of the Sugar Indians, "but without breakfast." On that day, near evening, they were ferried across the east branch of the Susquehanna to an Indian village inhabited by stray Cayugas and Mohicans. In vain the hungry men passed from hut to hut asking for food but heard pleas from famished Indians instead. They took quarters in the hut of a Mohican who directed his old mother to cook a soup of Indian corn. Weiser described this operation graphically: "She hung a large kettle of it over the fire, and also a smaller one with potash and made them both boil briskly. What she was to do with the potash was a mystery to me, for I soon saw that it was not for the purpose of washing . . . For the Skin of her body was not unlike the bark of tree from dirt which had not been washed off for a long time, and was quite dried in and cracked, and her fingernails were like eagle's claws. She finally took the ash kettle off the fire and put it aside until it had settled, and left a clear liquid on top, which she carefully poured into the kettle of corn." The Indians explained that this liquid would render the soup more palatable.

Weiser found that the soup was not as repulsive as the "dirty cook and unclean vessel." The interpreter left the hut while his companions were eating and induced an old woman to exchange some loaves of bread for needles and shoestrings. This bread he shared with Stump, his lone white companion. Meanwhile, the three Indians ate or drank too much of the old squaw's porridge and became sick.

Next morning the party set out once again, this time Weiser shared some of his bread with all companions. A guide who accompanied them to show them how to cross swollen streams fell into the water and saved himself by swimming in the opposite direction to which the party was traveling. Without a guide, they found their way to the Owego river. They were now in the province of New York.

Owego, a large Indian village, lay one mile away, across the broad river. It was the home of Tawagaret, who had assured his companions that his people could furnish food plentifully. The travelers fired their guns from the southern side of the river, but no natives heeded the signal. That night they tried to encamp on the ground, but a terrific storm made rest impossible, instead the men "stood the whole night around the fire." As dawn approached the cold became more bitter and the pools of water froze into ice.

After daylight, several Indian women came to the bank of the Owego on the opposite shore. They shouted that all the men of the village had gone in search of game and therefore they would not venture to bring their canoes across. Then Tawagaret called to them. Recognizing his voice a few of the more venturesome squaws rowed to the shore, where the five men waited. The white men were puzzled to note one of the women covered her face with a blanket. She was Tawagaret's wife. She had hidden her face out of modesty. "Such is the custom among the virtuous women of the Indian tribes."

Weiser found an unexpected welcome in the Cayuga village at Owego. Among the older members of the tribe, there were "some of them old acquaintances of mine from Shoharie"; some had "lodged at my house at Schoharie some fifteen or sixteen years ago." Now the Indians returned the hospitality and gave Weiser and his companions "food repeatedly, but each time only a little so as not to injure our health."

For two days Weiser and his three companions enjoyed the hospitality at Owego. Tawagaret "lodged in the hut of his mother-in-law." He was at home at least and tarried there. On April 2nd the two white men and two Indians reached an Onondaga village, where once again Weiser found welcome in the hut of an old Schoharie acquaintance. On the next day, they reached Otsiningo, another Onondaga village. Now Weiser was treading upon familiar territory. He records that he had visited the place in 1726, but he found his "old acquaintances of that period partly absent, partly dead." Here the Indians were starving. Weiser gave them food from the store which he had procured at Owego, even though his Indian companions disapproved, as they "showed great dissatisfaction." That night a thief stole the remainder of Weiser's provisions.

The snow was still knee-deep in the northlands and a five-day journey lay ahead before the Onondaga capital could be reached. Again, Weiser traded needles and shoestrings, this time for maple sugar juices, which proved to be an unsatisfactory diet, for all the members of the party "became quite ill." Stoffel Stump wished to die. His lone white companion appealed to Weiser to secure a canoe and float with the current down the Susquehanna to Shamokin and go home.

Now Weiser was obdurate and in his account, he states that he called upon God to give him strength. He called all the Indians at Otsiningo together and explained the object of his mission, pointing out its urgency and pleading for their help. An old Onondaga chieftain responded to his plea. A vacant hut was ransacked for provisions, two Indian runners traveling on show shoes were sent on ahead to apprise the capital of Weiser's approach. One of these was Kaloping, a Frenchman, who had been captive while he was a child, "but now an Indian in appearance if not worse." Meanwhile, Weiser and his companions waited for the return of the messengers. Old friends of the Schoharie days invited Weiser and Stump to supper occasionally and now and then mysteriously, loaves of bread were brought out of hiding. Doubtless, Shikellamy and Owisgera fared equally well in the huts of some of their friends and acquaintances. While the white men tarried Conrad heard the wise men of the villages lament the future fate of the Indians. Game was scarce, they said because white men induced the Indians to kill for skins, giving strong liquor in exchange. "Rum will kill us and leave the land clear for the Europeans," they avowed.

Weiser watched the children of the Indian village feeding upon bulbous roots that had been exposed by the rushing waters and heavy rains. The roots described may have been the wild Jerusalem artichoke, which Weiser called "wild potatoes or ground acorns . . . and look much in size and shape like black acorns." While he observed the children digging up the roots, Conrad was reminded of verses from the Book of Job 31:3-8 . . . "Then let me sow, and let another eat; yea let my offspring be rooted out." The fact that he recorded the fears of the elders and then noted the actions of the children reveals that Weiser too was giving some thought to the future of the Indian race.

"Hunger," wrote Weiser, "is a great tyrant, he does not spare the best of friends, much less strangers." Several days were spent in Otsiningo, which was known as the Den of Murderers because so many people were "swallowed up" each year. On April 8th, the party set out once more, but at noontime they met the two messengers returning, saying it was impossible to get through the snows. The old Onondaga chief had accompanied Weiser. His advice was to push on despite the discouraging reports. Rain and snow continued to fall alternately. The hungry weary men stumbled along, falling into "ditches and holes" along their course. "We all lost courage. I trembled and shook so much all over . . . I stepped aside and sat down under a tree to die."

This time it was the Indians who revived Weiser's spirit. Shikellamy remonstrated with him, reminding him of his religious convictions calling for faith. "Evil days," said Shikellamy, "were better for us than good, for the first often warned us against sins and washed them out, while the latter often enticed us to sin."

The old chieftain, who had not suffered during the weeks of fatigue, managed to go on ahead of the party and apprise the nearest Onondaga village of the mission and the plight of Weiser and his men. The final stages of the journey were eased by warmer weather and bare earth to tread upon. On the evening of April 10, four haggard men stumbled into Onondaga village. The huts were emptied to greet them. "You look like dead men," they were told. Weiser's acquaintances were "surprised at my miserable aspect; one said it is he; another said no, it is another person."

A message was sent to the chief village, the Onondaga capital, to announce that a message from Brother Onas (Governor Penn) had arrived. The messenger soon returned with an invitation to Weiser to come to them. His arrival was "anxiously awaited."

Here Weiser writes in his diary: "Honor and praise, glory and power be given to Almighty God, who rescued us from so many and various evils and dangers, and saved us from death and destruction, from doubt and despair, and other hazards."

On April 12, the Indian Council assembled to hear the message which Weiser had brought. There were "about forty men who all entered (Weiser's lodgings) with great gravity and pride." There were chiefs from all the Nations except the Cayugas. Weiser spoke to them in the Maqua tongue, which all understood. He presented a belt of wampum and a "string of eight *klafter* long," in the name of the Governor of Virginia and of Thomas Penn, Proprietor of Pennsylvania. His addressed stressed two points, namely, a truce with the southern Indians and an invitation to a treaty conference at Williamsburg in Virginia.

A feast followed the speech. Food was carried into the hut by the chiefs themselves and a pleasant time was had as Weiser recounted the experiences of his journey to them. Shikellamy and Stump ate too much and became very sick. No business was transacted on the next day, April 13. On the 14th, the council reassembled. This time all male Indians were present. Weiser's message was repeated in substance and he agreed that it was properly stated. Then the chief spokesmen of the tribe gave their answer. They would agree to the truce and keep their braves at home for one year. But they declined to accept the invitation to Williamsburg, suggesting Albany as the place of the congress of Indian tribes. Their pride would not permit them to enter the country of their enemy under a flag of truce.

With the object of his mission successfully achieved, Weiser indulged himself too much, "they showed every kindness to me, and we had no scarcity of food." He stated in his journal that he became very sick and expected to die. He lay in an unconscious stupor for half an hour. The Indians nursed him faithfully, prescribing medicines and sending him on brisk walks. On one of these walks, he was overcome with exhaustion and lay "insensible" on the ground. Some Indians found him, took him back to his hut and put him to bed.

In a few days, the three invalids had recovered and on April 18 they began their homeward journey, "if it should please the Supreme Being. The gods of the heathen are idols, the God of Israel created the heavens . . . He is God." This was Weiser's farewell to the Indian country. Stump and Shikellamy accompanied him southward. Owisgera remained at Onondaga. This time they were well stocked with provisions, furnished by the chiefs of Onondaga. Caxhayan, an Indian guide, was sent to accompany them for several miles.

Their journey proceeded without incident or accident. They re-crossed paths which had caused them so many hardships, but now the snow was gone and there was game to be shot in the forests. The traders were on the trails and they were generous with their rum. On April 28, Weiser and Stump reached Shamokin; Shikellamy had stopped at his village. "When I went on shore and looked into the forest the first object I saw was my horse, about 20 rods off, in fact not far from the spot where I left him, when going up," recorded Weiser. On May 1 the two men were at home in Tulpehocken.

WILLIAM COSBY
Twenty-fourth royal governor
of New York (1732-36).

Colonial governor of New York William Cosby

Map of southeastern Pennsylvania in colonial times

Klinger's Gap in Mahantongo Mountain near Klingerstown

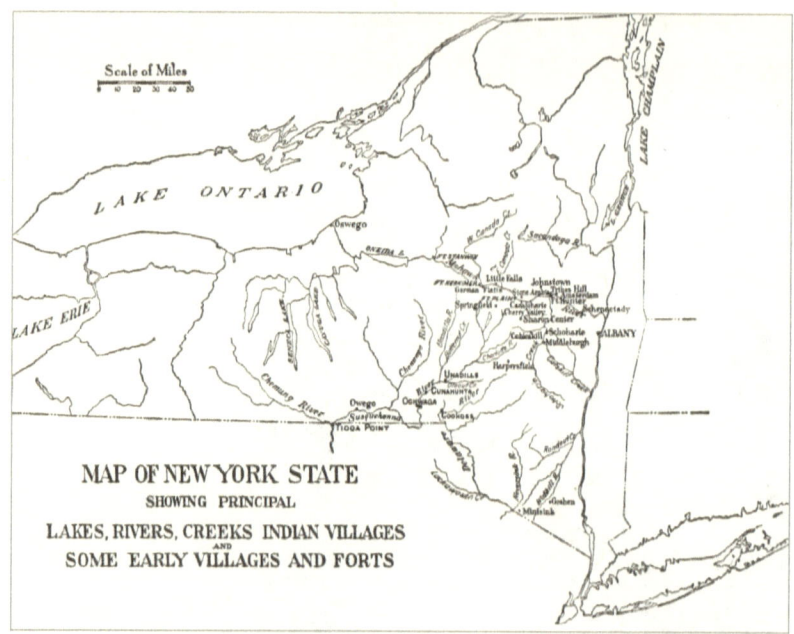

Map of colonial New York.

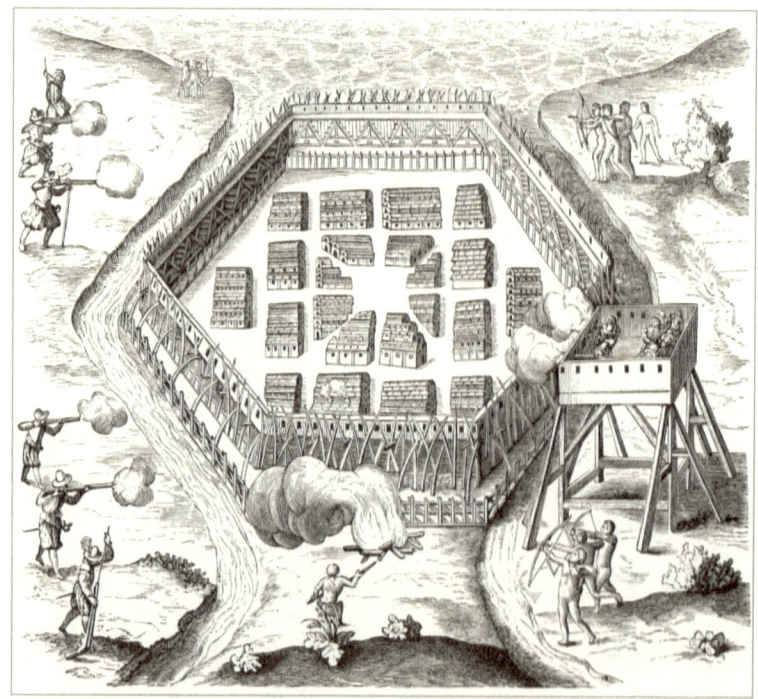

A palisaded Onondaga village

CHAPTER IV

Expanding Indian Affairs

The journey which Conrad Weiser made to Onondaga in 1737 on behalf of the governor of Virginia served to extend Pennsylvania's interest in Indian affairs beyond the borders of its own province. In former times the Penns had concerned themselves only with the tribes that shared the lands between the Delaware and the Susquehanna Rivers. Among these tribes were the Nescopecks, Conestogas, Conoys, Lenni Lenape, Wyominks, Minisinks, Susquehannocks, and others. The two important tribes were the Shawnees and the Delawares, the smaller groups being merged with or subordinate to the two larger nations. After Weiser participation in Indian affairs widened to include diplomatic relations with all the important tribes from the Great Lakes southward to Georgia. Weiser became almost indispensable to the Pennsylvania authorities, most of whom were Quakers. Earnestly desiring to play the role of peacemakers and, strategically, occupying the middle position between the two great Indian Confederacies, the governor and his advisors came to rely upon Weiser for his sagacity as well as his skill in interpreting.

But Conrad Weiser was wrestling with other problems during the years between 1736 and 1741. He was concerned about the heavenly kingdom and the redemption of the souls of men. In May 1735, he became an active Brother in the monastic order at the Ephrata Cloisters, contributing of his substance, proselyting for the faith and living the life of a self-abnegating monk. His fellow worshippers looked upon his worldly activities with disapproval.

To their way of thinking his employment in the interests of an earthly government conflicted with his spiritual obligations.[1] In deference to Conrad's scruples James Logan, Acting Governor of the province, called upon him for services only when it was necessary for dealing with inter-colonial matters. The affairs of the Delawares and Shawnees were entrusted to other hands for a time.

One of the penalties for being fixed in persons' minds as a leader is that one must frequently bear the blame for the evil things as well as the good. For almost two hundred years Conrad Weiser has been held responsible for the alienation of the Delaware and Shawnees Indians and the consequent series of Indian massacres which drenched the frontiers in blood during the French and Indian War. In his "Conrad Weiser and the Indian Policy of Colonial Pennsylvania," Joseph Walton charged that by espousing the cause of the Six Nations, Weiser bent the Indian policy of the province in such manner that the Pennsylvania tribes were outraged and eventually wreaked their vengeance with firebrand and tomahawk.[2] These charges will not withstand the scrutiny of the historian.

In a scholarly paper entitled "Conrad Weiser and the Delawares" Dr. Paul A. W. Wallace refutes the charge that Weiser was responsible for the alienation of the Delawares. "To the charges that Weiser's policy drove this tribe into the hands of the French, we reply that the alienation of the Delawares was an accomplished fact before Weiser appeared on the scene. His policy served to postpone the Delaware war and very nearly to prevent it altogether."[3]

The Delawares were conquered by the Iroquois long before Weiser came to Pennsylvania and they were made to wear "petticoats," which was a metaphor used by Indians to symbolize complete subjugation of a tribe.[4] Weiser had no part in this conquest

---

1. Hark, J. Max, Translation of *Chronicon Ephratense*, Lancaster, 1889, 82 et seq.
2. Thomson, Charles, *An Enquiry into the Causes of the Alienation of the Delaware and Shawanese Indian from the British Interest*, London, 1759.
3. Wallace, P.A.W., *Conrad Weiser and the Delawares*, Pennsylvania History, vol. 4, no. 3, 148.
4. There was a tradition among the Maqua Delawares that their one-time allies had betrayed them into a position in which the Lenni-Lenape, as they called themselves, had acted as peace negotiators. Since peace was effeminate, the negotiators accepted the status of "women" and figuratively, the word "petticoats."

and when he recognized the suzerainty of the Six Nations over the Pennsylvania Indians he was merely accepting the existing order of things. At the time Weiser became active in Indian affairs there was no keen resentment against this status on the part of the subject peoples. Fully aware of the vices of the Delawares, Weiser shared some of the prejudices which the Six Nations had against their loyalties. His insistence that the sovereignty of the Six Nations over their vassal tribes be recognized at all times was based upon his willingness to face realities. His prejudices, however, did not over-cloud his natural instincts as a peace-maker. In a fragment of one of his letters, written in 1748 or 1749 he advises that better relations between the Six Nations and their conquered tribes could be established if the term "petticoats" were avoided "and give them a Breech Cloath to wear" and also to substitute some other word for "cousins," which in the Indian tongue meant a subject people.

Weiser had no hand in the one overt act under which the Delawares chafed for twenty years. The notorious cheat of the "Walking Purchase" was engineered in 1737 at Pennsbury Manor, the summer residence of Thomas Penn, in conference with Nutimus, Lappawinzo and other Minisink and Jersey Indians.

Sassoonan, alias Allumpees, king of the Delawares, was not even invited to the conference. We know that a few weeks after the "Walk" the Delaware king visited Weiser at Tulpehocken and Pesquetomen, second Delaware of importance, was there too.[5]

While we have no record of the purpose of their visit, it may be surmised that they had gone to their friend Conrad to consult with him concerning the injustice done them. At least we can be certain that cordial relations existed because the king spent several days as Weiser's guest in August 1737.

It is true that Weiser prevailed upon the chiefs of the Six Nations to sign the Tulpehocken deed of 1736 which, inferentially, prevented the Delawares from selling any more land to Pennsylvania without the consent of the Iroquois. It is likewise true that Thomas Penn arranged the "walking purchase" with a view to making the deed to Bucks County lands doubly secure even to the extent of paying twice for the same territory.

---
5. Logan to Weiser, August 6, 1737, Peters MSS, 1:30.

It was the way this "walk" was conducted that angered the Delawares. Contrasted with the methods used by Conrad Weiser in Indian treaties, the walk was a fraud against tacitly recognized rights and an insult to the pride of a haughty nation. The terms of the sale called for the transfer of as much land as one man could walk in three days. Edward Marshall, a fast runner, was selected to walk out the distance. Instead of walking at a normal pace, as the Indians had intended, Marshall, and his relays ran and ran, outdistancing the Indian deputies who were sent to follow them. By this ruse, thirty miles were added to the domains which the Indians thought they were selling.

From 1737 to 1740, Weiser was not asked to act as interpreter in the various conferences with Pennsylvania Indians. The tasks were performed by James LeTort, a Frenchman, and George Miranda, an Indian trader.[6]

But Weiser was not idle in the interests of the province. In August of 1737, Logan requested him to "learn what number of Shawnees there are above or on or near Susquehanna, what towns of them and who are their chiefs."[7] The same letter requested Weiser to send a message to the Six Nations, informing them of Governor Gooch's transactions with the Catawba and Cherokee Indians.

Immediately upon receiving Weiser's account of his mid-winter mission to Onondaga, Logan had apprised the Virginia Governor of the results of the journey. The Six Nations had agreed to a cessation of hostilities for one year, but they designated Albany, rather than Williamsburg, as the place of meeting for ironing out inter-Indian squabbles. Gooch was "highly pleased" with Weiser's account and immediately dispatched a messenger to the Catawbas and Cherokees.

The reply received from the Cherokees was favorable to the formation of the treaty of peace, but the Catawbas were raising the hatchet. While Gooch's messenger was treating with them a sortie of Six Nation warriors had fallen upon a Catawba hunting party, killing three of their men and five of their horses. Despite the truce eight Catawbas had been killed by northern Indians

---

6. Colonial Records, 4:235–285 passim.
7. Logan to Weiser, supra.

"since their corn was planted," that is to say after the agreement which Weiser reported. The Cherokees too had met a band of Six Nations warriors in the woods, but these braves observed the terms of their agreement and for that reason, the Cherokees were willing to treat. The Catawbas had sworn revenge.

Peace-loving Quakers in Philadelphia were forced to send a message to the Six Nations in New York, warning them that they should be prepared to protect themselves against angry Catawbas. Had the Pennsylvanians not done this the Six Nations would have held the sons of Onas responsible for any surprise attack from the "Flatheads." But, at the same time, the Philadelphia Friends enjoined the northern allies to be peaceful lest "by their wars, they lessen their numbers and weaken themselves."[8]

In February 1738, Logan wrote to Governor George Clarke of New York, urging him to arrange a meeting at Albany between the northern and southern Indians. "Our Interpreter," wrote Logan, "an honest Dutchman, who lives about 70 miles from hence" had visited the Six Nations in the interest of Virginia and had succeeded in all particulars except in his effort to have the Iroquois come to Williamsburg in Virginia. The Iroquois had insisted upon meeting at Albany. Would Clarke assist in arranging such a conference? Meanwhile, Governor Gooch had sent a second messenger to the Catawbas and this time they had agreed to talk matters over with their foes in the northlands.[9]

Logan wrote to the governor of Virginia, explaining that the Indians of New York regarded Albany as their meeting place in treating with foreign nations. In this letter Logan urged Gooch to employ the services of Weiser at the Albany meeting . . . "but a good Interpreter will accompany them, they have good ones at Albany on their side, but for judgment and honesty none I believe exceeds ours, only he has a heavy Load of about ten small children to provide for."[10]

On February 15, 1738, Proprietor Thomas Penn sent a message to the Six Nations, informing them that Virginia's governor announced that the southern Indians had agreed to a cessation

---
8. Thomas Penn to the Six Nations, September 27, 1737, Peters MSS, 1:31.
9. Logan to Clarke, February 1, 1738, Logan Papers, 10:68.
10. Logan to Gooch, February 2, 1738, Ibid., 70.

of hostilities until a meeting at Albany could be arranged. "The Catawbas have maturely considered what passed last year, and are willing to believe that those from the northward who killed their People knew nothing of the Cessation of Arms, that for this reason they would Excuse the Action and are still desirous to make Peace, for which End they will meet the Chiefs of the Six Nations next summer at Albany."[11]

But no meeting between northern and southern Indians took place "next summer" or for several summers thereafter. In August 1738, George Thomas, the newly appointed deputy governor in Pennsylvania, arrived. He replaced Governor Patrick Gordon, who had died in 1736. The position of James Logan in colonial affairs was no longer preeminent in the administration of the province, although his influence continued to be felt for another decade. Governor Thomas, formerly a planter in Antigua, West Indies, was not a Quaker. The sons of William Penn had not espoused their father's faith and they selected their deputies without regard to religion. Reverend Richard Peters, an Anglican clergyman, became the secretary to the governor. Meanwhile, the Assembly continued to be made up of an overwhelming majority of Friends. Consequently, there was endless bickering between the executive and legislative branches of the government. Indian affairs, particularly those which concerned other colonies primarily, receded in the minds of the authorities, temporarily, at least.

Occasionally depredations of one sort or another forced the colony to pay some attention to Indian affairs during the year 1739. In April Secretary Peters called the attention of the new governor to a murder which had occurred in the "Shannandoah" and he wondered whether the Tulpehocken Treaty of 1736 gave Pennsylvania possession of those lands. Again, in that year William Webb, near Haycock Mountain, in Bucks County, was brutally assaulted by some Minisinks and suffered wounds which nearly proved fatal.

The War of the Austrian Succession commenced in 1740. Although the central issue of the struggle involved the central states of Europe, the conflict expanded into a struggle for empire ranging England and France upon opposite sides. In America,

---
11. Thomas Penn to the Six Nations, Peters MSS, 34.

the war is known today as King George's War, but colonial contemporaries referred to it as the Spanish War.¹² In a series of four colonial wars, the Indians held the balance of power between the British and French domains in the new world and their friendship was courted by both sides. Renewed concern about matters of forest diplomacy marks the year 1740.

In July 1740, Weiser informed Logan that a large group of Indians was on its way to Philadelphia. They were mostly Delawares and Shawnees but a few Six Nations Indians were among them. Logan showed Weiser's letter to Thomas Penn and replied to the writer, urging him to accompany the sachems as he did on former occasions. Weiser's original letter had stated that other matters detained him at home and he could not come. Logan sent a sum of money to help to defray the expenses en route and for entertaining the visitors. Logan's persuasions prevailed upon Weiser to come to Philadelphia and acquaint the proprietors, in advance, with the objectives of this unheralded visit.

At Stenton, July 30, 1740, Weiser informed Logan that the Shawnees had come to discuss the fur trade, the Delawares to talk about purchases, and Shikellamy, representing the Six Nations, wanted to know why his people had not been informed about the war which the great king over the seas had begun against Spain.¹³ The Iroquois were uneasy about their relations with their neighbors to the north and about the remainder of the goods which they were to receive in payment for their last sale of land. They feared that Great Britain at war would not be able to furnish the gunpowder which had been promised at reasonable prices.

Fortified by this advance knowledge the authorities were in a better position to cope with the problems which were presented when the conferees met in the Friends Meeting House and concluded the Treaty of 1740, August 1 to August 6. An Indian, named Freeman, acted as Interpreter for the Shawnees and Weiser served as interpreter for the questions which Shikellamy raised on behalf of the Six Nations.¹⁴

---

12. Spain entered the war on the side of Austria before France joined the allies against Frederick of Prussia. Sir William Gooch of Virginia lost interest in Indian affairs when the war began. He equipped and led an expedition against Carthegena, Spanish Cuba.
13. Pennsylvania Archives, 2nd ser., 7:236–237.
14. Colonial Records, 4:432–437.

The Western Indians complained that "your young men" had driven off all the game. "We want you to keep your young men away. We want our guns and axes mended free." Governor Thomas agreed to the demands and gave the Shawnees a handsome present. Said the Shawnees: "We are very sensible of the Fruits of Peace. We feel its benign influences, comfortable as the Sun Beams." To Sassoonan, king of the Delawares, the authorities showed courtesies as usual.

To Shikellamy was given the reply that the reason for not informing the Six Nations of the war in Europe was that France was not yet a party to the conflict. Then the proud sachem was regaled with a glowing picture of the might of Britain's navy and the prowess of her king.

In a letter from Logan to Penn, written on the eve of the 1740 conference, it becomes clear that Weiser's judgment, as well as his service, was enlisted in negotiating these matters. Logan wrote: "It is to be doubted whether it may be to satisfie them all with anything that may be reasonable to offer, and consequently the Treaty that was begun in perfect Friendship may end in or occasion a very wide misunderstanding. Therefore, as thou art sensible of Weiser's capacity in such matters, as well as honesty, no man can perhaps more fit to be advised upon the whole."[15]

By the Treaty of Tulpehocken, 1736, the Six Nations had sold lands west of the Susquehanna. Because this treaty was arranged at the frontier home of Conrad Weiser, far removed from the stores of supplies, there had been no exchange of goods to compensate the Indians. The Indians promised that they would collect that which was due them at some future time.

Early in 1742, Conrad Weiser received word from the Six Nations that they were planning to send deputies to Philadelphia in the early summer to collect what was due them. Weiser dispatched the messenger Caxhayan to Richard Peters, who, in his turn, informed Governor Thomas.

Late in February the governor instructed Weiser to send a message of welcome to the northern Indians. "You will put this in such a dress as will be most agreeable to the People it is to be carried to, which you understand." Again, Weiser was asked to

---
15. Pennsylvania Archives, supra.

escort the deputies to the capital city, to provide entertainment for them and to feed them at his Tulpehocken home.[16] "I hope nothing will happen to prevent your coming with them, for I shall not know what to do without you . . ." wrote Governor Thomas.

There was a reason for the governor's expressed concern about "Honest Conrad's" presence at the conference. Evil days had fallen upon the Weiser household and many members of the family were seriously ill. On March 16, 1742, one of Weiser's children, a seventeen-year-old daughter, Madalina, died in the Sister's house at Ephrata. In his autobiography, Weiser wrote: "My dear daughter Madalina went from Time to Eternity through an easy death after a long and tedious illness. Her Faith, Consolation, and Refuge were in the crucified Savior Jesus Christ, who she had vowed herself to in days of health with soul and body."[17]

Amid his own miseries, Conrad Weiser was solicitous for the welfare of others. The Pennsylvania Assembly was convoked into extraordinary session in January 1742 to consider the matter of building a hospital "for ye Reception of" the sick German immigrants who were supposed to be responsible for the dreaded malady known as Palatine fever. We have the testimony of Richard Peters that this special session was called "as ye Germans were by their friend Conrad Weiser importunate to have a hospital."[18] The projected "Pest House" plan led to a protracted controversy between the executive and legislative branches of the government during which the welfare of the poor Germans was forgotten.

Another reason which led Thomas to add a special plea to Weiser to attend the conference was the fear that the rules of the Ephrata Brethren would prevent their "Brother Enoch" (Weiser) from participating in Indian affairs. On this point, however, the governor had no real cause for worry. The arrival of Count Nikolaus von Zinzendorf had served to divorce Weiser from the ascetic life of the monastery on the Cocalico. The Count was vitally interested in the Indians because he wanted to convert them to Christianity. Weiser caught the fire of the missionary spirit and entered wholeheartedly into Zinzendorf's program.[19] Conse-

---

16. Governor George Thomas to Weiser, February 26, 1742, Peters MSS, 1:73.
17. Sachse, J. F., *The German Sectarians of Pennsylvania*, Philadelphia, 1900, 2:276.
18. Peters Letter Book, 5:3.
19. A subsequent chapter will deal with Weiser's interest in Zinzendorf's proselyting among the Indians.

quently, in 1742, he was quite willing to resume his leadership in Indian affairs.

Late in May, Caxhayan, the Cayuga messenger, together with his family of four, returned from Onondaga, announcing that the Six Nations were on their way to Philadelphia, to receive their goods. On June 10, Richard Peters sent a wagon to Tulpehocken, carrying among other things twelve pounds of tobacco, for the entertainment of the Indians. Weiser was instructed to provide for all their needs "with what Provisions you pleas & as far as you please." The magistrates in Philadelphia forbade the keepers of dram shops to sell rum to the visitors and the home of a Mrs. Butler was equipped to care for the visiting delegates.[20]

These instructions were sent by Richard Peters. On the same day, the venerable James Logan wrote to "Dear Conrad" urging that the Delawares be dissuaded from joining the trek of the delegates from New York. From long experience, Logan knew that the deputies would have a multitude of followers in their train, particularly when provincial gifts lay at the journey's end. Perhaps Allumpees, the Delaware King, at Shamokin, might be persuaded to come, opined Logan, but Weiser should discourage a mass migration of Pennsylvania Indians.[21]

The sagacious Logan had guessed correctly. Late in June, one hundred and sixty starving Iroquois were "now at Conrad's House." Weiser had informed Logan of the number of delegates from each tribe, to which Logan replied that he thought there should be "more of the Senecas and less of other tribes." The Senecas were the western nation of the Confederacy and therefore most directly concerned in negotiating for western lands. While the Indians lingered at Weiser's home their numbers were augmented by the arrival of stragglers until the bedraggled army of mendicants reached two hundred and twenty.[22]

Weiser led this shabby, filthy, horde of assorted deputies and camp followers to Logan's palatial home at Stenton, near Germantown. There the weary tribesmen insisted upon resting for three

---

20. Peters to Weiser, June 28, 1744, Peters Papers, 1:85.
21. Logan to Weiser, June 28, 1742, Ibid., 84.
22. Thomas Hockley to Thomas Penn, June 27, 1742, *Pennsylvania Magazine of History and Biography*, 27:435. Logan wrote to the Penns saying that there were 188 in the original group, but that they were joined by thirty or forty additional Shawanese, Conestogas, and other Pennsylvania Indians. Logan to Proprietors, July 12, 1742, Peters Paper, 1:89.

days before entering upon any deliberations. The first conference was held on July 2 at Stenton. Canassatego, the Onondaga chieftain, was the speaker for the Six Nations and Governor Thomas spoke for Pennsylvania. Conrad Weiser was the interpreter. After the customary preliminaries, the Indians apologized for the rash acts some of their young men committed on their present journey and received a mild rebuke from Governor Thomas. The first conference was held on Friday. On Saturday the Indians entered the city and on the following Monday, a meeting of Council and the main chiefs of the Indians was held at the Proprietor's house. Every effort was made to please these chiefs to hold them loyal during the war which was being waged by England against Spain, the sparks of which might set off a fire in the New World.[23]

At this conference, it was learned that the Senecas had not come because there was a famine in their land. Children were being eaten by their own parents, so terrible was the state of affairs in that nation. Although they could not attend the conference, the Senecas had empowered the other nations to act in their interest.

The Indians spent almost two weeks in Philadelphia. The great concourse of persons who attended these conferences made it necessary to conduct public affairs in the Great Meeting House. On July 6th the list of goods for the Indians was read, as follows:[24]

"500 lbs. Powder,
60 Kettles,
600 lbs. Lead,
100 Tobacco Tongs,
45 Guns,
100 Scissors,
60 Stroud Match Coats,
500 Awl Blades,
100 Blankets,
120 Combs,
100 Duffil Match Coats,
2,000 Needles,
200 Yards of Half thick,

---

23. Colonial Records, 4:560–572 passim.
24. Indian Treaties printed by Benjamin Franklin, 24.

1,000 Flints,
100 Shirts,
224 Looking Glasses,
40 Hats,
2 lbs. Vermilion,
40 Pairs of Shoes & Buckles,
100 Tin Potts,
40 Pair of Stockings,
1,000 Tobacco Pipes,
100 Hatchets
24 dozen of Gartering,
500 Knives,
200 lbs. of Tobacco, and
100 Hoes,
25 Gallons of Rum."

On July 10, an additional gift was made to the Indians, which increased the number of many of the above items and added another twenty gallons of rum, some tobacco, tongs, and sixty ruffled shirts.

Surrounded by this wealth, the Indians were concerned about their friend Conrad Weiser. They asked the governor not to fail to reward the Interpreter, "one in whom You and We can place a Confidence . . . He is a member of our Council, as well as of yours. When we adopted him, we divided him into two equal Parts, one we kept for ourselves and one we left for You. He has had a great Deal of Trouble with us, wore out his Shoes in our Messages, and dirty'd his Clothes by being amongst us *so that he is as nasty as an Indian.* And on our own behalf, we give him five Skins to buy him Cloaths and Shoes with." [25]

To this fine tribute, the governor replied that "We are pleased with the Notice you have taken of him, and think that he richly deserves it at your Hands. We shall not be wanting to make him a Suitable Gratification for the many good and faithful services he has done this Government." In effecting this pledge Council

---
25. Colonial Records, 4:581.

awarded Weiser thirty pounds for his services for "his Diligence & Labor . . . and his Skill in the Indian Languages and Methods of Business." They approved as "moderate" his bill for the expenses of the Indian journey from Tulpehocken and advanced a larger sum to him to help defray the expenses of the homeward journey.

While more than two hundred Indians were hard to be considered as welcome guests in Philadelphia, there is little evidence of any trouble caused by them during their stay. On the credit side, it was noted by the *Gazette* that the visiting Indians helped to put out a fire in the city.[26] Their good behavior can be attributed to the discipline imposed by Weiser because their conduct through the settled areas was orderly in contrast to the depredations they committed before reaching Weiser's home.

Before Weiser led his charges from Philadelphia, Logan wrote to him, urging that he should obtain information from the Indians "how many men for Service each nation consists of. What nations of Indians are at present in alliance with them" giving the names and locations of all allied tribes. Logan had his eyes upon the future. A war with France was looming ominously and it behooved leaders of the English colonies to take account of the strength of their Indian allies.[27]

Weiser waited until the body of Indians had returned to his home in Tulpehocken and there he secured the desired information from his guests. He learned of allies west of Lake Erie, thirty towns and two hundred warriors; of Indian villages on Lake Huron; on the branches of the Ohio, on the "great River Missysippy; of Indians in Canada who "live altogether on flesh, fish, roots, and Herbs, an "infinite Number of People, of late become Allies to the Six Nations." It is doubtful whether any provincial conference in America encompassed such a vast territory prior to this inquiry made by Weiser in his Tulpehocken home.

The Philadelphia Council of 1742 ended on July 12. In addition to receiving payment for western lands, the Iroquois used the final day of the conference to deliver a severe reproof to the Delawares for selling lands without permission from the Six Nations.[28]

---

26. Watson, *Annals of Philadelphia*, 2:161.
27. Logan to Weiser, July 11, 1742, Peters Papers, 1:88.
28. Minutes of Executive Council, Colonial Treaties, 4:586.

"You ought to be taken by the Hair and shak'd severely till you recover your senses and become Sober . . . This land that you claim is gone through your Guts. . . . You receive them (slanderous stories about settlers) with as much greediness as a Lewd Woman receives the Embraces of Bad Men. . . . You are Women." This vituperative chastisement was translated into English by Weiser and then translated into the Delaware tongue by Cornelius Spring.[29]

It was a happy assemblage that marched northward from Philadelphia in mid-July, along the road to Weiser's home in Tulpehocken. Gayly colored garments bedecked the stragglers, their faces painted with newly acquired vermillion dyes, tobacco fumes exuding from their mouths, and firewater exciting their senses with synthetic cheers as they followed Tarachawagon,[30] Conrad Weiser, along the winding Schuylkill.

---

29. Indian Treaties, supra, 21.
30. Tarachawagon—meaning "he who holds the reins of the Universe," the name given to Conrad Weiser by the chiefs of the Long House of Onondaga – W. F. Beauchamp.

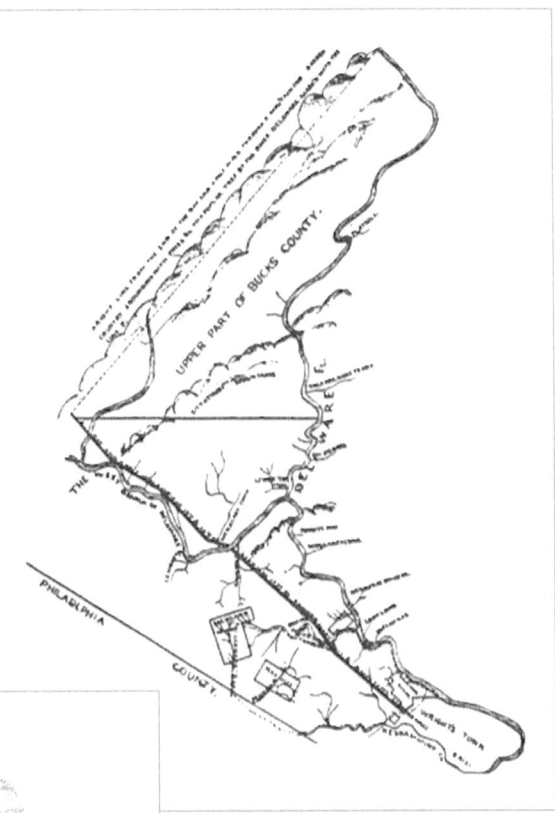

Map of the Walking Purchase

Richard Peters, secretary for the Penns

CHAPTER V

A Perplexed Christian

It is not possible to understand Conrad Weiser unless we make, at least, a casual survey of his religious experiences. Indeed, there are few historical characters in whom the things of the spirit are so inextricably woven into the fiber of their being. For the chronicler of this man's life, it is almost impossible to record the temporal aspects of the man's life as recorded in the deeds and services without overcasting the scene with matters of the soul.

Born in the cauldron of Europe, where religious clashes had scarred the lives of four generations before him, uprooting his own generation from its native soil, it is understandable that religious beliefs must have been very real to the thirteen-year-old-lad who, with thousands of other refugees, reenacted the scenes of the Old Testament Exodus. The wanderings of the Israelites and the experiences of the Palatines had many common features. Pastor John Tribekko, preaching to the exiles in London, was fond of calling attention to this parallel, but even Tribekko could not have foreseen that the denizens of the crown, quartered at Livingston Manor, 1710-1713, would be required to make "bricks without straw" in the abortive effort to produce naval stores for the British government.

These experiences left scars on the young boy's memory. "I had at a previous period of my life wished that I had never heard of a God," he wrote in his journal of 1737, "either from my parents or from other people, for the idea I had of him had led me away from him. I thought the aetheists more happy than those who cared much about God." This was written when the trying days of cold and hunger of the Onondaga journey were fresh in mind. However, in the next sentence, he rejoices—"Oh! How far Man is removed from God, yes inexpressibly far, although God is near, and cannot impart the least thing to corrupt Man until he has given himself up without conditions, and in such a manner as cannot be explained or described, but may be experienced in great anguish of body and of mind." Trial and suffering nurtured the roots of his faith.

The ancestors of Conrad Weiser were, without exceptions, Lutherans.[1] From Weiser's autobiography, we learn that he was baptized at Kupingen, in Württemberg. But merely to state that the family adhered to the Protestant teachings which passed for Lutheranism, late in the 17th century, should not create the impression that members of that confession reposed in spiritual comfort. There were powerful forces in southern Germany causing upheavals in the philosophy which shaped men's lives. Churchmen like Jacob Boehme and Jacob Arndt were lighting new fires in human souls and scholars such as Philipp Spener and Augustus Franke were fusing new concepts into old patterns of living. The spiritual forces that molded the youth of Weiser were not confined to persecution by Catholics. Debates and dissensions among those who professed his own family's creed must have sounded discordant notes to a lad searching to find an ordered world. In describing his early training Weiser wrote in his autobiography "I learned to pray to God and the Bible became a very agreeable book to me."[2]

A Reformed clergyman, Reverend John Frederick Hager, performed the marriage ceremony by which "I married my Anna Eve (Feg) . . . on the 22nd of November (1720), in my father's house in Schohary." The selection of a Calvinist divine for this ceremony may have been in deference to the faith of his bride, whose denominational preference we do not know. It may have been because, at the time of the marriage, there was no regularly ordained minister of the Lutheran church stationed at Schoharie.

---
1. Rev. C. Z. Weiser, *The Life of John Conrad Weiser*. Published Reading, 1899m o, 92.
2. Weiser's Autobiography, Library of Congress.

Of the four children born to the union prior to their emigration to Pennsylvania province, three were christened by Lutheran clergymen and one, Anna Madlina, by John Jacob Oehl, Reformed pastor.

REED'S CHURCH

In October 1727, four years after the first group of Palatines had arrived in Tulpehocken, they built the first German Lutheran church in Pennsylvania. Rieth's (Reed's) Church in Tulpehocken was built on an eminence northeast of the present Berks County village of Stouchsburg. Two days after the church was built the Weiser family arrived in Tulpehocken. Both Lutheran and Reformed folks worshipped there. Weiser and his family became members of the Lutheran congregation. As early as 1730 Conrad Weiser was a *Vorleser,* leading the services in divine worship.[3]

The Lutheran clergyman who served Rieth's was Reverend John Casper Stoever, a Lutheran of the old school who believed more in the outward signs of religion as it molds life and directs actions than in the pietistic concept of the soul's regeneration as advocated by Spener and Franke from the halls of Halle University in Germany. Reverend Theodore E. Schmauck, the historian of the Lutheran Church, is convinced that Weiser was fundamentally a Pietist. There is no doubt that he did subscribe to these views later in his life, but it is difficult to understand how a backwoodsman, who spent a great deal of his time with the Indians and who received no formal education, could have absorbed the abstract teachings of German philosophers at the early age of thirty-six, when he took issue with his pastor in 1732 and organized a movement to oust Stoever from the pulpit at Rieth's.

A more likely cause of his antagonism to Stoever is to be found in Weiser's admiration of the brilliant young clergyman who served the Reformed congregation at Rieth's. The Reverend Peter Miller preached inspiringly and stirred the emotions. The contrast between the two pastors resulted unfavorably for Stoever. Miller and Weiser became intimate friends, a relationship which

---

3. Schmauck, Theodore, E., *A History of the Lutheran Church in Pennsylvania,* Lancaster, Pennsylvania, 1903, 471.

survived many trying situations and lasted until death parted them.

THE TULPEHOCKEN CONFUSION

Weiser led the movement to secure an educated clergyman to replace the incumbent at Rieth's. Casper Leutbecker, a tailor by trade, joined in the campaign against Stoever and declared that he could secure the services of a young clergyman, trained at Halle. Professing to have some connections in London, where Lutheran clergymen served as Court Preachers to the early Hanoverian Georges, Leutbecker announced that a young cleric, named Bagenkopf, was on his way to America to serve Rieth's church. In 1734 a parish house was built for the expected preacher. Leutbecker, the tailor, moved into it. He busied himself organizing classes for confirmation and preached in the pulpit of the church. The new preacher never arrived. Leutbecker announced that Bagenkopf had died at sea and then installed himself as pastor of the church.[4]

At this point, Weiser became suspicious of the acts of Leutbecker. Rev. J. C. Stoever still preached to Lutherans in Tulpehocken, holding services in barns and farmhouses. Weiser and his followers could not gracefully support Stoever, whom they had attempted to depose and at the same time, they were distrustful of the self-appointed Leutbecker. The controversy led to the period of colonial church history known as the "Tulpehocken Confusion."[5]

The religious difficulty presented by the situation at Rieth's was not merely a local situation. It was more extensive than that. In the years prior to the arrival of Muhlenberg, there was religious anarchy in the outlying German settlements generally, finding its expression in many quaint and queer cults such as the New Born of Oley, the New Mooners, the Mystics, and the Seventh Day Baptists of Skippack and Ephrata.[6]

---

4. Ibid, 474–477. Also: Brownmiller, E. S., *Memorial Discourse*, Sesqui-Centennial of Reed's Church, 1887.
5. Ibid.
6. See Sachse, Julius F., *The German Pietists of Pennsylvania*, 1694–1708, and *The German Sectarians of Pennsylvania*, 1708–1742. Published at Philadelphia 1895 and 1899 respectively.

Not all the false prophets were charlatans. Many misguided simple souls constituted themselves as new messiahs. While new heresies sprang up on each hand the simple, uneducated Germans, deeply pious by nature, were tossed about with every new wind that blew. Since nothing was orthodox, their emotions were pitched hither and yon like a cannon loose from its moorings on the deck of a ship listing in the troughs and upon the crests of turbulent waves.

The Confusion at Tulpehocken had reached its ridiculous stage when, in 1735, the Stoever and Leutbecker parties vied with each other in suits at law to obtain sole possession of the church keys.

Torn between the two opposing factions, Weiser became an easy victim of the proselyting agents of the Seventh Day Baptists at Ephrata. The complete conversion of his friend, Rev. Peter Miller, the Reformed minister at Rieth's, was a powerful influence in turning Weiser to the fellowship of the Brothers in Wisdom at Ephrata.

As is often true in rebellion, the first results of the conversion we a complete swing away from his Lutheran tenants. In May 1735 Weiser joined with other recent converts in burning the Catechism and other religious books as a public act of repudiation of Orthodox Lutheranism. In that same month, Weiser and Miller were baptized and gathered into the Ephrata fold.

BROTHER ENOCH

Once a member of this new sect, he gave himself over completely to its teachings. He gave liberally of his substance to construct the cloisters there; he deserted worldly life to don the white garb of a monk; he fasted until his body grew thin and his features pale and wan; he allowed his beard to grow, and in every way joined with the other zealots in attempting to simulate the appearance of Jesus. Rev. Israel Acrelius, a Swedish missionary, records that Weiser on one occasion submitted to severe punishment when, upon returning from a visit to his home in Tulpehocken, he confessed, under inquisition, that he had slept with his own wife.[7] Since celibate rules meant that the Ephrata

---

7. Acrelius, Israel, *A History of New Sweden*, 399. Translated from the Swedish by William M. Reynolds for the Historical Society of Pennsylvania (1874).

Brotherhood was not self-perpetuating, proselyting activities had to be carried on vigorously by the members of the order. Lay brothers traveled in groups to distant places attempting to gather new members into the fold. Weiser joined these crusades which led the bearded brethren as far as New Jersey. Several attempts were made to draw the Schwenkfelders into the cloisters at Ephrata. One of the expeditions led Weiser and some solitary brothers to Skippack, where at the home of that Schwenkfelder pioneer, Christopher Wiegner, he met the Moravian bishop, Spangenberg, as early as 1736.[8]

Here we may pause to attempt to understand the religious nature of Weiser, this remarkable German, who was a very much perplexed Christian. Weiser's was an orderly mind. His correspondence, which has come down to us in volumes, proves him to have been a practical thinker, arriving at conclusions by almost severe logic. His occasional lapses into abstruse figures of speech are not flaws in his mental processes but are manifestly naïve efforts to imitate the styles and flourishes of his correspondents among whom he numbered such masters of the pen as Rev. Richard Peters, James Logan, and Thomas Lee. In his provincial reports, he never wanders from the simple statements of hard facts. His religious meanderings were certainly not the results of emotional instability.

He was, by nature, a respecter of constituted authority. A stoic sense of duty characterizes all his public actions. His wavering loyalties in religious matters can be explained only based on the lack of any recognized authority in church affairs, and his eagerness to follow new leaders is evidence of his hopes that they would find a way out of the prevalent condition of religious anarchy.

Another cause of his perplexities in religious matters grew out of the limits of his educational experiences. Possessed of an alert intelligence he had learned many things without formal education. One of the great disadvantages of the process of self-education is that it provides no anchors to fasten on while groping to learn the next lesson. The learner's feet are on the shifting sands of unrelated facts.

---

8. Schmauck, T.E. op. cit., 503. Dr. Schmauck raises the interesting suggestion that Weiser may have hoped to secure the services of a Lutheran clergyman through the aid of the Moravians.

Weiser was an earnest reader. The contents of his library as we know them from the inventory of his estate astound us when we observe that he owned such works as the writings of Voltaire, the life of Charles XII of Sweden, the works of Arnholtz, the Württemberg Genealogy, *The Nuremberg Calendar of Heraldry*, the religious tracts of the Unitas Fratrum (Moravians), together with many volumes on law and four Bibles—three in German and one in English.[9]

Such a varied diet of reading matter suggests a wide scope of interests for a humble German settler in remote Pennsylvania, whose early life, and much of his manhood was spent among native tribes who worshipped the mysteries of nature. Certainly, Voltaire and his Deistic conception of the supernatural could be understood by a man who had lived the life of an Indian. But how insecure in the tenets of orthodox Lutheranism would be any searcher after truth who was exposed to all those influences without the guidance of formal approaches to understanding.

Dissension at the Ephrata Cloister was frequent. Weiser objected to Beissel's transubstantiation of himself as divine; he mistrusted the claims to chastity professed by the monks who lived in the Sisters' House; as a magistrate, it became his duty to investigate charges of the murder of bastards in the convent; he resented the reflection cast upon his own acts as a family man and finally he wrote tracts opposing the economy instituted along the Cocalico, pointing out that the Brethren has fastened upon themselves, a bondage worse than that of Egypt, because there was no earthly escape possible.[10]

The Ephrata Brethren were quite tolerant and did not evict him from their midst despite his severe charges. His eminence as a public character gave prestige to their order. It was largely as a gesture to please Weiser that Governor Thomas in company with many dignitaries from Maryland and Virginia visited the Cloisters in June 1744, at the time of the great Lancaster Treaty. It was at this treaty that the Indians requested Governor Thomas to shave

---

9. Nolan, J. Bennet, *Conrad Weiser, His Inventory*, published in *Pennsylvania Magazine of History and Biography*, Philadelphia, 1932, 56:265–270.
10. Chronicon Ephratense, 83–87. See also *Letter of Conrad Weiser* to the Leaders at Ephrata, September 3, 1743. This letter was found among the papers of I. Daniel Rupp. It is published in C. Z. Weiser, op. cit., 128–130.

off Conrad's "Dumpler" beard because it frightened their children whenever he came to their villages on errands for the governor.

Although Weiser was connected with the Ephrata Brethren as late of 1744 he was not closely identified with the order after 1739. Affairs of state took him on long journeys into the wilderness. The arrival of Zinzendorf in 1741 diverted his activities to the Moravians.

BROTHER LUDWIG

Count Nikolaus Ludwig von Zinzendorf was the scion of a distinguished German family. Philipp Spener, the great pietist philosopher, had stood as a sponsor when the lad was baptized in an *ecclisiola* in Dresden, in 1700. Wealth, prestige, education came to the young man by inheritance, but it was an intense zeal for Christian service that made him the benefactor of distressed Moravians and sent him to "teach all nations, baptizing them in the name of the Father, and of the Son, and of the Holy Ghost." His enthusiasm was contagious and pious men like Weiser were easily brother under his influence.

Late in 1741 the Count arrived in Pennsylvania, heralded as a prophet and welcomed by the provincial authorities in a manner befitting his rank. He established his residence at the home of John Bechtel in Germantown and preached his first sermon in Market Square of the village. A few days later Henry Antes of Falckner's Swamp issued a call for German Christians to meet at the home of Theobald Endt, a clockmaker of Germantown, to hear the Count's message. This conference, or Synod, met on January 12, 1742, and Conrad Weiser's name heads the list of those who were in attendance.

The second Synod was held at George Huebner's house in Falckner's Swamp (near Boyertown) on January 25, and four weeks later a third conference was held in the DeTurck home in Oley. Weiser attended the Oley meeting "without having been sent for, but from my own curiosity as a private person." On this occasion, Weiser pleaded with the Count to secure the services of a Lutheran preacher from Halle University. He described the plight of the Lutherans at Rieth's Church and prevailed upon

Zinzendorf to accompany him to Tulpehocken "in order to see the Congregation itself."[11]

Zinzendorf's visit to Tulpehocken as Weiser's guest coincided with the time of Weiser's message to the provincial authorities, informing them of the plans of the Six Nations to come to Philadelphia to receive payment for lands sold in 1736. In the letters which Richard Peters and Governor Thomas wrote to Weiser in 1742 anent the preparations for the expected Indian deputies, there are several references to Zinzendorf's proposals which must have been suggested to Weiser in Tulpehocken and then relayed to the governor. Doubtless, the Count and the Interpreter discussed the opportunity which the Indian visit presented for Zinzendorf to ingratiate himself with the Indians and thereby gain an advantage for his proselyting plans.

On February 26, Thomas wrote to Weiser, gently forbidding Caxhayan, the Cayuga, who brought the message for Onondaga, to become Zinzendorf's guest in Philadelphia. In part the governor wrote "I shall be very well pleased if the Count could make them [the Indians] good Christians, but I would not have the Business of the Province depend upon his success with them, nor run the risqué of their being disobliged by being put into the hands of a Gentleman, who out of goodwill would restrain them from what they think there is no Crime in making moderate use of, Drunkenness is a very bad thing. . . ."[12]

Zinzendorf returned to Philadelphia from Tulpehocken on March 2, 1742. On that same day, Richard Peters wrote to Weiser "As the Count chooses that the Indians shall be conveyed from here to your house by the Moravian Brethren . . . the Count desires they might be maintained at his Expense in order to recommend himself to their favour." The closing sentence of this letter read "Do not let them want for anything that you shall judge convenient." [13]

Despite the objections raised by the Governor, the Count did act as host to Caxhayan when the Cayuga messenger reached

---

11. Mühlenberg, H. M. et al., *Hallische Nachrichten*, 1:363. Also in Schmauck, T. D., *History of the Lutheran Church*, The Pennsylvania German Society Proceedings, 12:504.
12. Thomas to Weiser, February 26, 1742, *Pennsylvania Magazine of History and Biography*, 29:452–454. Reprinted from the Peters Papers, vol. 1.
13. Peters to Weiser, March 2, 1742, Peters Papers, 1:77.

Philadelphia. For fourteen days the Six Nations delegate, together with his squaw and child, lived in Zinzendorf's house in Germantown.[14] This act of hospitality was destined to pay excellent dividends a few months later.

When the great assemblage of Six Nations Indians arrived in Philadelphia, Zinzendorf was out of the city on a missionary journey among the Delawares who lived in the Minisink Forks (Stroudsburg). It was while he was returning to Bethlehem that the Count had a presentiment that Conrad Weiser wanted him at Tulpehocken. According to Zinzendorf, an irresistible force impelled him "and in strong faith, I obeyed the call, although knowing neither why nor wherefore."

Obeying the mysterious summons, the Count and several of his companions set out for Tulpehocken, traveling in a southwest direction from Lehigh Gap, passing through Allemängel (Albany, Berks) and Ontelaunee, and crossing the Schuylkill at the point (near present-day Reading) where the Tulpehocken Creek empties into the Schuylkill River. It was the second of August 1742. Conrad Weiser's home was fourteen miles to the west. A camp was pitched near the Tulpehocken and Schuylkill junction.

While seated in his tent, awaiting the night-fall, Zinzendorf wrote a lengthy poem which he called Sicki-hille-hocken (Schuylkill-hocken?). The soul of a pious scholar was attuned to worship as he felt himself in communion with the Creator. On the banks of the Tulpehocken, he penned these lines.

> Hier schrieb ich enen Brief,
> Al salles um mich schlief,
> In der finstern Wusten
> *Sickihhillehocken.*
> Wie wenig Voglein nisten;
> Werd ich doch kaum inn
> Dasz die *Schuylkill* rinn'
> Ueber Nichbar *Green*
> . . . .

---

14. Zinzendorf's Account of his Experience Among the Indians presented to the Moravian Society in Fetter Lane, London, 1743. A Ms. Copy in the Moravian Archives, Bethlehem, Pa. Printed by Reichel, W. C., *Memorials of the Moravian Church*, Philadelphia (1870), 115–130.

Inzwischen opfr' ich Dir
Ein Theil der Nachtzeit hier,
In dem offnen Zelte
Am *Indischen Revier.*

. . . .

In Harmonie mit dem
Der Itzt in *Bethlehem*
Priesteramtes pfleget,
Seyn die die Zehen Stamm'
Zuerst ans Herz Gegleget.
Ach manch armes Schaaf
Fuhlt der Gelbsucht Straf
Die sein Volk betraf!

In *Tulpehocken* brennt's
Nun rund um alle Fence;
Denn die Nationen
Gehn durch dieselbe Grenz'
Zuruck hin, wo sie wohen—
Bringen Meinen Pfad
Mt dem Zeugenrad
Bald in ihre Stadt.[15]

TREATY OF TULPEHOCKEN

On the following day, Zinzendorf reached Weiser's home. There he found that Weiser was entertaining two hundred other guests. The Indian deputies had concluded their business at Philadelphia on July 12, but on August 3 they were still fastened upon the hospitality of their white friend Tarachawagon, the name by which Conrad was known to the Six Nations.[16]

The Count described his reception at the Weiser cabin as follows: "I came into a House where all the Kings of these Nations

---

15. Reichel, supra, 39–44. Copy in Moravian Archives may be original.
16. Weiser's name among the Maqua Indians was Ziguras. When he was adopted into the Six Nations he was given the name *Tarachawagon*, which is thought to mean "he who holds in his hands the reins of the universe." Painstaking research by many scholars has failed to determine the English meaning of the name Ziguras. W. C. Beauchamp noted student of Iroquois history, despaired of success after many careful investigations and study of Indian languages.

were assembled together. Kackshajim (Caxhayan) was among them with his wife and little Child who had all 3 been in my house at Philadelphia. The Child ran to me and fell about my Neck in the Presence of all the Indians, which made them look upon one another, and enquire among themselves how that came about."[17] All of the chiefs of the Indian nations were present to witness this extraordinary scene.

It must have appeared to the zealous missionary that a divine Providence had arranged the setting and the Count lost no time in capitalizing upon the opportunity offered.

With Weiser as his interpreter, Zinzendorf addressed the mystified sachems. He explained the objectives of the Moravian Brethren. The Brethren he said, "only conversed with the Souls of men." They did not meddle in affairs of state or traffic in wares. Could the rulers of the Indian nations see their way clear to grant permission to the missionaries to live in their villages "to speak together concerning what may be of Use to any Soul here or there"?

The Indians withdrew to ponder upon this strange proposal. One hour later they returned and Canassetego, the Onondaga who acted as spokesman at Philadelphia, made the following reply: "Brother, thou art come hither; we have known nothing of thee, nor thou of us; and thou art also come quite unexpectedly by us, as we by thee. The chief Spirit must have had some hand in this . . . We would only let thee know that thou and thy Brethren when they come, shall always be welcome to us."

To seal this pledge the Indians presented the Count with a belt of wampum of one hundred and eighty-six white beads.[18]

In this way, the vast domains of the Six Nations were opened to the missionary activities of the Moravians. No other Protestant churches approached the successes which the Brothers in Unity achieved in converting the heathen to Christianity. The influence of the Moravian missionaries proved to be a vital factor

---

17. The description of the treaty with the Indians is adapted from Zinzendorf's account referred to above. In evaluating its significance one must bear in mind that the Count was prone to embellish his narrative with spectacular turns. James Logan once referred to Zinzendorf as Don Quixote.

18. The string of wampum which figured in the Treaty was carried to London by Zinzendorf in 1743 and there given to Bishop Spangenberg, who gave the Count a receipt for it dated at Lamb's Inn, Essex, England, March 10, 1743. Notes and Queries: *Pennsylvania Magazine of History and Biography*, 39:231-232. For the services of Moravian Missionaries see Chapter IX: "Relations between the Pennsylvania Germans and the British Authorities, 1750–1775," by the author.

in protecting English colonial interests against French encroachments during the French and Indian Wars.

WYOMING JOURNEY

Early in September Zinzendorf asked Weiser to accompany him on a missionary journey to the Wyoming and Shawnees Indians. Governor Thomas tried to prevail upon the Interpreter to stay at home. "I am very much pleased," wrote Thomas, "with the particular account you give me of the several occurrences which have come to your knowledge, but am very far from being so with your intention to accompany the Count at a time that your Presence will be so much wanted to prepare your Countrymen against the ensuing Election. If you have any regard for the Proprietors & me, or rather, if you have any regard for the Peace of ye Province you will do all that's in your power to excuse Yourself from thy journey till the beginning of the next month, especially as you are very well convinced beforehand that it is no more than an Expedition."[19]

In Zinzendorf's account of the missionary journey to Wyoming, written at Shamokin September 29, 1742, he states, "Conrad Weiser finally concluded to be my guide to the Shawnees Country."[20] Setting out from Weiser's home in Heidelberg (Tulpehocken) the party of missionaries followed the same route northward which Conrad and his companions had followed on the hazardous mid-winter journey of 1737.

Near the crest of the Blue Mountain, the party paused for refreshment at a spring.[21] To this pool of fresh water, the Count gave the fanciful name of *Pilger's Ruh*. To the thickly wooded valley beyond the first mountain he applied the name *Anton's Wald* or Wilderness, naming it for Anton Seyfert, a Moravian missionary in Zinzendorf's party; the present Wiconisco Creek was named Erdmuth's Spring in honor of Zinzendorf's first wife, the Countess of Erdmuth; modern Peter's Mountain was named Thurnstein by Conrad Weiser for one of the estates owned by

---

19. Thomas to Weiser, September 9, 1742, Peters Papers, 1:94.
20. Reichel, W. C., supra. Reprint of Zinzendorf Diary, September 29, 1742.
21. Location of this spring has been marked by the Blue Mountain Eagle Climbing Club of Reading, "Pilger's Ruh" – Pilgrim's Rest.

Count Zinzendorf; "Lewis' Rest" in Wiconisco Township, Dauphin County, was named *Ludwig's Ruh* in honor of the Count who passed among his fellow missionaries as Brother Ludwig;[22] the beautiful pine-shaded stream which flows through the Gap in Mahantango Mountain was named *Benigna* in honor of Zinzendorf's daughter, the Countess Benigna; *Marienborn* in Northumberland was named for Zinzendorf's castle near Frankfort-on-the-Main. Somewhere between Peter's Mountain and Shamokin, the party crossed a creek which was given the name *Conrad Weiser's Creek*. There Zinzendorf noted evidence of Indian symbols painted on stones and the grave of an Indian hero.

At Shamokin, the Count made the acquaintance of Shikellamy, "whose presence I interpreted as a divine token." Weiser acted as guide, advisor, and interpreter for the missionaries. On Saturday, September 28, the Moravians at Shamokin wished to "pray the Litany," but the merry-making of the Indians disturbed them. Weiser was asked to inform Shikellamy that the white men were about to speak to their God. As soon as Conrad conveyed the message the "beating of drums ceased and the voices of the Indians were hushed."

The journey continued north of Shamokin. Weiser led them to the home of his old friend Madame Montour, the Indianized French woman.[23] When she saw these men of God she wept. When Zinzendorf told her that one of the Moravian towns was named Bethlehem, she interrupted to exclaim that the place in France where Jesus lived also was named Bethlehem!

Weiser left the party at the Montour village. The Madame's son, Andrew, was qualified to act as interpreter and guide for the remainder of the journey. Affairs of state called Weiser back to Shamokin.[24]

On November 25, 1742, Zinzendorf crowned his work in Pennsylvania when, with Conrad Weiser present, he dedicated the

---

22. On May 26, 1742, Count Zinzendorf made a formal renunciation of his rank and title before the provincial authorities. He preferred to be known as Brother Ludwig, or Louis, which was one of his Christian names.
23. Madame Montour, the daughter of a French army officer, who ruled an Indian village near present-day Montoursville, Pa.
24. Soon after the close of the Indian negotiations in Philadelphia, July 1742, new Indian problems were presented by the discovery of a plot, involving the Nanticoke Indians of Eastern Shore, Maryland.

First Moravian Church of Philadelphia. On the same day there arrived at the port of Philadelphia a young man who was destined to become the founder of organized Lutheranism in America; the progenitor off a remarkable dynasty of Pennsylvania German heroes; the Moses who led men like Weiser out of the wilderness of religious confusion, and not less significantly to become the son-in-law of Weiser himself. Henry Melchior Muhlenberg was not only a student from Halle—he was Halle transplanted into the new world.

LIGHT FROM THE HALLS OF HALLE

"The certainty of Death and the uncertainty of what should come afterward must forever have kept their Judgments in Bondage as well as subjected them to perplexing Fears and Apprehensions—a state of Mind very unfit for the discovery of religious Truths, but more so for the proper Behaviour in Circumstances of Distress and Calamity."[25] Thus, in part, wrote Richard Peters to his friend Conrad Weiser. Prior to his selection as secretary of the province, Peters had served as an Anglican clergyman in Philadelphia. Early in 1747 Conrad Weiser, still a perplexed Christian, had written to his English church friend, seeking guidance. Weiser had quoted a passage from Saint Paul's epistle to the Romans and Peters' use of the third person pronouns in the passage quoted above evidently refers to the Roman people.

Conrad Weiser's religious experience was a series of conflicting loyalties to changing concepts of man's relation to God. We have seen how he wavered between orthodox Lutheranism and the worship of the Divine Sophia at Ephrata Cloisters; how eagerly he sponsored the cause of the Moravians under the spell of Count Zinzendorf and how earnestly he longed for the leadership of a true disciple of Francke and Spener as their philosophy of Pietism was expounded at the German University of Halle.

In 1746, the German editor, Christopher Sauer, had written to Weiser, asking the interpreter to write an account of religious worship among Indians. To this request Weiser replied: "If by the

---
25. Richard Peters to Conrad Weiser, February 25, 1747, Peters MSS, 2:72.

Word Religion people meant an Assent to certain Creeds or the Observance of a Set of Religious Duties as appointed Prayers, Singing, Preaching, Baptism and so forth, or even Heathenish Worship, then it may be said neither the Five Nations nor their Neighbors have any Religion; but if by Religion we mean an Attraction of the Soul to God or a Union of the Soul with God, from which proceeds a Confidence in, and Hunger after the Knowledge of Him, then these people must be said to have a Religion."[26]

In reading this interpretation, translated from the German, one must conclude that Weiser was reading his own religious views into his descriptions of the faith of the Indians.

The irregularities and petty dissensions at Rieth's church in Tulpehocken had caused Weiser to sever his connection with that body as early as 1735. For a time, he espoused the cause of the brothers at Ephrata and in 1741, believing Zinzendorf to be a new Moses, he had become closely associated with the Unitas Fratrum, commonly called the Moravians.

On November 25, 1742, Henry Melchior Muhlenberg, a young Lutheran clergyman, recently from the halls of Halle University, came to Philadelphia, after spending some time in the newly settled province of Georgia. Within a few days after his arrival in Pennsylvania, the 31-year-old clergyman visited New Hanover in present Montgomery County. He was installed there as the Lutheran pastor before the end of 1742.

The sad plight of the Lutherans at Rieth's church, near Weiser's home, came to Muhlenberg's attention in 1743. The Tulpehocken situation was more confused than it had been when Weiser severed his connections with it. Now there were three parties, instead of only two, who were contending for the possession of the church. One faction was led by Reverend John Caspar Stoever, a second by one Gottlob Buettner, who had been installed there by Zinzendorf. Buettner was succeeded by another Zinzendorf appointed in June 1742. This man was John Philip Maurer, who added fuel to the confusion by attempting to oust

---

26. Weiser to Christopher Sauer, Society Collection, Historical Society of Pennsylvania. Also, for the German version, see *Pennsylvanische Berichte*, Jan 16, 1747.

Stoever completely. A third party was formed when a Lutheran clergyman, Valentine Kraft, drew a group of followers to himself. This third group withdrew from Rieth's church and built a new church, Christ Church, commonly known now as Long's, west of Stouchsburg. The cornerstone of the new church was dedicated in 1743.[27]

At this point in the history of the Tulpehocken Confusion, the Reverend Henry Melchior Muhlenberg was invited to Tulpehocken to give assistance and advice. The young clergyman from the halls of Halle was a welcome guest at the Weiser home. The perplexed Weiser was pleased to hear words of wisdom from the true representative of Pietism.

WEISER ACQUIRES A SON-IN-LAW

But Conrad Weiser was not the only member of that pioneer household to be attracted to the young clergyman. The dulcet notes of Muhlenberg's hymn-singing charmed Weiser's eldest daughter, Anna Maria. The romance of these young people culminated in their marriage in April 1745, thus founding one of the most remarkable families in Pennsylvania history.

The arrival of Muhlenberg did not end the controversies which disgraced the worshippers in Tulpehocken. His arrival did serve to alienate Weiser entirely from his Moravian associations, and the latter's duties as a magistrate plunged him into still greater difficulties in religious matters. Weiser was one of the magistrates whose duty it was to adjudicate the unseemly mess in Lancaster in 1745, when a Moravian preacher named Lawrence Nyberg had fomented trouble in the Lutheran congregation of that young city, ending in a case in litigation for possession of the church.[28]

In the same year, a new church was built on the site of the old Reed Church in Tulpehocken and Moravian clergymen, posing as Lutherans, installed themselves there. The true Lutherans entered suits at law for the possession of the church keys. Weiser, acting as a magistrate, aligned himself on the side opposed to

---
27. Schmauck, T. E., *Pennsylvania German Society Proceedings*, vol. 12.
28. Mann, William J., *Life and Times of Henry Melchior Muhlenberg*, Philadelphia, 1888, 176. See also various issues, numbers 70 to 87 of the *Pennsylvanische Berichte*, 1746–1747.

the Moravians. That controversy became so bitter that Weiser once remarked to friends that the Moravians were praying for his death.[29]

At the time when these controversies were at their height Muhlenberg introduced a new clergyman, just arrived from Halle, to serve the newly built Christ Church. The young bachelor, Rev. Nicholas Kurtz, made his home at Weiser's. With great tact and forbearance and aided by the frequent visits of Muhlenberg to the Weiser homestead, Kurtz succeeded in restoring peace and order among the Lutherans in the Tulpehocken area.

Although Weiser severed his connection with the Ephrata Cloister, he did not abandon all the tenets which he had professed while he was connected with the Brethren. Muhlenberg, his son-in-law, was much concerned about Weiser's soul, and on numerous occasions attempted to persuade him to return to the full communion of the Lutheran Church. The old pioneer refused to partake of the Lord's Supper, to attend services, or to observe Sunday as the Sabbath. He continued the Ephrata observance of Saturday as the Seventh Day. He still abstained from eating foods which were proscribed under the dietary laws of the Ephrata order.

THE FAITH OF HIS FATHERS

Such obstinacy exasperated Muhlenberg. Admitting his own failure and in fear of losing his temper, Muhlenberg appealed to his colleague, Peter Brunnholz, to attempt to show Weiser the error of his ways. With circuitous help from Providence, Brunnholz succeeded, where Muhlenberg had failed. During the conversation, Weiser admitted to Brunnholz that the Symbolical Books of the Lutheran Church were dear and precious to him; that he considered them essential to salvation and that he had never found anything in other religions even though he had tried them all. However, he declared he wished to wait a while longer before taking communion until he was certain that strife among Lutherans had ended.

This partial conversion was completed during the same evening. After the evening meal, Weiser became violently ill. A

---

29. Mann, William J., supra, 180–181.

stomach disorder which was chronic during the last two decades of his life caused intense alarm. His family and all neighboring clergymen were summoned to his bedside. In agonizing pain, he participated in a preparatory service and in the presence of Muhlenberg, Brunnholz, and Kurtz, he asked for the Lord's Supper. With great effort, he climbed from his bed and on bended knees, the sacrament was administered to him. Thus, Conrad Weiser returned to and remained steadfast in the faith of his fathers. He lived twelve years more after his conversion, but religious perplexity had vanished.

Each new page of Weiser's autobiography is introduced by a quotation from the Bible aptly chosen to symbolize some phase of his own experiences. One of those quotations from Lamentations V: 19-22 will serve to sum up his religious life.

"Thou, O Lord, remainest forever; thy throne from
 generation to generation . . .
Turn thou us unto Thee O Lord and we shall be turned;
 renew our days of old."

Through the bitter trials of his experiences, he had found peace and contentment for his soul after many years of perplexity and confusion. His last years found two great contrasts in his life. In temporal things, most of his early life had been devoted to pacifying and protecting the Indians, but death came while he was helping to crush them. In spiritual matters, he had engaged in many battles throughout his early career but as the shadows lengthened toward the evening of life he found solace and contentment in the bosom of the Faith of his Fathers.[30]

---

30. Portions of this chapter were extracted from Graeff, Arthur D., *Conrad Weiser, a Perplexed Christian*, Exile Herald, 1938, published by Schwenkfelder Exile Society, Norristown.

Model of Rieth's Church

Pewter chalice from Rieth's Church

Typical colonial attire in Weiser's time

The brothers' quarters at the Ephrata Cloister

A cabin at the Ephrata Cloister

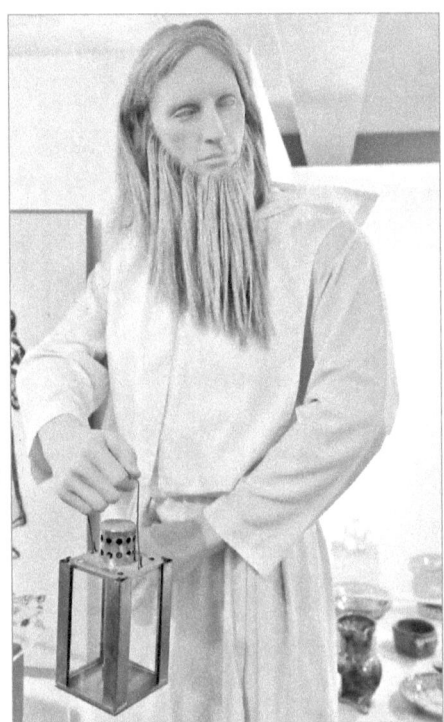

Monk attire at the Ephrata Cloister

Early pencil drawing of the Ephrata Cloister

Typical monk quarters at the Ephrata Cloister

The Ephrata Cloister today

Nikolaus Ludwig, count von Zinzendorf

Old postcard of the Deturk House in Oley

Historic marker for Pilger Ruh

Stone marker at the Pilger Ruh

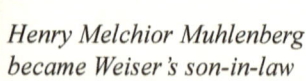

Henry Melchior Muhlenberg became Weiser's son-in-law

CHAPTER VI

A Man of Affairs

In America, the title "squire" is used to designate local officials who serve as magistrates or justices of the peace. In this sense of the word, Conrad Weiser was a squire. In this office, Conrad Weiser was following a Weiser tradition of three successive generations. His grandfather Jacob Weiser was *Schultheiss* of the village of Gross Asbach, in the county of Backnang, Württemberg. Conrad's father, Johann Conrad Weiser, held a similar office in the Palatine refugee settlements in Schoharie, New York, and Conrad served Tulpehocken township in Lancaster (Berks after 1752), Pennsylvania. His appointment to that position in 1741 was partly in recognition of his services to the province as an Indian agent and partly to place a German officeholder in the areas in which large numbers of Germans were settled in the hope of attracting their political support to the governor's party in opposition to the Quaker assembly.

Weiser's duties as a magistrate on the colonial frontier were more varied than similar positions would demand today. Stray cattle were brought to his barn to await redemption by their owners. The German newspapers carried extensive advertisements which were inserted by Weiser, describing the animals that were stabled in the magistrate's barn. The advertisements described the brands on horses' hoofs and hips or the incisions in the ears of cows. Colors were given in terms that are still familiar in the dialect today, such as "Schimmel," "schekkich," "hell brau," etc.

Among the most vexing problems to confront Weiser as justice were the recurring religious controversies growing out of the situation at Rieth's Church, near present-day Stouchsburg. Count Nicholas von Zinzendorf had succeeded in drawing some of the members of the Lutheran church into the fellowship of the Moravian Brethren. There were other parishioners who chose to be loyal to the Lutheran faith. A contest for the possession of the church keys forced Weiser as the local magistrate to enter the controversy. In 1742, while under the influence of the Count, Weiser had urged the Moravian members at Rieth's to secure a deed to the land. This was done, but the troubles did not end there. On April 5, 1743, Weiser attended a congregational meeting of the church in his capacity as a justice and witnessed a decision to open the church to all parties concerned. One month later a new Lutheran church was built a short distance west of Rieth's known as Christ Lutheran (Long's). The arrival of Reverend Henry Melchior Muhlenberg in 1743, finally brought order out of the confusion. Weiser's part in the solution of this problem did not grow out of his position as a magistrate, but because he was the father of a daughter whose charm captivated the young Lutheran clergyman and brought him frequently to Tulpehocken from Trappe and New Hanover.

On the lighter side, his duties made him the arbiter in several domestic squabbles between husbands and wives. One choice bit of recorded testimony reveals how a suspicious husband secreted himself to spy upon his unfaithful spouse and then descended upon her and her clandestine suitor at a most embarrassing moment. We have the testimony but, unfortunately, we do not know how the magistrate meted out justice.

Colonial magistrates were charged with the duty of collecting bad debts for creditors who lodged their accounts in their care. This was not a pleasant duty and no doubt it did not serve to increase Weiser's popularity among his German countrymen in Pennsylvania. In 1743 and 1744 Christopher Lauer operated a store in Tulpehocken, selling nails, tools, cloth, liquor, and dry goods to the settlers in the neighborhood. Money was scarce in this remote corner of the province and many credit transactions were made. When these accounts fell into default they were handed over to magistrate Weiser for collection. That he was successful in inducing debtors to pay is attested by the many accounts which are marked "Empfangen" (Received) C. W. Other accounts proved to be uncollectible because the debts had "gone to Virginia."

Among those who had to be dunned by Weiser was Tobias Bickel of Heidelberg. Bickel was one of the most extensive landowners in early Berks and Schuylkill Counties. His bill was paid to Weiser "in part." Adam Walborn and John Hollenbach were the progenitors of a large family group in the Bethel district of Berks and Lebanon counties. They paid their bills to Weiser. Others who made good on their obligations were Caspar Durst, Peter Loch, Wilhelm Hoster, Conrad Goldman, John Karsnitz, and others. Weiser collected Lauer's bill from Mathias Schmidt by taking wheat in exchange. The list of customers provides an excellent directory of names of persons residing in western Berks during the early years.[1]

The magistrate of Tulpehocken was rapidly becoming a man of affairs, projecting himself into the civic affairs of his province as well as his immediate community. In 1741 he embarked upon his first venture in provincial politics.

"A HOUSE DIVIDED AGAINST ITSELF CANNOT STAND"

Fully a century and a decade before Abraham Lincoln quoted the immortal words, declaring that "a house divided against itself can not stand," Conrad Weiser used the biblical metaphor in an appeal to the German voters of Pennsylvania. In 1741, Weiser addressed himself to his "worthy Countrymen in Pennsylvania" in an open letter which was distributed as a handbill at the time of the autumn elections to the Provincial Assembly. In April of that year, the Interpreter for the Province was appointed a Justice of the Peace for the northeastern district of Lancaster County. His elevation to this office marked him as a "governor's Man" in the political controversies which developed out of the struggle between Governor George Thomas and his Quaker-controlled assembly.

---

1. Lower, Christian, *Account Book*, Historical Society of Pennsylvania, MSS Division, Potts Papers, vol. 9.

Most of the Pennsylvania Germans sided with the Quakers in these contests, but as an officer, by executive appointment, Weiser's loyalty was owed to the governor's party. In his address to the German people, he aligned himself firmly on the side of the proprietary interests of the province as opposed to the "Sticklers" who advocated the continuance of Quaker domination in and by the Provincial Assembly.

Untoward fortune laid a heavy hand upon the early years of Thomas' administration as a deputy for the Penn heirs. The year 1741 was particularly trying. The War with Spain and France presented many vexing problems, chief among which was a disordered currency growing out of the refusal of the Assembly to support "the Arm of the Flesh" by voting funds for military purposes. Added to this there were more than the usual number of fires in the city; the winter was severe, subscriptions being made necessary to provide relief for the needy; riots had to be quelled; yellow fever, a West Indian infection, made necessary a curfew law for negroes; the infant city witnessed nearly eight hundred burials, many of these were charged to a disease known as "Palatine Fever," a form of typhus suffered by the German immigrants who disembarked from putrid redemptioner ships.[2]

Valiantly Thomas endeavored to cope with the many problems that faced the people of the province, but he was checked at every turn by a stubborn legislature, whose members thwarted his efforts repeatedly. By all sorts of specious arguments they sought to avoid their responsibilities and, niggardly, they tried to force the executive into submission by refusing to vote funds to pay his salary.[3]

During the summer of 1741, the merchants of Philadelphia addressed a petition to the King of England, complaining that the unfortified condition of the province made it easy prey for privateers. "We cannot but lament that we, only, of all your Majesty's subjects, are so unhappy as to have one branch of the legislature composed of people whose declared religious principles deny us

---

2. Scharff & Westcott, *History of Philadelphia*, Philadelphia, 1884, 1:210.
3. Graeff, Arthur D., *Relations between the Pennsylvania Germans and the British Authorities*, Norristown, 1939, 22.

that security which is the main end of society." Two hundred and thirty-three names were signed to the petitions.[4]

The October elections for representatives to the assembly provided an opportunity for the people to express their dissatisfaction with the policies of the incumbent members of that body. Conrad Weiser, more than any other citizen of the province, was responsible for dragging the issue out into the open in his "House Divided Against Itself" address to the German voters. His action suggested James Logan's well-known "Address to the Quakers Concerning War." The succession of events which brought this about will bear brief recital here.

One of Weiser's duties as a magistrate was to remand one Peter Reed to Lancaster jail. The prisoner took his revenge by circulating base remarks about Weiser which Thomas Cookson, Lancaster magistrate, designated as a scandal. However, after a time the young man repented and a brother of the offender prevailed upon Weiser to overlook the insult. On September 12, 1741, Cookson wrote to Weiser, stating that the prisoner "had signed a paper" acknowledging the injustice of "his reflections upon you." Cookson urged Weiser to prosecute the matter and secure an indictment against Reed. In the course of this letter, Cookson too occasions to dwell upon the political issues of the day.[5]

"The main arguments with the Dutch," wrote Cookson, "are that if the Governor's Party prevails they will be assured a high rate of tax and obliged to labor at erecting forts, etc., then putting them in mind of the Tyranny of their Princes."

The death of Thomas Ewing of Lancaster had created a vacancy in the delegation which the county sent to the provincial assembly. Cookson advocated the election of James Smith, a Scotch-Irishman, to succeed Ewing against the "precious schemes" of Samuel Blunston, the Quaker candidate for the position. "I hope you will propagate the same principles among your friends and acquaintances," Cookson suggested to Weiser.

---

4. Logan MSS, 10:68.
5. Thomas Cookson to Weiser, September 12, 1741. Weiser MSS, Pennsylvania History Society Tome, 1:6.

Immediately after receiving Cookson's letter, Conrad Weiser set out to consult with his friend James Logan, at Stenton, near Philadelphia. These two men put their heads together and drew up English and German versions of an appeal to the German voters of Pennsylvania to support the governor's position by electing representatives who would provide funds for the defense of the province. One day after Weiser's departure from the Logan home the President of Council sent a letter "so close after thy heels" urging several revisions of the text. "I have carefully looked over thy English paper that thou left with me and have proposed the alterations where I think it may be changed for the better." It is evident that Logan expected Cookson and Weiser to issue the address jointly because he suggested that "he may sign with and before thee as the elder justice in the Commission."[6] Items which Logan felt should be deleted were underscored and items to be added were placed in brackets in the revised version which Logan sent to Weiser. But it seems that Weiser chose not to follow Logan's suggestions in all particulars and to issue the address over his name alone.

Weiser's address, as it appears below, is preserved in Vol. 1 of the Weiser Manuscripts owned by the Historical Society of Pennsylvania. The manuscript was found among the papers of Mr. Horace Smith of the Falls of the Schuylkill. Since this form of the address appears here for the first time in print, it was thought desirable to retain all errors in spelling, grammar, and punctuation.

SERIOUS ADDRESS AND ADVICE TO OUR COUNTRYMEN AND GERMANS

Worthy Countrymen in Pensilvania:

It is with great Concern that I now speak to you on the ensuing Election of assembly man the importance of which is so great it must concern every Inhabitant of this province that possesses anything of temporal goods if it be no more than one's own live [life] if one loves it. The thing itself is that about a year ago a difference happened about the question Whether it was rendering tribute to

---
6. Logan MSS, 10:71.

Caesar or No. We the Germans in particular have hither to said No (to judge according to our deeds) in chusing such assembly man once and again who have ben far from complying with our gracious Sovereign about a contribution to his Wars That the house[7] quarreled with the governor and has not only given one farthing to them but to the governor not even his usual salary that has for above twenty years been allowed to the governor for the time being.

Permit me to put you in mind that as we for the most part retired into this country for Peace and Safety's sake and get our living easier then in Germany we not only have obtained our ends in all this but have also ben well received and protected by the governor of this Province especially by the present governor. And it is not yet a long time that His Majesty of Great Britain by an act of his Parliament invested us as protestants upon very easy terms with so many privileges and liberties whosoever that a native born Englishman can enjoy.

Consider whether this should not move us to actual thankfulness and to answer the above mentioned question with Yea (when without making reflections upon the favours we received) the laws of good order requires it and accordingly to chuse such an assembly man which will no longer oppose such reasonable requests as the present time requires and it is to be faired [feared] that if we as newly come to this country and have received so many favours do oppose the governor any longer into which under a Countinanace [continuance] of liberty it might not turn out to our best advantage to draw a particular displeasure upon us as many of the wisest Quakers themselves are afraid and show their dislike of the Behaviour of the assembly for this two years in Opposition to the governor. Whether or

---

7. Logan suggested at this point "who have been so far from complying with our gracious sovereign about a Contribution towards his Wars, That they have quarreled with the Governor and not only not given one farthing to the King. Logan suggested the last two words "and Countryman" but Weiser did not use them.

not it did not arise from private Pique I let time itself and the wiser judge.

It is at this present time more necessary to elect another assembly which may in the endeavor to put a stop to the difference between the governor and the country and to think upon men as which may bring peace and unity to prevail among us. [Sin]ce [manuscript torn here] we are every day in expectation of a French ware the French nation is many thousand strong in America and possessed of Canada to the north of us and to the west of us they are possessed of the great river Meshesying [Ohio] which extends in its several parts fare and wide one part of it ging where our traders go to deal with the Indians in the bounds of pensilvania in so much that between that and the west Branch of the Susquehanna is but a short land Carriage and all of the Indians near the foresaid water are in leage with the Enemy and it is an easy matter for the French with the help of these Indians to come to this Road and lay this province wast in a few days and in ruins or any of our neighboring provinces. And how cruelly those barbarians treat those which they take for their enemies is not to be expressed in a few words I wish heartily we may never have the Experience of it.

But for these Considerations if for no others we ought to be united as one people as we are told in the Gospel *a house divided against itself cannot stand* but in order to divide us many of you have been told it seems that if you took not care to chuse Quakers you would be brought in the same Slavery you came hither to avoid.

It grieves me to think that any should give themselves the liberty to invent and propagate such falsehoods. The Quakers are a sober and industrious and so far as they have ben concerned in government we have lived in their Protection but we see there are many amongst them who show the same Pashions and give way to them as much full as much as other men and we want such as will make up our Breaches and not widen them.

But as to the slavery that has been mentioned you may be assured that whom so ever you shall chuse by much the greater part of them will be English and there is no nation in the world more jealous and Carefull of their Laws than the English nation and you may therefore trust them. And that you may be directed by wisdom in your Choice and that peace, love truth and goodwill amongst men prevail is the hearty prayer of your friend Conrad Weiser.[8]

Tulpehocken in Lancaster County
20th of September, 1741 Conrad Weiser

Almost simultaneously with Weiser's appeal to the Germans appeared James Logan's "Address to the Quakers Concerning War." Even though he was a member of the Quaker faith, this veteran confidant of all the Penns placed the safety of the province above his religious scruples. Pointing out that Pennsylvania "is the Heart of the British Colonies," Logan pleaded for a law which would make possible the enlistment of men from "Germany and Ireland . . . who can bear Arms" . . . Parliament expects all Colonies to help in the War as the Assemblies of all others have in some Measure done except ourselves."[9] Logan's letter was referred to a committee of Quakers who refused to submit it to the Society in general because it dealt with civil and military affairs, matters which they deemed unworthy of the consideration of the Society of Friends.

Shortly after the election of 1741, Richard Peters, Secretary to the Governor, wrote a letter to Thomas Penn in England, stating that Logan had "sent for Conrad Weiser and the two cooked up a story which Conrad published in Dutch addressing it to his Countrymen and putting his name to it." This statement would lead us to believe that Logan inspired Weiser's words if it were not for a second letter from Peters to Penn, in which Peter presents a

---

8. There are at least three copies of the Weiser Address known to exist in manuscript form. The one reproduced here is taken from the collection of Weiser Correspondence which is designated here as Weiser MSS, Tome I, Official Correspondence, 3:164, and a manuscript which is in the Society Collection of the Historical Society of Pennsylvania. The last named was published in the *Pennsylvania Magazine of History and Biography*, 23:518–543. This version differs slightly from the one which is presented here.
9. *Pennsylvania Magazine of History and Biography*, 6:402. Logan's complete Address is printed.

different version of the authorship of the Address, declaring that it was Weiser's own.[10]

Modern political campaigns would find many of their counterparts in the pre-election activities of party zealots of the earlier years. Weiser's election broadside brought an answer from an anonymous writer who addressed the German people in their own tongue in a lengthy refutation of most of Weiser's arguments. Internal evidence found in this document leads us to conclude that its author was not a German even though he pretended to write to his "Countrymen" in the same sense that Weiser employed the term.[11]

The point which evoked the ire of the anonymous writer was Weiser's question as "to paying tribute to Caesar." The Assembly had done its share, but the governor chose to make unfavorable representations about their actions. The Germans could best prove their loyalty to their benefactors by remaining steadfast in their loyalty to the Quakers who had always served them well. It was defection from their former loyalties which would bring censure upon the Germans, in high places.

Weiser's own attitude, explained the anonymous letter, was the result of his appointment as a justice, making him subservient to the governor to whom he owed his appointment. The alarm about the danger from the French was belittled by the writer, they were "but a Handfull to us" and would have to pass through the domains of friendly Indians before they could inflict any harm. The address closed with a warning that a "snare is layd for you."

In describing the election of 1741, Richard Peters wrote "Every Dutchman was furnished with it (the anonymous paper) and they came down to the election with so much Zeal for the old Assembly that all the Arguments in the world would have had no Effect upon them, if there had been an inclination to contest the election."

Weiser's first venture into politics resulted in failure. He had championed the unpopular cause and his candidate James Smith was defeated by the Quaker-supported Samuel Blunston

---

10. Richard Peters to Thomas Penn, October 20, 1741, Peters Letter Book, 17. See also Richard Peters to John Penn, October 2, 1741, Logan Papers.
11. Penn Papers, Official Correspondence, 3:199. The anonymous letter was printed in Pennsylvania Archives and Series, 581-584. The heading is *Translations from the Dutch Press.*

of Lancaster. The defeat did not affect Weiser's standing with the executive branch of the provincial government. The succeeding years found him occupying higher and higher places in the councils of the province.

THE BARONY OF TULPEHOCKEN

During the seventeen years that had passed since his arrival in Pennsylvania, Weiser prospered. In 1744, he was the owner of a large plantation in Tulpehocken and possessed uncleared lands in Bethel, along the Swatara Creek. At least one contemporary writer referred to his estate as the "barony" of Tulpehocken. His pay for serving Pennsylvania and other provinces supplemented his regular income from farming and his fees as magistrate added another lucrative source of revenue. He was meticulous about collecting what was due him and on several occasions, he wrote rather pointed letters to his superiors reminding them that his bill for services was unpaid. The colonial authorities usually hastened to discharge their debts lest Weiser's services become unavailable because of default in payment. On numerous occasions, large sums were entrusted to him to defray the expenses of visiting Indians. All evidence goes to show that he spent these monies honestly and never were his accounts questioned by the authorities. His increasing wealth was honestly gained and diligently.

A large family made great demands upon his income. Four children had been born to him and his Anna Eve before they came into Pennsylvania. These children were named—Philip, Anna Madlina, Maria, and Frederick. Peter was born in 1730 in Tulpehocken. Then followed twins—Jacob and Christopher (1731), Elizabeth (1732), Margaret (1734), Samuel (1735), Benjamin (1736), Jabez (1740), Hannah (1742), and finally another Benjamin in 1744. In all, there were fourteen children. Seven of the children died before they reached maturity. In 1744 four sons and three daughters were living at home, Benjamin the youngest having been born in August of that year. Philip was a lad of twenty-two and Anna Madlina was nearing the age of twenty. Frederick was sixteen. Maria Magdalina, the second daughter, died in the Sisters' House in Ephrata in 1742. All the children living in 1744 survived him.

In 1745, Governor Thomas urged Weiser to undertake another journey to Onondaga on a peace mission to the Six Nations Indians, whose loyalty to the British interest was more vital than ever before. The War of the Austrian Succession found England and France fighting for colonies in the New World and the Iroquois Indians held the balance of power in the colonial contest in the New World. In his letter to Weiser, Thomas suggested that Conrad might prefer to stay closer to the settlements on his journey and in that way run fewer risks. The route by way of the Delaware and Albany might prove to be safer in wartime, suggested Thomas.

But Conrad Weiser declared that he had nothing to fear from Indians. He feared members of a family named Haines, who, according to Conrad, were threatening him and his household with bodily harm.

Late in 1744, a dastardly attempt was made to burn down Weiser's house while the family slept.[12] According to the account printed in the *Gazette* of November 29, 1744, some evil person placed a bundle of burning straw upon the low roof of a building which adjoined the Weiser cabin. They fastened the door of the house on the outside to prevent the egress of their intended victims "so that they might all perish in the flames." Some of the imprisoned Weiser children were awakened by the smell of smoke before the flames reached the main building. The shingles of the outhouse were already burning when Conrad and his sons managed to beat down the fastened door and extinguish the flames before any major damage had occurred.

Suspicion fell at once upon one Adam Haines, spelled Haen by Sauer's newspaper, "a vile profligate young man in the neighborhood." Haines had committed a crime and Weiser as the magistrate had bound him over to the Court of Quarter Sessions in Lancaster. It was reported that Haines had tried to bribe Weiser to suppress the charge and that Weiser, refusing the bribe, had ordered the arrest of Haines. The constable sent to apprehend the young man found that he had escaped.

Therefore, Weiser suspected that Adam Haines "with others of the same family" had resorted to arson in revenge.

---

12. For accounts of the attempts to burn Weiser's home see *Berichte*, December 16, 1744, and the *Gazette*, November 29, 1744, and December 6, 14, 18, 1744.

Governor Thomas issued a proclamation offering a reward for the arrest of Haines and his accomplices. The proclamation was published in the English and German newspapers in successive issues through three weeks in December 1744. On December 18 the Gazette announced that "the Persons suspected to have set Fire to Mr. Weiser's House are apprehended and committed to Prison."

The year 1744 was an eventful one in the life of Conrad Weiser. For this reason, we have broken the sequence of Indian affairs to preserve the chronology of Weiser's biography.

CHAPTER VII

A Diversity of Duties

THE NANTICOKE PLOT

Among other matters discussed by the Six Nations at Philadelphia in 1742 was a complaint against the province of Maryland, charging that settlers were clearing unpurchased lands. "And we expect as Owners of that Land to receive such a Consideration for it as the Land is worth," declared Chief Canassatego through Conrad Weiser, the interpreter. "We desire," continued the speaker, "you will press him (Governor Ogle of Maryland) to send Us a positive Answer. Let him say Yes or No; if he says Yes, we will treat with him; if No, we are able to do ourselves Justice, and we will do it . . ."[1]

This avowed threat against a neighboring province raised a troublesome point for the provincial authorities. Governor Thomas attempted to allay the tempers of the Indians by telling them that magistrates had been sent into the disturbed areas warning the squatters to remove themselves. At this point, the Indians did a very unusual thing. They broke into the governor's speech to refute that "so far from removing the people they (the magistrates) made Surveys for themselves, and they are in League with the Trespassers."

On the next day, the Provincial Council decided that the governor of Maryland should be informed of the attitude of the

---
1. Colonial Records, 4:570–571.

Six Nations. A messenger was dispatched to Annapolis carrying a copy of the threatening remarks made by the spokesman of the Six Nations. This letter was not sent until July 11th and the treaty ended on the following day. Consequently, there was not sufficient time to receive a reply from Governor Ogle before the Indians left the city.

It is difficult to determine whether it was by design on Weiser's part or whether Conrad's generous hospitality was the only motive for detaining the vast body of Indian delegates at his Tulpehocken home for three weeks after the close of the treaty. On August 3 Count Zinzendorf had found the chiefs lingering at Weiser's house.

The messenger to Maryland returned to Philadelphia with startling news from the south. Governor Ogle sent a handful of depositions taken from imprisoned Nanticoke Indians. These examinations revealed that there had been a plot to murder all the settlers on the Eastern Shore of Maryland. The arrest of the chiefs of the Nanticoke Nation had thwarted the scheme, but the audacity with which it was conceived gave the authorities of both provinces uneasy moments.[2]

According to the statements made by the prisoners, a group of twenty-three Shawnees and Senecas had visited the eastern shore of Maryland in May. These northern Indians had journeyed southward toward Philadelphia and then cut loose from the main body of deputies to enter Maryland province. There they urged the native Nanticokes to "join with themselves and the French against the English." Richard Peters wrote to Thomas Penn "It looked Dreadful at first and put the Marylanders into a terrible Consternation, all the counties were under Arms Night and Day from apprehension that the French were at the bottom of it."[3]

The messenger from Governor Thomas had reached Maryland just as the plot was discovered. His arrival and the message he carried helped to prevent civilian outbreaks against the culprits. The prisoners obediently recognized the sovereignty of the Six Nations.

On July 19, James Logan wrote to Weiser urging him to question the Indians who were still at Tulpehocken and to form some judgments as to the best steps to be taken.

---
2. Logan to Weiser, July 19, 1742, Peters Papers, 1:9.
3. Peters to Penns, August 25, 1742, Peters Letter Book, 24–25.

Weiser's answer was laid before Council on July 12. The Council of Chiefs at Tulpehocken had expressed surprise when Weiser told them of the actions of the Shawnees in Maryland. They promised to inquire into the matter on their homeward journey through Shawnee villages. Weiser's letters stated that the two strings of Wampum which were sent with it were, one to reprove the Nanticokes, and the other to plead with Governor Ogle for leniency in punishing the malefactors because they were a weak people who had been imposed upon by "the crafty and ill-designing Shawnees." The Indians repeated their demand for payment of the Maryland lands.

Thomas sent Weiser's letter to Ogle. Within a few days, the Maryland Governor dispatched a deputy to Philadelphia, empowered to treat with the Indians. The deputy, a Mr. Chase, was sent to Tulpehocken to meet Conrad Weiser. Late in August, the two men set out for Shamokin, the Pennsylvania capital of the Six Nations. Governor Thomas had instructed Weiser to consult Shikellamy.[4]

Upon his return from Shamokin, on August 31, Weiser sent two accounts of his transactions. One letter was carried to Logan by Conrad's son, the other was addressed to the Governor of Maryland. Since this is the first official document written by Weiser to officials outside of Pennsylvania, the significant portions of it are reproduced here:

> After my arrival at Shamokin I acquainted Shakalimin [Shikellamy], one of the Chiefs of the Six Nations of my Business being advised to go to him by His Honour the Governor of Pennsylvania. He telling me that it would be better to send Shikalimin to Onondago than to go myself, having a man who might be depended on which advice I followed and requested Shikalimin to the Chiefs of the Six Nations and acquaint them of the purport of Your Excellency's Instructions to me which Shikalimin promist to perform without loss of time and bring his Answer to Mr. Thomas who will give you such Information of it that

---

4. Ibid., The "Mr. Chase" referred to was the son of Reverend Samuel Chase, an eminent clergyman in colonial Maryland.

the Govr of Virginia may have timely notice to meet the Indians at Annapolis.

Shikalimin said he thought proper to acquaint some of the Inhabitants of Town [Shamokin] of this affair that they might be present when I opened my Instructions before he could proceed on his Journey that he might have there approbation August 31st 1742. Several of the Indians being assembled together (at which time) [crossed out] (when) [Ibid} I showed them the Strings of Wampon I had from Mr. Thomas which I gave Shikalimin to carry to Onondagues of which he accepted after this I in the presence of the Indns delivered (my) [crossed out] to them (the meaning of) [crossed out] my Yr Excellency's Message which they all seemed pleasd and desired Shakilimin to go to Onondagues to Inform them of this Business Skakalimin Informd me that as the Winter wass nigh & the Indians lived so far from Annapolis he Blieved they would not come before next Spring . . .[5]

It will be observed from the letter that Governor Ogle proposed a conference to be held at Annapolis and that Virginia was to be included in the transaction which was planned.

To Logan, Weiser wrote that a pass should be granted to Shikellamy. He reported that the Shawnees were disturbed by reports that they were to be punished and stated that Count Zinzendorf had requested his company on a missionary journey among the Wyoming Indians.

It was in response to this letter that Governor Thomas remonstrated with Weiser against accompanying the Count. "If you can think of no other way of excusing yourself to the Count, let him know, that I say, the services of the government require your presence in it 'till the next month."[6]

Three weeks later Conrad Weiser and Brother Ludwig (Zinzendorf) were pointing their horses northward to Shamokin. The Count expressed a desire to meet Shikellamy, but Weiser said that this would be impossible because the Oneida Chief was on

---
5. Weiser to Governor Samuel Ogle, n.d., Weiser MSS, 1:29.
6. Thomas to Weiser, September 9, 1742, Peters Papers, 1:94; Also Logan to Weiser, Ibid., 92.

his way to Onondaga. When the two pilgrims met the Six Nations' vice-regent at Shamokin, Weiser was surprised to find that his emissary had not yet set out and the Count regarded the turn of events as a revelation of divine providence working in his favor.[7]

When the party of Moravian missionaries reached the village over which Madame Montour reigned, Weiser decided to return to Shamokin, explaining that Shikellamy expected him there, Things were not working out as they had been planned. If Shikellamy had been intent upon going to Onondaga he could have joined the Zinzendorf party, but he had chosen to remain at Shamokin. It was October and the vivid memories of the winter journey of 1737 taught Conrad the dangers which would be encountered if the journey were postponed too long.

Prodded by Weiser the Oneida chieftain set out at once to carry the message to the Six Nations Council but, with characteristic Indian dilatoriness, he failed to complete his mission. En route Shikellamy met a party of Onondaga hunters and Caxhayan was among them. Shikellamy committed the message to Caxhayan on the promise that it would be carried to the Council and then the Viceroy returned to Shamokin. Caxhayan tarried too long "a Hunting and was somewhat neglectfull of which Shikelimo was informed some time this winter which gave a great deal of uneasiness and he (Shikellamy) was preparing for Onontaga" when other disturbing news detained him at Shamokin, awaiting a visit from Weiser. News had come from the "Shanadore," Shenandoah, that Shikellamy's son known as "unhappy Jake," had been killed in a skirmish there.

Early in October, Richard Peters sent a pass and other official documents to Shikellamy. On October 8, Governor Thomas issued a special Proclamation warning settlers to remove from all unoccupied lands.[8] At approximately the same time Peters informed the Penns in England that he had asked Weiser to sound out the Shamokin Indians about purchasing new lands in the borders of Pennsylvania. Weiser reported that the Indians were not willing to treat with the agents of the Proprietors "from an Imagination

---

7. Zinzendorf's Journal of September 1742. Published by Reichel, W. C. *Memorials of the Moravian Church.*
8. Pennsylvania Archives, 1st ser., 2:629–630.

that the Proprietors never leave the Keys of their money chest behind them." The Juniata lands, explained Weiser, "are favourite Lands" and the Indians were unwilling to sell, but that it might be possible to negotiate for Wyoming and other lands east of the Susquehanna. Peters informed the Penns that "Conrad is to attend the Six Nations to Annapolis in the Spring."[9]

THE RATTLESNAKE LEGEND

There is a tradition that after Weiser's return to Shamokin he had a premonition that Count Zinzendorf needed him. In his excellent account, *Otzinachson*[10], J. F. Meginness relates a story that Weiser set out to seek the party of Moravians and caught up with them just in time to save the life of Zinzendorf and others from execution by the Indians. In the absence of contemporary evidence, we must regard this account critically. There seems to be entirely too much of prescience in the relation between these two men to warrant full acceptance. Another legend which surrounds this journey of Weiser and Zinzendorf is the oft-told tale of "Zinzendorf and the Rattlesnake."

According to this legend, the Count was alone in his tent when a rattler, attracted by the fire, climbed upon his recumbent body and wound itself around a leg. Deep in the contemplation of his mission, the Count was oblivious to his danger. Indians peering into the tent were amazed to find this man of God unafraid and unharmed by the dreaded viper.[11]

FACTS ONCE MORE

Returning to the safer ground of recorded facts, we know that on November 21 Conrad Weiser visited Richard Peters and urged the authorities to sell a vast tract of land to the Moravians. In Weiser's presence, Peters wrote to Thomas Penn, stating that with proper encouragement 10,000 of the Brethren could be induced to migrate into Pennsylvania.[12] The occasion for Weiser's visit to

---
9. Richard Peters to the Proprietors, Peters Letter Book, 37–38.
10. Meginness, J. F., *Otsinachson, or the Valley of the West Branch of the Susquehanna*, Williamsport, Pa., 1889.
11. Neue Reading Kalender, 1874, *Zinzendorf und die Klapperschlange*. This account states that Weiser arrived soon after the incident took place.
12. Peters to Penns, November 21, 1742; Peters Letter Book, 5:41.

Philadelphia in November was to be present at the dedication of the new Moravian Church which Zinzendorf had built in that city at Moravian Alley and Race streets.[13] On the same day that the dedication took place, the Reverend Henry Melchior Muhlenberg arrived in Philadelphia.

Soon thereafter Indian affairs clamored for Weiser's attention. Shikellamy was waiting at Shamokin to learn the details of the death of his son in the Shenandoah.

THE VIRGINIA SKIRMISH

In 1737, Conrad Weiser had made a perilous winter journey to Onondaga in New York province on behalf of Governor Gooch of Virginia. The purpose of the journey was to prevail upon the Six Nations to send deputies to Williamsburg, the Virginia capital, there to iron out the differences between the Iroquois and the Catawba Indians of the South. Peace overtures met with the approval of the chieftains of both Indian groups, but the proud Iroquois were unwilling to travel to Williamsburg. Five years passed without effecting a treaty of amity. During these years Governor Gooch was active in leading a military expedition against Spanish Carthegena (Cuba) and the truce which Weiser arranged had expired.

In 1742, a party of Six Nation braves renewed the inter-Indian war. They traveled south through Pennsylvania into Virginia hunting Flathead scalps. Their routes of travel passed through white settlements in the Shenandoah Valley of Virginia. The Indians had no designs upon the lives of settlers, but they found it necessary to keep to paths where food could be obtained. Occasionally they were guilty of stealing chickens and hogs from lonely farmsteads on the frontier.

Naturally, the wronged settlers were incensed and the presence of Indians aggravated their sense of injustice. When the body of thirty-one Onondagas and Oneidas, under their captain, Jonnhaty, arrived at the Irish settlement in what is now Rockingham County in Virginia, they were met by irate settlers on horseback. A violent skirmish ensued in which several settlers and Indians were slain.

---
13. Ritter Abraham, *First Moravian Church of Philadelphia*, Philadelphia, 1857, 51.

The first reports of the skirmish reached Philadelphia on January 15, 1743. *The Pennsylvania Journal*, published by William Bradford, reported that three settlers had been found "shot dead in the Road" in the Irish settlement in the "back part of Virginia." The newspaper account made it appear that the Indians had been the aggressors in a bloody skirmish which took a toll of eight white and eleven Indian lives.[14]

On January 24, 1743, more information was brought by Thomas McKee, a trader, who owned a store near the Big Island in the Susquehanna (Lock Haven, Pennsylvania). Fearful of his life, McKee had fled from his station, abandoning his stores, to apprise the Pennsylvania authorities of the dangers which threatened the settlers of the province. In his deposition he stated that a band of Six Nations warriors had come to the Shawnee village at Big Island, complaining of their treatment by the settlers.[15] These Indians were bitter and vengeful. McKee listened to their recital of grievances against the Virginians as the Iroquois warriors appealed to the Shawanese for sympathy. He had tried to point out to the angry natives that Pennsylvania should not be blamed for the actions of Virginia, only to be told abruptly that all Europeans were alike.

The Shawnees readily espoused the cause of their brethren and McKee sensed danger to himself. Warned by a white woman who was a prisoner in the Shawnee village that the Indians planned to murder him, the trader fled from his station and hurried to Philadelphia with his message.

DIPLOMATIC DILEMMA

The full significance of McKee's words was at once clear to Governor Thomas and his advisors. A war between the Six Nations and Virginia could not avoid involving Pennsylvania. In case of such a conflict, the Iroquois Confederacy would call upon the sons of Onas (Penn) to live up to the treaties of friendship made with them. In Indian diplomacy, a treaty of any kind meant an alliance. It was, of course, unthinkable that His Majesty's province

---
14. *The Pennsylvania Journal and Weekly Advertiser*, January 18, 1743.
15. McKee's Deposition, Colonial Records, 4:630–631.

of Pennsylvania should join with Indians in a war against His Majesty's province of Virginia. The only escape from such a situation was to avert the outbreak of war.

On the advice of Council and with the approval of the politically hostile Assembly, Thomas ordered Conrad Weiser to go to Shamokin to offer Pennsylvania's services as a mediator. He sent Weiser all the information at hand and told him to use his own good judgment "as our Agent" in presenting the matter to the Indians. "I think I need say no more to you who knows so much."[16] The instructions were carried to Tulpehocken by Thomas McKee and together the two white men set out through deep snow for the Indian capital at Shamokin.

SHAMOKIN CONFERENCE

This time Weiser did not follow the Indian trail which led across the Blue Mountain as he had traveled on former occasions. On January 30, 1743, his course lay west to the Susquehanna River by way of Paxtang, which Weiser spelled "Backstone." When the Susquehanna was reached, McKee was greeted with the surprise of finding two of his men in canoes laden with skins. They had come from Chiniotte (Juniata) and reported that they had met the ten Iroquois warriors returning from Virginia. The Indians had been civil to the traders, whose gifts of food they accepted, but they had not mentioned anything about the news from Virginia. This was an ominous sign. Settlers at Paxtang were uneasy because they had observed Shawnee scouts watching their movements.

Journeying northward from Paxtang, Weiser and McKee met up with the Shawnee scouts at a trader's house. The Indians were sullen and carried their weapons unsheathed when Weiser tried to speak to them. Their hands trembled when Conrad proffered his hand in a friendly gesture. These Indians were strangers and Weiser could not speak their language. When McKee told them in Shawnee who Weiser was and the mission on which he was sent, the Indians were pleased and agreed to accompany the them to Shamokin.

---

16. Ibid., 634; James Logan sent a message of goodwill with Weiser, Peters MSS, 2:106.

A few days later, Weiser, McKee, and the Shawanese scouts reached the Indian capital. They were greeted by Shikellamy and Allumpees, the Delaware king. The ardor of Shikellamy's greeting was tempered with sorrow. One of his sons had been slain in the Virginia skirmish and the sachem was in mourning. Weiser announced that he had come to "wipe of[f] the Tears from your Eyes."

To the twenty-five chief men at Shamokin, Weiser became Governor Thomas because it was official words he was speaking. He reminded them of the treaties of friendship existing between the two governments and suggested that Pennsylvania should be given a chance to mediate the troubles with Virginia. His proposal won immediate favor in the Council and the next day Shikellamy and Saghisdowa were instructed to set out for Onondaga.

A grandson of Shikellamy was one of the survivors of the Virginia encounter. He was present at the Shamokin conference and gave Weiser a detailed account of the skirmish with the Irish settlers "at Jonontore" (Shenandoah). The Indians' side of the story differed greatly from the report which Colonel James Patton of Virginia made to Governor Gooch. According to the warrior at Shamokin, the whites were the aggressors and the Indians had fought only to save themselves from destruction. This account Weiser transmitted to Governor Thomas on February 9, 1743.[17] Richard Peters wrote to Thomas Penn that he was "rather inclined" to believe the Indian side of the story after reading the testimony of Shikellamy's grandson.[18]

Meanwhile, Governor Thomas had written to Gooch, offering Pennsylvania's services as a mediator. After a considerable amount of blustering Gooch accepted the proposal and Conrad Weiser was sent to Shamokin a second time.[19]

COLONEL LEVIN GALE

It was not on behalf of Virginia alone that Weiser made his second journey of 1743. The differences between the Six Nations and Maryland were still unsettled. Governor Ogle had been

---
17. Weiser's Journal, January 31–February 9, 1743, Colonial Records, 4:640–642.
18. Peters to Penn, February n.d., 1743; Peters Letter Book, 5:50. Account in Bradford's Journal, January 25, 1743, places the blame upon the Irish settlers.
19. Gooch to Thomas, February 8, 1743, Peters MSS, 1:109.

succeeded by Governor Thomas Bladen and some delay had occurred in providing the goods which were to be given to the Indians as a present. In March 1743, Colonel Levin Gale arrived in Philadelphia, commissioned as Maryland's agent to deal with the Six Nations. Gale promptly begged Weiser to come to Philadelphia, "as everybody agrees no person can be so serviceable as you."[20] Thomas wrote to the interpreter on the same day "Your presence is absolutely necessary here."

Weiser obeyed the summons and met Gale at Philadelphia on March 10, 1743. Complications had arisen in the plans for a conference at Annapolis. Thomas Cresap, one of the factors in the so-called Cresap's War, was conniving with the Indians to have the treaty held at his farm near Old Town on the north fork of the Potomac. Quite naturally this interference was resented by both Pennsylvania and Maryland authorities. Weiser was consulted and gave as his opinion that Cresap was not "in favour with the Indians. They look upon him as a man that either wants wit or honesty."[21] A lengthy account was written by Weiser, explaining the status of Maryland's relations with the northern Indians. Two days later Colonel Gale dispatched a "special messenger sent from Conrad Weiser, Esq. to His Excellency Thomas Bladen" with orders to all sheriffs in Maryland to "give him [the messenger] all the assistance you can."[22]

To Gale's question whether the pending Virginia matter might interfere with the settlement of Maryland's problem, Weiser answered that the two would not conflict, but suggested that the joint conference be held within the borders of Pennsylvania.

SHAMOKIN AGAIN

On the ninth of April, Weiser reached Shamokin. On the same day, Shikellamy and Saghisdowa returned from Onondaga with the answer of the Six Nations. In the conference which followed, Weiser spoke for Pennsylvania, Maryland, and Virginia and the chieftains spoke for the Six Nations and their allies. The setting

---

20. Levin Gale to Weiser, March 5, 1743, 113.
21. Weiser to Gale, n.d., 1743, Peters MSS, 2:4. Cresap wrote to Shikellimy April 2, 1743, inviting the Six Nations to meet at his home at Antedam (Antiedam), 1:118.
22. Peters MSS, 1:117.

was unique. At Shamokin [Sunbury] where the two great branches of the Susquehanna meet, messages were exchanged between those who dwelt near its northernmost headwaters and the governors of the provinces which formed along its widening course.

The Indians welcomed the offer of mediation but studded their remarks with veiled threats and declarations of prowess. They said that they were accustomed to regard the first "blow" as the act of disorderly people, but when they received a "second blow, we rose and knock'd down our Enemies with one Blow, and we are still able to do the same; but we leave our Case to you. We have ordered our warriors with the strongest Words to sit down and not to revenge themselves."

To the invitation of Maryland, the Indians replied that they would not be able to come (this summer) but they would come to Pennsylvania "tomorrow morning," meaning the next spring. It is to be noted that they did not mention a treaty place in Maryland or Cresap's plantation at Old Town but specified a spot named by them, Canataquamy, near present-day Harrisburg.[23]

When Weiser had a chance to speak with Shikellamy alone, he asked a direct question as to why the Six Nations were unwilling to treat that summer in either of the southern capitals. Shikellamy explained that his people could not "come down with a Hatchet Struck in their Head; the Governor of Virginia must wash off the Blood first and take the Hatchet out of their Head and Dress the Wound." It was the opinion of the vice-regent that unless this was done there would be a war between the Iroquois and Virginia. This opined the sachem, was the real reason for postponing the journey for one year, and unless something was done soon to "wash off the Blood," the next year's journey would be on the warpath instead of on a peace path.

The Delaware king, Allumpees, sent the following message to Governor Thomas at the close of the Shamokin conference. "When we first heard the news, all was dark about Shamokin, we could not see at the Least Distance from Us, and our hearts were filled with many Apprehensions; but when Conrad arrived with your Message the Clouds were Dispelled, the Darkness ceased. . . ."

---

23. Gale to Weiser, March 10, 1743, Maryland Archives, 28:296; Pennsylvania Vol. Records, 4:647.

On the morning of April 22, a German and two Indians were waiting at the door when the governor's council assembled. Shikellamy and Saghisdowa had accompanied Weiser to Philadelphia to report what they had learned at Onondaga. Weiser's translation of the report was sent to Governor Gooch.[24] In a letter to the Virginia Governor Thomas referred to Weiser as a "man of great probity and a thorough Knowledge in Indian Affairs," hinting that the Pennsylvania Interpreter be employed by Virginia to go to Onondaga to "take the Hatchet out of their Heads."

In his reply, Gooch requested Thomas "to send your honest Interpreter once more to the Indian Chiefs." The blood could be washed from their faces with a gift of goods worth 100 pounds sterling at the expense of Virginia.[25]

Accordingly, Conrad Weiser received his instructions to go to Onondaga a second time, on behalf of Virginia. There he was to promise a gift of goods to the amount stated by Gooch and to fix upon a place for selling the lands in dispute.[26] On July 6 three men who figured prominently in the affairs of Colonial Pennsylvania set out together from Weiser's house for destinations far to the north. They were John Bartram, bent upon studying the flora and fauna of the forests; Lewis Evans commissioned to draw official maps for the province, and Conrad Weiser, peace ambassador from Virginia, Maryland, and Pennsylvania, to the powerful Indian nations.

Among the many activities of the many-sided Benjamin Franklin was the organization of a club known as the Junto, which later evolved as the American Philosophical Society. The Junto was formed to serve both social and cultural purposes for the enlightened persons in Philadelphia. Scientific experiments and explorations were encouraged by the organization. They readily agreed to study the flora and fauna of interior America. Franklin's newspaper, *The Gazette*, urged public support for the subscription being raised "for the encouragement of Mr. John Bartram to travel through New York, Pennsylvania, New Jersey,

---
24. Thomas to Bladen, April 25, 1743. Maryland Archives, 298. Thomas to Gooch, n.d., Colonial Records, 4:653.
25. Gooch to Thomas, May 7, 1743, Ibid., 654.
26. Thomas to Weiser, June 18, 1743, Ibid., 655.

and Maryland, in search of curious vegetables, fossils, etc., which it is hoped will meet with success."[27]

Lewis Evans, a cartographer, who was very much esteemed by the Penn Proprietors, accompanied Bartram to the home of Conrad Weiser early in July of 1743. Together the three men set out for New York province.

REMOVING THE HATCHET

Weiser led his companions northward over the Indian trail which crossed over the Blue Mountain at Pilger's Ruh and entered the Schuylkill Valley, which Zinzendorf had named Anton's Wilderness. From the top of the Blue Ridge, Evans viewed the broad valley which spread out to the north. In his journal, he described the scene as "varied here and there with swelling hills, looking at a distance like cleared land, but are covered with dwarf oaks, about shoulder high, and bearing acorns, or the best gallnuts of any as we have."[28]

These observations would seem to fit the pen of Bartram, the naturalist, rather than that of Evans, the map maker. But Bartram was more concerned with the danger of rattlesnakes. Five of these vipers were killed on the first day of the journey. At night Bartram complained that he was disturbed by small gnats. On the second night, at Mahonoy, the naturalist complained of fleas. The next evening the party reached the Indian village of Shamokin and this time Bartram could not sleep because the Indians got drunk and caroused during the night. The travelers tarried at Shamokin on the fourth day, but that night Bartram and Evans "went out to the mountain to sleep." Weiser stayed in the Indian village.[29]

---

27. *Pennsylvania Gazette*, March 10, 1742.
28. Lewis Evans "*Observations.*" Quoted in Watson's *Annals of Philadelphia*, Part II, 561.
29. Bartram, John, *Observations*. Printed for George Perkins Humphries, Rochester, N.Y., 1895. See also Ernest Earnest, *John and William Bartram*, University of Pennsylvania Press, 1940. In 1749 the Penn Proprietors wanted Evans and Bartram to accompany Weiser on the trip which Weiser made exploring the Ohio country. Weiser objected to their company. See Gipson, Lawrence Henry, *Lewis Evans*, Phila. 1939. Peters wrote to Penn, Feb. 16, 1750. "We must give way to Conrad without who the back parts can never be safely reconnoitered." Page 38. Mr. Gipson states that the reason for Weiser's opposition to their company is not clear, pointing out that in March 1749 the New York Gazette stated that Conrad Weiser agreed to receive subscriptions for Evans' maps at his home. The author submits this as evidence that good relations must have existed between Weiser and Evans. I submit that Weiser declined the company of these men because they were not good travelers.

North of Shamokin they passed the home of Shikellamy who, with one of his sons, had joined the party at the forks of the Susquehanna and traveled with them. But natural hardships continued to annoy the naturalists. Heavy rain made them uncomfortable until the Indians improvised a bark cover to shield the white men.

The travelers were deep in Penn's forests on July 11. On this day Shikellamy and his son shot a deer and a feast of venison was prepared on the following day. Now came the turn of Weiser's white companions to josh the leader of the expedition. Conrad was not feeling well and could not eat the portions placed before him. Bartram and Evans ate Weiser's share "by proxy" and doubtlessly indulged in some good natural bantering.

One day later, Weiser's party met a group of eight Shawnee Indians. Both groups sought a shady tree and squatted under it, smoking pipes which were lit for them by a squaw. Weiser explained to the Shawnees that he was on his way to the Six Nations Council, there to offer mediation in the affairs between the Iroquois and Virginia. To this piece of news, the Indians shouted "To-Bay," an expression of approval. Bartram records the reply to Weiser. The Indians said that they "were sensible with what an unwearied diligence Weiser had hitherto been instrumental in preserving peace and good harmony between the Indians and the English and that as they could not but now commend the prudence and zeal with which he had affected this laudable purpose, so they earnestly entreated and sincerely hoped he would still persevere in the same endeavors and with the same success and that his good offices may never be wanting on any future occasion.[30]

Somewhere between the Pennsylvania line and Onondaga Weiser's two white companions, Bartram and Evans, parted company with him and continued their journey to Lake Ontario. His two red companions Shikellamy and his son stayed on the path to Onondaga. This path led to Cachisdasche, the first town of the Onondaga Nation. The Iroquois Long House was five miles farther north. Advance messengers were sent ahead to inform the chiefs that Conrad Weiser had come with a message from Onas on behalf of Assaryquoa, the Indian name for the Governor of Virginia.

---

30. Bartram, *Observations*, 22.

ONONDAGA WELCOME

The chief town of the Onondagas prepared a grand welcome for Weiser, whom they called Tarachawagon.[31] A feast of dried eels, boiled in hominy, was set before him and mats were brought for his comforts. Canassatego, who led the huge delegation of deputies to Philadelphia in 1742, came to pay his respects and politely inquired about the welfare of the authorities of Philadelphia. Weiser and the chiefs smoked a pipe of "Philadelphia Tobacco" and chatted about matters of general interest. When Tocanuntie, the Black Prince of Onondaga, came to call he brought with him Caxhayan, the messenger who had been befriended by Zinzendorf a year earlier. To these old friends, Weiser spoke in a humorous vein. To their greeting that he always brought good news, Conrad replied: "It was enough to kill a Man to come such a Long & bad Road over hills, Rocks, Old Trees, and Rivers, and to fight through a Cloud of Vermine and all kinds of Poisen'd Worms and creeping things, besides being Loaded with a disagreeable Message, upon which they laugh'd."

This was the shrewd Weiser's way of diverting discussion from the main purpose of his journey until a more auspicious moment could be found. On the twenty-third of August, Conrad and Shikellamy prevailed upon Canassatego to "meet us in the Bushes," that is privately, and then explained the object of their mission to the supreme chieftain of the Six Nations. At a council of the Onondagas Weiser was officially welcomed as Assaryquoa and Shikellamy as Onas. No business could be transacted however until the chiefs of all the Six Nations were present. Messengers were sent to invite the representatives of the confederacy and while the Onondagas waited they arranged a feast in honor of Weiser. Jonnhaty, the captain, who had led the warriors in the ill-fated Virginia skirmish, was the host at the banquet.

A cask of rum was rolled into the Jonnhaty hut. Virginia and Pennsylvania were toasted in song and the Sun was thanked for giving light. The cask was opened and Canassatego drank the first cup, toasting the health of Assaryquoa and Caheshcarowana

---

31. The description of the events at Onondaga is extracted from Weiser's Journal of 1743, July 31 to August 2. Colonial Records, 4:660–668.

drank to the health of Onas and then the cups were filled for all those present to confirm the sentiments expressed by the chiefs. On the second round of drinks, Jonnhaty handed the first cup to Conrad, who toasted the "wise counsellors of the united nations" and his sentiments were endorsed by all who were there, each one drinking a gill of rum. A kettle of soup was passed and every guest was welcome to dip from its contents with a wooden spoon. After all the rum, two gallons of it, was drunk, the feast was ended. The assembled chiefs and deputies shouted *Jo-haa* and departed.

While the Onondagas were feasting, a delegation of Nanticoke Indians, from far-off Maryland, arrived at the Six Nations capital. The southern Indians could speak no Maqua and the Onondagas did not know the Nanticoke tongue. Consequently, the Indians could not converse with each other. At this juncture, Weiser spoke to some Nanticokes in English and found that they understood. The Black Prince, Tocanuntie, observed this conversation and directed "We will hear you with our English Ear and speak to you with our English Tongue. There is the Man (pointing to Weiser) who is the Guardian of all the Indians." In this way it came to pass that a German-born American interpreted between Iroquois and Nanticokes, using English as the common basis for communication.

CEREMONY IN THE WOODS

During the days which followed Jonnhaty's feast, the delegations began to arrive from the allied nations. With the Oneidas came a venerable chief, Aquoyiota, whom Weiser had known during his boyhood days in Schoharie. New ceremonies and repeated Jo-haas greeted each new group of deputies. On the 28th of July, the full Council was assembled and two fires were lit, one for the Six Nations and one for Virginia. The Six Nations tended the one and Weiser stood guard over the other.

There followed a long recital of incidents which led to the unhappy state of affairs which made the meeting necessary. Many belts of wampum were hung upon a stick. Kettles of hominy and loaves of Indian bread were placed before Assaryquoa, Weiser, who was designated as the "Divider." The announcement of Virginia's gift brought forth Jo-haas of joy and Weiser was told that he was about to receive an answer.

Then, after thanking Onas for his meditation, Tocanuntie addressed Virginia, "You have healed our Wounds . . . an evil Spirit was the promoter of the late unhappy Skirmish . . . we thank you for removing your Hatchet . . . Let this Belt of Wampum serve to remove our Hatchet from you and not only bury it but we will fling it into the Bottomless Pitt, into the Ocean."

The Six Nations promised both Maryland and Virginia that they would come down to Harris Ferry in Pennsylvania "after eight moons are passed by." They made it clear, however, that they were in no mood for peace with their enemies, the Catawbas, but promised to restrain their young braves and prevent them from making their warpath through the areas where white men were settled.

A song of joy marked the conclusion of the statements by the Black Prince. The Iroquois put out their fire and Weiser "put out the fire on behalf of Assaryquoa and Onas." After an exchange of civilities, Weiser set out upon his homeward journey. He had every reason to feel that his mission had been successful.

Soon after Weiser's return to Pennsylvania the *Gazette* informed its readers that "the misunderstanding between the colony of Virginia and the Six Nations . . . is now happily accommodated by the Mediation of our Governor . . . when all past offenses were sunk in the Ocean, never more to be seen or heard of."

The optimism expressed by Franklin's newspaper was somewhat premature. True, the Hatchet had been removed and the blood had been washed off by the intercession of Weiser in his capacity of ambassador without portfolio, but the demands of the Six Nations against Virginia and Maryland had not yet been satisfied. The plans for the inter-colony-Indian treaty had been made, but time was to prove how much more remained to be done before peace was certain. In the negotiations which followed Conrad Weiser's services became indispensable to Pennsylvania, to Maryland, to Virginia, and to the Oneidas, Senecas, Tuscaroras, Cayugas, Mohawks, Onondagas, and their many allies.

THE ARMSTRONG MURDER

The German settlers of Pennsylvania were not traders nor can they be designated properly as frontiersmen. The pioneers who lived on the edges of civilization and traded with the Indians who dwelt beyond these limits were mostly Scotch-Irishmen. These men were rugged individualists, ever ready to maintain their rights against any odds and contemptuous of Indians. The Quaker methods of appeasing the Indians drew the scorn of the doughty frontiersmen who lived and traded with the natives. There was always danger of a frontier war along the reaches of the Susquehanna River.

With many issues at stake in 1744, it was vitally important that there should be no overt act of hostility between whites and Indians in Pennsylvania when hundreds of Six Nations Indians were in the province. The interests of neighboring provinces were involved as well as those of Pennsylvania. An incident of a hostile nature might well frustrate all plans and lead to dire consequences.

For these reasons the murder of John Armstrong and two of his white companions by some Delawares, threatened the peace of the province in April 1744, only a few weeks before the northern Indians were expected.

When the gruesome news of the murders reached the Philadelphia Council, Conrad Weiser was promptly dispatched to Shamokin to ferret out the facts and prevent trouble. The following narrative has been constructed from Weiser's findings and the depositions of witnesses to some of the phases of the crime:

John Armstrong, a Scotch-Irish trader living at Paxtang, held Mushemeelin, a Delaware in his debt for several pelts. To secure this small debt, Armstrong had seized Mushemeelin's horse and a rifled gun, taking a value of seven pounds for a debt estimated by Christopher Sauer at forty shillings. The rifle was given to James Smith, one of Armstrong's helpers, and the horse was sold or lent to a neighboring trader, James Berry. During the winter of 1743-1744 Mushemeelin had offered Armstrong an ornament valued at twenty shillings, demanding the return of his horse. Armstrong refused the proffered payment, declaring that the debt had been increased recently. Sharp words followed and the men quarreled.³²

When the snows melted, John Armstrong, accompanied by two of his servants, James Smith and Woodward Arnold, set out upon their annual journey to the Allegheny, loaded with stock and stores for the Indian trade. Enroute they passed Mushemeelin's cabin. The Delaware's wife was at home alone. She demanded that Armstrong return the horse which he had taken because it was her property. Her demands were ignored.

Mushemeelin came home from a hunting excursion and listened to his wife's tale of her encounter with Armstrong. Accompanied by two young Delawares who had been on the hunting trip with him, Mushemeelin set out in pursuit of Armstrong and his party. He told his companions that they were going to the "Great Hill to hunt Bears." Correctly guessing the route taken by Armstrong and his men, the three hunters followed the Juniata River and soon came close to their intended victims. The smoke of Armstrong's fire could be seen in the distance.

"Now they are not far off," said Mushemeelin to Jemmy and Neshellamy. "We will make ourselves black, then they will deliver up the Horse immediately and I will tell Jack (Armstrong) that if he don't give the Horse I will kill him." Shikellamy told Weiser that Mushemeelin laughed as he spoke.³³

Mushemeelin daubed his face with black charcoal and the three Indians crept forward to the Armstrong camp. Only James Smith was there. In reply to a question as to Armstrong's whereabouts, Smith said he had gone on ahead. Mushemeelin went on alone, while his two companions joined with Smith in preparing a meal of turtles.

While the preparations for the meal were going on a gunshot was heard in the woods. It was at this time that Woodward, alias English Arnold, was murdered as was learned afterward. Soon Mushemeelin returned demanding, "Why did you two not kill that

---

32. *Pennsylvania Berichte*: Christopher Sauer's Newspaper Accounts in issues of April 26, May 3, May 10, and May 16, 1744.
33. Conrad Weiser's Report of his journey to Shamokin, April–May 1744. Colonial Records, 4:680–684. The conversational dialogue reproduced in this chapter is almost an exact transcription of the account which was supplied to Weiser by Shikellimy and recorded by Weiser. The only editing that has been done by the author is in the arrangement of the paragraph forms, and the comments which follow the dialogue.

white man (Smith) according as I bid you? I have laid the other two down."

As we shall see, only one settler had been slain.

Jemmy, a young brave, was startled by this announcement and ran away. Mushemeelin charged the remaining Delawares: "How will you do to kill Catawbas if you cannot kill white men? You Coward! I'll show you how you must do it."

Saying this, the enraged Delaware picked up an ax and with three strong blows split the helpless Smith's head. "Smith never stirred."

After the awful deed was done the murderer set out to find the fugitive Jemmy. When the frightened youth rejoined his two companions the maddened Mushemeelin informed the lad that it became his duty to kill the third white man, since he and Neshellamy had dispatched the other two. In this way, he tried to have Jemmy believe that Neshellamy had killed Smith.

Bloodthirsty, Mushemeelin pressed on along the trail, his horrified companions following reluctantly. Before long they met John Armstrong. Breathing his rage Mushemeelin demanded: "Where is my horse?"

"He will come by and by, you shall have him." Armstrong was playing for time.

"I want him now."

"You shall have him. Come let us go to that fire and let us smoke and talk together." This was said in hope of placating the mad man.

"Go along then," said Mushemeelin.

"I am coming," said Armstrong, "do you go before, Mushemeelin, do you go foremost." Armstrong looked like a dead man and bent forward toward the fire.

Mushemeelin shot him in his back and then leaped upon the fallen body of the trader, plunging his hatchet into his victim's head while he shouted: "Give me my horse, I tell you."

After the terrible deed was done the murderer pledged his companions to secrecy and forced them to accept portions of the trader's stock and stores. In this way, he sought to implicate them in the crime. Soon afterward the three conspirators met several other Indians, who naturally questioned the source of their wealth. Mushemeelin was forced to explain that he had murdered Armstrong and another division of the spoils was designed to seal the lips of the new arrivals. These Indians would have none of the loot, but they were willing to help Mushemeelin hide the goods.

Jemmy left the party and returned to the Indian village of Shamokin. Soon news trickled out of the village that Armstrong and his party had been murdered and it found its way southward along the Susquehanna to Paxtang, where Alexander Armstrong was concerned about the fate of his brother and the two servants.

The irate settlers at Paxtang met at the home of Joseph Chambers and there decided to ask the Delaware king to send some scouts to help the white men search for Armstrong.[34] Eight Indians were promptly sent to the house of James Berry, but three of them ran away before the scouting party was organized. Nine white men and five Indians set out along the path which the traders followed. James Berry was the first to find a sign of the tragedy.

Near a white oak tree which had three notches cut into it, Berry found a shoulder bone, which it was believed was that of Armstrong. This led the searchers to believe that Armstrong's body had been eaten by the Indians. When the bone was handed to one of the Delaware Indian scouts "his Nose gushed out with Blood." This was interpreted as evidence of guilt by the other Indians.

Some "Bawld" Eagles circling above the treetops near the narrows of the Juniata (Jack's Narrows, near Newport, Perry County) led the searching party to the corpse of James Smith. The bald eagles continued to circle at a point farther on. Following this sign, the white men found the remains of Woodward Arnold. The Indian scouts had deserted the party. A fearful night was spent in the woods by the nine Scotch-Irishmen. A barking dog kept them awake; he seemed to be warning them against the treacherous Delawares who had absconded during the day. On the following day, they buried the corpses of Smith and Arnold and then followed a circuitous route back to Paxtang by way of John Harris (Harrisburg). They felt that they might be waylaid by the wily natives if they followed the regular trader's path.

Meanwhile, Allumpies, King of the Delawares, and Shikellamy realized that the guilty persons would have to be brought

---

34. The Deposition of Alexander Armstrong et al., Pennsylvania Archives, 1st ser., 1:643.

to justice. Shikellamy sent a message to Weiser, begging him to come to Shamokin, to help him in his difficult position. But Conrad was not at home when the letter reached Tulpehocken. Left to his own resources Allumpies, on the advice of his council, employed an Indian conjurer (or ker, as Weiser informs us) to find out who the murderers were. The seer was busy all night long and in the morning, he named Mushemeelin as the murderer. Three chiefs called upon the designated criminal and obtained a confession from him.

When the report of the examination was given to Shikellamy, orders were given to arrest the perpetrators of the crime. This announcement caused consternation in the Indian village. Many Indians fled into the woods and none were willing to seize the person of Mushemeelin. Allumpies himself was frightened and begged Shikellamy's protection.

Finally, Shikellamy's sons prevailed upon a few tribesmen to help them take Mushemeelin and Neshellamy into custody. Both were bound and placed in a canoe. But no one could be found to take the canoe to Alexander Armstrong at Paxtang.

The brother of the deceased trader had written several messages to the Indians at Shamokin, demanding that justice be done.[35] The tone of these letters was quite civil, but John Shikellamy (later Black Logan) made use of the knowledge that such letters had been received to threaten the frightened Delawares that if they were afraid to take the live prisoners to Paxtang they "might separate their Heads from their Bodies and lay them in the Canoe, and carry them to Alexander to roast and eat them; that would satisfy his revenge, as he wants to eat Indians." This persuasion worked and two canoes were sent southward along the Delaware, each carrying a bound prisoner.

Only one of the prisoners reached Paxtang. Somewhere along the route, Shikellamy's sons released Neshellamy, on the strength of his protests of innocence. The Paxtang people sent their lone prisoner to Lancaster jail, where he was questioned by the magistrate, Thomas Cookson.

The murderer admitted that he had killed Woodward and Armstrong, but maintained stoutly that Neshellamy had tomahawked

---
35. Armstrong to Allumpies, April 25, 1744, Ibid., 647–648.

Smith. He was bitter in denouncing his captors for freeing his confederate Neshellamy. Mushemeelin told the Lancaster Magistrate that he expected to be held in Lancaster until the Six Nations chief arrived from the north and then to be dealt with according to their laws.

CONRAD WEISER, DETECTIVE

An Indian held in Lancaster jail, charged with the murder of white men, appealing to the deputies of the Six Nations assembled in conference was a situation which the authorities in Philadelphia felt had to be avoided. Late in April, Conrad Weiser was sent to Shamokin to get the whole story of the murders and to carry belts of wampum to the Delawares as an earnest of goodwill. During his interviews with the chief men at Shamokin, Weiser learned the story as it has been set forth here. In a letter to Christopher Sauer, written two years after the journey, Weiser stated that the Indians had prepared a huge feast to welcome him when he came with the[36] message from the governor. "Over one hundred persons present, who ate a large fat bear in great silence." A venerable chieftain made a speech in which he expressed his joy that "the Sun would not set (no war) but only a little Cloud go across it . . . Thanks to thee thou Great Ruler of the World, that thou allowest the Sun to shine again and hast driven away the Cloud."

Mushemeelin was removed to the Philadelphia jail before the Six Nations' delegates arrived in Lancaster. On August 9 the widow of John Armstrong applied to the Assembly for a pension for herself and her children. On the same day, the Assembly voted Weiser a reward of thirty pounds for his services in the Armstrong affair.[37] On August 21, after the conclusion of the Lancaster Treaty between the Six Nations and Virginia and Maryland, Weiser and Shikellamy came to Philadelphia and were present at the denunciation of the Delawares uttered by Governor Thomas to a

---

36. Weiser to Christopher Sauer, December n.d., 1746. From the Abraham Cassel Collection. Translated by Helen Bell. Printed in the *Pennsylvania Magazine of History and Biography*, 1:166-167.
37. *Votes of the Pennsylvania Assembly*, 3:548. The Votes were printed by Benjamin Franklin. In 1931 the State of Pennsylvania printed the Eighth Series of the Pennsylvania Archives, in which the Votes were reproduced. Conrad Weiser appeared in person, before the Assembly, to present his bill for the Shamokin Journey. Pennsylvania Archives, 8th ser., 4:2920-2925.

delegation of that nation led by Quidahickgunt, substituting for Allumpies, who was sick. The Delawares were penitent. "Let this string of wampum," they declared, "clear the air that was foul . . . and serve to take the Overflow of Gall out of your Entrails for such a foul offence."[38]

By the orders of the governor, the Delawares brought with them Mushemeelin's companions, Jemmy and Neshellamy.[39] Although the Indians protested vigorously that these men were not involved in the crime directly, Thomas explained that they would be needed as witnesses at the trial. As a matter of general counsel Thomas warned "Tho' the Indian Traders are not the best sort of People and may do you hurt, yet you are not to Revenge yourselves, but apply in all such Cases to Conrad Weiser."[40]

COLONIAL JUSTICE

The transfer of trial from Lancaster to Philadelphia was not legal. Pennsylvania colonial law required that capital offenses had to be tried in the county in which the crime was committed. On October 16, 1744, the Assembly passed a bill for the speedy trial of any Indians charged with capital offenses. The law was ex post facto in that it was made to apply to former offenses yet untried. A change of venue was provided by this special act by declaring that all such cases be tried in Philadelphia before the Supreme Court or Justices of the Courts of Oyer and Terminer and Gaol Delivery.[41]

Governor Thomas promptly affixed his signature to the bill and it became law in time to try Mushemeelin under its terms. In this way, justice was dispensed in colonial Philadelphia. Weiser was present at the trial which took place late in October and early in November. Mushemeelin was sentenced to die. On November 14 Mushemeelin was hanged and John Armstrong's murder was avenged.[42]

---

38. Colonial Records, 4:742-743.
39. *Pennsylvania Gazette*, August 23, 1744.
40. Colonial Records, supra.
41. Mitchell, J. and Henry Flanders, *Pennsylvania Statutes at Large* (Harrisburg, 1898), 5:56. See also Colonial Records, 4:571-572.
42. *Pennsylvania Journal and Weekly Advertiser*, William Bradford, Publisher; November 15, 1744.

A Diversity of Duties

Colonial governor Samuel Ogle of Maryland

The botanist John Bartram

Painting of Count Zinzendorf (left of center) meeting with Shikellamy. Conrad Weiser is in the middle of the picture.

CHAPTER VIII

The Treaty of Lancaster

Virginia was a royal province in 1744 and its governor, Sir William Gooch, held his commission from the Crown of Great Britain. The governors of the two proprietary provinces, Pennsylvania and Maryland, held their positions as the deputies of proprietors resident in England. Virginia's governor assumed a haughty attitude in 1744 when he wrote to Governor Thomas of Pennsylvania, arranging the preliminaries for the long-awaited Indian treaty. Richard Peters phrased it well in writing to Weiser, early in February, saying, "Gooch seems to sneer and talk big."

GOOCH DOES NOT UNDERSTAND

The incident to which Peters referred was Gooch's letter of January 11, in which the Virginia governor indulged in caustic criticism of Weiser's arrangements for the proposed treaty.[1] He objected to the time and the place which he thought Weiser had arranged. During the preceding summer, Weiser had visited the Six Nations Capital at Onondaga and had obtained the pledge of the Six Nations Capital at Onondaga and had obtained the pledge of the Iroquois to come to a point north of Harris Ferry in Pennsylvania. Gooch averred that he had been given to understand that the meeting would be held at Cresap's plantation in Maryland. "Harris Ferry," declared Gooch, "seems the most inconvenient that could be thought of, agreed upon by your honest Interpreter,

---
1. Gooch to Thomas, January 11, 1744, Peters MSS, 2:1.

Mr. Weiser, but what induced him to make the change I cannot tell, and whereas they promised to meet the latter end of April or the beginning of May, this gentleman [Weiser] has pleased to alter it to the *first* of April." This early date, complained the Virginia governor, would greatly inconvenience his commissioners who would be forced to cross swollen rivers and "miry" roads at that season of the year.

To Gooch, it seemed unfair that his agents would have to travel "three times as far as the Indians." This, he argued, showed too much "indulgence" to the Indians. Therefore, would Thomas arrange "through your Auxiliary" to have the meeting held at Philadelphia or New Town [Lancaster]?

Alas! The proud royal governor was pitiably ignorant of Indian ways and of North American geography. On January 20 Pennsylvania's governor wrote his reply and in it, he administered some elementary lessons in these subjects. In geography, Gooch was shown that the distance from Williamsburg to Harris Ferry was "not near as great" as the distance from that point northward to Onondaga, and Lancaster was only thirty miles south of the Ferry. Firmly Thomas declared that no more Indian treaties would be held at Philadelphia because of the disorder always occasioned by the presence of many Indians. As for New Town or Lancaster, it so happened that Weiser had already arranged to hold the meeting in that town. This change in plans had been made in November and was not in deference to Virginia's request.

Weiser's report to his employers, written after his return from Onondaga in 1743, was couched in Indian phraseology. The sachems had told him: "We will set out from our several villages after eight moons are passed by when the ninth is just to be seen, this present Moon, which has just begun, not to be reckoned"

Thomas carefully pointed out to Gooch that this meant mid-May or early June before the deputies could reach the place agreed upon. The Virginians had mistaken the time of departure for the time of arrival.

Concerning the plans to meet at Cresap's place. Thomas explained that the Maryland gentleman had connived with several irresponsible Indians to gain their approval of his estate as a treaty place, but the responsible chiefs of the Six Nations had disavowed the act of their subjects, declaring that they would not enter Maryland so long as they had differences with that province.

Nobly, Pennsylvania's Governor defended Conrad Weiser. "I know him to be an honest, sensible man," he wrote to Gooch, "and that he will be found to have acted in everything agreeable to this character. And it is my opinion *that neither our government nor that of Maryland will be able to carry on the treaty without him.* For these reasons I engaged him in the service of both, very much against his own inclinations."[2]

In sending a copy of Gooch's letter to Weiser, Richard Peters wrote: "I suppose he will take shame for it."[3] And, as shall be seen, he did.

Governor Thomas Bladen of Maryland did not join with Gooch in the complaints against Weiser's transactions, but he helped to confuse the plans in other ways. Jointly with Virginia, Maryland asked that Weiser should be directed to arrange with the Indians so that each province could make a separate treaty. This was contrary to the wishes of Pennsylvania and Conrad received orders from his own government to prevent separate treaties.[4] In March, Bladen revived the Cresap issue by sending a message to the Six Nations, inviting them to meet at the plantation on the Potomac. This message passed through Weiser's hand. It is endorsed in Conrad's handwriting, but his name is not signed to the endorsement.[5] There could be no harm in sending on the invitation when Weiser knew that the temper of the chiefs was set against entering Maryland province.

From the standpoint of the southern provinces, the treaty at Lancaster was to be a real-estate transaction. Large quantities of assorted goods would have to be purchased in advance of the meeting in order that the exchange could be made as soon as the terms were agreed upon. Both Maryland and Virginia were hopelessly ignorant of the kind of articles which would satisfy the wants of the northern Indians and in this, as in many things, they were forced to rely upon Weiser's advice. The articles which Colonel Levin Gale had purchased in Philadelphia in 1743, were

---

2. Thomas to Gooch, January 20, 1744, Peters MSS, 2:2.
3. Peters to Weiser, February 2, 1744, Weiser MSS, 1:9.
4. Peters to Weiser, February 13, 1744, Ibid., 10.
5. Bladen to the Six Nations, March 23, 1744, Peters MSS, 2:6.

deemed unsatisfactory in 1744. In February, Weiser made inquiries about the whereabouts of the Maryland purchasing agent, only to learn that the colonel had gone to England, ostensibly, for purchasing goods there. March and April passed without any word from Gale. Then Maryland was forced to designate the Philadelphia merchant, John Galloway, as their purchaser, informing him that "if Weiser should happen to be at Philadelphia he will inform you both as to time and place."[6] Weiser must have received directions in this matter directly from Maryland because he wrote to Peters that he "must see John Galloway." Weiser's letter was dated April 28 and the one written to Galloway from Maryland bears the date April 29. Still, other complications arose when Colonel Patton, the Virginia officer involved in the Virginia skirmish of 1743, came to Philadelphia to try to convince the Pennsylvania authorities that the Six Nations warriors were the aggressors in that unfortunate encounter.

These matters came to a head when Weiser was busy with the Armstrong murder case. After his return from Shamokin early in May, he visited Philadelphia and arranged with Galloway for the treaty goods.

THOMAS LEE OF VIRGINIA

Stratford, in Virginia, was the name of the mansion belonging to Thomas Lee, founder of the great American family of Lees. It was from Stratford that the Virginia commissioners to the Lancaster treaty set out for the north. Thomas Lee was one of the commissioners and his associate was William Beverly. Accompanying these two was William Black, secretary of the commission, who recorded the treaty procedure at Lancaster. It is from *Black's Journal*[7] that we are permitted to learn many of the most intimate facts connected with the tri-colony-Indian Treaty of 1744. The commissioners had reached Annapolis in Maryland on May 20, when they learned of the alarm occasioned in Pennsylvania by the murder of Armstrong and his men. They informed their governor

---

6. Maryland Archives, 28:314.
7. Journal of William Black, 1744. Published in three installments in Volume I of the *Pennsylvania Magazine of History and Biography*, Philadelphia (1877).

that it was feared that the northern Indians would not come to the treaty because of this disturbance.

Suspicion of Weiser was fixed in the minds of the commissioners as they journeyed northward. They told Gooch that the Maryland people "have here great Suspicions of Mr. Weiser and they will not Solely rely on him." They asked the Governor of Virginia whether this information would serve to alter his instructions "which are positive as to Weiser" but, that if he wished to change them, he should send a post to Philadelphia, giving them the liberty to choose some other agent. Less than a week later they wrote from Baltimore, saying that they had received an "Artful Letter from Conrad Weiser, which they say is Logan, though Weiser signs it," describing the expenses to which Pennsylvania was forced to go on Virginia's behalf. They feared that they would be confronted with difficulties if Weiser is to be their only interpreter.[8]

A new problem was presented by word from Weiser that the Indians would talk only to governors. These Virginia gentlemen did not realize that the Indians had ways of clothing emissaries with gubernatorial titles. On many occasions, Weiser played the part of Onas (Penn). Maryland, too, was disturbed by the news which Weiser sent and changed the personnel of its commission. A bitter controversy between the governor of Maryland and his Assembly developed over this issue. The Virginians believed Governor Bladen might decide to go to the treaty in person. Weiser's letters were sent to Maryland by way of the Principio Iron Works in Cecil County. He was under express orders to keep the governors of the southern provinces informed about the progress of treaty plans and to forward prompt notices of the approach of the Indians.

"POOR CONRAD IS ILL"

These intercolonial and inter-Indian responsibilities forced Weiser to make many trips to Philadelphia, though not all his time was spent in the interests of diplomacy. When in Philadelphia Conrad Weiser visited Dr. Thomas Graeme, one of the eminent

---
8. Ibid.

physicians of colonial Pennsylvania. Weiser was afflicted with a chronic stomach ailment which he called "Fever." This malady plagued him at recurring intervals from middle-age until he finally succumbed in 1760. In 1744 he consulted Dr. Graeme.

In the same year, Conrad received a "Memorandum" from his forest friend Madame Montour, prescribing a remedy for "Fever."[9] This rare bit of Indian lore Conrad wrote on the last page of an account book which he carried with him on his mid-summer journey to the Susquehanna. Here we have an Indian prescription, given to Weiser by a French woman and written in the German language. Rendered in English it reads: "Take a good thimble full, tie it in a rag, and let it dissolve in a half pint of water, and throw the rest away. It dissolves like salt. The few remaining crumbs are thrown away. When the fever comes the patient must be given this half pint of water, to be drunk, and if the fever returns, it is repeated. For a child, according to proportion."

Late in May, just at the time when the Indians were daily expected to arrive at Harris Ferry and the commissioners of both southern provinces were in Philadelphia with treaty goods, Weiser became violently and dangerously ill. For a time, it was feared that all the well laid plans for the treaty would come to naught. Tarachawagon was ill! He who "held in his hands the reins of the Universe" had written that he was "resign'd to Divine Providence" and "very low down." For fourteen days he had not partaken of any food and the fever kept him from sleep at night. "Poor Conrad is ill," wrote Peters to Thomas Penn in England.[10] By special messenger, Dr. Graeme sent a prescription to Tulpehocken. It was "a Vomit, gentle and easy." The medicine was a "paper Bark." Governor Thomas sent word to Weiser, urging him to follow the physician's directions, stating that he himself had, on occasion

---

9. *Memorandum of "Madame Montour"* appears on the last page of an account of Indian expenses incurred by Weiser in 1744. Peters MSS, 2:16. It is difficult to say precisely at what time Weiser procured this prescription. Madame Montour was present at the Lancaster Treaty and accompanied the Indians in their journey to that city. It is possible that Weiser obtained information after he recovered from the illness. But the fact that it appears on the *last* page of a booklet which he must have carried with him from Tulpehocken when he went to meet the Indians suggests that he may have inscribed the note before he left his home. We know that he carried the account book on the journey because it contains the signatures of persons at Paxtang from whom he bought supplies.
10. June 7, 1744, Peters Letter Book, vol. 6.

been "relieved by the Bark, as if it was a Charm." Peters appealed to Conrad as a "sensible man" not to fail to take the medicine.[11]

The alarm about Weiser's health was shared by the members of the Virginia Commission, who had reached Philadelphia late in May. Conferences with authorities in that city had assured them that Weiser's services would be indispensable at the treaty and the fear that they might not be available caused Thomas Lee and W. Beverly to inform Governor Gooch of the unfortunate turn of events. Their letter reveals, eloquently, how ignorant they were of affairs in Pennsylvania. It was feared, they reported, that Weiser would refuse to take "physic because of his views on religion. He has been, it seems, brought up in a Sect called the Dumplers (Dunkards), a particular sect of Enthusiasts." According to their version of Conrad's illness was caused by worry about scandals at the Ephrata Cloisters. They hinted that one of his daughters was involved. To their governor, they explained: "We thought that it woud not be uninteresting to you to leave the Road of Business, and to touch a little upon Particulars relating to this useful man!"[12] Fearing that Weiser would not be able to serve them at Lancaster, the Virginians appealed to Richard Peters to act as their agent, a proposal which Peters did not relish.[13]

While Weiser lay sick at Tulpehocken his friend Shikellamy arrived with a message, informing him that the advance guard of the Indians had reached a point near Shamokin. These deputies came to herald the approach of the main body of the Six Nations representatives. Having made his report, Shikellamy hastened to return to Shamokin, promising to send a fleetfooted messenger with a second message when the exact whereabouts of the main body of delegates could be determined. Weiser held a horse and rider in readiness to dispatch the news to Philadelphia and to the Principio Iron Works in Maryland the moment Shikellamy would send him word. This word arrived on June 11, and at Weiser's call, the authorities delegated by Maryland, Virginia, Pennsylvania, and

---

11. Peters to Weiser, June 4, 1744, Peters MSS, 2:2. Also Ibid., June 7, 1744, and Weiser to Peters, June 2, 1744, *Pennsylvania Magazine of History and Biography*, 1:414–415.
12. Thomas Lee and W. Beverly to Gooch, June 7, 1744, Black's Journal, supra.
13. Peters Letter Book, vol. 6.

the several Indian nations were converging on the small inland town of Lancaster on the banks of the Conestoga Creek.[14]

Dr. Graeme's bark had "worked like a charm." When Weiser learned that the company of deputies with their train of hangers-on had reached Shamokin he set out to meet them. He, Taracha-wagon, would play the part of host to the guests of Pennsylvania.

LANCASTER HOSPITALITY

When Conrad Weiser set out from his home in Tulpehocken in June 1744, to act as host to the visiting delegations of Six Nations' Indians, he did not go empty-handed. An itemized account of his expenditures for the guests of Pennsylvania reveals that he dealt lavishly of food and drink to the motley aggregation of Indians whom he escorted from a point near present Millersburg to Lancaster, fifty miles. His prodigality was not in the interest of generosity alone, because the advance of the Indians could be hastened if they were not obliged to forage for food along the way.

As soon as he learned of the approach of the deputies Weiser sent an order to Joseph Chamber's mill for more than a half ton of flour. Two hundred and forty-five Indian men, women, and children had to be fed. When Weiser met the company at James Berry's house, twenty miles north of Harris Ferry, he arranged to have an ox slaughtered for a feast and another 200 pounds of flour was purchased for their needs.

On June 16, Weiser records that he purchased bread and milk from Simon Girty, Sr., the father of the notorious renegade of the Pennsylvania frontier. This was not the last encounter which Weiser was to have with the Irish trader at Sherman's Creek.

The Nanticoke Indians had come to Pennsylvania from Maryland and were settled on the Ionyaty, which probably was the present Pine Creek of Schuylkill County. Weiser spent the night of June 17 in their midst. To these Indians, Conrad sent five hundred pounds of flour. The Nanticokes were involved in the transactions which were to take place with Maryland.

The whole company of visiting Indians consumed almost 300 pounds of flour each day. Rum and tobacco had to be purchased

---
14. T. Cookson to Peters, June 11, 1744, Pennsylvania Archives, 1:657–658.

for the chief men of the nations at traders' stores and at traders' prices. On leaving the trading post of Chambers the Indians begged for "one dram more," which Weiser says, "I could not deny them."

A change of menu was possible when the travelers neared the settlements. When they reached the post of John Harris, Weiser furnished them with two sheep, forty loaves of bread, and several "Beals [Bbls?] full of middling Bear." The cost to the province for this repast was nine pounds, sixteen shillings, and eight pence, approximately fifty dollars in modern currency.[15]

Southward, toward Lancaster, the long line of assorted natives filed through the forests, consuming a full week in traveling the fifty miles from Chamber's mills to the appointed treaty place. The sick and lame had to be cared for; animals had to be killed and dressed for the cooking pot or fire spit, and wayward hunters, bent upon adding wild-pigeons to their feast, had to be recalled. On June 20th Weiser had foreseen these delays and sent a special messenger forward to Lancaster to announce the probable time of arrival as Friday, June 22.

On June 21, the Maryland commissioners, Edmund Jennings and Philip Thomas, reached Lancaster. Witham Marshe was secretary of this delegation and his copious notes, combined with the records of William Black, the Virginian, enable us to reconstruct a vivid picture of the Lancaster treaty. Governor Bladen, Maryland's governor, sent word to Weiser that ill health prevented him from coming to Lancaster in person. These officials established headquarters at the house of Peter Worrel and awaited the arrival of the Indians, which was expected on the next day. In his journal, Marshe complained that the limestone water in Lancaster "gave me a looseness and dulled my appetite."[16]

With great fanfare and a brilliant coterie of gentlemen, Governor George Thomas set out from Philadelphia to attend the Lancaster treaty. The Virginia commissioners went with him. Altogether there were thirty-four gentlemen in his party.[17] This group reached Lancaster in time to greet Weiser and his two hundred and fifty charges when they arrived on Friday, June 22.

---

15. Weiser's Account of Expenditures, June 1744, Peters MSS, 2:16.
16. Witham Marshe's Journal of 1744. First published by Samuel Hall in Boston, 1801. Also in the Massachusetts Historical Society Collection, 7:171–185.
17. *Pennsylvania Gazette*, June 21, 1744. Also Sauer's *Berichte*, same date.

PARADE OF THE INDIANS, 1744

It was dinner time when the strange parade of denizens of the woods entered Lancaster. Some squaws were riding on horses. They carried children in their arms. Marshe tells us that a great "concourse" of Lancaster people joined in the procession and the march was conducted in good order. The braves carried bows, arrows, and tomahawks. They were dressed in filthy clothes, the shabby remnants of gifts received at former treaties.

Canassatego, the great chieftain, marched at the head of the procession. When he came to Worrel's house, where the Marylanders were staying, he paused and sang an Indian song, which the commissioners interpreted as a gesture of friendliness. Canassatego was tall, Marshe tells us, and full chested. He had a manly bearing, a good-natured smile and his brown arms gave the impression of great physical prowess, despite his sixty years. The Maryland delegates welcomed the Chieftain and his second in command Tocanuntie.

Tocanuntie, who figured so prominently in Weiser's 1743 mission to Onondaga, was known as the Black Prince. His dark skin led some to believe that he had some African ancestry, but his physique was that of a Native American. He was tall and thin and among his people was regarded as the greatest of warriors. It was said that the Governor of Canada always refused to treat with the Six Nations unless Tocanuntie was personally in attendance.

"Weiser, the Interpreter," wrote Marshe, "is highly esteemed by the Indians and is one of their council of state though a German by birth." It is to be regretted that the writer did not furnish us a description in this instance.

Weiser led the Indians to the outskirts of Lancaster, where poles and boards were available for the building of wigwams and cabins. The Indians preferred this arrangement to being quartered in houses. The cabins were arranged according to the rank of each nation in the Grand Council at Onondaga and the Onondagas were placed on the "right hand upper end." Having disposed of his guests Weiser asked that word should be circulated to the curious multitude that gathered about the camp, cautioning against giving offense by indiscreet laughing. He warned that the Indians would resent being the victims of ill-chosen remarks, explaining that many of them understood some English.

Once the cabins were set up, Weiser invited a few men from each delegation to join him in a visit to the cabins while the Indians rested. Later, in the afternoon, the Indians painted themselves "divers sorts of Colours." They made themselves frightful by rubbing grease on white painted visages. Before sundown, Weiser led some of the chiefs to the courthouse, where they were officially welcomed by Governor Thomas. The commissioners of all provinces concerned were present at the ceremony, the English seating themselves at a table and the Indians on ascending stairs. Punch was drunk and pipes were smoked as greetings were exchanged. No business was transacted because the Indians wished to rest for a few days.

THE GOVERNOR VISITS EPHRATA

While the Indians rested, June 23, Weiser escorted a different sort of entourage to Ephrata twenty miles northeast of Lancaster. The Virginia gentlemen were curious to know more about the strange sect of Seventh Day Baptists, who dwelt in the Ephrata Cloisters. Governor Thomas and his staff availed themselves of an opportunity to inspect the institution which had at one time diverted their Interpreter's attention from affairs of state. Conrad Weiser, formerly Brother Enoch of the order of Kedah, guided the distinguished party through the bakery, the Saal and Saron, where the Order of Spiritual Virgins lived. They were shown the illuminated writings and the rare pictures which formed a part of the treasures at the Cloisters. A Maryland gentleman expressed a desire to purchase an ornate sketch, whereupon the Prior, Conrad Beissel, made him a gift of the picture.

The Ephrata Brethren treated their distinguished guests with courtesy, but they were not overawed by the high titles of their visitors. Governor Thomas remarked that he found things at Ephrata to be not as he had "pictured them." The Ephrata institution was a "Dunkers Nunnery" in the accounts of Marshe of Maryland, written prior to the visit, and Lee, of Virginia, had referred to it as a "Nunnery under the Care of Men."[18] Christopher Sauer, the editor of the German newspaper in Philadelphia, never missed an opportunity to publish scandal rumors which emanated from the Cloisters. Sauer's wife had deserted him to join the Sisters in Saron and he was bitter. Very likely the visitors had expected to find a society steeped in sexual irregularities and found, instead, a devout people working out their spiritual salvation and economic well-being in the Cocalico pastures.

The officials returned to Lancaster before sundown and interest shifted to the Indian camp on the outskirts of the village. The Indians staged a dance for the entertainment of the crowds which flocked to their encampment. Some of them begged money from bystanders. Among the spectators, there were many German settlers, some of whom carried guns. Canassatego showed his displeasure at this unfriendly evidence and the offenders deferred to his wishes. There was no drinking, even though bystanders offered liquor. The Indians were determined to stay sober during the treaty which was to come.

The Indian dance was repeated on Sunday evening to larger crowds of onlookers. That night Marshe of Maryland had a very distasteful experience. Three Indian traders had usurped his bed at Worrel's. With the help of the landlord, the rascals were evicted, but the young Maryland gentleman was forced to sleep on a wet floor. The room had been washed. "By this means the fleas and bugs were defeated of their prey."[19]

FRIVOLITIES

Lancaster, Pennsylvania, was the scene of a great diplomatic conference and the little town did its best to rival the dazzling whirl of social splendor which marked old world capitals on the occasion of international conferences. The elite of Pennsylvania were there. In addition to the governor and his Council. William Logan, the son of the great James Logan of Philadelphia was one of the younger set. Andrew Hamilton, Junior, joined in the festivities

---

18. Lee and Beverly to Gooch, June 7, 1744, Black's Journal, *Pennsylvania Magazine of History and Biography*, 1:418.
19. Marshe's Journal, supra.

of the Governor's dinner, which was held on Monday evening, June 25. The scion of this famous family joined with a young Indian in dancing a jig to music played by two German fiddlers. These fiddlers had serenaded the governor under the window of the dining hall and Thomas ordered them to be brought upstairs. Their music, says Marshe, was not harmonious, but it was diverting. After the great feast which the governor provided for all his assorted guests, the tables and chairs were cleared away and the young folks danced long into the night.

By Wednesday evening, June 27, the treaty was in progress, but the delegates sought recreation by attending James Hamilton's Ball at the Lancaster Court House.[20] The host opened the festivities by dancing a minuet with one of the ladies. The dance, according to Marshe, "was wilder than any of the Indians' dances." The German fiddlers were once more pressed into service. The Lancaster ladies who attended the ball did not impress young Marshe favorably. He writes disparagingly of the "German-Scotch-Irish females." However, his evening was brightened by the presence of some ladies "not long since from New York, well dressed and of agreeable behavior."

In company with Colonel Nathaniel Rigbie, of Maryland, Marshe visited the Indian encampment on Thursday evening where the men tossed pennies to the ground and were amused to watch the "scramble among the papooses" searching for the coins. Their visit carried them to the cabin of Madame Montour, the French-Indian friend of Conrad Weiser. The Madame had brought her two daughters Margaret and Esther with her.[21] Both young women figure prominently in Pennsylvania Indian history a decade after 1744. The Maryland gentlemen found these half-breed Indians quite civil, even polite. On the evening of the 29th, Friday, Marshe visited a Mr. Adams, whom he described as a German doctor, reputed to be an expert organist. According to Marshe the man was a reformed rake and his music was not as great as his enthusiasm for it.

---

20. James Hamilton was the son of Andrew Hamilton, the famous lawyer, who defended the German, Peter Zenger, in the historical trial in New York, for the freedom of the American Press. Marshe's use of the name Andrew is probably in error. Andrew Hamilton died in 1741. Later James Hamilton was governor of Pennsylvania.
21. French Margaret and Queen Esther. See Darlington, W. F., "The Montours," *Pennsylvania Magazine of History and Biography*, 4:218-224. Marshe questioned the mother about her French origins when he visited the tent in Lancaster.

Meanwhile, Conrad Weiser found no time for social amenities. Perplexing problems confronted him on every hand. Hungry and mischievous Indians strayed from camp and pilfered from neighboring farms. The bark was stripped from John Musser's walnut trees and there was constant friction between the townspeople and their quaint guests.[22] According to Sauer the Indians were sensitive at the beginning of the treaty and refused to talk until the crowds were removed from the courthouse. Weiser denied this statement, however, when in August 1744, he wrote to Sauer to correct some of the erroneous statements which had appeared in the *Berichte*.[23]

THE TRI-COLONY TREATY

The first Lancaster County Court House served as the county seat from 1739 to 1784, when it was replaced with a new structure. It was a brick building, two stories high and stood on Lancaster's center square. For nearly half of a century, it was the scene of many notable events in the colonial history of Pennsylvania. In 1777 it served as the capital of the united American colonies when the Continental Congress was forced to flee from Philadelphia to escape the invading British army under General Howe. In 1744 the Court House was the scene of the Tri-colony Indian treaty which was negotiated, largely, by Conrad Weiser.

Great care had to be exercised in arranging the preliminaries of treating with the Indians. Ceremony was always an integral part of any negotiations into which the Six Nations entered and of all the distinguished company of commissioners from Maryland and Virginia and the big-wigs of colonial Pennsylvania, only Conrad Weiser was versed in Indian diplomatic courtesies.

With each pronouncement of fact or decision, a belt of wampum had to be placed upon the conference table by the spokesman who proclaimed the statement. To show that all deputies concurred in the remarks, the Indians joined in chorus to exclaim Jo-haa! As a sign of approbation. When some particularly telling point was made, the Indians were wont to shout Jo-haa! Woh!

---
22. Votes of the Assembly, 3:555.
23. *Berichte*, August 16, 1744.

Wugh! As the equivalent of the English Huzzah! Or Hurrah! Lest the visiting sachems misinterpret the silence of the white men during similar declarations, Weiser was instructed to interject the Jo-haa! Woh! Wugh! At the proper intervals.

Thus, at one and the same time Conrad was forced to act as interpreter and cheerleader. The task of interpreting was exceedingly difficult. The delegations from the southern provinces were not in a mood to deal mildly with the Indians. The English version of their remarks contains a suggestion of swaggering defiance of the claims of the Iroquois, while the adroit replies of the Indians were filled with specious reasoning and special pleading.[24] To Weiser fell the task of couching these charges and counter-charges in words and tones which would prevent an open break between the negotiators.

Because he was the official host to all delegations, Governor Thomas opened the proceedings in Lancaster on Monday, June 25, 1744. After perfunctory greetings, he outlined the succession of events which led up to the meeting in session and proffered the continued good offices in Pennsylvania as a mediator in the differences which might arise in the future. In a special address to the commissioners of the two southern provinces, he spoke quite frankly of the strategic position held by the Six Nations in the conflict with the French enemies of England. To the Indians, he spoke of keeping the Chain of Friendship despite French perfidy and the covert designs of the Governor of Canada to sever that covenant Chain. Promising to address them at some later session on questions relating to Pennsylvania, Thomas concluded his remarks by placing a belt of wampum and the Indians shouted "Jo-haa!"

It was Maryland's turn to present their case first.[25] Speaking for the Governor of that province Weiser gave a belt of wampum as a gesture of welcome and it was greeted with a Jo-haa! The Indians were told that the threats uttered against them by the Six Nations were inconsiderate and that the Maryland people were

---

24. A full account of the Lancaster Treaty is published in *Indian Treaties*. Printed by Benjamin Franklin, 1736–1762. Published under the auspices of the Historical Society of Pennsylvania (1938).
25. Thomas Lee gave Weiser thirty "pistols" and ordered him to induce the Indians to treat with Virginia first. The Indians refused to be bribed. Peters Letter Book: Richard Peters to Thomas Penn.

numerous and well-armed, ready to defend themselves. But the "old and wise People" of Maryland had counseled patience with such "rash Expressions" and urged that a conference should be held to determine "What right they have to the land in Maryland." A belt of wampum confirmed that the commissioners had come to Lancaster for that purpose. To this, the Indians shouted Jo-haa!

Maryland's claims to her lands were based on royal grants of long-standing explained her governor through Weiser. The patents were confirmed by treaties with the Susquehanna Indians and other treaties, made and renewed, with the Six Nations themselves, by which they secured all or nearly all lands east and west of the Chesapeake. Without specifically naming it, the commissioners referred to the so-called "Dongan" deed by which the Iroquois ceded vast areas of lands to the southward to Governor Thomas Dongan of New York, in 1683.

Canassatego replied to Maryland on the following day. "Rash expressions," he said, were needed to prompt the Maryland people to action. Mild words had failed on former occasions because they were ignored, but strong words, spoken without ill design, had brought about the present conference. Then, taking up the challenge of former treaties, Canassatego embarked upon a lengthy oration, replete with metaphors, trying to establish the antiquity of the Indians' claim upon new world lands. His historic account changed to the recital of grievances which began soon after the English came among them. His people suffered from famine because the deer had become scarce and they had been wronged "from that Pen and Ink work that is going on at the Table." Saying this, the speaker pointed to the secretaries.

It was true that they had heeded the advice of the governor [Dongan] of New York and had given their lands in his care so that he might keep them in trust against the evil designs of others. But "he went away to England and carried our Land with him, and there Sold it to Our Brother Onas" [Penn]. However, the generous Onas realized the injustice done his brethren and promptly "paid us for our [Susquehanna] Lands over again."

The treaties made with Susquehanna and Conestoga Indians, declared Canassatego, did not cover the claims of the Six Nations. It was the western reaches of the Potomac for which the Iroquois had received no payment and it was for these lands that they had come to be paid.

COVERT MACHINATIONS

Behind the scenes at Lancaster, the Virginia commissioners were striving to turn some of Canassatego's early remarks to their own advantage. Early in the treaty, the chieftain had said that the Indians had nothing to say to Virginia, meaning at that moment. Thomas Lee, Virginia commissioner, twisted this phrase to mean that the Indians had no claims on Virginia. At times the statements made by the Virginians were so barbed that Weiser was hard put to interpret to the Indians. On one occasion Canassatego importuned the interpreter to break the silence caused by Weiser's confused effort to phrase his Indian words without the sting which the Virginian's English carried with it. Once Colonel Lee charged that the interpreter gave the wrong "turn" to a sentence which he translated, but other persons agreed that Weiser had rendered the sentence correctly.[26]

On June 27, the Virginians addressed the Six Nations, setting forth arguments like those which had been advanced by Maryland, but claimed that, in 1742, the Six Nations had made claim only upon Maryland lands. By what right, they asked, did the Indians now extend their claim to Virginia? However, they promised that "we are willing to make you satisfaction. We have a Chest of New goods and the key is in Our Pockets."

TOCANUNTIE'S SPEECH

"By the right of conquest!" answered Tocanuntie, the great warrior, now assuming the duties of spokesman for the Indians. His fame as a fighter had preceded him and at Lancaster, he proved that he was mighty in the debate. The whole world knew, said he, that his people had subjugated the tribes in Pennsylvania, Maryland and "on the Back of the Great Mountain in Virginia" and that "if ever the Virginians get a good Right to it, it must be by Us." He reminded the Virginians of a pledge they had made

---

26. Ibid.

to keep their own people "on your Side of the Middle of the Hill (Alleghenies) and told us that if any of the Warriors of the Six Nations came on your side of the Middle of the Hill you would hang them and you gave us liberty to do the same with any of your People." He charged that Virginia had allowed settlers to encroach upon Indian lands in the Shenandoah. For many years the Six Nations had moved farther and farther westward but "your People came like Flocks of Birds." The Six Nations declared the Black Prince Tocanuntie had come to get "Justice for what is Past and to come to a thorough Settlement for the future."

MARYLAND SETTLES CLAIMS

Without admitting the justice of the Indians' claim, the Maryland commissioners decided to give the goods to the Indians on Thursday, June 26. They demanded a written release for all lands in Maryland upon which the Six Nations had any claim whatsoever. In this way, they would "take care that the links of Our Friendship be not rusted."

Conrad Weiser had the Maryland treaty goods brought into the Court House and spread upon a table. The commissioners instructed him to explain the prices and qualities of the goods to the sachems who came to inspect them. After examining the assorted duffels, strowds, shirts (200) and other articles, including four dozens of jewsharps, the Indians indicated that they wished to confer, privately, with some of their chiefs and with Conrad Weiser. They withdrew from the treaty room and Weiser joined them in their discussions. When they returned to the treaty chamber they had agreed upon their selection of goods and the prices which they were willing to allow.

The terms of the treaty with Maryland were agreed upon and drawn up on Friday, June 29th, and signed on the following day by several Six Nations chieftains. The Indians relinquished all claims to and in the settled areas of Maryland and it appeared that the transactions could be readily completed when Shikellamy, the vice-regent of the Six Nations, surprised everyone by refusing to sign the deed.

Shikellamy's attitude was particularly annoying to the Maryland commissioners. Without the signature of the vice-regent, a deed would be of little value. The Maryland officials became suspicious of the integrity of the Pennsylvania authorities, charging that they had induced the sachem to withhold his approval for some selfish reasons of their own.[27]

At this juncture, Conrad Weiser allayed the fears of Maryland by assuring the commissioners that he would "deal with Schickellimy." The interpreter's confidence in his own powers of persuasion was correct. On Monday, July 2, Shikellamy signed the deed. At the behest of the Indians, Weiser signed twice, once as Tarachawagon, witness, and again as, Conrad Weiser, interpreter.[28] The Maryland people marveled at the sagacity of this German immigrant, who could solve so many problems.

THE VIRGINIA AGREEMENT

The matters at issue between the Six Nations and Virginia were debated at great length. Both sides dipped into former treaties and their interpretations. The Dongan deed was used by the Virginians and the Indians countered that their right of conquest was not to be offset by treaties. The King of England had never conquered the Six Nations, "but it looks to us that God did not approve of it, if he had, he would not have Placed the Sea where it is as Limits between us and you."

The Virginians charged that the Six Nations had not heeded the overtures of peace which were made by the Cherokee and Catawba Indians when the Governor of Virginia sent Conrad Weiser on a peace mission to Onondaga in 1737. The wars between the Six Nations and the Southern Indians brought with them perplexing problems for Virginia. Roving bands of warriors passed through the Shenandoah Valley, disturbing the settlers. In 1743 a bloody skirmish had taken place during one of these forays. By purchasing the Shenandoah lands the Virginians hoped to put

---

27. Marshe's Journal. It must be remembered that the Mason and Dixon Line, fixing the boundaries between Pennsylvania and Maryland, was not surveyed until 1763, nineteen years after the events herein related.
28. Shikellimy signed the deed as Swatane, his Oneida name. The final signing was done at the home of George Sanderson in Lancaster. A list of the names of the Indians at the Lancaster treaty is printed in the Pennsylvania Archives, 1st ser., 1:656-657. The Maryland deed is printed in the Maryland Archives, 28:337. It is explained there that the Indians' marks of X were made "by their friend, Conrad Weiser." Weiser signed his European name in the column which the colonists signed.

an end to these incursions. At Lancaster, the Six Nations were charged with failure to keep the peace.

To this charge, Gachradoda, the Cayuga chieftain replied that the Catawbas had refused to come to Onondaga "and sent us word that we were but women; that they were men and double men, for they had two penises." Vehemently the Cayugas condemned the Virginia Indians, declaring that war would continue between the Flatheads and Six Nations until "one of us is destroyed."

Despairing of the futility of debates, Gachradoda reminded the Virginians that they had said that the key to the chest of goods was in their "Pockets." The Indians wished to see the goods and "to come to some Conclusion." It was Saturday. Virginia promised to open the chest on the following Monday. That afternoon all the parties to the treaty and many guests attended the great treaty banquet which was held on the second floor of the Court House. Twenty-four chiefs were there, together with all the commissioners and many notables. Five tables were laden with a great variety of foods and drinks. The sachems occupied two tables, Canassatego being seated at the head of one of them, the other chiefs being arranged according to rank. Thomas Cookson, Lancaster judge; William Logan, son of James Logan, and Colonel Rigbie, of Maryland, presided at the other tables and carved the meat. Cider and wine were served, mixed with water. The chiefs ate heartily. Their fingers served as forks.

During the feast, Conrad Weiser stood between the table at which Governor Thomas was seated and the Indians' tables in order that he might translate the toasts as they were uttered by Indians and whites. As a part of the festivities, the Indians coined a name for the governor of Maryland. Pennsylvania's Governor was Onas; New York's Governor was Corlear; Canada's Governor they knew as Onontijo and Virginia's as Assaryquoa. Lots were drawn to determine which one of the Six Nations should have the honor to select a name for Maryland. The Cayugas won the drawing of lots and their spokesman Gachradoda rose "with all the dignity of a Warrior, the Gesture of an Orator" and announced that hereafter they would call the governor of Maryland Tocarryhogan, denoting excellency or living in the middle, between Onas and Assaryquoa. Now it was the turn of the colonials to utter cheers and they responded with three huzzahs and drank to the health of King George and the Six Nations. The Maryland treaty was signed after the banquet.

Witham Marshe, secretary of the Maryland delegation, as he wrote in his journal: "Thus we happily affected the purchase of lands in Maryland by the dexterous management of the interpreter, notwithstanding the storm on Saturday [Shikellamy's refusal to sign] that threatened to blast our measures—and hereby gained some 100,000 acres of land to Lord Baltimore, who had no good right to them before this release."

The published accounts of the Lancaster Treaty reveal only those statements and facts which could be submitted to the scrutiny of the world and posterity. Behind the scenes, there were ugly deeds and harsh words which did not find their way into the official records. The colonial delegations mistrusted each other and maneuvered for advantage for themselves. Colonel Thomas Lee of Virginia was suspected of crafty manipulation and concealment of letters relating to the treaty. At one point Maryland suspected Pennsylvania of double-dealing. When Conrad Weiser learned that the Virginians had written to Governor Clarke of New York, requesting an interpreter to serve in his stead, he sulked and refused to have any part in the councils.[29]

Weiser's action forced the intercolonial bickering upon the attention of the Indians. A delegation of chiefs called upon Richard Peters, imploring him to take a hand in adjusting the impasse which had risen. The Indians feared that without Conrad's services they might be drawn into a controversy with the southern provinces and that Pennsylvania might not be able to understand their position.

The Maryland commissioners were loyal to Weiser and the instructions which Governor Gooch of Virginia had sent to his representatives were strict as to the employment of the Pennsylvania interpreter. Governor Clarke had answered Lee's letter on some of its points, but completely ignored the request for an interpreter. A general conference of all commissioners was called to straighten out the difficulties and Conrad Weiser was present. Governor Thomas acted as mediator. Weiser produced his

---

29. Peters to Penn, August 2, 1744, Peters Letter Book, 6:24-26.

instructions from Gooch and Peters supported his position with copies of other letters. The neutral Maryland commissioners decided in favor of Weiser and Colonel Lee of Virginia was shamed for his "wrong-headedness."

On Monday, July 2, 1744, the transactions between Maryland and the Six Nations were concluded, but Virginia's problem was still unsettled. A chest was opened by Virginia's delegates and the Indians were shown the goods which they would receive in exchange for a release of all lands in Virginia. Two hundred pounds in gold were placed upon the conference table and the Indians were told that the gold and the goods were theirs in exchange for their signature to a deed which was shown to them.

Weiser explained the terms of the deed to the chiefs. A gaming-board was placed upon the treaty table and lines were drawn upon it to represent boundaries. It is unfortunate that we have no records of the interpretation which Weiser gave to the Indians because the Six Nations and the Virginians differed afterward about the specifications of the treaty. The Six Nations interpreted a phrase "west to the setting sun" to mean to the crest of the farthest range of the Allegheny Mountains, while the Virginians took the position that the Indians had relinquished their claim to all lands which lay within the original Virginia charters, "west and northwest."[30] In 1744, however, they agreed to sign the deed and receive their presents of goods. The gold was given to them in amounts of one hundred pounds on each of the succeeding days.

Before the close of the treaty, the Virginia commissioners suggested that the wise men of the Six Nations should send three or four of their young boys to live in Virginia, where they could be educated and grow up to serve as interpreters in future conferences. "Our Friend Conrad Weiser, when he is old, will go into the other World as Our Fathers have done," said Colonel Lee. If boys could be trained they could, like Weiser, "have the Ears and Tongues of our Children and yours." To this suggestion, the Indians replied: "We hope Tarachawagon will be preserved by the

---

30. Virginia interpreted this phrase to mean all of the territory due west within the latitude originally granted to the Virginia Company and the extension by her second charter which would have included all of the area later known as the Northwest Territory, including Ohio, Indiana, Illinois, Michigan, and Wisconsin. Due west she claimed present-day West Virginia and Kentucky east of the Mississippi River.

Good Spirit to a good old age. When he is gone under the Ground it will then be time to look out for another . . . who will serve both Parties with the same Fidelity as Tarachawagon does: while he lives there is no room to complain." This was a complete vindication for Conrad Weiser hurled back at the scheming Virginians.

JOHAA! WHO! WUGH!

The Pennsylvania delegation had no land purchases to make at Lancaster. The officials were ever mindful of duties as host to the visiting deputies and rarely did Governor Thomas inject any matters relating to his province. During the early stages of the conference, he took advantage of a lull in the discussions to review the Armstrong murder case and to explain to the Six Nations that the English courts held accomplices guilty of crimes. He insisted that the companions of Mushmeelin, the murderer, should be sent to Philadelphia for trial. This the Indians promised they would do.

After the southern provinces had concluded their land purchases, Thomas regaled the Indians with glowing accounts of British victories, on land and sea, in the War against France. His obvious purpose was to impress the powerful Iroquois with the might of Britain in order that the tribes might be held firm in the English interests. His remarks were received with lusty Jo-haas, especially, when he announced that Pennsylvania would brighten the Chain with a gift of three hundred pounds expended in goods. Jo-haa! Who! Wugh!

"You tell us you beat the French," replied Canassatego, "if so, you must have taken a great deal of Rum from them and can the better spare us some of that Liquor to make us rejoice with you in the Victory." Was it cunning or cupidity? The governor found it hard to decide but responded to the broad hint by ordering a dram of rum for each of the deputies to be given in a small glass, calling it a *French glass,* symbolic of French stinginess.

On the following day, Canassatego resurrected the issue of the glasses. Now, he suggested, let us drink from English glasses. Caught in this battle of wits, Governor Thomas ordered rum in

English glasses to "show the Difference between the Narrowness of the French and the Generosity of the English."

More to the point, however, the Six Nations assured Pennsylvania that "we shall have your Country under our Eye" and prevent the French from invading the English settlements. They had already warned the governor of Canada against sending soldiers through New York.

After a belt had been placed in confirmation of this settlement, Weiser informed the English delegates that Canassatego had forgotten something and begged permission to say something which should have preceded the token of wampum and the Johaa ceremony. Permission was readily granted. Then the spokesman revealed that the power of the Six Nations was so great that they would undertake to restrain other Indian tribes from aiding the French. This the subordinate tribes had agreed upon before the delegation had departed from their villages. "We have put the Spirit of Antipathy against the French in those People." This was welcome news indeed to Governor Thomas and his associates and they were glad that Canassatego had remembered.

The Six Nations pledge of benevolent neutrality came at an opportune moment in the affairs of colonial Pennsylvania. On the same day that it was given alarming news reached Philadelphia from Virginia, stating that the Creek Indians in Georgia had joined with the Spanish to attack the English colonies. In reporting this news, Christopher Sauer stated that some persons in Maxatawny Township, Berks County, had already fled to Oley, upon hearing that the Northern Indians were on the warpath against them.[31]

CELEBRATION

After the Treaty of Lancaster, on July 4, 1744, the Indians gave a belt to Governor Thomas, begging him to shave off the remaining half of Conrad Weiser's beard. They stated that they had removed the one half and it remained for Thomas to remove the other because Weiser belonged half to the Six Nations and half to Pennsylvania. They did not like him to wear a beard because it frightened their children. It is difficult to determine how much of

---

31. *Berichte*, July 16, 1744.

this was meant in earnest and how much was in fun. The Indians never gave the belt of wampum facetiously and it is conceivable that Weiser's beard, a survivor of his ascetic days at Ephrata, might have puzzled Indian children who never saw bearded men in their own villages. But when Governor Thomas promised to obey their wishes in tonsorial matters the impression is given that it was a joke, unless all parties were speaking in metaphor, but then, why the reference to the frightened children?

At the close of the final session of the treaty, the Virginia delegates made Canassatego a present of a scarlet coat of camel's hair and Maryland gave to Gachradoda a broad hat, trimmed with gold lace. Conrad Weiser had earned thirty pounds. Toasts were drunk to the health of George the Second of England and to the Six Nations and the treaty ended on a noisy note when the entire company joined in three cheers.

The celebrations held in the chambers of the courthouse were too mild for the Indians. The occasion called for a more spectacular demonstration. On the evening of July 2nd, after the Maryland goods were distributed, the Indian camp at Lancaster gave the locals a great spectacle.

The Indians painted their faces in horrendous hues, donned their feathery headpieces, and ran to Thomas Cookson's house, where Governor Thomas was staying. They shrieked and whooped as they rushed along raising and lowering their tomahawks as their bodies dipped and bowed in a fiendish dance.

The actors of this strange pageant formed a circle in front of the governor's quarters and one of their number stood in the center of the ring, while the other performers flourished their weapons in menacing gestures toward him. All the while they kept up their unearthly cries and pranced up and down in their war dance. The demonstration lasted for seven or eight minutes and then they withdrew temporarily only to repeat their performance. In this way, the Six Nations serenaded Pennsylvania's governor.

William Marshe interpreted the dance as being symbolic of an Indian attack against a fort. The men in the middle of the circle were the fort. The act of withdrawing after the first attack meant that the besiegers had been driven back. The return to the dance represented a renewal of the attack.

To show his appreciation of the tribute to the serenade, Governor Thomas treated his noisy visitors to glasses of sangaree, after which the noisy natives returned to their cabins.

On July 5, the deputies started for their homes. Maryland and Virginia commissioners traveled southward, Governor Thomas and his party set their faces eastward, and two hundred and fifty Indians, laden with their newly acquired wealth, set foot northward into the mountains. Tarachawagon accompanied them to Harris Ferry. The responsibility of providing for their needs ended when they reached the Susquehanna and Weiser returned to the peaceful pursuits of farming in Tulpehocken.

A QUESTION OF REPORTING

Repercussions of the Lancaster Treaty came in September 1744, when Sauer's newspaper, the *Berichte,* published an "eye witness" account of the incidents connected with the treaty. This account corresponded closely to that presented by Witham Marshe, the secretary of the Maryland delegation. On September 16, the editor published a letter from Conrad Weiser, in which the interpreter set himself to the task of correcting some of the false statements which had appeared in the newspaper. Weiser denied that the white people got the Indians drunk; that none of the Indians had horses; that the Indians sacrificed a white calf in the woods in some occult fashion; it was untrue that the Virginians secured no advantages from the treaty, quite to the contrary they fared better than the Marylanders. These are but a few of the twenty errors which Weiser tried to correct.

On July 31, Governor Thomas expressed his satisfaction with the Lancaster Treaty in an address to the Provincial Council and ten days later the usually hostile assembly commended the governor for his "prudent management." It was Colonel Thomas Lee of Virginia who paid Weiser tribute. The commissioner who had come to the treaty questioning Weiser's integrity wrote to the Interpreter on August 30, 1744, declaring among other things "You should have a pension for life."[32]

---

32. Thomas Lee to Conrad Weiser, August 30, 1744, Peters MSS, 2:19.

Thomas Lee of Stratford Hall in Virginia

Drawing of the colonial-era courthouse in Lancaster, Pennsylvania

CHAPTER IX

Two Missions to New York

The Treaty of Lancaster had served to establish permanent peace between the governments of Maryland and Virginia. The Iroquois had been appeased and there was excellent promise that their nation would remain loyal to the English interests in the war with France which was currently being waged. Unfortunately, however, the treaty of 1744 had done nothing to allay the bitter, age-old, struggle between the warring Indian tribes themselves.

Despite repeated pledges and wampum-sealed pacts, the hostility between the Six Nations and the southern tribes of Catawbas and Cherokees continued. In 1737 Conrad Weiser had undertaken a hazardous journey through midwinter snows, carrying a proposal of peace from the Virginia Indians to the Six Nations' Capital at Onondaga in New York province. The immediate purpose of that journey had been successfully carried out when Weiser secured a pledge of cessation of hostilities until a treaty could be effected.

But the years passed and no treaty was made. Iroquois braves resumed their murderous sorties into the Flathead country as the land of the Catawbas was known to them. In December 1744 a British officer stationed at Oswego, near the border of Canada, described a feast which the French officers had given to some Six Nations' Indians to draw them to their own cause. Several fat cattle were killed and French soldiers staged an Indian war dance, carrying the heads of the beasts as they shouted. "Thus, we will carry the Heads of the English." The Indians took up the dance in the same manner, but shouted: "Thus we will carry the Heads of the Flatheads."[1]

Five hundred miles farther south in the valley of the Shenandoah, a company of Six Nations' braves was trying to make good the boast at almost the same time that it was uttered. On January 2, 1745, Conrad Weiser informed Richard Peters of an encounter between northern Indians and Catawbas in Virginia. Weiser's son, Philip, had been sent to Virginia to collect a debt which had been placed in his father's hand, as a magistrate, for collection. The son returned with the news that a skirmish had taken place between the rival Indian parties. The most vital fact now seemed to be that one of Shikellamy's sons, named "Unhappy Jake," had been slain in the encounter along with a Six Nations captain and five other warriors.[2]

The grief of the vice-regent of the Six Nations had to be assuaged. Weiser suggested to Secretary Peters that a gift be made to Shikellamy, to help him wipe away his tears. With the approval of the colonial authorities, Weiser set about to procure a fitting present for his friend. He tried to make a purchase in Lancaster but failed to find a suitable article. He sent his son to Philadelphia to the merchant Edward Shippen, with orders to buy three stroud matchcoats and "1/2 duzzend of silk Handkercher." The young man returned, bringing with him three pieces of stroud in addition to the other items specified.

"Honest Conrad," as Weiser was saluted by Logan, Thomas, and Peters, in numerous letters, was perturbed about the excess materials. "I think it would be extravagant to give it to Shikellamy," he wrote to Peters. "I think there must be some mistake, I hope it is not in my order." Just as Weiser always tried to protect the Indians from being imposed upon by greedy white men, he was just as determined to see to it that the province should not be defrauded or put to unnecessary expense.

Four months before the sad news about Unhappy Jake reached Tulpehocken, Weiser had spent three weeks of September 1744 in Shamokin, building a log house for Shikellamy. The work was performed by "Eight young men of my Country people,"

---
1. Letter from Oswego, Pennsylvania Archives, 1:665.
2. Weiser to Peters, Ibid., 666.

as Weiser expressed it. The house was almost fifty feet long and almost eighteen feet wide, "and covered with Singels" [shingles].

On this occasion, Weiser had learned many items of news of Indian affairs through his friend Shikellamy. This information Weiser put into a letter to the venerable James Logan, who was living a semi-retired life in his mansion at Stenton. The letter contained evidence of the various overtures which the French governor of Canada had made to the chiefs of the Six Nations seeking to draw those Indians to the French cause or to "stand newtar." The struggle for the trading post at Oswego was described. The Indians reported that a commissioner from Albany had requested the sachems at Onondaga to send warriors to man the post until enough British forces could be mustered to relieve them. The sachems did not agree to this proposal but sent a message to Onontijo, the French governor, informing him that they did not approve of the French occupation of the post, saying "it would look very mean in their father Onontijo to attack the English on their Back . . . to act more Honorable as becometh a Warrior, and go Round by Sea and face the English."[3]

Weiser's reason for addressing this letter to James Logan instead of Peters or Thomas, who were then incumbents in provincial offices, indicates that the writer realized that Logan's interests in the fur trade made him more familiar with the problems involved and more appreciative of the significance of the events related. As a postscript, Weiser added the information that the Shawnee Indians, long suspected of knavery by Logan, had cast their lot with the French and planned to war against the Six Nations and the English. This letter to Logan, dated September 29th, 1744, found its way to the desk of Governor Thomas.

Not long after Weiser's disturbing news from the north and west came to the attention of Governor Thomas, another Indian problem presented itself from the south. Once again, the Catawbas were asking Pennsylvania to arrange a treaty with the Iroquois. In their letter to Governor Gooch, of Virginia, the chiefs of the Catawbas explained that they had previously asked the governor of South Carolina to intercede for them, but the only answer to that plea was a recurrence of attacks from the Six Nations. "We

---
3. Weiser to Logan, Ibid., 661.

desire that a letter may be writ to Conrad Weiser," they asked of Gooch, urging him to act once more as the agent of Virginia.[4]

The Catawba letter was written in October 1744, several weeks before the skirmish in which Shikellamy's son was killed. On November 22, Governor Gooch wrote to Thomas requesting that Pennsylvania should extend her good offices once more in the interests of inter-tribal peace. A copy of the Catawba letter was enclosed. Several months passed before Gooch's letter reached Thomas. On January 31, 1745, the governor sent Weiser copies of the Catawba letter and that of Colonel Gooch, together with his own letter, stating that he had accepted the responsibility of trying to negotiate a settlement of the Inter-Indian strife. Would Conrad be willing to undertake the mission "to put a finishing hand to so good a work?"

"With a little of your good management," continued Thomas, "There could be no doubt that the Six Nations would agree to send deputies to some neutral place. Will you undertake another journey to Onondaga this spring?" Shikellamy's late loss of his son rendered him unsuitable for the errand, thought Thomas, because he might thirst for revenge. The governor, solicitous for Conrad's welfare, warned that "you may run a risqué of being made a prisoner by the French in the journey."[5]

How little did the provincial governor know the mettle of the man to whom he wrote!

Certainly, he was "very willing to undertake a journey to Onondaga . . . and I do not doubt of success," came Weiser's reply. Concerning the danger from French forces, he declared "they will have more to fear from me than I from them." Weiser's own fear, he said, was for the safety of his family from the evil deeds of the Haines family of Tulpehocken and Heidelberg. "They are worse than any French or Indians," he wrote. Weiser's duties as a magistrate had forced him to perform acts which incurred the enmity of some of his neighbors.

As for Shikellamy, Conrad had his own ways of dealing with the Oneida chieftain. He knew that Indians continue in mourning for bereaved ones only so long as no new duty presents itself.

---
4. Catawba Chiefs to Governor Gooch, Ibid., 664.
5. Thomas to Weiser, Peters MSS, 2:23.

With a new commission mourning ceases. He would sound the sentiments of his old friend and if he proved to be inclined to peace he would tell Shikellamy of the Catawba request, and if the vice-regent proved to be revengeful Weiser would not mention the matter. Anyway, it was auspicious that he, Conrad, was soon to go to carry mourning presents to the chief at Shamokin. This circumstance promised to provide the proper mood for a proposal of a peace mission.

In evaluating the sincerity of the Catawbas' plea for peace, Weiser minced no words in condemning the southern Indians for duplicity in their dealings and for the lack of tribal government. "Their King," wrote Weiser, "is often the greatest fool among them, the rest don't mind him and after all sends him to the grave with a Broken head." The prospect of securing a binding agreement with such people was not very good, but it was worth trying. It would have been better, thought Weiser, if two venerable men of the Cherokee and Catawba nations had been sent to accompany him to Onondaga. The interpreter regretted that the Catawba letter did not bear the signatures or marks of some of their chiefs. Later this point proved to be significant.

The trip to Shamokin, scheduled for early February, was delayed when Weiser scalded his foot badly, late in January "and I suppose I made it angry" he wrote to Richard Peters.[6] He had called in the services of a physician and hoped "that it will soon be better" in order that he might pay his respects to Shikellamy at Shamokin as soon as possible. On February 25 the ailing extremity had healed sufficiently to enable Weiser to visit the vice-regent of the Six Nations.

Once again Weiser was successful in bringing the old Sachem at Shamokin to his point of view. Shikellamy agreed to accompany Weiser to Onondaga and to take one of his surviving sons with him. However, the old chieftain informed Weiser that something should be done to regulate the liquor traffic among the Indians. The Six Nations were incensed against traders who got them drunk and then cheated them out of their pelts. Weiser reported this complaint to the governor of the province. Shortly before the mission set out for the northern villages, the Pennsylvania

---
6. Weiser to Peters, Pennsylvania Archives, 1:673.

Assembly enacted strict liquor laws "to strengthen Weiser's hand at Onondaga."[7]

Governor Thomas sent his formal instructions to Weiser on April 24, 1745.[8] The Six Nations were to be prevailed upon to send not more than five deputies to Williamsburg in Virginia to treat with an equal number of deputies from the southern Indians. If Williamsburg could not be agreed upon, then Philadelphia might be suggested, but Weiser was to be very, very careful to keep the number of deputies to not more than five. Philadelphia did not want a repetition of former treaties when hundreds of natives fastened themselves upon the hospitality of the city. Weiser was to keep an account of the expenses of the journey. The costs would be paid by the province of Virginia.

Early in May, an additional duty was added to Weiser's instructions. The troublesome Shawnees were at it again. Their leader was Peter Chartiers, a half-breed trader who professed loyalty to the English when it suited his purpose and turned traitor when out of sight. James Letort, a trader stationed in Conoy, Lancaster County, was supposed to have joined in the desertion from the English cause. These Shawnees had left their villages on the Ohio and had gone north into Canada to join the French. They were led by the renegade Chartiers. On May 14, five days before Weiser's party was scheduled to set out for Onondaga three traders had appeared before their factor, Edward Shippen, in Philadelphia, making depositions to the effect that they had been robbed by Chartiers and his Indians. They reported that there were seven or eight hundred Indians, with a few Frenchmen on the march to a branch of the river Wabash, which lay in the French possessions.[9]

On the same day that these depositions were made, Thomas commanded Weiser "you must lay the whole matter before the Council of the Six Nations at Onondaga and press them as far as is consistent with prudence, to demand restitution on my behalf of the Shawnees for the goods taken and that they deliver up Peter Chartiers to me forthwith." And then in a more moderate

---

7. Colonial Records, 4:759–761.
8. Peters MMS, 2:29.
9. Peters Letter Book, 6:40. Depositions by Peter Tostee, James Dunning and George Croghan. We shall meet Croghan again.

tone "As this is a matter of some delicacy much must be left to your own Discretion."

A delicate matter indeed, calling for discretion! In one hand Tarachawagon carried the olive branch offered by the Catawbas whom the Six Nations hated, in the other he carried a threat that the Six Nations must act against the Shawnees and at all and the same times, must strive to keep the most powerful Indian confederacy securely on the British side of the War of the Austrian Succession. He was an ambassador extraordinary!

THE CHILDREN OF GOD

It was an odd assortment of humankind that assembled in May 1745 to travel northward through Pennsylvania forests to Onondaga, New York. The party of seven men included Conrad Weiser, the leader, ambassador from Virginia, Pennsylvania, and the Catawbas, a German by birth, an Indian by adoption and an American by choice. There were two Indians, Shikellamy and his son Andrew, one French-Indian Andrew Montour, son of Madame Montour, two Moravian missionaries, Brothers Augustus Spangenberg and David Zeisberger, and an American born missionary of English parentage named John Joseph Bull, or Shebosch, as he was known to the Indians.

Although these men differed in character and origins they had one motive in common. Each one was going north as a peacemaker. But the specific peace objectives which they entertained differed vastly. To Shikellamy and his son it meant peace with the Catawbas; to Weiser, it was primarily an errand to strengthen the English alliance with the Six Nations. Andrew Montour, half French and half Indian, counted himself an Iroquois warrior. He had recently returned from an excursion against the Catawbas. His home was in Pennsylvania. His life was one of conflicting loyalties to native, English, or the French.

The three Moravian missionaries were men destined to achieve high distinction in their chosen work. Spangenberg had already attained a high place in the councils of the church. Zeisberger and Shebosch were to become the founders of the first white settlements in Ohio at Schoenbrunn and Gnadenhutten in Tuscarawas

County. Their immediate duties sent them on a mission to the Six Nations to plead for the right to move their converts among the Mohican Indians of Dutchess County, New York, to Wyoming in Pennsylvania. The settlers of Dutchess County were unwilling to tolerate the presence of Indians in their community, though they were converted to Christianity. It was a mission of peace upon which these men of God were bent.[10]

Conrad Weiser had met Spangenberg at Christopher Wiegner's home in Towamensing, in present-day Montgomery County, when the Moravian bishop made his first visit to America in 1736. Through his Moravian friends, Weiser learned of the plight of the Mohican Indians and it was at his invitation that a delegation of Moravian clergymen accompanied him to Onondaga. This was in order because it was at Weiser's home in 1742 that Count Zinzendorf had made the treaty with the Six Nations, granting perpetual rights to the Brothers of that faith to enter the Iroquois villages.

We have Spangenberg's day-by-day journal, describing events which took place as these men wove their way through forests over streams and across mountains into the Indian country.[11] In reconstructing this narrative of Conrad Weiser we have already described the details incident to the two earlier journeys to Onondaga. In the first instance (1737) we drew upon Weiser's own account of the journey. In 1743 we had the journals of the naturalist John Bartram and the cartographer Lewis Evans upon which to draw. On a third journey (1742) which did not extend so far, we had Count Zinzendorf's diary as a record of events.

Spangenberg's journal supplies a more detailed account of events along the route of the journey. Since we have told the story of the routes in other accounts we will extract only the more striking incidents from Spangenberg's account.

Many persons accompanied the travelers to the top of the Blue Mountain, where the party made their first night's encampment

---

10. Spangenberg and his companions were successful in gaining the permission of the Six Nations to move the Mohicans to Wyoming. The Mohicans, however, refused to move to that part of Pennsylvania. They were moved to the Moravian settlement at Gnadenhütten.
11. Spangenberg's Notes of Travel to Onondago in 1745, edited by John W. Jordan, published in Volumes II and III of the *Pennsylvania Magazine of History and Biography*, 1878 and 1879, Philadelphia, Pa. In Dr. Jordan's translation of the journal all dates appear to be adjusted to the new style calendar. Weiser's journal dates events eleven days earlier than those listed by Jordan. The new style calendar was not adopted by the British colonies until 1752, seven years after the journey to Onondago.

at Pilger's Ruh, the mountain spring named by Zinzendorf. The expedition left Tulpehocken on May 14, 1745. On the second day of the journey, the local people who had traveled a part of the way returned to their homes. Weiser's two sons, Philip and Frederick, continued with the party until they reached Shamokin and then returned to Tulpehocken with messages.

Several days were passed at Shamokin while the white men waited for Shikellamy and Andrew Montour to return from hunting trips upon which they had set out separately. The time was spent visiting Weiser's old acquaintances among the Indians. Spangenberg noted that there were several Indians residing at Shamokin who had formerly lived at Tulpehocken.

During one of their conversations, Weiser related to Spangenberg that Thomas Penn had recently written to him suggesting that some younger person become closely associated with him (Weiser) in order that an interpreter competent to succeed him could be trained. The name of David Zeisberger was suggested, but whether the name was brought forward by Weiser or by Spangenberg it is not possible to determine with certainty. It is significant that, in 1752, Zeisberger did live at Onondaga for a time, to learn the Six Nations dialects.

While at Shamokin, the travelers learned that a Christian preacher, who they guessed was the Presbyterian David Brainerd, had come to the Indians at that place, promising to make his home among them and minister to them. Shikellamy had declined, for the Indians saying significantly "We are Indians and do not wish to be transformed into White men. The English are our Brethren, but we never promised to become what they are. As little as we desire the preacher to become Indian, so little ought he to desire the Indians to become preachers." The preacher left Shamokin after this statement was made.

On May 27, the entire party was collected and the expedition set out following the same route which Weiser described in his 1737 journal, except that by 1745 several place names were given to points en route. Between Tulpehocken and the Muncy Creek, most of these names had been given by Zinzendorf and his party in 1742. Spangenberg too, invented names for points north of the Lycoming Creek, choosing fanciful terms rather than the names commemorating personal or religious experiences as Zinzendorf had done.

In this matter of assigning names, the Indians in the party felt that they too should take a hand, and so they gave Spangenberg the Indian name Tigerhitonti, meaning a row of trees: Zeisberger they designated at Ganonsseracheri, meaning "on the pumpkin" and Brother John Joseph they named Hagingonis, meaning one who twists tobacco. Andrew Montour's Indian name already was Sattelihu, and Weiser's Tarachawagon, meaning he who holds in his hands the reins of the universe.

As they penetrated more deeply into the woods, the party met with several warriors who were returning from sorties against the Catawbas. These braves joined the expedition. Weiser selected a fleet-footed warrior, furnished him with provisions, and then sent him on ahead to inform the Chiefs at Onondaga of the approach of his party. This precaution proved later to be a very wise one.

There was no vexing problem of supplies on the 1745 journey. This time the travelers had horses and they found plenty of food for themselves and their animals. Indian villages through which they passed welcomed and feasted them. All of this was in contrast with the grueling experiences of Weiser and Shikellamy on the 1737 expedition in mid-winter. On June 7th, ten days after leaving Shamokin, the party reached the Onondaga capital.

The travelers were given a grand welcome in the Indian capital. Canassatego, the King, invited them to his house for entertainment. On the day following their arrival, the Indians staged a parade through the village to the music of violins, flutes, and a drum. They serenaded the house in which Spangenberg and his followers were lodging. The night of June 9 three hours of entertainment were provided. Spangenberg described the Indian dance as follows: "One beat a drum and about twenty danced around the fire. The leader was distinguished by having rattles around his legs. All yelled savagely, and after having danced a quarter of an hour, the sweat ran down as if water had been poured over them. The men danced abreast, and the women follow, and whoever can appear the most grotesque, and leap the highest, receives the most praise."

This warm reception to Weiser and his party was made possible because of the notice which Weiser's messenger had brought three days before their arrival. Many of the Seneca and Cayuga Chiefs had already been summoned. Some Six Nations deputies had already gone to Oswego, planning to meet the French governor on the day following the arrival of the messenger. Others had already gone into French Canada and were beyond recall. But, for those chiefs who were notified, a message from Conrad Weiser carried more import than an invitation from the governor of New France. These sachems returned to Onondaga to greet Tarachawagon and give ear to the tidings he brought from Onas.

Prior to the formal meeting of Council, Weiser sounded the sentiments of the Six Nations on the matter of their relations with the French. Did the Governor at Albany know of their projected visit to French Canada? What did the Albany commissioners of Indian affairs say about the French overtures? The reply which the Indians gave showed that they were struggling to maintain their neutrality and to profit by courting both contending groups of white men. They had always had cordial relations with the governor of France, they said, and they wished to continue in that way even though the French were known to "be a crafty People." Their intention, they declared, was to report everything that transpired to their English Brethren. They had already agreed to reject any proposal that the French might make to them. A shrewd man, such as Weiser was, must have sensed the difficulties which Indian affairs would soon present for the British colonies of North America. Wisely he avoided any further discussion of the war against the French.

After consulting his old friend Canassatego, he presented the Catawba peace proposal to the Indian Council. The Catawba letter asked that a delegation of Iroquois Chieftains come to their villages in Virginia to negotiate terms, but in interpreting the message Weiser suggested Williamsburg as the meeting place. "It would have caused Suspicion," he told Governor Thomas, if he had mentioned the Flathead towns.

Tocanuntie, the Black Prince, gave the answer of the Indians after the Council had deliberated for one day. The matter was of such great importance, declared the spokesman, that the members present in Council were not willing to pass final judgment. All the Allies of the Six Nations would have to be consulted and because many of them were on their way to visit the French governor no action could be taken until their return in the fall of the year. One thing that had been decided, however, was the Six Nations would not travel to Williamsburg. No council fire was lit there and there was no road open to them into the domain of Assaryquoa, the governor of Virginia. A cessation of hostilities was agreed upon, pending a treaty of peace. This was the best that the Six Nations would promise at that time.

In the matter of securing condemnation for the perfidy of Peter Chartiers and the treason of the Shawnees, Weiser was far more successful than he was in the Catawba proposal. As he cited the accounts of the plundering of traders and of the Shawnee's withdrawal from their villages into French territory, the assembled chiefs "clamored" against the faithless ones. They promised to apprehend Peter Chartiers and make every effort to secure restitution of the stolen goods. However, significantly, they must "go now to Canada and take your Belt of Wampum with us" in order to call the matter to the attention of the French who would be called upon to pay the bill for the theft. Adroitly Tocanuntie couched his reasons in the following words: "We look upon what has happened as a blow on the side of the French against us, and the Blow that is given as if it were given on our own head . . . We are very glad that this News has reached us before we set out for Canada."

The concluding lines of the extract from Weiser's journal declared that it seemed to him that the Six Nations "expect nothing less than War with the Shawnees and peace with the Catawbas."[12]

After the conference Weiser, Spangenberg, Shikellamy, and Montour visited the fur trading post at Oswego on Lake Ontario. Six bark-canoe loads of Indians went with them. When they returned from this excursion they were met by Canassatego, who had prepared a meal as a welcome. On June 18 the party started homeward. While they were still in the Province of New York the travelers divided. The Moravians and the two Shikellamys followed

---

12. Extract of Conrad Weiser's Report of his Journey to Onondago, Colonial Records, 4:778–780.

one path, while Weiser and Montour followed another, farther to the west.[13] Both paths converged at present-day Muncy.

THE ALBANY CONFERENCE

Lake Ontario formed a silvery boundary between the new World domains of Louis XV of France and George II of Great Britain. Its littoral was dotted with two lonely fortresses frowning at each other across the lake. Oswego, a fortified fur trading post, guarded the interest of England in this remote corner of the world and the French Fort Frontenac waved the white flag of the Bourbons in defiance. Oswego was one hundred and fifty miles northwest of Albany and the French outpost almost as far from Montreal. Both were deep in the Indian country of that day and beyond the outer edge of civilization.

And yet both outposts were regarded by their royal owners as prize jewels of the crown. The gala fête at Versailles could be interrupted by any messenger who brought news from Frontenac and at times it appeared that the word Oswego called for more attention in the Court of St. James than did such names as Charleston, Boston, or Philadelphia. Royal purses were fattened on the lucrative fur trade which centered on Lake Ontario.

Bark canoes bearing the pelts from the other Great Lakes to the west were paddled along Ontario, bringing their precious cargoes to the white man's marts. But which group of white men, English or French, should get them? Certainly, the pelts would go to the post which first attracted the Indians who brought them. If Frontenac was successful the furs could be sent on to Montreal,

---

13. Weiser MSS, 1:12. An expense account of Weiser's Journey of 1745, charged to the government of Virginia.

	£ s/d/
To Bread, Rice, Rum and Sugar	1-2-0
To several Pieces Ribbon, Ferrit Knives, Scizzars	4-19-8
Vermillion bought from William Parsons to serve as Money	
To paid for Carriage sent to Shamokin	1-10-0
To paid Capt. Visher at Oswego on the Lake of Frontenac For provision on my return	4-13-0
To paid the men of the militia of the said for to carry me And my company from Oswego to Onontago	1-7-0
Spent in Onontago for myself and companions, Shikalamy and his son	5-7-0
Total	18-18-8
Conrad Weiser, Interpreter, By an Amanuensis.	

down the St. Lawrence, and across the seas to France, where ladies of leisure craved new adornments with which to dazzle the glamorous court at Versailles. If Oswego traders could induce the Indians to part with their goods, then the pelts were borne to Albany, down the Mohawk and Hudson to New York, there to enter the extensive trade of the British Empire.

The fur trade was the most profitable trade in colonial North America. The Spanish had found raw gold in New Spain, but the French fared almost as well in their early monopoly of the fur trade. The Holland Dutch, settled along the Hudson River, had challenged this French monopoly in the seventeenth century and by 1727 English traders had pierced the woods to Oswego, there to trade with the French on almost equal terms. The friendship of the Six Nations had made this, the Oswego outpost a safe venture for Englishmen. Iroquois villages dotted the area south of the post and their warriors could be depended upon to keep open the road from Albany to Ontario.

The shrewd Iroquois knew how to bend friendship to profit. They too were hunters and had pelts to trade. If the French were forced to compete with the English in bidding for trade, better prices could be realized by the Indians.

The strategic position of the Six Nations was increased greatly when England and France were at war and the struggle for colonies set the white men north and south of Lake Ontario against each other in deadly combat. The Iroquois Confederacy had to be relied upon by the British to form a buffer between the settlements to the south and east and only the steadfast loyalty of the Six Nations could prevent the disaster of Oswego falling into French possession before British forces could be marshaled to guard it.

East of the Hudson the settlers of Massachusetts and Connecticut were being harassed by marauding French Indians. The New England colonies were clamoring for aid from New York and Pennsylvania and for active participation in warfare by the wards of the sister colonies, the Mohawks, and other nations of the Iroquois Confederacy. The Yankees wished to set these tribes against the French Indians.

Traders returning from the west in September 1745 brought startling news. According to the testimony, the Shawnee Indians were fortifying positions in the Ohio country and that four hundred Six Nations braves were marching to destroy the Shawnees because they believed the western Indians were allied with the ancient enemy, the Flatheads, or Catawbas.[14] This report raised the threat of an inter-Indian war which might decimate the strength of the Six Nations and certainly would draw their fighting men from Oswego and farther still from New England.

When Conrad Weiser had visited the Indian capital at Onondaga in June 1745, he learned that some of the chiefs were determined to accept the invitation of the governor of Canada to visit him at Montreal. He was powerless at the time in his efforts to dissuade them, but he had extracted a promise from the sachems that a full report of their visit would be given to the Indian commissioners at Albany and to Onas, the governor of Pennsylvania.

Early in September 1745, Governor George Clinton of New York heard a disturbing bit of news about the results of the Six Nations' visit with the French Governor. The French interpreter had tossed a belt of wampum at the feet of the visiting Iroquois delegates and had challenged them to pick it up. The belt had a hatchet design woven into the beads and to accept it meant an alliance with the giver in warfare. According to the report the deputies of the Six Nations had picked up the belt, figuratively, and literally taken up the hatchet. Then they joined with French Indians in a war dance, rounding out the ceremony of a military alliance, as these children of the woods understood it.

Alarmed about the safety of Oswego and northern New York, urged by the pleas of New England the solicitous for English interests in general, Governor Clinton wrote to the governors of all neighboring provinces calling a conference on Indian affairs to meet in Albany in October.

Prompted by Governor Thomas, Pennsylvania's Assembly voted a gift of goods of the value of 250 pounds to be given to the Indians and appointed Thomas Lawrence, a member of the governor's Council; Isaac Norris, Speaker of the Assembly, and John Kinsey, a prominent member of the Assembly, to act as commissioners and Conrad Weiser as official interpreter.[15]

---

14. *Pennsylvania Gazette*, September 12, 1745. Also Sauer's *Berichte*, September 16, 1745.
15. Colonial Records, 5:7–8.

It was Weiser's second journey to New York province in the year 1745. On this trip, however, the Philadelphia gentlemen did not choose the overland route through Pennsylvania mountains, trod by Weiser and his companions on former occasions. With Albany as their destination, they followed the Delaware north to Trenton, cut across north Jersey to New York, and ascended the Hudson by boat to Albany. Weiser joined the party at Bristol, having traveled directly eastward, avoiding Philadelphia. The journal of this expedition was written by Isaac Norris and Weiser is accorded scant recognition in the entries. When he is mentioned it is only in his official capacity, The Philadelphia gentlemen were wined and dined in the homes of rich settlers as they progressed along their way. In Trenton, they visited New Jersey's governor, Robert Hunter Morris, an individual who was destined to figure prominently in the lives of these men, including Weiser, a decade after 1745.[16] In New York City the Pennsylvania men enjoyed the lavish hospitality of wealthy Dutch Patroons and as they neared Albany they were the guests of Philip Livingston, scion of the Livingstons of the Manor, upon which the Weisers and thousands of hapless Palatines were indentured in 1711.

Even though Norris fails to mention Weiser's activities during the journey, it is not difficult to reconstruct the thoughts which must have passed through the mind of this man of fifty years as he revisited the scenes of his boyhood. Those were days of subservience, of the humiliating mass indenture, of exodus and wandering in the wilderness, of hunger and privation. There was the village of Germantown, over which his father had once presided as a leader; there too was the schoolhouse erected in 1711 which he had attended and close by was the old Lutheran church and the cemetery where the headstones bore inscriptions and names which recorded the deaths of those who had suffered with him. Remarkable how these same names were being carved into sandstone in Rieths' cemetery, at Host and in Heidelberg and Tulpehocken, in Pennsylvania. Yes, there at the Hudson's edge he had seen his countrymen embark on an expedition against the French during Queen Anne's War in 1712. He had seen them

---

16. For day by day account of the journey, see the Journal of Isaac Norris, *Pennsylvania Magazine of History and Biography*, 27:20–28.

return, only to be stripped of their weapons by ungrateful officers who mistrusted these Palatine wards of Governor Hunter and good Queen Anne.

There were the scrub pine trees, desolate second growth of the majestic monarchs which were girdled by the refugees from the Palatinate in the vain hope of converting their sap into pitch and tar.

As the sloop which carried him reached Albany he must have remembered the night he spent in the Dutch gaol, because as a youth he had the temerity to resist the sheriffs who tried to evict his people from their newly found homes in Schoharie. Thirty-five years! And now he had come to try to help quiet the alarms of those who had used him and his people badly. But enough of dreaming. He came as an officer of Pennsylvania and his duty must be performed.

On October 4, the Pennsylvania commissioners arrived in Albany and presented their credentials to Governor Clinton. On the same day, Governor Roger Wolcott of Connecticut reached the city on the upper Hudson. Four hundred and sixty Indians entered the town on that day. No Senecas were among them. On the next day, the Massachusetts delegates arrived, bringing with them their own interpreter.

New England was smarting from wounds recently inflicted by murderous bands of French Indians. The Yankees thirsted for revenge and were in no mood to temporize. Nothing short of an outright declaration of war against the French by the Iroquois and the other colonies would satisfy them. Massachusetts was already at war and haughtily disdained proffers of moral support from her sister colonies or benevolent neutrality from the Six Nations.[17]

The New York commissioners and Governor Clinton were not insisting upon warlike procedures so much as they wanted assurances that Oswego would be safe and the Six Nations steadfast in their neutrality.

The Pennsylvania gentlemen came laden with costly presents to appease their Indian friends. The Quaker assembly in Philadelphia had forbidden them to make any warlike commitments,

---
17. Colonial Records, 5:8–18 passim.

even though Governor Thomas had strenuously urged that the province should offer military aid. The Assembly had taken every precaution to see to it that the commissioners would heed their injunction. Two of the three commissioners, Norris and Kinsey, were ardent Quakers whose consciences forbade them to give countenance to warlike acts.

With such diverse motives, amounting almost to cross purposes, the prospect of unified action by the northern British colonies was remote indeed as the Albany conference of 1745 was opened.

The domains of the Six Nations spread fanwise from the upper reaches of the Susquehanna into the province of New York. The Oneidas, Onondagas, Cayugas, occupied the middle position, while the Senecas were the rulers of the area west of the Five Finger Lakes and the Mohawks dominated the eastern end of the province, along the Mohawk River Valley, the upper Hudson and the borders of Connecticut and Massachusetts.

Early in 1745, an evil report was circulated among the Mohawks which had caused that tribe to be alarmed. Rumor had it that the English were planning "to cut them all off by surprise." The New England commissioners learned of this rumor and fearing reprisals from neighbors, the Mohawks tried to get to the bottom of the alarm by inquiring among the representatives of the Maquas present at the Albany conference of 1745. Without asking the permission of the Pennsylvania delegation, the New England commissioners engaged the services of Conrad Weiser to act as interpreter during their investigation. On October 8 Weiser obliged the New England delegates by acting in this capacity.

When Isaac Norris and John Kinsey, the Pennsylvania commissioners, learned that Weiser had served the northern provinces, they were not pleased with his conduct. They ordered him to confine himself to his duties in the services of Pennsylvania and "if at any time he should be sent for, not to go without having had an application first to us."

At this point, Joseph Murray, a member of the Executive Council of New York, representing Governor Clinton, appeared before the Pennsylvania commissioners to apologize for the oversight and to plead for the continued services of Weiser in the inquiry into the Mohawk alarm. The commissioners gave their consent and Weiser continued to serve the New England provinces. With his aid, it was learned that the Mohawks attributed the origin of the rumor to one Andrew Petar, "an old Dutchman." But, on oath, Petar denied the charge and his inquisitors believed him. Finally, the blame was fixed upon a Mohawk named Indian Henry.[18]

On October 10, Governor Clinton invited all the delegates from other colonies to hear the speech which he intended to make to the Indians. The tenor of that speech was in sharp contrast to the traditional Penn Indian diplomacy. It was a series of charges against the Six Nations for past transgressions and breathed a challenge that only by a declaration of war against the French could the Indians redeem themselves. The tone was haughty and the metaphors ill-chosen. In speaking of the perfidy of the Canadians the governor said that he had hoped in vain that they would "carry on the war in a Christian-like manner." Such words must have sounded like blasphemy to the ears of devout Quakers such as Isaac Norris and John Kinsey!

The Pennsylvania delegates refused to accept the address as an expression of their sentiments. Governor Clinton objected to their attendance at conference sessions with their hats on their heads and the two Friends were insistent upon their right to wear them. The consequence of this class of opinion was that most of the Pennsylvania delegation absented itself from the conference when Clinton made his speech and Penn's colony was forced to treat separately with the Six Nations.

Clinton upbraided the Indians for many isolated misdeeds of their warriors and cited breaches of treaties of which the Pennsylvanians had known nothing. He warned them against permitting the carrying place at Oswego from falling into French hands. When the Iroquois admitted that they had had meetings with Frenchmen at Oswego, claiming that they had met them only in the interests of preserving peace, Clinton scoffed at their explanation and called it "pretence."

On October 14th, the Governor of New York, having passed upon the address which the Pennsylvanians wished to make, turned the discussions over to Pennsylvania province. The commissioners instructed Weiser to summon the chiefs of the Nations

---

18. The account of this inquiry and Weiser's part as it appears in the Journal of Isaac Norris.

to the meeting place, but the conference was delayed by new complaints from New England. New atrocities had been inflicted by a party of French and Indians at a place called Great Meadows (Saratoga).[19] The New England delegates were impatient, demanding that Clinton urge the Six Nations to an immediate declaration of war. At this suggestion, New York's governor lost patience. He refused to act upon the demands of Massachusetts and Connecticut, declaring that the former had been to precipitate in declaring war in the first place. Stubbornly he took the position that he would make no further move until he had consulted his own legislature.

Meanwhile, the chiefs of the Indians became uneasy. Sensing that something was wrong, they asked Conrad Weiser to arrange a meeting at Clinton's private quarters. There they hoped to explain their position to him through Weiser's interpretation.

Clinton slammed the door in their faces. He refused to receive a delegation of Indians and hurriedly left Albany without attending the sessions of a conference between the Six Nations and the Pennsylvania delegates. This was a complete disavowal of a promise which Clinton had made in his address to the Indians, in which he had promised to listen to their side of the story. When James Logan, in Philadelphia, heard of this shabby treatment of Weiser and the chieftains, he was "so filled with Indignation against that monster of a Man," that he wrote to Governor Thomas, condemning Clinton's rash actions. In using the phrase "Monster of a Man," Logan extracted a phrase from Conrad Weiser's report of the Conference in Albany. In reporting this incident Weiser could not restrain himself from taking sides with the Indians in their hurt pride.[20]

The Pennsylvania delegates did all they could to assuage the wounded feelings of their native brethren when the separate conference finally took place. They had several grave charges to present against the actions of some Indians which were not in

---

19. James Logan was greatly concerned about the strategic position of Saratoga. On October 29, 1745, the venerable statesman wrote to Conrad Weiser, asking him to furnish information about the place. Logan wanted to know the number of guns that the captured fort had held: what garrisons had defended it; the number of inhabitants and the exact distance from Albany. Peters MSS, 2:46.

20. James Logan to Richard Peters, for the attention of the governor, October 8, 1745, Logan MSS, 10:73.

accordance with recent treaties, but with Weiser acting as interpreter, these charges were couched in mild phrases. The chief burden of the address was to urge the Six Nations to call back to their villages those of their number who had joined the French.

Canassatego, speaking for the Six Nations, spoke wisely when he stated the position of his people, declaring their neutrality. They "looked upon this War as a War between English and French only and did not intend to engage on either side; for that the French and English made War and made Peace at Pleasure, but when the Indians once engaged in War they knew not when it would end."

To the Pennsylvanians, the Indian spokesman revealed the details of the conference which Iroquois delegates had had with the Governor of Canada. This visit to Canada had been one of the chief reasons for calling the conference of 1745. The Governor of Canada, who called himself the Father of the Indians, had urged them to support the cause of the French as the duty of the Indians, his children. He had promised that those warriors who joined his cause should want for nothing, guns, pistols, swords, ammunition, tobacco, and paint would be furnished to them.

It was at this point in the conference at Montreal that a belt of wampum had been tossed on the ground, challenging the Iroquois warriors to pick it up as a token of their joining the French forces. Without any consultation between themselves, a few of the thoughtless young braves had joined in war dance which followed the challenge of the wampum belt, but this hasty action in no way committed the Six Nations to an alliance with the French and even those who had accepted the challenge rued their action a short time afterward.

Concerning the promise they had made to Weiser in June of that year, to make every effort to apprehend Peter Chartiers and recover the goods stolen from Pennsylvania traders, they reported that they had made their representations to the governor of Canada, but that gentleman professed to know nothing about the matter. The Indians were helpless to do anything more about it. They had sent orders recalling their people who had crossed to the Canadian side, but orders were ignored and the chiefs of the Six Nations had no means by which to enforce them.

In all the positions taken by the Iroquois at the Albany Conference, it was obvious that they were striving to maintain their neutrality in the struggle between England and France. In this course of action, they were encouraged by the Quakers of Pennsylvania and by their friend and confidant Conrad Weiser.

Augustus Spangenberg

David Zeisberger

Isaac Norris

David Brainerd preaching to the Indians

Fort Oswego

CHAPTER X

Standing "Newter"

"Can a man of your interest and warm Heart sit still at Tulpehocken?" Conrad Weiser was nearing his fiftieth birthday when Secretary Peters wrote the above to him on July 9, 1746.[1] The circumstances which prompted the appeal did not grow out of any reluctance on Weiser's part to perform the duties imposed upon him as magistrate and interpreter. Quite to the contrary he and only he remained steadfast in his efforts to avert inter-Indian wars and to secure the safety of the British colonies from the horrors of Indian massacre and French invasion. Richard Peters turned to Weiser when it appeared that all else had failed and implored the aging Tarachawagon to keep his hold upon the reins of the universe.

Intercolonial Indian diplomacy had come to an end after the shabby treatment the visiting delegates had received from Governor Clinton at the Albany Conference of 1745. This breach in the united front which the colonies tried to show in their earlier dealings with the natives threatened the loss of the Indians' friendship at a time when alarms were being heard on every hand. The winter of 1745–1746 had brought accounts of huge bands of French Indians being collected along the southern shores of the Great Lakes and as far west as the Mississippi River. The treason of Peter Chartiers was frequently mentioned as an underlying cause of the widespread native uprising.

---

1. Peters to Weiser, Weiser MSS, 1:15.

In Philadelphia, three companies of volunteer troops were raised to defend the province. Two English companies and one German company were inducted. The captain of the German company was one Doctor Diemer, whom we shall meet again. An attempt was made to raise an additional German company at Tulpehocken. Governor Thomas issued a proclamation urging enlistments and Conrad Weiser was requested to translate the proclamation into German. The settlers of Tulpehocken were indifferent to this appeal and Conrad Weiser himself, declined a captain's commission, offered by the Governor in a letter addressed to "Capt. Conrad Weiser, Esquire." Weiser declined the post after discussing the matter with his "neighbors and others."[2] Peters then asked Weiser to translate the Governor's proclamation, calling for troops into German. "Is there no way to spirit up the people?" he asked.[3]

Secretary Peters' appeal to bestir himself did not grow out of Weiser's failure to raise a military company. Diplomacy had broken down. Desperately Clinton of New York had called for another conference at Albany and his call had met with a cool reception in the Pennsylvania Assembly. That body declined to send delegates but indicated that it was willing that Governor Thomas should attend if he wished.

Governor George Thomas was a sick man, and affairs of state were subordinate to his failing health. Increasing "pains in his chest," as Weiser described the Governor's ailment, finally forced him to resign his position. John Penn, one of the proprietors, died in 1746. James Logan was a chronic sufferer from the ague, his letters written during this period showing the effects of palsy in the uneven script of his handwriting. "I am in the midst of all these troubles and a very hot spell of weather," added Richard Peters to the letter, in which he begged Weiser to aid him.

Meanwhile, the pugnacious governor of Virginia, Colonel Gooch, was directing his attention toward fitting out a military expedition against the French. He had wearied of his attempts to bring about peace between the Catawbas of the south and their ancient enemies, the Six Nations.[4] On most of his long journeys

---
2. Weiser to Thomas Lee, July 5, 1746, Ibid.
3. Peters to Weiser, June 11, 1746, Peters MSS, 2:58.
4. The Catawbas and Cherokees had a quarrel among themselves at the time, the former

into the wilderness, Weiser carried a commission from Virginia, but after the collapse of negotiations at Albany in 1746 Gooch had lost patience and in a letter to Governor Thomas washed his hands of any further part in the role of peacemaker, declaring "it would be a good Policy to leave them (the Indians) to determine their Differences between themselves" and then in bitter sarcasm he added, "and then they (Six Nations) may want leisure to travel to Canada and Montreal."

Governor Thomas gave vent to his disgust at Gooch's retreat from the peace plans. "Thus all Mr. Gooch's Humanity is ended in a politick permission to the People to cut one another's Throats as fast as they can," wrote Thomas to Weiser. It remained for Pennsylvania alone to prevent the annual excursions of Six Nations' braves in quest of Flathead scalps.

The Catawbas had informed Gooch that they would treat with the Iroquois if the latter sent presents and were willing to come to Williamsburg in Virginia. Thomas instructed Weiser to employ Shikellamy to carry this message to the Six Nations Council at Onondaga. Even if Virginia was negligent in her duty, Pennsylvania must not be remiss in hers.

Even though Governor Gooch had put Indian affairs out of his mind, there was one man in Virginia who was sensible of the danger involved. That man was Colonel Thomas Lee of Stratford, the founder of the remarkable family which brought up so much distinction to the name of Lee during the early days of the republic. Colonel Lee had met Conrad Weiser in Lancaster, at the time of the Tri-colony Treaty of 1744. At that time these two men had become fast friends and a correspondence between the two had continued without interruption. Lee sought information from Weiser on Indian marriage customs, copies of Indian folk songs, delivery of stalks of Rhenish grapes to be planted at Stratford, and many related subjects. Weiser supplied the desired information as the exchange of letters continued through the years intervening between 1744 and the crisis of 1746.

In one of the letters, Weiser warned Lee of the dangers of Indian wars. The Virginia colonel still held his office as commissioner of

---

charging the latter with giving shelter to stray Iroquois warriors. *Philadelphia Gazette*, June 26, 1746.

Indian Affairs and he took up the problem of arranging a conference between the Six Nations and the Catawbas after Governor Gooch abandoned the cause. Lee urged Weiser to prevail upon the Iroquois to send delegates to Frederick in Maryland as a midway point between the longhouses of the contending tribes.

When Clinton of New York called for Pennsylvania delegates to attend a conference at Albany, his invitation was spurned. The Pennsylvania Assembly refused and the Governor was ill. An Indian Conference with the Six Nations involving the momentous question of taking up the hatchet called for the presence of some Pennsylvania representative. With no one there, the Indians would feel that Onas had deserted them when they needed his counsel most. This was the state of affairs when Peters wrote to Weiser, pleading that he should go to Albany to represent Pennsylvania. Weiser agreed to go.

Once again, he carried a message from Virginia, this time at the request of Colonel Lee. The Virginia Assembly had voted Weiser a reward of thirty pounds for his services on former occasions. Forty ounces of gold were sent to the Six Nations in the name of the governor of Virginia, with the promise that more would be given after the treaty which was planned to be held at Frederick.

In a letter to Lee, April 16, 1746,[5] Weiser stated that he had just returned from Shamokin, where he had learned something about the attitude of the Indians toward participating in the war against the French. "I, for my part, always thought it would be a very Difficult for us to Engage them against the French, but much more Difficult for the French to Engage them against us, as they may seem to be absolutely resolved to stand newter, but as we live in an age where the Steadfast of mankind is not to be Depended on and most Nations are guided by Self Interest, it would not be a great Wonder if the poor Indians would look out for gain and more so as the French are Ever busy about them . . ."

The neutrality of the Six Nations was wearing thin. The New York authorities were bringing heavy pressure upon them to take up the hatchet against the French. On August 28, 1746, Sir William Johnson, aged only thirty-one years, was appointed "Colonel

---

5. Reference to Weiser-Lee Correspondence may be consulted in the two tomes of Weiser Correspondence in the Historical Society of Pennsylvania.

of the Forces to be raised out of the Six Nations." Johnson's close association as a trader at Oswego and a favorite among the Mohawk nation placed him in a strange position.[6]

On the other hand, the French were using every ruse possible to win the Six Nations to their cause. Mohawk braves captured at Crown Point were sent home with French presents. These Indians told their people that the French would not disturb Mohawk country if the Six Nations remained neutral. They, the French, would attack only New England as revenge for the loss of Cape Breton. The effectiveness of the French inducements to the young braves of the Six Nations was proven by the discovery of some Oneidas who had fallen in battle against the English at Saratoga. These evil portents Weiser communicated to Richard Peters in a letter sent from Albany on Sept. 27, 1746.[7]

This same letter reported, dejectedly, "I wish I was able to write a agreeable letter to you, but I find nothing at all agreeable in the affair of the Expedition (and Elsewhere). It appears to me very dismal. Our friends, the Six Nations, have promised to fight, but . . . it was only their Lipps that spoke and not their Hearts. So many accidents happened which are looked upon by the Indians as bad Omens. Soon when they came down (to Albany) they were soon catched by the Small Pox and the other Distemper called the Long Fever. Both Distempers carried off about 200 Albany people and makes sad Work among the Indians, most of them fell sick before they came home and a great many died." This statement must refer to the Indian visit of 1745.

There was no Indian powwow at Albany in 1746. The convergence of troops upon that city was in the form of a military expedition. Colonel Gooch planned to take his Virginia battalions to Albany and Colonel Lee had informed Weiser that Gooch would meet him there. But Virginia's governor, like Pennsylvania's, became very sick at the last moment and did not make the journey. In commenting on his disappointment in Gooch, Weiser quoted Scriptures in writing Peters, "The Fool has the Rod in his hand, which in Justice ought to be on his back."

---

6. Pound, Arthur, *Johnson of the Mohawks*, New York, 1930, 98–113.
7. Weiser MSS, 1:13.

Conrad Weiser, as the peace emissary from Pennsylvania and Virginia, was the only person at Albany interested in securing any form of peace in 1746. The outskirts of the city were converted into a military camp. Weiser's description of the encampment and the provisioning of the provincial troops will be of interest here.

"Now for our own people—a Sett of Man that can Damn Gott and swear are the Head of the Affair (Expedition against Canada) who suffer no Body about them that does not agree with them and the very Counsellors of the King . . . are not heard . . . The Soldiers that are quartered on both Sides of the River, up and down, killed many Cattle and Sheep and play the Mischief . . . Drinks and Damns and the cursing Albany labours under is Un-Expressable, and no Expedition is expected nor intended by G. C. (George Clinton), who is now made a colonel, if he can help it this Fall.

"Waggons are now making to carry the Canons and Orders will be sent to Mr. Livingston's (Livingston Manor) Furniss to run some Canon Balls . . .

"The four Pennsilvany Companies are posted about 13 miles above Albany on the west Shoer (Shore) at a place called the Half Moon. They have no Blankets yet, no Great Coats, their Stockings hang over their Shoes of some of them . . . I advised Captain Diemer to go to the Governor for some Blankets . . ."

From these remarks, we gather that Weiser was not a warlike man in 1746.

"WE THE, ENGLISH"

The Anglicization of Conrad Weiser was complete when in 1747 he counted himself among "we the English." It is true, of course, that in choosing this phrase, the sturdy Pennsylvania German pioneer was merely distinguishing between the two nations then at war and the term "English" was used in opposition to "French." The seven-year-old War of the Austrian Succession was reaching its climax in Europe and its full impact was being felt on the American continent.

The Mohawk Indians, easternmost nation of the Iroquois Confederacy. had declared war against French Canada. Encouraged by Colonel William Johnson and Henry Lydius, New York agents, these Indians had taken up the hatchet in the British interest and a few straggling warriors belong to the Oneida and Onondaga had joined them. Governor William Shirley of Massachusetts informed Pennsylvania authorities of this declaration of war in the spring of 1747. Massachusetts province, already at war with the French, quite naturally welcomed their new allies, and Governor Shirley wrote to the other English colonies, hoping to prod them into joining the struggle. If Pennsylvania did not choose to go the full length of declaring war, the governor hoped that the province would see fit to send supplies to aid the Mohawks, who were one of the Six Nations, in alliance with Penn's province.

Shirley's letter reached Pennsylvania at a time when there was no stable executive authority functioning in the province. Governor George Thomas, ill and discouraged, had departed for England, John Penn had died during the previous year, and James Logan, tottering under his four-score-years, had retired from active participation in the affairs of state. Only Richard Peters remained to guide Anthony Palmer, the president of Council, who assumed the executive authority of the province. In dealing with the problems which Shirley's request presented, the Pennsylvania Assembly and Council were forced to rely upon Conrad Weiser's advice and counsel.

A copy of the Shirley letter was sent to Weiser, asking him to express his views. Accompanying the letters there were instructions sending the interpreter to Shamokin with a message to the Indians, informing them of the death of John Penn and the departure of Governor Thomas. The instructions also exhorted Weiser to make extensive inquiries among the Indians at Shamokin concerning the state of affairs at Onondaga.[8]

Before setting out for Shamokin, Weiser wrote to Peters expressing his reactions to Shirley's request. His disapproval of the actions of Johnson and Lydius in enlisting only one of the Six Nations in the campaign without the general approval of the other five nations. While he would not know whether the Iroquois Confederacy had declared war against the French until after his prospected visit to Shamokin, he would advise against sending

---
8. Colonial Records, 5:73. Also Pennsylvania Archives, 1:748–749.

presents and supplies to the Mohawks only, lest the five nations interpret such an act as a show of preference or an inclination on the part of Pennsylvania to treat separately, where all treaty obligations required that transactions should be carried on only with the Confederacy.[9]

In June 1747, Weiser set out for Shamokin by way of Paxtang. He was fortunate in meeting a group of Shamokin Indians at the home of Joseph Chambers, a trader whose house was south of the Indian capital. Shikellamy was one of the group he met and there were enough members of the tribe to conduct the conference at the Chambers' house.[10]

During this conference, Weiser learned many facts, some of which he included in his official report to the Council, others he wrote in a separate letter to Richard Peters, and still others which, for reasons best known to himself, he did not divulge.

The Six Nations had not declared war against the French. The Cayugas and Senecas were opposed to such an act. The latest news from Onondaga reported that some members of these nations were in Niagara in response to a French invitation to come there to receive presents. The wily French had induced them to come by declaring that the Mohawks and Onondagas had always appropriated the larger share of presents which the English made to the Six Nations, cheating the two western nations out of their just dues. Now, said the French, they would even matters by making a special present to the two defrauded peoples.

This bit of information might have been disturbing to the English, had it not been toned down considerably by Shikellamy's expressed opinion that the Six Nations would "stick together, notwithstanding the Presents received from the French." In a personal letter to Peters, Weiser stated, however, that he was far from certain that the Six Nations would join the British cause.[11] The Indians were taking advantage of the state of affairs to court both sides of the war in the hope of gaining the best advantages for themselves. Very bitterly, Weiser condemned the inactivity of the British armed forces, charging that the Indians chided him

---
9. Weiser to Peters, June 15, 1747, Pennsylvania Archives, 1:749–750.
10. Weiser's Account of his Journey to Shamokin, Colonial Records, 5:84–88.
11. Weiser to Peters, June 21, 1747, Pennsylvania Archives, 1:750.

about the cowardice of the English. The charge was made that the English were trying to push the Indian into the brunt of the battle, "and think we English will leave them in the Lurch."

Notwithstanding these sentiments, it was Weiser's conviction that even though the Six Nations would strive to remain neutral, they would never join the French against the English.

At Shamokin, Weiser learned of two tribes of Ohio Indians whose warriors had come to the English trading post at Oswego, offering to fight against the French. These tribes were in rebellion against French control, which they claimed had become unbearable and they hoped for their independence. Information on the point was rather vague at Shamokin.

A few days before Weiser made his report on the Ohio Indians, Richard Peters had received information from George Croghan, a fur trader, that a group of Indians on the south side of Lake Erie had expressed a desire to join the English cause and he recommended that a present be sent by Pennsylvania to encourage them. Weiser was asked to suggest the articles which should be included in this present.[12]

Weiser's advice was that a small present be sent through Croghan at once, along with the promise of a much larger present to be delivered by next summer. Weiser intimated broadly that he would deliver the larger present himself. A journey to the Indian villages on the Ohio and Lake Erie would afford him an opportunity to "see with my own eyes" the Indian settlements in the western portion of the province.

In October 1747, Weiser made a second trip to Shamokin. This time he went to minister to his sick friend, Shikellamy. A plague had befallen the Indian settlement on the Susquehanna and death had claimed at least three members of the aging chieftain's immediate family. Equipped with medicine furnished by Dr. Graeme of Philadelphia, Weiser prevailed upon his friends to take the white man's medicine. In describing Shikellamy's ailment to James Logan, Weiser said it was a combination of "Feaver and Ego."[13] Very kindly, the venerable Logan took time to correct Weiser's spelling, pointing out that word was "ague" and

---

12. Peters to Weiser, September 26. 1747, Peters MSS, 2:79. Also Pennsylvania Archives, 1:771.
13. Weiser to Logan, September 27, 1747, Logan MSS, 10:76–77.

not "ego."[14] "Doctor" Weiser ministered to the stricken Indians at Shamokin and his concoction cured all the surviving members of Shikellamy's family. Allumpies, the drunken king of the Delaware, had succumbed before Weiser arrived with his medicine, but Shikellamy and others were on their feet again in a few days.

During this visit, Weiser learned that the struggle for neutrality among the Indians had encountered new obstacles. The French governor had called upon all Indians in the region of the Great Lakes, to take up the hatchet against the English and two of them had accepted, while other western tribes had sent belts of black wampum to the Delaware and Shawnees on the Susquehanna, urging these Pennsylvania Indians to join in a war against eh French.

At the home of the traitor, Thomas McGee, Weiser reported having seen a human scalp, alleged to be the scalp of a Frenchmen. Some Ohio Indians had brought the scalp to McGee's house with the intention of requesting the trader to take it to Philadelphia, as proof that the western Indians were attacking the French. McGee was not at home when the scalp was delivered. The messenger who brought the scalp tried to prevail on Weiser to accept it in the name of Pennsylvania. This Conrad refused to do, declaring that Pennsylvania had not "given the Hatchet or employed anybody to kill Frenchmen." The scalp was taken "in time of Peace . . . all white People would look upon such Action with Contempt."[15]

In his report of his second Shamokin journey, Weiser included an appeal for a present for Shikellamy, who was impoverished by the costs of sickness and death in his family. "In his Sickness the Horses have eat all his Corn; his Cloaths he gave to Indian doctors to cure him and his Family all in vain; he has nobody to hunt for him, and I cannot see how the poor old man can live."

In November 1747, Weiser was summoned to Philadelphia to pass upon the goods purchased for presents to Shikellamy and to the Lake Erie Indians, whose loyalty was attested by George Croghan.[16] Just before answering the summons to come to Philadelphia, Weiser was in Lancaster attending to some of his

---
14. Logan to Weiser, September 30, 1747, Peters MSS, 2:81.
15. Weiser to Peters, September 27, 1747, Weiser MSS, 1:13.
16. Colonial Records, November 6, 1747, 5:139.

duties as a magistrate. While there, he met ten Ohio Indians who were on their way to Philadelphia to inform the authorities there concerning the state of affairs in the distant Ohio country. This information made Weiser's presence in Philadelphia more urgent than before.[17]

In the conference with the Ohio warrior, Weiser was given a free hand in dealing with the western emissaries. From these warriors, it was learned that the Six Nations had urged western tribes to "stand neuter" while the English and French destroyed each other. Message and message had come from Onondaga to the tribes living on the branches of the Mississippi, counseling neutrality. The older men in these tribes were inclined to defer to the council of Onondaga, but the younger warriors had decided "to take up the English Hatchet against the will of the old People, and to lay their old People aside as of no use but in time of Peace."

In characteristic metaphors, these warriors spoke of "building a Fire under the Kettle and putting Frenchmen's Heads in it." They had observed that the English fire "was almost out." They presented a string of wampum "to encourage you . . . to put more Fire under your Kettle."

Before answering the Indians, the Pennsylvania Council asked Conrad Weiser to inquire into many detailed matters concerning these western Indians. Their history, their sincerity of purpose, their future designs, their numbers, and villages.[18] Also, Council desired to know what James Logan thought about the matter. Weiser and Peters were instructed to visit Logan and learn his "sentiments."

The results of these inquiries and interviews were presented to Council by Weiser in the forenoon of November 16, 1747, prior to the conference with the Ohio Indians, which was scheduled for the afternoon of the same day.

An act of Providence, said Weiser, brought the Ohio Indians to Philadelphia. One Ohio tribe of Indians had listened to the French and had taken up arms against the English. This act was a signal for the young warriors of the more powerful tribes to

---
17. Ibid., 140–145. Also see *Pennsylvania Gazette*, November 11, 1747, and November 19, 1747.
18. Logan MSS, 10:78.

declare in favor of the English, lest other small tribes desert to the French. It was the custom among these tribes that in time of war the older men put the management of affairs in the hands of warriors, and therefore the warriors in Philadelphia now were empowered to speak for the tribes. Weiser recommended that a handsome present be given these warriors and held out the hope that securing their friendship might serve to gain the friendship of all the Indians of the area we now know as the middle west.

Council accepted Weiser's recommendations and in the conference with the Ohio Indians that followed, the newly formed alliance of friendship was sealed with one hundred and fifty pounds worth of presents. At the same time Council, acting upon Weiser's advice, purchased goods to be given to the Lake Erie Indians and to Shikellamy.

COORDINATING INDIAN AFFAIRS

There were many difficulties to be encountered by Weiser and the Pennsylvania authorities before the contemplated mission to the Ohio Indians could be gotten underway. Indian affairs touching or involving nearly all the English colonies claimed the attention of the farmer of Tulpehocken. Into Weiser's stone cabin came many kinds of disturbing messages from Onondaga, from Philadelphia, from Aughwick, Logstown on the Ohio, Boston, New York, Annapolis, Stratford, Williamsburg, Shamokin, Wyoming, even from far away Charleston, South Carolina.

The Pennsylvania Assembly realized that Maryland and Virginia as parties to the Lancaster Treaty of 1744, would have an interest in the lands beyond the Allegheny Mountains. Accordingly, President of Council, Anthony Palmer, wrote to the governors of those provinces, inviting them to join Pennsylvania in making a present to the "farr" Indians. Both governors, Ogle of Maryland and Gooch of Virginia, expressed a willingness to "encrease" the size of the present and agreed to trust Weiser with the delivery of the goods on their behalf.[19]

---

19. Palmer to Gooch; Palmer to Ogle, January 25, 1748, 189–190; Ogle to Palmer, February 15, 1748, 202; Gooch to Palmer, March 7, 1748, 221; Ogle to Palmer, March 8, 1748, 209; all Colonial Records, vol. 5.

In February 1748, Weiser was called to Philadelphia to advise Council on the purchase of goods for the western Indians.[20] The huge Pennsylvania present represented an expenditure of nearly one thousand pounds, Pennsylvania currency. Included in the items was an expenditure for the purchase of a hammock for Conrad Weiser. The fifty-two-year-old agent of the Penns desired some comforts on his long journey. He had suffered severe illness due to exposure during his November journeys in 1747 and his recurring malady of stomach disorders called for reasonable cautions.

Arrangements were made to collect the goods at George Croghan's at Aughwick, west of the Susquehanna. Croghan had sent his own cargo of trading goods westward before March 28, 1748, and was waiting at home to help Weiser to carry the presents to the Lake Erie and Ohio Indians. He had collected twenty horses for carrying the burden.

The expanding realms of Indian diplomacy increased the difficulty of coordinating the plans for an expedition into the interior of the country. Winter snows blanketed the foot trails in the mountains and moccasined messengers did not stir from their villages. Bewigged legislatures in Philadelphia, seated before their cavernous fireplaces could do no more than guess about the events which were stirring in the wooded hinterland. The well-laid plans for the Ohio journey were destined to meet with unforeseen difficulties when springtime messages brought new problems of forest diplomacy.

Late in March 1748, Richard Peters and James Logan sat before the glowing embers of a fireplace in Stenton mansion and pondered a communication from Weiser. For some reason which they could not determine, Conrad was reluctant to undertake the journey to Ohio.[21] With the disappearance of the snows, Shikellamy had visited Weiser at Tulpehocken and had advised against undertaking the mission. Two of the Ohio warriors who had been present at the Philadelphia conference during the previous autumn had lingered at Shamokin throughout the winter. Weiser had accompanied these warriors on their homeward journey, en-

---
20. Ibid., 197.
21. On the night of March 28, Peter lodged at Stenton and discussed with Logan, Weiser's apparent unwillingness to go to Ohio. Logan to Weiser, Peters MSS, 2:100.

tertaining them at Tulpehocken for several days and then escorting them to the Indian village at Shamokin. Eight of the braves had struck out into the wilderness, Ohio bound, but two had lingered on the banks of the Susquehanna.

During the long winter evenings, spent at the log house which Weiser had built for Shikellamy, these warriors had become talkative, revealing several matters which led Shikellamy to advise against the Ohio journey. Chief among these revelations was the fact that the western Indians had not declared war against the French, as had been stated in Philadelphia.

To the great credit of Logan and other Philadelphians, it must be pointed out that their interest in cultivating the friendship of the western Indians was not motivated solely by a desire to gain a military alliance. Logan, and perhaps others, envisioned the long-range advantages which would accrue from such a friendship, and Weiser, too, must have known that the underlying purpose of the mission was predicated upon the future rather than the mercenary plans to secure allies. Because both Peters and Logan knew that Weiser would not let a military matter deflect him from the grand purpose, they were puzzled to know why he now counseled against an undertaking which he had sponsored until recently. On March 31, both Weiser and Shikellamy were summoned to Philadelphia. "It is expected that neither of You will make any Excuses nor the least Delay," said Peters, because "you will not suffer it to be said that any Harm to the public Weal thro' Your, or either of Your Faults."[22]

On April 11, Weiser and Shikellamy appeared before Council and stated their reasons for requesting postponement of the journey to Ohio. A messenger from the Onondaga Council had informed Shikellamy that the Six Nations were planning to send deputies to Philadelphia early in 1748. The matters to be dealt with were of such delicate nature that Conrad Weiser's presence at the conference would be absolutely necessary. The vice-regent of the Six Nations did not know all of the matters that needed settlement, but he did explain that it would be necessary to elect a successor to Allumpies, the late king of the Delawares.[23]

---

22. Peters to Weiser, Colonial Records, 5:213.
23. Ibid., 222–223.

On the surface, it would not appear that a tribal election would be vital enough as a matter of state to require Weiser's presence. However, the Council deferred to the wishes of Weiser and his native friend and postponed the Ohio journey until such time as the Six Nations could be dealt with. An extensive list of instructions which had been prepared for Weiser's Ohio mission by President Palmer was tabled.

One month later, a delegation of Cayuga Indians came to Weiser's home in Tulpehocken with an ominous piece of news. An English messenger had come into Cayuga villages, urging those Indians to make war on the French. It was a matter of self-defense he had warned them. The Indians met in Council and decided not only to refuse the proffered English hatchet but to rebuke the English for their artfulness in trying to draw the Indians into the war. Then, very unwisely, the Englishman had threatened the Cayugas with reprisals, saying that if they would not be allies they must be regarded as enemies.

Naturally, the Indians resented such treatment and let the Englishman know that his welcome was worn thin.

Shikellamy had not accompanied the Six Nations delegates to Weiser's home, because he was too ill. He had sat in Council, however, when the delegates made their report at Shamokin and advised that some part of the story must be false because he could not conceive of an Englishman acting in this manner. Two of Shikellamy's sons were dispatched to inform Weiser of the old chieftain's views and the Cayugas were notified by Shikellamy that Tarachawagon (Weiser) would soon learn the "Truth of the Matter."

Duly impressed with the ominous character of Weiser's report, Council acted speedily, dispatching a letter to Governor Clinton by express and tacitly demanding an immediate reply, while Weiser waited in Philadelphia. The Cayugas remained at Tulpehocken, awaiting Weiser's answer.

Governor Clinton's reply came after three days' time. Clinton stated that he knew nothing about the message referred to. He said that he had sent Colonel Johnson to the Six Nations to "prevent their going to Canada," but Johnson's treaty contained no mention of the matters presented by the Cayuga Indians. If any such message was delivered "surreptitiously" it was contrary to his "directions and knowledge." He continued, "I look upon such (whoever that may be) aiming at nothing less than a total Defection of those tribes." A copy of Johnson's treaty of Onondaga was sent with Clinton's letter. Secretary Peters prepared copies of the letter and treaty and gave them to Weiser in order that he might properly interpret them to the Indians when he reached his Tulpehocken home.

While Weiser was detained in Philadelphia, a letter arrived from Logstown on the Ohio. George Croghan had gone on ahead when Weiser's journey was postponed early in April and he had delivered the present to the Erie Indians. He promised that a larger gift would reach them on August first, delivered by "Mr. Weiser," to whom they were to state their wishes and complaints. The Indians acknowledged the gift by giving another "French scalp" and stated that they looked forward to the forthcoming visit of Mr. Weiser, "who could never come in at a better time, as we have a large Body of our Brethren that are lately come to supply as well as ourselves."

The complaints to which Croghan referred grew out of the liquor traffic. The Indians protested against the evil of firewater, commended the Pennsylvania Assembly for passing strict prohibition laws—and then, in the same speech begged that some rum be delivered, because some of the French Indians who had lately joined their nation, had never tasted English rum, so they hoped that the traders would continue to bring it in order that the Erie Indians might entertain their guests.

Another letter reached Philadelphia while Weiser tarried there awaiting Clinton's reply. This letter stated that a delegation of Twightwees Indians from the Wabash River in Ohio was on the Allegheny Road, planning to discuss some matters in Philadelphia. These Indians indicated that they wanted the council fire lighted in Lancaster because Philadelphia was "too sickly."

This message puzzled the members of Council. They did not recognize the names of Indians signed to it. Weiser was summoned and he brought with him Andrew Montour, half-breed son of Madame Montour. Weiser recommended Montour to the

Council, stating that he had employed him on a previous occasion and found him trustworthy. Montour identified the names of some of the signers of the letter and stated that the Twightwees were "a very considerable nation, and That it was happy that they and their Friends shew'd an inclination to be well with the English . . ."

Council deliberated upon the matter of sending commissioners to Lancaster for several weeks. Finally, in mid-July, a commission of four members of Council was appointed to meet the Twightwees at Lancaster. William Logan, son of James Logan, was one of the members of the commission.

Conrad Weiser was the interpreter at the Twightwees Treaty in Lancaster 1748. The chief spokesman for the Indians was Scarroday, an Oneida, who lived among the Ohio Indians. As an Oneida, Scarroday spoke the Six Nations tongue, which Weiser understood very well.[24]

The Twightwees were "desirous to enter the chain of Friendship with the English" and wished to "open a Council Road to the English Governments." Most of the transactions growing out of the Twightwees Treaty dealt with the terms of alliance with the English and the clearing of the path for Weiser's projected journey to Ohio. These details will not call for recounting here, because the War of the Austrian Succession, otherwise known as King George's War, had been terminated by the Treaty of Aix la-Chapelle and news of the peace reached Lancaster while the Indian conference was being held.

But Conrad Weiser's duties did not terminate with the end of the struggle. The mission to Ohio was not abandoned. Added to the tasks already assigned to him on his journey was the duty to carry the governor's proclamation against rum, to stave the casks of traders along the route and to try to find a citizen of South Carolina named Haig, who, according to Governor James Glen of that province, had been captured and taken to Ohio.

The Lancaster Treaty ended on July 23. George Croghan had promised that Mr. Weiser would deliver the presents on August 1st. While in Lancaster, Weiser received a letter from Richard

---

24. Thomas Cookson to Peters, July 14, 1748, Pennsylvania Archives, 2:19. Cookson informs Peters that it was fortunate that Weiser was there.

Peters, telling him that there was no money in the treasury at Philadelphia. "Beg, borrow, or steal your supplies," came the very worldly order from the erstwhile Anglican clergyman, Peters. And then when you reach Ohio, "Send up a little Flagg."[25]

Massachusetts governor William Shirley

Dr. Thomas Graeme of Philadelphia

George Croghan's house near the Conodoguinet Creek in Cumberland County, Pennsylvania, as it appears today.

---

25. Peters to Weiser, July 14, 1748, Peters MSS, 2:106.

CHAPTER XI

To the Ohio Country

Westward the star of the empire takes its way! Prior to 1748, forest diplomacy was carried on along the Indian footpaths which led northward and southward through Pennsylvania. The valleys, cut through the mountains by the Susquehanna and its tributaries, were traversed by native and white men, commissioned to negotiate treaties with royal and proprietary deputies residing in the capital cities of the various colonies found along the Atlantic seacoast.

The routes of the westward were trodden by traders carrying their packs of the trade goods, when westward-bound, and returning laden with pelts for old-world markets. During the first half of the eighteenth century, all matters of diplomacy, as they related to the western nations, were entrusted to these traders, who for the greater part of them were wily, unprincipled scoundrels whose cupidity was checked by no consideration beyond their personal safety. After the middle of the eighteenth-century diplomatic missions moved east and west through Pennsylvania. Conrad Weiser pioneered these trails.

At the Treaty of Lancaster, in 1744, the Six Nations sold lands westward to the setting sun. Figuratively, the Indians meant to the crest of the Appalachian Mountains, but white men interpreting the term literally, regarded purchase in terms of their "sea to sea" charters, embracing all the mysterious land between the two oceans.

Late in 1747, the Pennsylvania Assembly had decided upon Weiser's suggestion to send a large present to the Ohio Indians in the hope of holding their loyalty to the British cause during King George's War (1740-1748). This decision was coupled with another plan to send a present to the Lake Erie Indians whose villages lay along the southern shores of the eastern lakes. The prospect of drawing these western tribes to the British interest led Thomas Lee of Virginia, founder of the great Virginia dynasty of that name, to write to Conrad Weiser saying that "with the help of these Indians we can drive the French out of North America."

When we bear in mind that almost all the tribes east of the Mississippi and south of the Great Lakes were under the suzerainty of the Six Nations, we can appreciate the strategic position which Conrad Weiser held in conducting negotiations with them. As the one European who held the full confidence of the Council at Onondaga, Weiser, more than any other individual, was responsible for setting up the impenetrable barrier against French incursions south of the St. Lawrence and north of the Ohio. Truly it may be said that this German immigrant to New York and Pennsylvania was an empire builder. The services of this one humble denizen of the crown repaid many times over all the monies paid out by the royal treasury to succor the distressed Palatines from 1709 to 1712. It was he who planted the first British flag in the rich Ohio country and blazed the trail for the establishment of an Anglo-Saxon civilization beyond the Appalachian Mountains.

Here we reproduce the first three weeks' account of Weiser's Ohio journey as it appears in:

THE JOURNAL OF CONRAD WEISER, ESQR.[1]
INDIAN INTERPRETER TO OHIO

Aug. 11th: Set out from my House & came to James Galbreath that day, 39 miles.
(James Galbreath, at Donegal, near Harrisburg)

12th: Came to George Croghan's, 15 miles.
(Croghan's place in Cumberland County, near Silver Spring in the township of the same name.

---

1. Weiser's Ohio Journal, 1748, Colonial Records, 5:348–358.

13th: To Robert Dunnings, 20 miles. (Robert Dunning, a trader. His post at Big Spring, Cumberland County near Carlisle).

14th: To Tuscarroro Path, 30 miles.

15th and 16th: Lay by on Account of the Men coming back Sick & some other affairs hindering us. (While Weiser's party camped in the Tuscarora Path, Conrad wrote a letter to Richard Peters, describing the problems growing out of the white men squatting on unpurchased lands. A postscript note to the letter states that "Mr. Franklin's son (William Franklin) is very well." (The younger Franklin was commissioned as an Indian agent at the Lancaster Treaty of 1748.)[2]

17th: Crossed the Tuscarroro Hill & came to the Sleeping Place called the Black Log, 20 miles. (Black Log Valley—Juniata County).

18th: Had a great Rain in the afternoon; came within two Miles of the Standing Stone, 24 miles. (Standing Stone early name of Huntingdon, Pa.)

19th: We traveled about 12 miles; were obligate to dry our Things in the afternoon.

20th: Came to Frankstown, but so now House or Cabins; here we overtook the Goods, because four of George Croghan's Hands fell sick, 26 miles. (Frankstown, near Hollidaysburg, Blair County, Pa.)

21st: Lay by, it raining all Day.

22nd: Crossed Allegheny Hill & came to the Clear Fields, 16 miles. (Clearfield Creek, Cambria County, Pa. Allegheny Hill in township of the same name, Blair County).

23rd: Came to the Shawonese Cabbins, 34 miles. (East of Schellsburg, Bedford County).

24th: Found a dead Man on the Road who had killed himself by Drinking too much Whiskey; the Place

---

2. Weiser to Peters, August 15, 1748, Pennsylvania Archives, 1st ser., 2:15.

being very stony we cou'd not dig a Grave; He smelling very strong we covered him with Stones & Wood & went on our Journey; came to the 10 Mile Lick, 32 Miles. (Ten Mile Lick, near Spring Church, Armstrong County).

25th: Crossed Kiskeminetoes Creek & came to Ohio that Day, 26 miles. (The Kittanning Path which Weiser followed from Black Log to the Kiskiminitas Creek terminated in Kittanning, Armstrong County. The word "Ohio" is used by Weiser to indicate lands west of the tributaries of the Allegheny River which forms & junctions with the Ohio River within the limits of present-day Pennsylvania).

26th: Hired a Canoe; paid 1,000 Black Wampum for the loan of it in Logs Town. Our Horses being all tyred, we went by Water & came that Night to Delaware Town; the Indians used us very kindly. (Logstown, nearly twenty miles north of the Forks of the Ohio River, near Economy, Pennsylvania, the site of the Harmony Society of the Rappites of the nineteenth century, Butler County).

27th: Set off again in the morning early; Rainy Weather. We dined in at Seneka Town, where an old Seneka Woman Reigns with great Authority; we dined at her House, & they all used us very well; at this & the last mentioned Delaware Town they received us by firing a great many Guns; especially at this last Place. We saluted the Town by firing off a 4 pair of Pistols; arrived that Evening at Logs Town & saluted the Town as before; the Indians returned about One hundred Guns; Great joy appear'd in their Countenances. From the Place where we took Water, i.e. from the old Shawonese Town, commonly called Chartier's own, to this Place is about 60 Miles by Water & but 35 or 40 by Land.

The Indian Council met this Evening to Shake Hands with me & to show their Satisfaction at my safe arrival; I desired of them to send a Couple of Canoes to fetch down the Goods from Chartier's Old Town, where we had been oblig'd to leave them on account of our Horses being all tyred. I gave them a String of Wampum to enforce my Request. (Chartier's Town, Chartier's Old Town, near Tarentum, Allegheny County).

28th: Lay still.

29th: The Indians sett off in Canoes to fetch the goods. I expected the Goods wou'd be all at Chartier's Old Town by the time the Canoes wou'd get there, as we met about twenty Horses of George Croghan's at the Shawonese Cabbins in order to fetch the Goods that were then lying at Franks Town.
This Day news came to Town that the Six Nations were on the point of declaring War against the French, for reason the French had Imprison'd some of the Indian Deputies. A Council was held & all the Indians acquainted with the News, and it was said that the Indian Messenger was by way to give all the Indians Notice to make ready to fight the French. This Day my Companions went by Coscosky, a large Indian Town about 30 Miles off.

30th: I went to Beaver Creek, an Indian Town about 8 Miles off, chiefly Delaware, the rest Mohocks, to have some Belts of Wampum made. This afternoon Rainy Weather set in which lasted about a week. Andrew Montour came back from Coscosky with a Message from the Indians there to desire of me that the ensuing Council might be held at their Town. We both lodged at this Town at George Croghan's Trading House.—(Coscosky—Weiser may refer to *Goschgoschunk* or Goschgoshing, a Delaware village which stood near the present village of Tionesta, Forrest County. However, the distance between Logstown and present Tionesta is twice as great as the thirty miles stated by Weiser. Considering that

Weiser was only reporting what he had heard about the distance, it is quite probable that his information was incorrect.)

31st: Sent Andrew Montour back to Coscosky with a String of Wampum to let the Indians there know that it was an act of their own that the ensuing Council must be held at Logs Town, they had ordered it so last Spring when George Croghan was up, and the last Treaty in Lancaster the Shawonese and Twightwees have been told so, & they stayed accordingly for that purpose, & both would be offended if the Council was to be held at Coscosky, besides my instructions binds me to Logs Town, & could not go further without giving offence.

Sept. 1st: The Indians in Logs Town having heard of the message from Coscosky sent for me to know what I was resolv'd to do, and told me that the Indians at Coscosky were no more Chiefs than themselves & that last Spring they had nothing to eat, & expecting that they shou'd have nothing to eat at our arrival; order'd that the Council should be held here; now their Corn is ripe, they want to remove the Council, but they ought to stand by their word; we have kept the Twightwees here & our own Brethren the Shawonese from below on that account, as I told them the Message that I had sent by Andrew Montour; they were content.

2nd: Rain continued; the Indians brought in a good deal of Venison.

3rd: Set up the Union Flagg on a long Pole. Treated all the Company with a Dram of Rum; the King's Health was drank by Indians & White men . . .

For several days after September 3, Weiser was "very sick of the Cholick." The diarist does not tell us whether his indisposition resulted from too much drinking to the King's health. We have every reason to believe that Conrad was a temperate man, and we know that stomach ailments were a chronic malady with him. In the days that followed he greeted the deputies of the various nations assembled at Logstown. There were Senecas, Shawnees, Wyandots, Twightwees, Mohawks, Mohicans, Onondagas. Cayugas, Oneidas, and Delawares were represented by deputies.

On September 8, Weiser heard a rumor that the Wyandots had changed their minds about allying themselves with the English. He sent Andrew Montour to Beaver Creek to investigate this rumor and it proved to be false. On the same day, the deputies of the Wyandots showed Weiser a curious belt of Wampum which they had received as a token from the Governor of New York, "more than fifty years ago." Threaded into a design, in black beads, there were seven "images" in the belt, each figure joined by the holding of hands. The Wyandots told him that the first figure represented the King of England, the next five stood for each of the Five Nations (Tuscaroras were not yet in the Confederacy at the time that the presentation was made) and the seventh figure represented the Wyandots.

A host of Indian deputies collected in Logstown, anxiously awaited the arrival of the pack of horses carrying the presents of Virginia and Pennsylvania. The goods were delayed, but Henry Norland, a Maryland trader, an Indian, brought great quantities of whiskey to Logstown, getting the Indians drunk and causing trouble for Weiser. Faced with this problem Weiser and Croghan staved some of Norland's whiskey to prevent it from causing more trouble.

The delay in the arrival of the treaty presents caused Weiser to fear that the goods might have fallen into the "hands of the enemy." He prevailed upon the Chiefs to send some warriors to meet the carrying party and not to return until they could report on the goods. In a few days, these warriors returned reporting that they had seen nothing of the presents. Weiser was vexed at this turn of events when he learned that the scouts had traveled on farther eastward than Shawanese Cabins (Bedford County). Yet why should the pack horses and their leader be detained? Weiser's party had met them at Frankstown on August 20 and now it was September 14, almost four weeks later and Croghan's people had not yet reached Shawanese Cabins, a mere seventy-five miles?

It appears that the Indians were patient while they waited at Logstown. Weiser employed his time confirming treaties of friendship and investigating the problems presented by Governor Palmer of South Carolina concerning several settlers who had been taken prisoner by the Seneca. Many belts of wampum were exchanged confirming pledges of Indian loyalty to the English. Weiser told them that the war with France was ended because the "French King's People have almost starved" but that "after their Bellies are full they will quarrel again and raise a War . . . we the English are your true Brethren at all Events."

On September 16, two days after the empty-handed return of the Indian scouts, the treaty goods arrived at Logstown. The porters explained that heavy rains had caused the creeks to rise so high that they could not be crossed for days. Further delay had been caused because of illness. The failure of the Indians scouts to locate the party remained unexplained. The presents were distributed on September 17 and the Indians expressed their great satisfaction.

In Weiser's accounts, we find very little expression of humor. It is fitting, therefore, that we extract a portion of the speech he made when he presented the presents:

"Brethren:
You have of late made frequent Complaints against the Traders bringing so much Rum to your Towns, & desir'd it might be stop't; & your Brethren the President & Council made an Act accordingly & put a stop to it, & no Trader was to bring any Rum or strong Liquor to your Towns. I have the Act here with me & shall explain it to You before I leave you; But it seems it is out of your Brethren's Power to stop it entirely. You send down your own Skins by the traders to buy Rum for you. You go yourselves & fetch Horse loads of strong Liquor. But the other Day an Indian came to this Town out of Maryland with 3 Horse loads of liquor, so that it appears you love it so well that you cannot be without it. You know very well that the Country near the endless Mountain affords strong Liquor, & the moment the Traders buy it they are

gone out of the Inhabitants & are traveling to this Place without being discover'd; besides this, you never agree about it—one will have it, the other won't (tho' very few), a third says we will have it cheaper; this last we believe is spoken from your Hearts (here they Laughed). Your Brethren, therefore, have order'd that every—of Whiskey shall be sold to You for 5 Bucks in your Town, & if a Trader offers to sell Whiskey to You and will not let you have it at that Price, you may take it from him & drink it for nothing."

A marked change in the relations between the provincial authorities and their Indian neighbors took place after the peace of Aix-la-Chapelle, in 1748. The cessation of hostilities against the French encouraged many settlers to penetrate more deeply into the woods to pioneer new homes and the need to placate the Indians to keep their support no longer appeared to be as vital in the safety of the province. Land hunger supplanted peace diplomacy in negotiations between Indians and whites and Conrad Weiser, as the agent of the province, became more and more involved in land purchases. It is not surprising that land hunger gripped him too, as it did the members of Penn's official family and members of the provincial legislature.

Another factor which led to the alienation of Indian accord was the death of Shikellamy late in 1748. The sagacious vice-regent of the Six Nations had always maintained an attitude of opposition to the indiscriminate land transactions between his people and the white trespassers. He had opposed the sale of lands at the Treaty of Lancaster in 1744 and always viewed new proposals with mistrust. True, he was a staunch friend of Weiser and had given every evidence of a kindly attitude toward the sons of Onas in Philadelphia, but it must be pointed out that his zeal for service was in the interest of maintaining peace and not in the profit for himself or his people.

Early in December 1748, Shikellamy had visited Bethlehem. In his last years he was a convert to Christianity as it was preached by the Moravian missionaries. On his homeward journey, he stopped at Weiser's home in Tulpehocken to visit Tarachawagon. When he returned to Shamokin, in company with the missionaries David Zeisberger and Henry Fry, he found his people suffering for want of food. On December 7, the aged sachem was taken ill with a fever. Zeisberger attended him in his illness which grew steadily worse, the patient losing his sense of hearing and speech, and on December 17 he died.[3] The body was prepared for burial by painting it in bright colors. Henry Fry built a wooden coffin and the great chieftain was buried on the bank of the "winding River," near a great buttonwood tree which stood guard over the grave until the early years of the present century. Today there is a fine monument erected over Shikellamy's grave within the limits of Sunbury on the Susquehanna Trail of the Lakes to Sea highway.

Governor Hamilton dispatched Weiser to Shamokin in April 1749 to carry condolences to the children and grandchildren of the sachem. Because of this visit, Weiser commissioned John Shikellamy, Tachnachdoris, the eldest son of the deceased vice-regent, to assume his father's position as the friend of Onas; but events proved that Shikellamy's place could never be filled. No longer could Conrad Weiser hear the innermost secrets of the Onondaga Council Fire from the lips of a tried and trusted friend.[4]

The year 1749 found Conrad Weiser engaged in many and varied activities. His duties as magistrate took him to Lancaster courts on several occasions; his diligence in tracking down debtors to Christian Lauer consumed much of his time; his reconversion to Lutheranism made him the outstanding layman to whom the coterie of Lutheran clerics brought their problems; his own expanding land interests called for surveys and the execution of patents and legal documents and he was commissioned as a seller of lots for the new town of Reading, any one of these activities was enough to consume the time and energy of an ordinary man. But Conrad Weiser was not ordinary.

Meanwhile, far to the northward in the leafy realms of Pennsylvania's woods, hundreds of Six Nations deputies were gathering to march to Philadelphia. With the French peace of 1748,

---
3. Snyder, Charles F., *Conrad Weiser and the Susquehanna Valley*, Northumberland County Historical Society Proceedings, 6:41.
4. Weiser to Governor Hamilton, April 22, 1749, Pennsylvania Archives, 2:23-24.

the strategic position they had held for eight years as a buffer between the warring white men, had come to an end and so too had the wooing of their favor by both sides. The Senecas, the Oneidas, and the other tribes would come to Philadelphia to see how things stood with their white brethren. Their visit was unheralded, uninvited, and unwelcome.

For some reason, unexplained, the plans of the Indians did not work out as they had intended. Wyoming, in Pennsylvania, was designated as the rallying point for all the nations but only forty assorted representatives arrived on the day specified. These forty decided to proceed to Philadelphia without waiting any longer and on June 28 they entered the city, escorted by Conrad Weiser, who had had no advance intelligence of their coming.[5]

After the customary perfunctory greetings, during which Governor Hamilton and Council did their best to conceal their irritation, the deputies set forth their complaints. Settlers were squatting on unpurchased lands. They prayed "that they be made to remove instantly with all their Effects, to prevent the sad Consequences which will otherwise ensue." Adroitly they pleaded poverty and hinted that some of their tribes had never received full payment for their lands. Obviously, they wanted a present and the Council decided to give them a hundred pounds worth of goods.

But Governor Hamilton was not inclined to give something for nothing. On July 7, he instructed Weiser to sound out the Senecas in the group on the question of the purchase of lands west of the Susquehanna.[6] The Indians were assured that the squatters would be forced off the unpurchased lands and their request to have their guns mended would be honored.

Sauer, the publisher, noted in his *Berichte* that this group of Indians conducted themselves quietly and contrasted their behavior with the poor behavior of Philadelphia children. On July 8, the group of forty deputies set out on their homeward journey, accompanied by Conrad Weiser. No land transactions had taken place. On July 18, the Governor issued a proclamation ordering persons living on unpurchased lands to vacate at once. It appeared that Indian affairs were settled for the time

---

5. *Berichte*, July 16, 1749.
6. *Berichte*, Pennsylvania Archives, 2:588–589.

being. The Indians fastened themselves on Weiser's hospitality at Tulpehocken, while Weiser used his opportunity to discuss the prospect of further land purchases with his guests.

If the people in Philadelphia thought that they were done with Indian affairs for 1748, they were badly mistaken. Early in August, the Governor received word from Conrad Weiser that the delayed delegation of deputies had finally arrived at his home. There were almost three hundred persons in the party. Despite all that Conrad would say or do, they were bent upon going to Philadelphia and demanding satisfaction.[7]

Weiser tried hard to dissuade the chieftains. On the evening of August 9, he held a "Council" in his own home, at which thirty-eight chieftains were present. The memorandum of the meeting was sent to Richard Peters. Canassatego once more was the spokesman for the Six Nations.

> "Brother Tarrachawagon:
> You told us last night that you looked upon our going to Philadelphia to be imprudent and you said that we brought too many of our allies with us . . . we have never been reprimanded for it after this manner, perhaps it is because you got all our Lands you wanted from us—our fate is the Same as our Cousins the Delawares and Mohicans. We asked for nothing, but you say we must not expect a Present, no, not our Belly-full of Victuals because we are so numerous . . ."

To this Weiser replied that his advice was based upon his own thinking and not upon instructions from Philadelphia "that this was not the first time I advised them. If they approved my advice well & good, if not it was well and good again as to what belonged to me."

On to Philadelphia marched the deputies, the first group returning with their tardy comrades. For nearly two weeks they had feasted at Weiser's expense at Tulpehocken and the whetted appetites were unrestrained as they wended their devastating way

---
7. Weiser to Hamilton, August 10, 1749, Colonial Records, 5:397.

toward Philadelphia. Farmers' livestock, orchards, and gardens were ravaged by the undisciplined deputies and their nondescript followers and hangers-on. Weiser's patience was severely tried as he attempted to hold their rapacity in check on the southeastward journey to Philadelphia.[8]

On August 18, the Governor and Council heard Canassatego renew the complaints against the squatters. The Governor's recent proclamation was a fine gesture, but it must be made effective. Especially objectionable was the occupation of the lands along the Juniata River which the Indians regarded as the best hunting grounds for deer. There were complaints about the murder of a nephew of Canassatego by white men and against the treatment given to the Nanticokes in Maryland.

To these complaints, the Governor and Council lent a sympathetic ear. They readily agreed to meet the requests and decided upon a present of five hundred pounds of goods. Then, the question of a new purchase was broached and after numerous conferences between Weiser and the chieftains, the limits of the new purchase were agreed upon.

The deed of 1749 is a ponderous document listing the names of all the deputies who were empowered to act for the several nations whose interests were involved.[9] Stripped of its technical terms the area sold by the Six Nations in 1749 included all the land north of the Blue Mountains between the Delaware and Susquehanna north to the junction of the Lehigh and Delaware rivers on the east and to present-day Line Mountain, south of Sunbury on the Susquehanna. All this land was purchased for the sum of five hundred pounds, paid in addition to the same amount given as a present to the Indians.

Laden with their gifts and well satisfied with themselves, the Indian cohorts left Philadelphia on August 25, 1749. Conrad Weiser was commissioned to escort them to the Susquehanna and to provide food for them along the way. From Weiser's account of this journey northward we learn that the march reached Whitemarsh, outside of Germantown, on the first day. Most of the Indians were drunk, Weiser tells us.

---

8. Watson's Annals of Philadelphia, 1:99. Also Colonial Records, 5:403–404.
9. Deed of 1749, Conrad Weiser, Interpreter, Pennsylvania Archives, 2:33–36.

On August 26, Weiser was forced to wait at Whitemarsh until the straggling drunkards caught up with the group. On this day he purchased 384 lbs. of beef from Christopher Raby, as well as other supplies for his charges. On the next day, the group crossed the Perkiomen Creek at present-day Collegeville and were fed at John Shrack's hostelry. After stopping at Marcus Huling's place, near Pottsgrove (Pottstown), the group reached the infant town of Reading on the 28th. There William Hartley's widow, Finney's tenant, supplied the necessary 490 pounds of beef and 150 pounds of flour and other necessaries. On this day Jarvislawis, a Cayuga chief, died and was buried somewhere between Reading and Tulpehocken. On the 30th of August, in driving rain, the bedraggled entourage of nearly three hundred persons arrived at Weiser's home in Tulpehocken.

There the party lingered for several days, consuming nearly 1000 pounds of beef, mutton, and pork; 575 pounds of flour; and 63 loaves of "Bread at a pens a Loaf," as Weiser itemized his account.

On September 2, the marching delegates crossed the Blue Mountains on the old Shamokin Trail between present day Bethel, Berks County, and Pine Grove, Schuylkill County. On the third, they reached James Galbreath's trading post and on the next day, they came to Chambers' Mill on the Susquehanna. There Weiser purchased a "fat cow" from the Widow Chambers. The price was three pounds and ten shillings, or approximately eighteen dollars.[10]

On September 6, Conrad gave his charges a farewell glass of liquor and "took my leave of them." His bill to the province totaled £64-3-8. There was an additional account for the care of eleven Indians who stayed at Weiser's home during the Philadelphia treaty because they were too ill to travel. Also, there was a charge for wages and wagoners who carried the sick and lame from Philadelphia.

The sons of Onas had treated their native brethren well, but from the beginning to the end, the entire responsibility was Conrad Weiser's.

---

10. Bill of Indian Expenses,Weiser MSS, 1:21.

EVICTING THE SQUATTERS

A conflict between the land claims of settlers and Indians was inevitable. Treaties and purchases served to postpone the issue during the two decades preceding 1750, but the expanding white settlements were rolling back the frontier of Pennsylvania more rapidly than diplomacy could secure title to the lands which lay beyond the confines of most recent purchases.

Land-hunger gripped rulers and subjects of the English colonies. Members of the provincial Council acquired vast tracks of wooded hillsides and fertile valleys without seeing or surveying. The Penn heirs, in whom all titles truly belonged, were enjoying the rustic life of Stoke Poges, in England, only vaguely aware of the machinations of land speculators in far-off Pennsylvania, by which their inheritance was being appropriated by greedy agents who used their salaries to pay nominal sums to their employers in exchange for patents which they made out and surveyed for themselves. Conrad Weiser's services were extremely useful to the Penns in securing Indian titles to lands which were already theirs by royal grant. We have seen how Weiser negotiated purchases from the Six Nations equal in area to several European states or several English shires for paltry-sums expended in buying gaudy garments and baubles whose glisten delighted the child-like senses of these forest children.

So too, Conrad Weiser was extremely useful to the land speculators who carved out huge manors for themselves, paying only fees simple to their liege lords of Stoke Poges. Thomas Penn's provincial agents were profuse in sounding Weiser's praises into the ears of their absent master. Was it not he who could negotiate the purchase of new lands with the Indians, whose claims must be satisfied if tenants were to take up homes in security? Certainly, the Indians' claims were nebulous and their concepts of land ownership were absurd in the light of property laws of white men. And yet, it was a very convenient arrangement for the land-hungry speculators to have the Indians appeased by token payments from the Penn treasury while they studied maps and drew up patents to themselves.

In performing his duties as an agent for the Penns, Conrad Weiser was acting in the interests of his employers and not as an accomplice of the speculators. In his relations with the Indians, he respected their interests and held their confidence. In his correspondence with Thomas Lee, of Virginia, he endeavored to advance the interests of the newly formed Ohio Company and at the same time secure fair returns to the Indians, whose lands were being purchased by Virginia. He was straightforward in these transactions, a wholesome character casting its honest shadow over an age of duplicity and subtle schemes of avarice. Perhaps he was not astute enough to detect the selfish purposes of other men, for men such as he never can think in devious ways, but he was never the dope of grasping men. He worked for his employers and tried to remember that Shikellamy had once said to the Council, "One half of Conrad belongs to the Indians."

If men of high estate in the Councils of the province were victims of land-hunger, it is not surprising that smaller men were afflicted with the same malady. Settlers' families spilled over the treaty boundaries in search of new homes and fairer fields. They squatted upon unpurchased lands in the fertile valleys west of the Susquehanna; into Sherman's Valley; into the Cumberland and along the blue Juniata, which Peter Kalm, the Swedish traveler, so aptly named the "noble river." The first trespassers were a few German families who built homes and cleared lands along the Juniata in 1740. The Indians protested and made it an issue of the treaty of 1742. Governor Thomas issued a proclamation against squatting on unpurchased lands and in 1743 these Germans were evicted by the governor's deputies. This earnest of goodwill appeased the Indians for a short time, but the problem was destined to rise again in more serious form.

Very jealously the Pennsylvania Indians guarded their rights to the Juniata region. This was the earthly "Happy Hunting Grounds" for deer. The towering mountains and crags of the upper reaches of the Susquehanna provided poor shelter for the animals and the slashes of the Allegheny slopes were unsuited for hunting. Only on the plateaus and in the foothills, could the deer be tracked. But the gentler slopes of the Juniata, the gushing streams, the dense foliage, and luxurious undergrowth of the Juniata Valley provided a natural habitat for the fleet-footed creatures and a paradise for hunters.

The eviction of the first group of trespassers did not halt the westward trek of land-hungry pioneers. They continued to enter the valleys west of the Susquehanna and the smoke curling from their cabins was viewed with alarm by Indians who felt that their domain was invaded.

The situation created by these squatters was made more complex by the fact that some of them took up their homes in the lower sections of Cumberland, an area that was in dispute between Pennsylvania and Maryland at the time. Whose duty was it to force them to leave?

Because the English colonies were at war with France during the years between 1740 and 1748, the Indians made no demands upon Pennsylvania to evict the unwelcome intruders. However, in 1749, when nearly three hundred Indians virtually invaded the city, formal demands were made upon Governor Hamilton to burn down the cabins of the trespassers on unpurchased lands. Governor Hamilton promised that the squatters would be removed.

Quite naturally the eviction proceedings became the duty of the magistrates and Conrad Weiser was a magistrate of Lancaster County, the county nearest to the disputed lands. As an expert on Indian affairs, Weiser was asked to undertake the expedition against the settlers, most of whom were Scotch-Irish, who had defied the governor's proclamation ordering them to evacuate their cabins and return to purchased lands. Weiser's advice to the governor was positive in its insistence that the tenants should be removed from the unpurchased lands. He willingly accepted a portion of the responsibility and used his influence to prevail upon other magistrates to join the expedition. Because of the delicate nature of the mission, Governor Hamilton directed his personal secretary, Richard Peters, to lead the group of provincial officials, empowering him to appoint special deputies and to call upon the sheriffs of the outlying counties.[11]

Weiser and Peters set out from Philadelphia, together, on May 5, 1750. These two men had served the province for a score of

---

11. Richard Peters: Account of his expedition to evict the squatters, Colonial Records, 5:440–449.

years and had always worked together in the solution of problems growing out of Indian affairs. Now they were associated in action as well as in planning. They traveled to George Croghan's farm in Cumberland and there they were joined by several Indians. Some of the Delaware of Shamokin were invited to accompany the expedition as witnesses that the terms of the treaty were observed. The two sons of Shikellamy were among the Indians who joined the punitive expedition at the rallying point at Croghan's farm. At a conference held at Croghan's home, Weiser made his speech to the gathering of Lancaster and Cumberland magistrates and the other deputized officials, prevailing upon all to unite themselves in the venture.

On May 22, the band of officials and their Indian associates reached a white settlement on the Juniata, approximately 25 miles west of the Susquehanna. There were five cabins built at that point. The tenants were ordered to appear before the magistrates to defend themselves as best they could. The defendants pleaded that the land belonged to the Penns and therefore they had assumed their rights. They admitted that they had ignored the governor's proclamation and pleaded for mercy. Three of the trespassers submitted to arrest and agreed to appear in court, but two brothers, named Galloway, resisted arrest and escaped.

The magistrates and sheriffs then entered the Galloway cabin, removed all the furnishings and Richard Peters took possession of the hut in the name of the province. There arose the question of what to do about the empty cabin. Weiser insisted that it should be burnt to the ground, "giving it as his firm Opinion that if all the Cabins were left standing the Indians would conceive such a contemptible Opinion of the Government that they would come themselves in the winter, murder the People and set the Houses on Fire." Acting on Weiser's advice the Galloway cabin was destroyed.

The official party moved eastward along the Juniata and came to the home of Andrew Lycon, a squatter. Lycon pointed a loaded musket at the magistrates and the sheriff seized him. This action took place in the presence of some Indians who had camped near the Lycon cabin. The Indians demanded that the cabin should be burned and Peters was forced to bow to their demands.

Peters offered no explanation of Weiser's reasons for asking to be excused before the mission was completed. In his report, he suggested that perhaps Conrad would make his position clear in his own way. This Weiser attempted to do in a letter to Peters, dated June 20, 1750, a letter designed to justify his own conduct in his eyes of the "Honorable Proprietors" on two counts:

> Notwithstanding my Obligations by the Honorable Proprietors and my goodwill to serve them on all Occasions and my late promises to reconnoiter the province with C. & P. (Croghan and Peters) am very scrupulous in my mind and find great difficulty o perform because I know I cannot do it without giving great Offense to the Six Nations.

He goes on to explain that his presence on the trail which led to the Ohio country would cause a great deal of speculation among the Indians of the West. They would conclude that he was coming as an ambassador with a message and with gifts. So long as he had stayed north of the Tuscarora Path his activities would not be misinterpreted. "What shall I say to the Sinnikers (Senecas), Cayugers and Onontagios . . . they would certainly suspect the governor of Pennsylvania of having something in view in their detriment in undertaking the journey." To travel on that path without the advance knowledge of the Onondaga Council would be unsafe, he declared and then added significantly, "I could get Andrew Montour and Shikellamy's son to go long but they would shelter behind me as well as John Bartram and Lewis Evans and say, you are a great man among the Six Nations, what you do we leave you to answer for the whole . . . and if things would turn out wrong they would lay the whole blame on me."

This letter, obviously, is designed to excuse his previous action in deserting the magistrates at Shippensburg and to decline a further suggestion that he undertake another mission to the Ohio. While it is not clear just what errand had been required of him, it is very clear that he was unwilling to act without the expressed approval of the Six Nations Council whose jurisdiction he recognized.

There is a second possible explanation of his reluctance to continue in the expedition to evict the trespassers. Conrad Weiser was in the employ of Maryland while he was serving Pennsylvania as an agent. Thomas Cresap, a Maryland agent, had encouraged settlers to clear lands in the disputed territory despite the Pennsylvania proclamation. The lands at the lower Cumberland were claimed by the Penns and the Calverts and the eviction proceedings involve both provinces. Complaints against Cresap had reached Weiser before the party of magistrates set out for Cumberland and he had communicated them to Edmund Jennings, the Indian commissioner of Maryland. Weiser did not receive a reply from Jennings until after his return from Cumberland. In a letter dated August 29, 1750, Jennings assured Weiser that Colonel Cresap had acted without the approval of Maryland. It appears that the Indians had reported that Cresap had had encouragement from his superiors. Jennings assured Weiser that this alarm was "without Foundation, and I cannot question your effective Endeavours to set us right in the opinions of our good Friends, and the Six Nations, if they have been abused with false Reports."

The final boundary between Pennsylvania and Maryland was not fixed until 1760 when David Rittenhouse, a Pennsylvania German, surveyed the line which in 1763 was re-surveyed by Mason and Dixon. In the struggle for the disputed areas, both provinces found it to their advantage to people the lands with settlers who would be loyal to their parent colony. Weiser must have sensed the troubles which would arise if Marylanders were evicted from their settlements by Pennsylvania magistrates and his own position as an agent of Maryland would have been very trying.

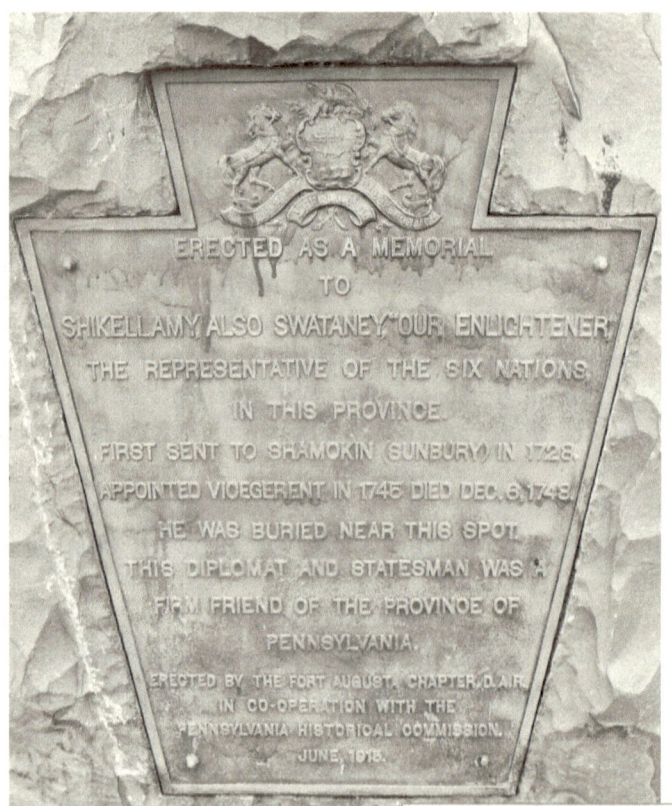

Marker near Shikellamy's grave in Sunbury, Pennsylvania. The actual grave is likely paved over and was allegedly dug up in the 1800s.

Colonial Governor James Hamilton of Pennsylvania

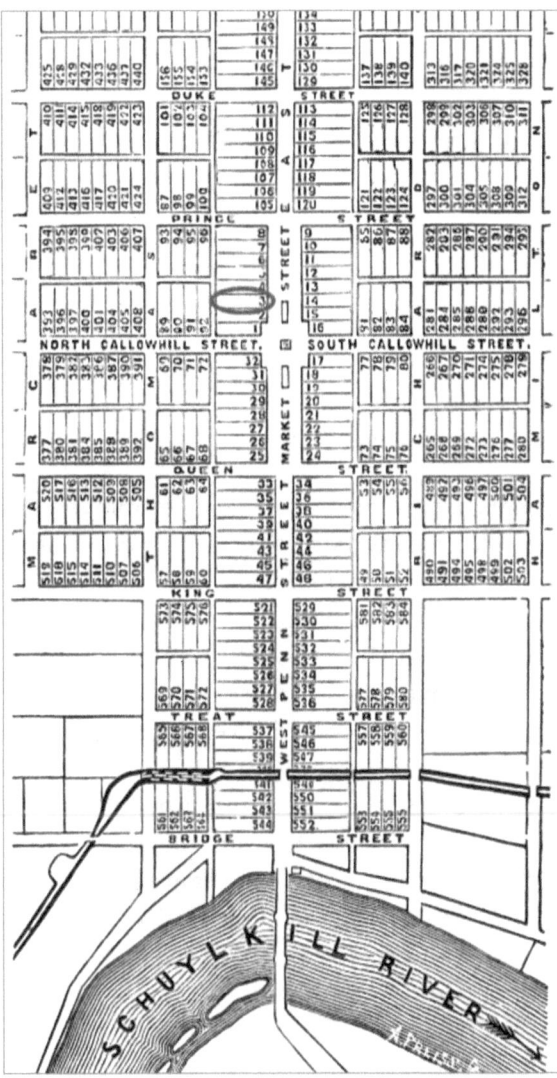

Lot plan for the City of Reading. Weiser was responsible for selling the lots and purchased Lot 3 for himself. Nearby were lots for the Muhlenbergs and Peter Knorr.

CHAPTER XII

Rival Claims

THE OHIO CONFLICT

Christopher Gist, a surveyor, was employed by Virginia in staking out the land claims of that province west of the Alleghenies. A Delaware Indian asked Gist the following question: "The French claim all of the land north of the Ohio and the English claim all of the land south of the Ohio. Just where is the Indians' land?" We do not have Gist's answer, but it has been suggested that the Happy Hunting Grounds were somewhere above, in the Ohio skies.

In the struggle for the vast domains of the colonial west, France and England vied with each other so intently that the Indian's claims were frequently disregarded or, at best, treated very lightly. In 1748, Conrad Weiser had raised the English flag on the banks of the Ohio River. In 1749, Celeron de Bienville, a French officer, buried some leaden plates in the earth near the confluence of the rivers at the forks of the Ohio. The plates bore an inscription in French claiming all that region in the name of Louis XV of France.[1]

---

1. Translation of the inscription: "In the year 1749, during the reign of Louis XV, King of France, W. E. Celeron, Commander of a detachment sent by the Marquis de La Gallissoniere, Commander-in-chief of New France to restore tranquility in some native villages of these districts have buried the plates at the confluence of the Ohio and Tchadakion, on this 29th of July, near the river Ohio, as a monument of our having retaken possession of the said River, and of those that fall into it, and of all the lands on both sides as far as the source of the said rivers, as well as of those of which the former kings of France has possessed, partly by force of arms, partly by treaties, especially by those of Ryswick. Utrecht and Aix-la-Chappelle."

Two European giants were struggling for empire in the wilderness of the New World, each party in the conflict courting the favor of the natives in the hope of appeasing them and gaining them as allies in the conflict. Despite all promises and blandishments, the ultimate objective of both giants was to acquire the Indians' lands for their own empire. In such a contest the premium was high on cunning and adroitness on the part of the principal actors in the absorbing drama.

One tremendous advantage lay with the French. There was only one New France, but there were thirteen daughters of England, all jealous of each other and disinclined to act in unison. From Onontijo, the governor of Canada, the Indians heard messages which were as true on the Miami or Ohio Rivers west of the setting sun, as they were on Lake Champlain or up the St. Lawrence River. But messages in English from Onas in Pennsylvania, from Corlear in New York, or from Assaryquoah in Virginia, contradicted each other and the Indian was confused. The English cause was weakened in the struggle for Indian support.

The Ohio country lay west of the settlements of Pennsylvania and Maryland. The charters of both proprietary colonies fixed definite limits in their western boundaries and Lord Baltimore's domain stopped far short of the disputed area. The western limits of William Penn's grant were undetermined in 1750, but it was reasonable to assume that the forks of the Ohio at present-day Pittsburgh, lay well within the specified five degrees west of the Delaware River, which Charles Stuart had warranted to him. Virginia's dominion by her second charter, extended vaguely into space, allotting to her all lands west and northwest of her latitudes, whatever that might be made to mean.

Early in the eighteenth century, Pennsylvania had taken the lead in the fur trade with the western Indians and it was a Pennsylvanian, Conrad Weiser, who first laid claim to the western lands in English interests. But Weiser was an agent of Virginia as well as of Pennsylvania and some of the presents he had carried to the Ohio in 1749 were given in the name of the royal province of Virginia. Once the English claims were fixed in the Ohio Valley it was urged that Pennsylvania should build a fort at the forks of the Ohio, but the Quaker Assembly of that province was unwilling to compromise with its policy of peaceful penetration. In this way, Penn's province lost its leadership in the west and the more aggressive Virginians seized the opportunity to exploit the rich areas "west and northwest." Enterprising Virginians, led by Colonel Thomas Lee and Lawrence Washington organized a vast real estate venture which was known as the Ohio Company and the lands they marked for sale lay largely within the present borders of Pennsylvania.

At the Lancaster treaty of 1744, the Six Nations had sold lands to Virginia "west of the setting sun." In the figurative speech of the Indians, this phrase might have meant two things. In one sense it would have been interpreted in the terms of the English's "sea-to-sea," or, as the Indians later maintained, it might have meant only to the summit of the highest peaks of the Alleghenies. The Virginians chose to apply the broader interpretation and at Lancaster, they promised a present at some later time to pay for these far-away lands.

Colonel Thomas Lee of Stratford Manor, near Williamsburg, Virginia, was the moving spirit of the negotiations at Lancaster and through the six years that intervened between 1744 and his death in December 1750, the founder of that illustrious American family of Lees never lost sight of his objective. It will be remembered that Colonel Lee was skeptical about trusting Conrad Weiser at the Lancaster treaty. But the close association of these two men at Lancaster led to a friendship which was carried on by correspondence without interruption until Lee's death.

Among the papers of Weiser, there are numerous letters from the distinguished Virginian to the German friend in Tulpehocken. Would Conrad collect Indian songs and have them set to music; what were the marriage customs among the Indians; did they esteem chastity before marriage or were they promiscuous in their sexual relationships? These are but a few of the questions Lee asked of Weiser. In some cases, we have copies of official reports which Weiser sent to his Virginia friend, but how interesting would be the letters Weiser wrote to Lee in replying to those intimate affairs of the Indians. We should learn Indian lore two generations older than either George Henry Loskiel or John Heckewelder were able to observe.

One request which Lee made to Weiser will bear discussion here. Could Conrad secure some Rhenish grapevines and send them to Stratford? Would they thrive in the southern climate? A subsequent letter from Lee acknowledged receiving such grape vines. The Rhenish grape was brought to Pennsylvania by the early German settlers and it flourished for a time, but later the vines were destroyed in a blight.

> John Adams in Massachusetts begged his friend Benjamin Franklin to send him twigs of the Rhenish grape. As a guest in Philadelphia, Adams had tasted superior wines and had learned that the wines owed their delicacy to grapes of a peculiar variety grown by the German settlers of Pennsylvania. Franklin obliged his legal friend and sent a parcel of twigs, explaining that he had secured them from a settler "over sixty miles from this place."

On February 27, 1750, Colonel Lee wrote to Weiser as follows: ". . . ever since I have known you I have found you a very honest man and that you have made use of that Influence you have with the Indians for the good of His Majesty's subjects, as well as for the Indians whose real interest is to be Friends with us . . . and in the Light I have constantly represented you to this Government (Virginia)."

Lee then explained that he had arranged for the "King's present," ordering the goods directly from London. This present was to be given to the Six Nations as payment for lands sold to Virginia at Lancaster in 1744. Could Weiser prevail upon the deputies from the Six Nations to come to Fredericksburg in Virginia to receive their gifts—"I shall rely upon you to bring the Indians Here and to assist me." Because Virginia was a royal colony, the grant to the Ohio Company came "immediately from the King" Lee explained, and therefore Weiser would be exerting himself in the public good and in His Majesty's service. The appeal for Weiser's aid in this matter was based upon making "a strong Settlement and carry on a fair and extensive Trade, by these means to gain the Indians to the British Interest" in spite of the crafty French. The letter is worded carefully, submerging the interests of Virginia and the Ohio Company, declaring that there were "no selfish ends where the Public good is greatly concerned, this I assure you is the principle I shall be governed by and because you have the same way of thinking I have the greatest Esteem for You."[2]

It is evident that Weiser had convinced Lee that the power of the Six Nations extended over all Indians, in Ohio, as well as in New York and Pennsylvania. Therefore, the Indians to be appeased by the Ohio Company were the New York sachems who would, in turn, command the Delawares, Shawnees, Miamis, and Wyandots to relinquish their lands to the English. And yet, before the Six Nations could be approached, Weiser had to be won over to Virginia's cause and the adroit phrasing of Lee's letter was designed to minimize the land interests of Virginia gentlemen while the public weal was stressed.

Fredericksburg on the Rappahannock was farther south than Annapolis and we have seen that the wise men of Onondaga consistently refused to travel southward beyond the limits of Pennsylvania. The old feud between the Six Nations and the Catawbas was not ended despite a series of truces which Weiser had arranged. The prospect of a treaty place on the Rappahannock did not appeal to Weiser and he pointed out to Lee that the Six Nations would not venture so close to Catawba lands. However, Weiser informed Lee that he had instructed Shikellamy's sons to send a message to Onondaga saying that the treaty goods would be distributed on the Rappahannock.

On June 20, Lee replied, stating that he was disappointed that the Indians would not come to Fredericksburg, "The King's present is now here." What should be done with the goods? The woolens "may be spoiled and Powder is a dangerous Article to keep." Lee complained that he thought Weiser could have prevailed upon the Indians to "make a brisker notion to receive the King's present." Now, urged Lee, try again, and promise a bigger Present than ever before.[3]

Beyond the towering Alleghenies, events were moving swiftly. Weiser was receiving complaints from Shamokin that Indians

---
2. Lee to Weiser, Peters MSS, 3:5.
3. Ibid., 9. Again Lee stressed that his only interest was to promote the King's service.

were being murdered by settlers. Joncaire, the Frenchman, was building a chain of forts in the Ohio country. Governor Clinton of New York sent out alarming letters to the English governors, warning that the Ohio Indians were all going over to the French.[4]

Once again Conrad Weiser was dispatched to Onondaga in the summer of 1750. It was hoped that he could stem the tide. Even though the English colonies were disunited in their dealings with the Indians, there was one voice that could speak to the Six Nations in the united interest of all of them, and that voice was Conrad Weiser's.

WARRAGHIYAGEY

Warraghiyagey was the Mohawk name of Colonel William Johnson, the Irishman who came to New York in 1738, aged twenty-three. Asked by his wealthy uncle, Admiral Peter Warren, a sea dog of the Elizabethan school, young Johnson set up trading posts in the Mohawk country of the upper Hudson and soon gained the favor of the easternmost tribe of the Six Nations, the Mohawks. With lavish hands, he wined and dined them in his home at Mount Johnson on the banks of the Mohawk River. His trade flourished briskly because his store counters were popular from the Susquehanna at Oquaga, near present-day Binghamton, to Oswego on Lake Ontario.

Soon after his establishment in Mohawk country, Johnson had purchased a Palatine immigrant girl's redemption time and for five years he and Catherine Wissenberg lived as man and wife, even though the marriage ceremony did not occur until shortly before Catherine's death in 1745. Life and morals were loose at Mount Johnson and drunken Indians delighted in accepting generous gifts from their wealthy friend Warraghiyagey. In less than ten years, Johnson had made himself the white father of the Mohawk nation.

The other five nations of the powerful Iroquois Confederacy did not sit at Warraghiyagey's table and did not share in the presents that their Maqua brethren received from Johnson's bountiful store. When in 1746 William Johnson was commissioned as a

---
4. A series of letters, Pennsylvania Archives, 2nd ser., 6:75–77.

colonel by Governor Clinton, in order that he might organize an invasion of Canada, the Mohawk followed cheerily, but the other five nations remained inactive, silent, and glum. The Six Nations were about to become the Five Nations of the Confederacy as they had been for centuries before 1709 when the addition of the Tuscaroras had augmented the number to six. The Mohawks were under the spell of Warraghiyagey.

Conrad Weiser, too, had his early Indian training in the villages of the Mohawks. But by 1750, thirty-two years had come and gone since the boy Conrad departed from his father's household in Schoharie to make his home among the Maqua. A full generation of time had passed since Weiser had migrated from his farmstead south of "Mohocks Indian Town" to go to Pennsylvania. The younger members of the Mohawks' nation did not know Weiser.

Even though Conrad had made many journeys into the Indian country during the years between 1737 and 1750, his route of travel had not brought him into the Mohawk Valley, where he might have renewed his old associations. On most of his journeys, he had reached the Onondaga Councils west of the Mohawk Trail by climbing the mountains of central Pennsylvania and southern New York. His trips to Albany in 1745 and 1746 had been by way of the Hudson River and north of Albany, not northwest, the direction from which the Mohawks River flowed into the Hudson. By 1750 he was known only as Tarachawagon, his Onondaga name, and Ziguras, as he was known to the Mohawks, was forgotten.

If their brothers, the Mohawks, were being showered with gifts from Mount Johnson, why should the remaining Five Nations not look to the French Governor in Canada for favor? It was natural that they should.

On August 15, 1750, Conrad Weiser set out from his home in Tulpehocken, turning the faces of his two horses eastward as he passed through Maxatawny, Bethlehem, and Nazareth, to arrive at Smithfield on the Delaware on August 18. He was on his way to Onondaga to urge the Six Nations to come to Virginia to receive payments for lands which the Ohio Company wished to acquire. He was on his way to investigate the causes of many disturbing rumors which tended to show that the Six Nations were deserting to the French. His route would take him through the Mohawk country, through Schoharie, to Mount Johnson where Warraghiyagey reigned, through the land of the Oneidas, through the villages of the Cayugas to Onondaga. He traveled alone.[5]

While Weiser rested on the Delaware, Colonel William Johnson was listening to ominous words spoken by old Hendricks, one of the colonel's Indian lieutenants. At a conference held at Mount Johnson on August 18, Hendricks charged that Johnson, as well as all other Englishmen, were secretly conniving with the French to destroy all Indians. Johnson wrote to Governor Clinton: "I cannot omit acquainting your Excellency how insolent Nickus & Henrick etc have behaved now at my House. They entered it in a great Passion, would not even shake hands with me."[6] Nickus, the Indian, had just returned from Canada, where the European's plot against all Indians was known "by all in Canada" and that the Governor of Canada had shown a council of Indians a huge belt of wampum, supposedly sent to him by Governor Clinton in confirmation of the scheme. But Onontijo would not enter into the nefarious plot, he told his Indian audience. "This . . . gave me three days of hard work," wrote Johnson to Clinton, but he succeeded in convincing the Indians present at the conference that the Governor of Canada was lying. In his report to Clinton, Johnson warned that he had heard that the French were planning to build a fort at Onondaga.

The Treaty of Aix-la-Chappelle, ending the War of the Austrian Succession, did not end King George's War in the New World. Actual hostilities ceased for a time, but the rivalry between France and England in America went on more keenly than ever. In Europe, there were eight years of peace between 1748 and the Seven Years' War which began in Europe in 1756. Open conflict between armed forces began in western Pennsylvania in 1754, two years before England and France were embattled in Europe. Statesmen would have been blind, indeed, if they had not foreseen such an eventuality in 1750. Governor Clinton, alarmed by Johnson's reports, again urged Governor Hamilton of Pennsylvania to act to

---
5. Weiser's Journal, Colonial Records, 5:470–480.
6. William Johnson to Governor Clinton, August 18, 1750, Pennsylvania Archives, 2nd ser., 6:79–82.

secure the steadfast loyalty of the Ohio Indians. Hamilton replied that he saw no cause for immediate alarm.[7] Unfortunate for him, his two most trusted agents in dealing with Indian affairs were absent from Philadelphia. Richard Peters was in Cumberland evicting squatters as Conrad Weiser was on his way to Onondaga on horseback.

On August 25, Weiser reached Albany. He had traveled by way of Kingston and at Catskill, he crossed to the east bank of the Hudson "for the sake of a better Road," as he reports in his journal.[8] Perhaps the east bank held other inducements for him, as well as convenience, for we find him spending August 24 at the "Manor of Levingston," or the spot in which he had spent several days of boyhood, as one of the Palatine refugees, indentured to Livingston Manor to work out their passage money by tapping pine trees for resin, pitch, and tar.

On Sunday, August 26, Weiser met with the Mohawks, Hendricks, and Nickus, in Albany, the chiefs who had reported the European's plot to Johnson a few days earlier. To Weiser these chiefs said nothing about the plot, at least there is no mention of it in Conrad's journal and a matter of such significance would have been noted by him. Instead, they told him that they had engaged in the recent war against the French and had been prisoners in Canada. They complained that the French had abused them.

Weiser entertained his two native friends, Hendricks and Nickus, at a public house, where he loosened their tongues with "several Bottles of Wine." He learned that almost all the Onondagas had accepted the "French Religion." His Mohawk companions informed him that Colonel Johnson had a commission from the Governor of Carolina to try to effect peace in the ancient quarrel between the Six Nations and the Catawbas. The commission came from Carolina, said the Mohawks, but Weiser noted that they spoke of Assaryquoah, which was the Indian name of the Governor of Virginia, as Weiser so well knew, because it had been conferred upon him for the first time at Onondaga when he acted in the capacity of Governor Gooch. According to the account given

---

7. Ibid., 75–76. Governor Clinton complained to the London Lord's office that the Governor of Pennsylvania was "too confident."
8. Pennsylvania Archives, supra.

him, Johnson had already approached the Six Nations Council on the matter. Hendricks told Weiser privately that Johnson would not succeed as a peacemaker but if he, Hendrick, were well paid for his trouble, he was sure he could bring about a peace between the ancient enemies. The wily old chieftain had guessed, incorrectly, that Weiser's mission was once again on behalf of Virginia to negotiate a peace with the Catawbas and that therefore he could secure funds from Weiser.

From Albany, Weiser rode westward to Schoharie and three days were spent renewing his old acquaintances who "were very glad to see me" after twenty-one years. In his conversation with Indians in Mohawks Indiantown,[9] he heard once again the story of the defection of the Onondagas, Cayugas, and Senecas. They were all turned Frenchmen. Some Oneidas were inclined to join them. The Mohawks complained that they were abused by the other nations because they remained loyal to the English. Indian affairs were being neglected and the governor of New York refused to speak to the Indians.

On the last day of August, Weiser took leave of his old friends and set out for Fort Hunter on the Mohawk, three miles from Mount Johnson, the home of Warraghiyagey. He was caught in a heavy downpour of rain and lost his way. Fortunately, he met two Mohawks in the woods and the braves guided him to the neighborhood of Fort Hunter.

In the heart of the Mohawk country, Weiser held a conference with the Indians on September 1. Two chiefs, Brant and Seth, were among those present. The Brant mentioned could not have been the notorious Joseph Brant, who scourged Cherry Valley during the Revolutionary War. Joseph Brant was only seven years old in 1750. The full name of Nickus mentioned earlier in this account was Nickus Brant and it is possible that he is the one mentioned by Weiser as being present at Hunter's Fort.

It will be recalled that Hendricks had broached the matter of a Catawba peace to Weiser in Albany *privately*. Therefore, Nickus Brant would not have heard what took place over the wine bottles in the Albany public house. At the conference, the assembled

---

9. There are reasons to lead us to believe that the Mohawks' Indiantown referred to was the place of abode of young Weiser and his family before coming to Pennsylvania in 1729.

Mohawks wanted to know the purpose of Weiser's mission and they asked pointedly whether it had anything to do with the Catawbas. Weiser told them that his errand grew out of some provisions of the Lancaster Treaty of 1744 and that the King of England had sent a fine present to the Six Nations.

The Mohawk conference was held in the forenoon of September 1. When it was ended, Conrad Weiser made his way to Mount Johnson, there to be cordially received by the master, Colonel William himself. For a full day of twenty-four hours Conrad Weiser, Indian agent, and interpreter for Pennsylvania, Maryland, and Virginia, was the guest of Johnson, commissioner of Indian Affairs for the province of New York.

Conrad "was hospitably entertained by the colonel." The two men discussed Indian affairs at great length and each confided to the other matters of their immediate interests. Weiser told Johnson the purpose of his mission and Johnson showed Weiser a copy of a letter which the Governor of South Carolina had written to Clinton, urging New York's intercession in bringing about a Catawba peace. Johnson explained that he had already undertaken to arrange a treaty between the Catawbas and the Six Nations, the plan being to invite several Catawba chiefs to Fort Hunter, near Mount Johnson, and then negotiate there.

"We both agreed," records Weiser, "that it was best for me not to say anything about (at Onondaga) the Catawbas because he had made, it is to be hoped, a good beginning."[10]

THE RUSTED CHAIN

The Chain of Friendship, which for twenty years had been brightened by a series of treaties between Pennsylvania and the Six Nations, was losing it luster when Conrad Weiser visited the New York Indian Council in 1750. The holy water of the French priests was proving to be more potent than the firewater of the English traders, and external sprinklings in the sacrament of baptism gained more loyal supporters for Onontiquoah, the French king, than alcoholic spirits working internally could win for the deputies of the king of England. The nations west of the Mohawks

---
10. Weiser's Journal, supra.

were converted to Catholicism and their loyalties were rapidly turning away from the English to His Most Catholic Majesty, the King of France.

These ominous facts were learned by Weiser while he traveled westward from Colonel William Johnson's home on the Mohawk River. Everywhere he went he heard the same story from the Indians who confided with him "out in the Bushes," or secretly.

Westward from the Mohawk country, Weiser sought the hospitality of the Pickert family at Canajoharie, near Palatine Bridge. One of Weiser's sisters had married Nicholas Pickert and Conrad's visit resulted in a reunion of family ties. During his visit, Conrad was impressed by the evidence of the attainments of his young nephew. John Pickert, who had already mastered English and Dutch and could speak the Mohawk tongue "tolerable well." Later Weiser recommended John Pickert to the Mohawk Council to become his successor as interpreter "after I have grown old and no longer able to travel." The interpreter was now fifty-four years old.

Another advantage that Conrad extracted from his sister's family was to exchange his tired Tulpehocken horses for fresh mounts just before he entered the wilderness leading to the land of the Oneidas. One horse was exchanged at Pickert's and another at George Coat's, the last English settlement on the Mohawk.

On September 6, Weiser reached the Oneidas' town and on the following day, a Council was summoned. The wise men of Oneida were informed of the mission on behalf of Virginia and invited to send deputies to a larger Council at the Six Nations capital at Onondaga. This, the Oneidas, agreed to do and in addition, they sent fleet messengers forward to inform the Onondaga chiefs of Tarachawagon's coming. Among other things the sachems of Oneida plied Weiser with questions about negotiations for peace with the Catawbas but, very adroitly, Conrad parried them and avoided making any statements about the progress of Colonel Johnson's plans to effect a settlement.

At Oneida, Weiser heard the grievances which the Six Nations had against the English. They complained of the men at Albany; of the neglect shown their warriors during the recent war; of the suffering of the families of braves who were captured by the French and held prisoners in Canada while the needs of their wives and children were not heeded by the English at Albany. Corlear, Governor Clinton, would not speak to them or listen to them. He learned of the success of proselyting priests in converting "Onondagas to the French Religion." Much of this he learned from the lips of the aged Disononto, an Oneida chieftain, who had fought under Colonel Pieter Schuyler during King William's War.

At Tuscarora Town, eighteen miles west of Oneida, Weiser was confronted with more distressing news. Canassatego, "the Word" of the Six Nations, had died a few hours ago. Canassatego, the friend of Weiser, who had led the many delegations of the Six Nations to treaties in Pennsylvania, was no more. He was the greatest man of all the nations and his name meant, the Word. Shikellamy was gone; Tocanuntie, the Black Prince, died in a French prison camp during the recent war; and Caxhayan, the trusted messenger and protégé of Count Zinzendorf, had succumbed during the return trip of the deputies to their northern villages after the Philadelphia purchase in 1749. Twenty other chiefs had died during that excursion. Of all the coterie of chiefs with whom Weiser had dealt, only Saristaquoah[11] still lived at Onondaga.

The death of the "Word" increased Weiser's difficulties. No Indian Councils could be held with all the Six Nations in mourning for their chief spokesman. To appear in Council would be an affront to the memory of the deceased until a ceremony of wiping away the tears was performed. Such a ceremony might ordinarily require weeks or months of lamentation in preparation of the funeral ritual.

If we needed to find conclusive testimony that Conrad Weiser was highly esteemed by the Six Nations it would be proven beyond a doubt by the import of the second message Weiser received while he lingered in Tuscarora Town. "The Council had upon a second thought resolved to hear me, though contrary to the ancient custom" and "notwithstanding the melancholy Event that befell Onondaga."

On the morning of September 9, Weiser left Tuscarora Town and set out for Six Nations capital. He was accompanied by Gechdachery, an old man who sang a song of lamentation as they rode

---

11. Saristaquoah was one of the Indians who had befriended Weiser and his party during the trying experience of the mid-winter Journey of 1737. See Chapter 3.

along the Indian path. The theme of the mournful song was that former friends were no more, that evil Spirits reigned the earth, that they would "bring forth Thorns and Briars." Gechdachery's brother, Soterwanachty was one of the chiefs who had died during the return trip from Philadelphia a year earlier. Weiser comforted the bereaved man with thoughts of God's omnipotence to which the Indian "said Amen in his way."

Deep gloom shrouded Onondaga. Saristaquoah came to see Weiser in his cabin, explaining that the other chiefs were in mourning. Four days passed while Weiser awaited the assembling of the deputies. The Cayugas and Senecas sent word that they could not come. The Senecas gave no reason for their failure to appear. The westernmost nation was almost completely under the spell of the French. Jean Couer, or Joncaire, as the English called him, had recently passed through the Seneca country on his way to building French forts in the Ohio country. He had boasted that he would drive away the English with the assistance of the Indians. The Cayugas empowered the Oneidas to act for them at the general council. The Mohawks were not interested. They were the wards of the generous Warrachiyagey, William Johnson, whose larder never became empty.

While Weiser waited for the deputies of the other three nations (Onondagas, Oneidas, and Tuscaroras) to assemble, he learned many things which confirmed the rumors he had heard about defections to the French. The French priests were giving presents of silver and gold; converts were taken to Montreal to be greeted by Onontijo in person; Onontijo told them he would be their Guardian, they had no need for the council fires any longer.

Some of the older chiefs looked upon the turn of events with apprehension. They told Weiser that hey had warned their people that the French would "make Slaves of them." Some of the chiefs mocked the converts, saying "Go and get baptized by your Father and bring home fine Cloathes, that we may get some drink." Weiser's comment on this is worth observing here. "I saw plain that they do not pay any Respect to any Religion, let it come from where it will, if they do not get (gain) by it."

Before the Council could enter upon the business for which it was summoned, it was necessary that appropriate tributes be paid to the deceased Canassatego. Weiser, as the representative of Assaryquoah, the governor of Virginia, gave a large belt of Wampum "to cover the grave" of the "Word." After the ritual was performed, the ambassador was invited to state his business.

Very briefly Tarachawagon told the Council that Virginia had purchased the presents to be given in exchange for lands sold at Lancaster in 1744. These presents were at Fredericksburg in Virginia, where the English king would kindle a council fire on the banks of the Potomac, "where you may sit in Safety as under the Shadow of a great Tree."

Even though Weiser requested an immediate answer to his invitation to come to Virginia, the Six Nations Council chose to deliberate for several days. On September 15 they told him that they would send their answer by messengers who would follow Weiser's homeward journey. Two days later, while Weiser was in Oneida Town, the messengers from Onondaga arrived and a Council of Oneidas was summoned.

The Six Nations declined the invitation. The white man's country was filled with evil spirits "that kill us and we are now . . . Orphans." The last journey to Philadelphia had cost too many lives and Fredericksburg was much deeper in the "Land where White Man Dwell," therefore the evil spirits would be deadlier. Why did Assaryquoah not send the goods to Albany by water?

Weiser was at a great disadvantage. The Oneida Council could not act for the entire Six Nations, even if he could prevail upon the members to change their position. The best that he could do was to warn that Virginia might see fit to give the presents to the Ohio Indians themselves if the Six Nations did not come to claim it. The Oneidas replied that the Ohio Indians were their wards and had no right to receive presents unless the Six Nations gave them their share of a general present. At Onondaga, Weiser had been told "over and over" that the Ohio Indians had no right to sell lands.

Following the same route of travel he had used to reach the Indian country, Weiser set out on his homeward journey, reaching Bethlehem in Pennsylvania on September 30, 1750. From that town he wrote to his friend Richard Peters, deploring the defection of the Indians.[12] "He that is now on the head of affairs

---

12. Penn Papers, Official Correspondence, 5:63. Also in Colonial Records, 5:467.

is a professed Roman Catholic, and altogether devoted to the French. The French priests have made a hundred Converts of the Onondagers; that is to say, Men, Women and Children, and they are all cloathed and walk in the finest Cloathes, dressed with Silver and Gold, and I believe that the English Interest among the Six Nations can be of no consideration any more. The Indians speak with contempt of the New Yorkers and Albany People, and much the same of the rest of the English Colonies." The chain of friendship had tarnished.

On October 1, Weiser reached his home in Tulpehocken. Three days later he wrote to Colonel Thomas Lee,[13] Commissioner of Indian Affairs in Virginia, stating that his mission had failed, but Lee never read Weiser's letter. The founder of the great Lee dynasty of America had breathed his last, late in 1750, on the same day that King George II in England affixed his signature to a document appointing Thomas Lee of Stratford, royal governor of Virginia.

On October 10,[14] Richard Peters relayed Weiser's ominous accounts to the Penns in London.[15] On the 16th, Christopher Sauer's German newspaper published detailed accounts of the success of the Jesuit missionaries working among the Six Nations.[16] On the same day, Governor James Hamilton recommended to his Executive Council that Conrad Weiser should be sent to Albany with a present for the Six Nations as a "message of Condolence on the death of their Sachems."[17] The Chain of Friendship had grown rusty and dull, now Pennsylvania would try to brighten it once more.[18]

---

13. Weiser MSS, 1:28.
14. Penn Papers, Indian Affairs, 1:56–69.
15. On October 3, 1750, Richard Peters wrote to Weiser, informing him that Professor Kalm, the Swedish traveler, had reported that the French were erecting forts on the Ohio River; Peters MSS, 3:30. Also *Pennsylvania Magazine of History and Biography*, 29:455–456.
16. *Berichte*, October 16, 1750.
17. Colonial Records, 5:487.
18. Much of the material contained in the account of the Onondaga Journal is extracted from Weiser's Journal (supra), but there are additional references to be found in the Penn Papers, Indian Affairs (supra), Logan MSS, 11:35, and Weiser MSS; Case 18 of the Historical Society of Pennsylvania.

Sir William Johnson

CHAPTER XIII

Building Bridgeheads for Peace

The scope of Indian affairs was greatly increased after 1750. Thousands of immigrants were crowding American shores, hoping to find new homes and farms in the new world. The impact of this mass migration was felt most directly by the middle colonies, New York and Pennsylvania. Glowing accounts of rich farmlands had been carried back to the distressed people of the old world, and longingly they sought a chance to begin life anew. Provincial proprietors welcomed the influx of new settlers, particularly those skilled in agriculture. Their arrival would rapidly increase the value of lands in the "back country" and their homesteads near the frontiers would serve as a buffer of protection against Indian incursions.

To secure title to these interior lands, many purchases had to be made from the Indians. With each purchase, the wigwam villages of the Indians were pushed farther westward and northwestward until the new frontier bordered upon and spilled over into lands which were coveted by Frenchmen. There just was not enough land in North America to continue the practice of rolling back the frontier indefinitely.

During the first half of the 18th century, the provincial authorities of Pennsylvania were concerned with Indian affairs only as they affected the proprietary lands of the Penn family. The tribes that shared these domains with white men were the Delawares, Shawnees, and minor tribes whose villages stood near the inland rivers of the province. In treating with these small units, the services of white traders had been used satisfactorily, but when the Iroquois Confederacy of New York province extended its sovereignty over subordinated Indian nations, it had become necessary to employ the services of Conrad Weiser whose strategic position as an adopted son of one of the Six Nations made him almost indispensable to the Pennsylvania authorities.

The extension of diplomatic relations, outside of Pennsylvania, began during the third decade of the 18th century when Conrad Weiser entered the employ of the Province. After nearly twenty years of Indian diplomacy confined to treating with the sachems at Onondaga and their inferiors, the colonial governors of Penn's province found themselves in a pivotal position in Indian affairs on many fronts instead of only one.

The vexing problem of French encroachments in the northwest country brought Pennsylvania into negotiations with the Twightwees, Wyandots, and Miamis in the west. The ambitious plan of Virginia and her Ohio Company called for attention in the west. The problems of the Cherokees and Catawbas in the Carolinas remained unsettled despite the many intercessions which Pennsylvania and Virginia, through Conrad Weiser, had made between 1737 and 1751. At the same time, the old problem of holding fast the loyalty of the powerful Iroquois Confederacy was fraught with new dangers as Weiser had learned, to his dismay, during his eventful visit among the Maqua villages in 1750.

An untoward chain of circumstances occurring just when these vexing problems were increasing added to the perplexities that confronted the deputies of the Penns and other colonial governors and their executive Councils. Late in 1750, Thomas Lee, Virginia's commissioner of Indian affairs, breathed his last breath. Lee had never confided his knowledge of Indian matters to his associates, as shown in a letter from Richard Peters to Weiser, in which the secretary to the governor of Pennsylvania asked Conrad to supply information to the Council of Virginia, declaring that it appeared that Colonel Lee had never transmitted any of the information obtained through his extensive correspondence with the Pennsylvania agent. In 1751, James Logan, the venerable pillar of the province of Pennsylvania, passed into the beyond and the benefits of his vast experiences and wise counsel were gone forever. The turbulent political confusions of New York province caused Colonel William Johnson, commissioner of Indian affairs for that province, to resign his commission in high dudgeon early in the spring of 1751. Governor Clinton of New York sulked in his office, jealous of Pennsylvania's (Weiser's) influence with the Six Nations, whom he regarded as his wards, even though he despised them and ignored their pleas.

Added to these difficulties, Penn's province found itself lamentably short-handed in available trustworthy men to negotiate with the Indians. Conrad Weiser could not be in two or more places at one time. In dealing with the western Indians, Governor James Hamilton was forced to rely upon George Croghan, a trader whose integrity was frequently questioned, and Andrew Montour, son of Madame Montour, a French-Indian, whose loyalty to the English case was suspect. Only Conrad Weiser could be depended upon.[1]

We have seen that death removed most of the leaders of the Indian tribes. Allumpees, king of the Delawares; Shikellamy, Vice-Regent of the Six Nations; Canassatego, the "Word" of Onondaga; Caxhayan, the Moravian convert; and many other wise men had ceased their earthly labors and were gone to the Happy Hunting Grounds.

It became more and more apparent that someone ought to be trained to assist Weiser and, when fate so decreed, to be ready to succeed him. Daniel Claus of New York was brought to Pennsylvania to act as a tutor of Weiser's son Sammy, instructing him in the Mohawk language. But mere tutoring was not enough to bring about the desired results.

Soon after his return from the Indian country, 1750, the colonial assembly directed that Weiser should be sent north once again to carry messages and gifts of condolence on the death of Canassatego, the "Word." Such sentiments were mere gestures on the part of the provincial legislators. It was expedient to be sorrowful and perfunctory messages of bereavement were to be used more to brighten the rusting chain of friendship than to wipe away the tears of the "Word's" forest children. According to

---

1. See *Governor Hamilton to the Lords of Trade*, Feb 4, 1751, Pennsylvania Archives, 2:60–63. Also Peters to Weiser, March 12, 1751, Peters MSS, 3:28. Also March 20, Ibid., 30.

Indian custom, deceased persons were never referred to by their given name, hence Canassatego is named "The Word."

Weiser was willing to undertake the mission to Albany in 1751, particularly when it appeared that a conference of colonial governors would be called at Albany and his services as an interpreter would be required. Punctilious in matters of state, Conrad realized that he as a Pennsylvanian could not deal with Governor Clinton's wards without permission from New York province. In February 1751, he wrote to Colonel William Johnson tactfully requesting permission to confer with the Six Nations at some place of Johnson's choosing.[2] But the hot-headed Irishman, whose meteoric rise to political position had placed him at the head of New York's Indian Affairs, was in one of his sulking moods and, unknown to Weiser, had resigned his commission. (This letter to Johnson was written from Philadelphia, obviously by an amanuensis, the handwriting and the syntax of the letter are not in the Weiser style, but the endorsement on the reverse side of the letter is certainly in Weiser's own hand.)

While a journey to Albany was planned, the colonial assembly was wrestling with the problem of appeasing the northwestern Indians. Jean Coeur (Joncaire), the Frenchman, was moving about from village to village along the Allegheny River boasting that the French would help the Indians living there to drive the English into the sea. Disgruntled Delawares and Shawnees disposed of their Susquehanna lands were listening to the Frenchman's promises and the defections among the Senecas, westernmost of the Six Nations, reported by Weiser in 1750 made it appear that the English hold on the western regions was tenuous indeed.[3]

To help in counteracting the French influence, Weiser was asked by Governor Hamilton to carry presents to these western tribes and thereby wean the tribes away from Joncaire.[4] In reply to this request, made in March 1751, Conrad pointed out that he could not travel to Allegheny and return in time to carry the message to Albany scheduled for mid-summer. He recommended that Croghan and Montour be sent in his stead. Faced with the choice

---
2. Weiser to Johnson, February 8, 1751, Weiser MSS, 1:65.
3. Colonial Records, 5:513.
4. Hamilton to Weiser, Peters MSS, 3:38.

of only one journey, Weiser, consistent with his fundamental policy of dealing directly with the Six Nations in Council, chose to go to New York. His nomination of Montour and Croghan for the westward journey was the best solution he could offer.

It is important to note here that Weiser's suggestion of Croghan as an agent was not an unqualified recommendation. "If Mr. Croghan's Integrity is questioned," wrote Conrad, "some of the Traders of Ohio might be required to be present, who will not spare or favor him . . . Moreover, all these Ohio Indians are subservient to the Six Nations, whom we will treat with at Albany."

Governor Clinton had invited all English governors to Albany, but most of the officials of the middle and southern colonies declined to attend. The Pennsylvania Assembly, hesitating to commit itself to military pledges, decided to send Conrad Weiser to bring back knowledge of what was being planned. Accordingly, on May 2, Governor Hamilton called Weiser to Philadelphia, declaring "You understand Indian Affairs much better than any of us."

Having failed to secure permission through Colonel Johnson, Conrad requested Governor Hamilton to appeal directly to Governor Clinton for permission to speak to the Indians at Albany. Clinton replied that permission would be granted, provided Weiser could agree to conform to conditions.[5]

In June, Conrad Weiser and his son, affectionately referred to as Sammy in all accounts, set out for Albany, traveling by way of Philadelphia, Bordentown, and Amboy to New York City.

Samuel Weiser was born to Conrad and Anna Eve Weiser on April 23, 1735. In April 1751, he passed his sixteenth birthday. It was planned that Sammy should serve as an understudy to his father and, perhaps, he would find a home among the Indians for several months, there to repeat the experience of the father a generation earlier.

While in Philadelphia, Weiser asked the sanction of Governor Hamilton to place Sammy in a Mohawk family. Hamilton was pleased and gave his agent a letter to Governor Clinton, requesting the permission of New York. One of the first acts of the Weisers after reaching New York City was to call upon Clinton at

---

5. Hamilton to Clinton, May 15, 1751, Pennsylvania Archives, 2nd ser., 6:94. The reply: June 6, Ibid., 95.

his home in Flushing and present Hamilton's request. Clinton said that the matter would be laid before council. Two days later, Edward Holland, Clinton's secretary, informed Weiser that the New York authorities had agreed to the proposal.

While in New York, June 17-24, Weiser met his son-in-law, Reverend Henry M. Muhlenberg, who was in that city on some ecclesiastical mission. This meeting must have been prearranged because Weiser delivered several letters to the clergyman, letters which his daughter had given him for transmission while he and Sammy had passed through Trappe on their way to Philadelphia.[6]

Weiser's stay in New York City was not confined to arranging family matters. Among the assorted delegates awaiting sloops to carry the governor's party in Albany were several strange Indians. William Bull, commissioner of South Carolina, and an interpreter named Cool had brought a delegation of "Flatheads," Catawbas, to make a treaty of peace. Governor Glen of South Carolina had listened to the entreaties of William Johnson, and now, after fourteen years of negotiations, the chieftains of the warring nations were to meet in peace conclaves.

KING NARSKEEKEE

According to Weiser's own testimony, the meeting was purely accidental. It was only natural that a man of his interests should seek out the quarters of these Catawba delegates and cultivate their acquaintance. On June 19, Conrad made a point of visiting the southern Indians and to his delight, found one of them who could converse in the Maqua language. The Catawba had spent a portion of his youth as a prisoner in the Mohawk towns and had learned some of their language.

Through this acquaintance, Weiser met the Catawba king, Narskeekee, apparently quite a remarkable fellow. Out of respect and "brotherly love to the English" the King had come northward to "make peace" with the Six Nations but not to "sue" for it. His people would "spend the last Drop of Blood" rather than humble themselves. But would Tarrachawagon, a friend of the Six

---

6. Mann, William J., "Diary of Henry Melchior Muhlenberg," *Published Life and Times of Henry Melchior Muhlenberg*, Philadelphia (1888), 277. Also Weiser's own account, Colonial Records, 5:541.

Nations, "endeavor in bring about a Peace?" Narskeekee was tired of "Wars" and wished that those now born "might live in peace and die of age."

To this plea for help, Weiser promised that he would give all aid in his power, but reminded the Catawba King that he had tried for many years to effect this very matter, "but without any Sensible Success." Boldly Conrad reminded Narkskeekee that it was the Catawbas who usually broke the true agreement which had been made through the Governor of Virginia. To this, the wise old chief replied that "If all old Stories would be told over again there could be no Peace . . . on his part he would never repeat any."

"Was it safe?" inquired the Catawba King, "for me and my people to go to Albany, among our enemies?"

"Yes, in Albany," answered the German, "where the governor's protection was in force, but if it should turn out that no peace is made the Six Nations Council will tell you to go home in peace and . . . they will send after you and kill you in your own country."[7]

William Bull, Commissioner of South Carolina, sought Weiser's advice before the party left New York. He confided that the government of South Carolina was far more concerned about the ending of inter-Indian hostilities than the Catawbas themselves were. Weiser advised that humility should be the keynote of all speeches the southern Indians should make to the Six Nations, fearing that Narskeekee, in his present mood, was "a little too Haughty in his Mind." On the 20th of June, the South Carolina commissioner furnished a banquet to his charges and Conrad Weiser, the agent of Pennsylvania, was invited as a special guest. It was a formal affair and the Catawba deputies were dressed in their finest clothes of blue, the King himself wearing "red Breeches" as Weiser noted.

The next day, Weiser received another invitation, one which might have flattered the vanity of a man of small stature; it was to join the governor's party on Clinton's own sloop, to go up the Hudson to Albany. This time Weiser declined. He preferred to travel to the treaty place on the same boat with his new friends, Narskeekee and the Catawbas. Perhaps it was vanity after all that determined his choice, for was not Narskeekee a king, while

---
7. Weiser's account, supra.

Clinton was merely an erstwhile governor of one of England's many domains? Or, was it that Conrad heard a still small voice enjoining him, "Blessed are the Peacemakers; for they shall inherit the earth?"

On June 27, the sloop carrying Weiser and his son and the Catawbas arrived at Albany and the Pennsylvanian found lodging at the private home of Robert Rosebloom. Gradually the delegations from the Six Nations reached Albany. Senecas, Cayugas, Onondagas, these sought out the quarters of Tarachawagon to bid him welcome. Had he brought the Flatheads to sue for peace? The commissioners of Massachusetts and Providence Plantations came asking whether Weiser had come to negotiate new land purchases.

The Mohawks came, among them Brant and his wife. Would the Mohawks receive Sammy into their village as their fathers had adopted Tarachawagon thirty-seven years ago? Yoha, shouted the Brants as they embraced Sammy "with tears in their Eis" that their home was lonely because their own son had left to study English in Albany. Weiser was pleased, recalling to them that it was into Brant's wife's family that he himself had been adopted in 1714.

Schoharie Indians came to renew acquaintance with their old friend and neighbor. The Rosebloom house was the busiest spot in Albany. Catawba chieftains came there, furtive glances betraying their apprehension. They had fared well enough with the Mohawks, but when the other Iroquois tribesmen came they feared that they might "cut their throats." Weiser allayed their fears and saw to it that a sentry was placed at the door of their lodgings.

Where was Governor Hamilton, asked some Onondagas; will Thomas Penn come, asked others—will there be Indian commissioners from Pennsylvania, a Seneca chief wished to know. No, only Tarachawagon from Pennsylvania and his son, Sammy, who had come to learn the culture of the Indians, had come from Pennsylvania to bring that province's condolences on the death of the Six Nations chieftain.

On the 2nd of July, twenty canoes carried French Indians from Canada. The Mohawks were disturbed. Why did the governor of New York permit the French Indians to come to Albany, when Mohawks were forbidden to visit Canada, asked the Mohawks of their adopted son, Tarachawagon? This apostle of peace explained that the French Indians too had come to offer their condolences. Why did Corlear, Clinton, tarry so long in his tent without speaking to the Six Nations? Would not Tarachawagon deliver his message early in the morning "before the governor would rise?" No, replied Weiser, his instructions were to hold his tongue until Corlear had spoken.

Meanwhile, Clinton was growing jealous or suspicious of Weiser's frequent powwows with the Indians. The governor demanded the speech he intended to deliver. This Weiser refused to do, stating that he would pledge not to exceed his instructions which had been read and approved by Clinton's Council. A sergeant was sent to escort Weiser into Clinton's presence. Again, Clinton asked for a written copy of the intended speech, but Conrad was obdurate. Then Clinton reprimanded Weiser for his many private conferences at his lodgings; indeed, matters had reached the point where Clinton could not assemble the deputies to listen to him. By inference, this meant that Weiser was detaining them elsewhere. "As for the Indians coming to see me," Weiser replied, "I could not loke (lock) meself up nor did I care to offend them." In his report to Governor Glen of South Carolina, Weiser observed "If Governor Clinton had asked his Interpreter and Colonel Johnson where the Indians had been all that day and what they had been about, they could have told him if they would."

On July 4, Weiser requested permission to deliver his message. It was denied. Five days later he repeated his request only to meet with further rebuffs. Clinton's negotiations ended on July 9 and Weiser was notified that he would be permitted to speak on the next day.

But the next day found Governor Clinton abroad his sloop returning to New York. He had deserted the conference without bidding the Indians farewell and refusing to listen to their entreaties. Before departing, however, Clinton sent word to Weiser, asking him to assist Mr. Bull of South Carolina and Arent Stevens, the New York Interpreter, in dealing with the Catawba matters. And these matters certainly required a skillful hand.

Negotiations between the Flatheads and their traditional enemies were not proceeding smoothly. When the Catawbas were sent for by the Mohawks, Weiser was asked to conduct them to the conference chamber. They entered rattling their calabashes and whirling feathers in their hands, singing their weird tribal songs. Once seated, the King offered the calumet pipe of peace and it was smoked by the chiefs of the Six Nations. Then the Catawba warriors passed the peace pipe while Narskeekee rose to speak.

But the words of the Catawba King were unintelligible, for even Mr. Jool, the South Carolina interpreter, found it difficult "to English it." Jool was unequal to translating anything into the Maqua. Then one Captain Gallick, a member of the Massachusetts delegation, tried his skills but failed. Tarachawagon was asked to translate, "which I did to their Satisfaction." The first meeting had ended amicably enough.

Later that day, Jool asked Weiser to come to the Catawba lodgings. Narskeekee thanked Tarachawagon for his services earlier, but there was something troubling the southern Indians. Mr. Bull, their own commissioner, had made some statements during the conference "which sounded very rash." Once again, Conrad poured oil on troubled waters, appeased the wounded pride of the Indians and restored confidence.[8]

None of the matters concerned Weiser's appointed mission to Albany; he served his fellowmen without any expectation of reward, even after Arent Stevens refused to translate for the Catawbas unless he was paid for it.

When the time came for Tarachawagon to speak on behalf of Onas, he took great pains to see to it that the condolences were offered in the proper manner. Because there were a "great deal of Serimonies which no European can perform," an Oneida Indian was engaged to intone and mumble the incantations of lament. After the ceremony, the Oneidas announced that Tarachawagon brought a message commanding all to listen attentively. Punctiliously, Weiser offered condolences, naming the departed chiefs, presenting strouds, matchcoats, and wampums to cover their graves and gifts to wipe away the tears of the living.

Then Abraham Peters, a Mohawk Chief, thanked Weiser and made a speech welcoming Sammy Weiser, "We will take care of

---

8. Account of Catawba Treaty and South Carolina Commission, William Bulluqun to Conrad Weiser, September 7, 1751, Weiser MSS, 1:21. Also Peters MSS, 3:49.

your Son, we look upon him as one of our own Children, we will use our best Endeavor to learn him to speak our Language well, we are very glad you brought him to us as to your Town, it shows that you retain the same Love as you did formerly to us."

CROSS PURPOSES

The conference at Albany had accomplished very little. The arrogance of Governor Clinton, the sulking of Colonel Johnson, and the inefficiency of William Bull served to vitiate the noble efforts of Weiser. Bull did not deem it necessary to escort his charges on their homeward journey. Instead, he left instructions to have them meet him in Philadelphia. There Governor Glen's commissioner tarried until late autumn, waiting for his wards to appear. Perplexed to know what had happened to them, Bull wrote to Weiser complaining that only one warrior had reached Philadelphia in late September. He had no idea where the others tarried.

While Conrad Weiser was negotiating at Albany, George Croghan and Andrew Montour were carrying Pennsylvania presents across the Alleghenies to Logstown on the Ohio River. The loyalty of the western tribes, the Wyandots, Miamis, Twightwees, and others, had to be secured to the British interest and an effort had to be made to prevent the defection of the Shawnees and Delawares.

In 1748, Conrad Weiser had run up "a little Flagg," claiming the vast region beyond the Appalachian range for England. One year later, Celeron de Bienville had planted leaden plates, claiming the same land in the name of France. Some Six Nations Indians stole one of the plates and sent it by messenger to their Council in New York, where its message was translated to them and the western Indians concluded that the French were trying to steal their lands. Weiser had chosen the symbol of running up a flag to claim possession—the French had committed themselves to record words. Following their claim to the territory, the French had sent Jean Coeur, Joncaire, to live in the Ohio country for three years to plan the building of forts along the western river. Joncaire explained that these "stone houses" would help the Indians carry on their trade to the Great Lakes.[9]

---

9. Pennsylvania Archives, 2nd ser., 6:114–119.

In May 1741, the Pennsylvania deputies reached Logstown on the Ohio with the presents for the western Indians. Joncaire stood among the Indians and watched the distribution of English goods. According to Croghan's account, the French agent tried to dissuade the Indians from accepting the gifts, only to be rebuked by the Indians. "Is it not our Land," the spokesman cried stamping the Ground and putting his finger to John Coeur's nose. "What Right has Onontijo to our Lands? I desire you may go home directly."

Such language and conduct appear to be out of character for an Indian. Certainly, none of Weiser's journals record such vituperative expressions directed against an individual and the gesture of putting a finger to the nose is unique in Indian lore. There is much in Croghan's report of the Logstown treaty that does not ring true.

A few weeks after the conference at Logstown, this same Marquis de la Jonquiere conducted a conference with Six Nations Indians in the northern Ohio country during which the Indians informed the French that they had "summoned the English to withdraw from the other side of the mountain in order that the earth be free." In his turn, the Frenchman warned the Iroquois "The English are much less anxious to take away your peltries than to become masters of your Lands; they labor only to debauch you; you have the weakness to listen to them and your blindness is so great that you do not perceive that the very hand that caresses you will scourge you like negroes and slaves, so soon as it will have got Possession of those Lands."

But in Croghan's account of his own dealings at Logstown, he records his own condemnation of the French and gives the impression that the Indians were bitter against the common foe. If the sentiments of the Indians were as inimical to the French as Croghan records them, then Joncaire could not have found a welcome among them, while on the other hand, if Croghan spoke the sharp words against the French as he records them, then he and Joncaire could not have become such close friends as subsequent events made them appear to be.

In one portion of his journal, Croghan reports that Joncaire confided to him that he personally was not opposed to English rule in Ohio, but that the Governor of Canada had ordered him to act as he did. Either the Frenchman's guile was too subtle for Croghan's powers or there was collusion of some sort between these men. Joncaire prevailed upon Croghan to carry a letter to Pennsylvania's governor on his return trip. This letter was written in French and it is probable that Croghan either did not know or could not read the contents, but its delivery at Croghan's hands did not raise that Irishman in the esteem of those who were guarding English interests in Pennsylvania.

The wily Joncaire had sent his answer to the protests of Hamilton and Clinton by which the English governors had warned that the War of the Austrian Succession was ended and that the French penetrations of the Ohio country were invasions of English domains.

Very subtly, Joncaire admitted that French occupation of the Ohio was a contravention of the peace terms of Aix-la-Chapelle, provided the English regarded the Six Nations as their *subjects*, but if the Six Nations were a *free* people, then there was no breach of peace. Thus the crafty Joncaire maneuvered the English into the position of claiming the subjugation of the Iroquois or relinquishing their claims upon the disputed lands. Neither position was tenable for a royal or proprietary governor of an English colony and Hamilton as well as Clinton must have smarted under the lash of Joncaire's logic.

It was indeed a diplomatic coup for a French pretender to all the lands from the mouth of the Mississippi to "la belle Riviere," the Ohio, to employ the kindness of an agent of the English king to carry a threat to the governor of Pennsylvania, for that was the essence of the letter.

Governor James Hamilton was irate when he read the contents of Joncaire's letter and his Assembly, at loggerheads with him in some of his executive acts, seized the opportunity to chide him for employing agents, "who carry letters" from every inferior French officer who shall presume to send down his threats or pretended Claims . . . to give himself an Air of Authority among our Indian Allies."

Croghan was under a cloud and his companion, Montour, shared the criticism for mismanaging and misrepresenting facts.

There were some implications in the dealings of these two that might warrant even more serious charges. When the two Pennsylvania agents returned to Aughwick, in Cumberland, Croghan wrote a strong letter of recommendation to Colonel Cresap of Maryland, urging the employment of Montour in that province. When this became known, Richard Peters wrote a strong letter to Weiser charging him with the blame of the half-breed's defection. Justifiably, Weiser denied any responsibility for the act and Peters apologized. It had been learned that Croghan prevailed upon Montour to sign a letter charging Weiser with misconduct of Indian affairs. To join the service of Colonel Cresap was almost treason to Pennsylvania because of the disputed boundary lines and because of Cresap's previous attempts to wrest the administration of Indian affairs from Pennsylvania's control.[10]

The onus of blame now fell upon Croghan himself. Exactly what charge was raised against him is not clear. Weiser made no direct accusations, declaring only that he would withhold judgment until he could hear Croghan's side of the story.[11]

Whatever differences may have existed, they appear to have been submerged when, early in 1753, Colonel Cresap personally appealed to Weiser for help in solving some knotty problems for Maryland. The governor of Virginia was appealing to Weiser through Cresap. Maryland and Virginia, both, wanted to deliver presents to the western Indians at Logstown on the Ohio. They knew nothing about wampum belts and the ceremonies in which they were used, would Weiser procure some for them? What "Quantity of Liquor" ought to be provided "as we are strangers in the nature of treating with the Indians occasions me to request this trouble of you."

Cresap informed Weiser that Colonel Patton had Virginia's Indian affairs in charge and that the hot-headed Irishman merely uttered threats against the Indians when he was sent to Allegheny

---

10. Peters to Weiser, September 25, 1751, Peters MSS, 3:48. Also Ibid., 47.
11. Peters to Weiser, September 19, 1751, Ibid., 47. Suspicions of a very serious nature were directed against George Croghan—later. See "George Croghan and the Westward Movement" by A. T. Votweiler, Cleveland, Ohio, 1926. Also by the same author in the *Pennsylvania Magazine of History and Biography*, 47:134. He was suspected in 1756 of being the "Filius Gallicae," author of letters to Duc de Mirepoux. See Arthur D. Graeff, *Relations between Pennsylvania Germans and British Authorities*, Norristown (1939), 69, and Proceedings of the Pennsylvania German Society, vol. 47.

to invite them to a treaty at Logstown. The Indians had journeyed to Cresap's on the Potomac to learn what Patton's visit meant."[12]

Among the recommendations which Croghan made in his report to Governor Hamilton was a plan to build a fort in the juncture of the three rivers where Pittsburgh now stands. The Quaker assembly was totally unwilling to contribute funds for such a warlike enterprise. The legislators even began to balk at appropriating money for Indian presents, maintaining that the Penn proprietors would assume this burden. Hamilton countered their demands by declaring that the proprietors were paying Weiser in lands which were more valuable than money "and are at this Time at the Expense of Maintaining His Son (Sammy Weiser) with a Tutor (Daniel Claus) in the Indian Country to learn their Language and Customs for the service of the Provinces."

The assembly commended the governor for such "care and concern" but took occasion at the same time, to oppose the plan to build a fort in the Ohio country as recommended in Croghan's report. They feared "the person in whom the governor confided the management of the Treaty (Croghan)" had misrepresented the true state of affairs in Ohio.

Late in 1751, Richard Peters wrote to Weiser stating that another trip to Onondaga would be required in 1752. However, Conrad made no extended journeys during that year. Other matters claimed his time and other affairs demanded his presence. At various times there were plans to have the Pennsylvania interpreter go to Williamsburg to advise the Virginia governor on the selection of presents for the Ohio Indians and there was some talk about sending Weiser to Logstown in 1753.[13] The deterring factor always was the realization that the Indians would be expecting military pledges from Pennsylvania and Weiser was not empowered to make any such promises.

Governor Hamilton wrote to Weiser stating that he had an objection to his going to Williamsburg, the capital of Virginia, or to Logstown, the Indian capital of the Ohio country, but, urged Hamilton, "you will not forget that you live here, nor fail on all

---
12. Thomas Cresap to Weiser, February 20, 1752, Peters MSS, 3:54.
13. Peters to Weiser, May 25, 1751, Peters MSS, 2:41. The suit grew out of the distribution of lots in the newly founded city of Reading.

proper occasions to support the Honour and Interest of it (Pennsylvania) to the best of your Power."

In January 1753, Governor Robert Dinwiddie of Virginia wrote to Governor Samuel Ogle of Maryland, declaring that he would be "glad if (Andrew) Montour will move to Virginia, so that we may have an Interpreter." Previously Montour had asked permission of Governor James Hamilton of Pennsylvania to set up a plantation in the Juniata Valley. To this request, Hamilton replied that the young French-Indian should apply to Conrad Weiser.[14]

Prior to 1751, Weiser and Montour had been good friends and the older man had recommended Madame Montour's son to the provincial authorities as a possible successor to himself. But the dubious conduct of Montour and Croghan at Logstown in 1751 had cooled this friendship. We do not know whether Weiser opposed granting lands to Montour but in 1753 we find the half-breed entering the employ of Virginia and from thence forward, Weiser's influence in the southern provinces waned. Andrew Montour was employed to carry Virginia's message to the Six Nations in 1752. "Andrew's pride will render him odious to the Onondaga Council," wrote Weiser to Peters.

At Logstown, in 1751, the Indians friendly to the English were warned that the French were collecting troops at Niagara for attacking the Indian settlements on the Ohio. This warning was sounded by Croghan and Montour. Quite naturally, the Wyandots and Miamis begged the provisional governments of Pennsylvania, Maryland, and Virginia for military aid in meeting the danger that impended. Virginia was quick to promise such assistance, but the Quaker assembly in Philadelphia, opposed to war in any form, was unwilling to provide the necessary funds for a military expedition. Due to the pacifistic attitude of Pennsylvania, the more militant Virginia assumed the lead in the management of Indian affairs in the Ohio country and Pennsylvania was forced, gradually, to confine her activities to the lands lying east of the Alleghenies.[15]

Throughout most of the year 1753, Weiser was busy superintending the building of houses in the new city of Reading. He was commended for sticking to his duties in Reading instead of

---

14. Dinwiddie Papers, 1:37. Also Ibid., 17.
15. Colonial Records, 5:567.

embarking on Indian treaty-making expeditions, by no less a person than Thomas Penn, who wrote from London, early in 1753: "I am well pleased that Conrad Weiser excused himself from going to the Ohio, as I think negotiations there, not the most likely to secure the Indian to the English Interest. When we enter into Treatys with them we should consider how they are to be supported in case they are attacked." In the absence of testimony from Weiser, we may assume that he had advanced this objection in asking to be excused from going to Logstown.[16]

When Andrew Montour returned from a journey to Onondaga in 1752, he brought ominous news. He had failed to accomplish his original mission. As an agent of Virginia, he was to invite the Six Nations to treat with the Catawbas at Winchester in Virginia. In this Montour had no more success than Weiser had had on former occasions when Virginia employed Conrad's services on similar errands. But Montour did bring news that the French were loading boats and collecting their soldiers in preparation for a large-scale invasion of the Ohio country. This report was carried to Governor Dinwiddie of Virginia, who in turn relayed it to Governor Hamilton. On August 2, 1753, Hamilton informed Dinwiddie that he had sent Conrad Weiser to get "to the Bottom of Matters with the Six Nations," explaining that the Ohio Indians would not act without the knowledge of the council in New York province.

On July 26, 1753, Weiser was summoned to Philadelphia and given his instructions. He should learn whether the Six Nations allowed the French to build forts on the Ohio; whether the French had forced the Onondaga council to accede to their demands; whether the Six Nations had ordered English traders out of Ohio; how the chain of Friendship between themselves stands; will the Six Nations oppose the French, and in what manner; what assistance was expected from Pennsylvania. The only promise Weiser was permitted to make was that "Pennsylvania will do all that can be in reason expected as to furnish Cloathing and so forth."

A few minutes before Weiser boarded a "stage-boat" bound for Bordentown in New Jersey, he received additional orders. Six Pennsylvania traders, all from Lancaster County, had been captured by the Indians and were held in or near Montreal, Canada.

---
16. Peters MSS, 3:63.

A letter signed jointly by the six of them appealed to Governor Hamilton to bring about the release. They were being held for ransom by French Indians, the governor of Canada refusing to purchase them as slaves. These men believed that a protest from the provincial governors of New York and Pennsylvania would induce their captors to release them. Weiser was commissioned to investigate the case when he reached Albany.

Weiser's instructions carried a strict injunction that he must wait upon Governor George Clinton at his house in Flushing, New York, and deliver him Governor Hamilton's letter, explaining the purpose of the mission to Onondaga. Previous experience had shown how keenly New York's governor resented independent action on the part of Pennsylvania in dealing with the Six Nations. Hamilton wished to observe all the amenities.

On August 1, Weiser arrived in New York a sick man. In order that no time should be lost, he sent his son, Sammy, to the governor's mansion in Flushing, but Clinton was not home. Sammy entrusted Hamilton's letter to the governor's "Lady" and three days later Weiser boarded a sloop for Albany without having seen or heard from Clinton. One week after this letter was left at the governor's home, Clinton wrote to Weiser at Albany. This letter contained strict orders to Weiser not to go to Onondaga unless it be in company with Colonel William Johnson and not to make any applications to the Six Nations or deliver a message unless approved by Johnson "and in his presence."[17]

In Albany, Weiser called upon Mayor Robert Sanders, who had written to Governor Hamilton on behalf of the six Lancaster traders being held prisoners by the Indians of Canada. Sanders received Weiser cordially and proceeded to call a conference of New York's Indian commissioners on that same day. During the conference, an Indian squaw named Susanna was sent for by the commissioner. Susanna had one of the captives, Jabez Evans, in her own custody. The man was given to her, she explained, to compensate for the loss of one of her relatives.

Through the information secured from Susanna, Weiser acting as interpreter, it was learned how the men became captives during a recent inter-tribal war. The squaw supplied information

---
17. Clinton to Weiser, August 8, 1753. Clinton reprimands Weiser for failing to wait.

as to where the other five could be found and ways were devised to secure the release of all of them.

Susanna interpreted the proceedings to ask Weiser how he, a Pennsylvanian, had learned to speak the Indian tongue so fluently. Unwilling to divulge his name, Weiser informed her that he had lived at Schoharie during his younger years and had, since then, "travelled up and down among the Indians."

Colonel Johnson, now reinstated as Commissioner of Indian Affairs, received Weiser kindly on August 11th. He raised no objections to Conrad's discoursing at length with the Mohawks at Mohawk's Castles and Mount Johnson, but he failed to invite his Pennsylvania guest to accompany him to Onondaga, the chief Council of Six Nations. Johnson showed Weiser his commission and instructions from the governor of New York. Even though Conrad told his host that he had similar instructions from Pennsylvania, Johnson still did not extend an invitation. "I perceived some Coolness in him as to my going. I thought it best not to proceed any further at this time." Weiser and his son, Sammy, were handsomely entertained at Johnson's home and when they departed for their homeward journey, they were invited to make "his House my Home" and a request that Weiser should send "now and then a Letter."

Even though Weiser did not reach Onondaga in 1753, he secured a great deal of the information he was sent to obtain. In his informal talks with Abraham Peters, Seth, Hendricks, and other Mohawks he learned that the French passed Oswego with "a numerous army of Men—well armed and some great Guns; that they were bound for Ohio, where they would build Strong Houses at the Carrying Places;" that they threatened to remove all English traders and exterminate the Indians allied with the English.

The Senecas had sent a message to Colonel Johnson, asking him how long they had to live. The Colonel had told them that they must fight to save themselves and their honor.

Abraham Peters told Weiser that "the English had lost Ground in the Time of the Last War;" that the sending of clothing and even ammunition would not save the Six Nations from the French; only English fighting men could help the Indians to resist.

In effect, all the points of Weiser's instructions were covered at Mohawk's Castles in Johnson-land. On August 27, Weiser returned to Flushing and called upon Governor Clinton. He was admitted and after assuring the governor that he had not exceeded his orders, the Pennsylvania agent was well received. Conrad apologized for his abrupt departure earlier in the month. "His Excellency said it was well" and the conference was terminated with an invitation to "stay and eat a Bit of Victuals first."[18]

THE CARLISLE TREATY

Two days after Conrad Weiser left Philadelphia in 1753 to carry a message to Onondaga, word reached Pennsylvania's governor that Andrew Montour had recently returned from a second visit in the Six Nations capital. Through Montour, the chiefs of the Iroquois in New York urged the English governors to preserve peace with the French, but "If our Indians should be struck it will be very kind to help them; it is better to help them than Us." By this statement, the Six Nations were urging aid for their western allies "for we are near New York and can be supplied easily from thence. Col. Johnson . . . has assured Us We may always have what we want there . . . but our Young Men at Ohio must have their Supply from You."

Montour's message was not convincing. It was attested by the names of five Indians, three Onondagas, one Oneida, and one Tuscarora. In Conrad Weiser's list of the chief men of the Six Nations, prepared several weeks earlier, there was no mention of any of these signers. It appears to be quite out of character for the Six Nations to urge that supplies be sent to the other tribes and there is little evidence to show that any of the Six Nations excepting the Mohawks held great affection for Colonel William Johnson.

Montour was not above double-dealing in his conduct of Indian affairs. Shortly before the message reached Philadelphia, Richard Peters, Secretary to Governor James Hamilton, was exasperated by the "Accounts from Ohio, as there were none but

---

18. Recorded in Weiser's Journal of 1753. Clinton wrote to Hamilton, stating that he was displeased with Weiser, August 27, 1753, Colonial Records, 5:647.

Indian Traders to apply to for Information who were too partial, ignorant, and too much concerned for their own Interest to give true or Intelligent Accounts." Along the same line, Governor Hamilton wrote to Governor Dinwiddie of Virginia, declaring: "Whilst the Traders are men of dissolute lives, without Prudence or abilities, and whilst the Indians are perpetually kept under the Influence of strong Liquor, who of either sort can be trusted? What intelligence can be depended on? How can the Behaviour or real Disposition of the Indians be known?"

Virginia had assumed the lead in dealing with the Ohio Indians. Her interests in the Ohio Company made it imperative that the Old Dominion should gain the favor of the tribes living on the lands she wanted to occupy. Pennsylvania was not yet interested in land transactions west of the Alleghenies and concerned herself mostly with the fur trade of the Ohio country. With the employment of Andrew Montour as agent, the Virginians established direct contact with the Iroquois Confederacy in New York, thus freeing themselves from dependency upon Conrad Weiser in their Indian negotiations. From this moment onward, Pennsylvania's leadership in Indian affairs diminished.

Another factor which accelerated the ascendency of Virginia was her readiness to engage in military endeavors whenever her Indian allies asked for such assistance. The Quaker assembly was unwilling to compromise the religious tenets of most of its members and therefore refused to build "strong houses" or forts along the Ohio and its tributaries.

The long-anticipated French invasion of the Ohio country began in August 1752. The first blow was struck against the Miamis, or Twightwees. A message from Carlisle informed Governor Hamilton that fifteen Indians and one settler were killed in the skirmish. The Indians sent a scalp with their messenger as gruesome proof of the horrors they had experienced. They had seen their king, Old Britain, killed "and eaten within a hundred yards of the Fort, before our Faces."

The Pennsylvania Assembly was willing to vote money as a gift of condolence for the Miamis and in May 1753, they appropriated an addition six hundred points "to the other Indian Nations in our Alliance." It appears that the Assembly intended that the second present should be offered to the Indians at Onondaga; hence the disavowal of the Six Nations as purported in Montour's message partially quoted at the beginning of this account.

The spending of the appropriations was left to Hamilton's judgment. For some reason, not quite clear, the governor assumed that the terms of the act creating the present were binding upon him to distribute the monies only upon the specific requests of the Indians for war materials. In explaining his delay to the Assembly, Hamilton stated that he feared that wagon-trains carrying goods might fall into the hands of prowling parties of enemy troops; that the good effect of a large present would be lost if not distributed on the Indians' own villages and that he could not find reliable persons to deliver the gifts.

Conrad Weiser returned from his Albany journey of 1753 on the first of September and within a few days, he received orders to accompany the Pennsylvania commissioners to treat with the Ohio Indians at Carlisle. Through Governor Dinwiddie and Montour, the Ohio Indians had learned of Pennsylvania's appropriation of money for their aid and in August 1753, they asked that the goods be sent to Carlisle.

The commissioners were Richard Peters, secretary to the governor; Isaac Norris, speaker of the Assembly; and Benjamin Franklin, Esquire, a newly-elected member of the Assembly and newly appointed postmaster-general of the colonies. Conrad Weiser was not designated as a commissioner; officially he was to be only the interpreter, but events proved that his counsel was sought on most of the issues which arose.

The commissioners and Weiser reached Carlisle before the wagons carrying condolence presents caught up with them. The Indians reached the treaty place on the same day, September 26. They were on their way home to Ohio after a visit to Virginia and Carlisle was chosen as a treating place, because their journey westward would begin there. Andrew Montour and George Croghan were with the Indians; the former assisting Weiser in the work of interpreting.

Two hundred pounds had been appropriated as condolence for the Miamis. This sum had been expended upon goods which were rolling toward Carlisle. The other six hundred pounds voted by the assembly had not yet been converted into treaty goods.

The Miamis knew that the condolence gifts would be distributed at Carlisle. During the first days of the treaty, they refused to enter any discussion until their tears should be wiped away. Accordingly, the commissioners sent out messengers urging their wagoners to hurry in order that conferences might begin.

In addition to the Miamis, there were many representatives of other Indian nations assembled at Carlisle. The report of the commissioners stated that there were "some of the most considerable Persons of the Six Nations, Delawares, Shawonese with Deputies from the Twightwees (Miamis) and Owendats (Wyandots)." During the days wasted in waiting for the wagons, Conrad Weiser used the time to good advantage by holding private conferences with the chiefs, learning many details which helped him to arrive at the decision he was called upon to make at the close of the conference.[19]

Through these conversations, supplemented by his general knowledge of Indian affairs, he prepared his list of the "principal Indians" present at the treaty, listing them by name, tribe, and rank. Appended to the list, Weiser prepared another, "List of the Names of the Chiefs now entrusted with the Conduct of Publick Affairs Among the Six Nations." On the second list, Weiser made notations showing which of the chiefs were "enclined to the French."

When the condolence presents arrived at Carlisle and were properly distributed, the conference began. The Indians recited a long train of injustices inflicted upon them by the French. They avowed their continued loyalty to the English and begged for war materials. The Virginians were going to build the strong house (fort) at the junction of the Ohio and Monongahela rivers. They had asked Pennsylvania to do this in earlier years. Now the sons of Onas must come to their rescue. They had declared war against the French and their English allies must help them.

Two other points were stressed by the Indians. First, no English settlements should be built west of the Allegheny Hills until

---

19. The negotiations of Carlisle, October 1–4, 1753. May be found in Colonial Records, 5:670–684.

the war with the French was ended, and, second, they begged the English traders should be forbidden to sell rum. "These wicked whiskey sellers when they have once got the Indians in Liquor make them sell the very Clothes from their Backs."

On this question of the liquor traffic, it is interesting to note what Benjamin Franklin wrote about his observation of the Carlisle Treaty of 1753: "We strictly," says Franklin, "forbade the selling any liquor to them; and, when they complained of this restriction, we told them, that, if they could continue sober during the treaty, we would give them plenty of rum when the business was over. They claimed and received the rum. In the evening, hearing a great noise among them, the commissioners walked to see what was the matter. We found they had made a great bonfire in the middle of the square; they were all drunk, men and women, quarreling and fighting. Their dark-colored bodies, half naked, seen only by the gloomy light of the bonfire, running after and beating one another with firebrands, accompanied by their horrid yellings, formed a scene the most resembling our ideas of hell that could well be imagined; there was no appeasing the tumult, and we retired to our lodging. At midnight a number of them came thundering at our door, demanding more rum, of which we took no notice. The next day, sensible that they had misbehaved in giving us that disturbance, they sent three of their old counselors to make their apology. The orator acknowledged the fault, but laid it upon the rum; and then endeavored to excuse the rum by saying, 'The Great Spirit, who made all things, made everything for some use, and whatever use he designed any thing for, that use it should be always be put to'; now, when he made rum, he said, 'Let this be for the Indians to get drunk with; and it must be so.' And indeed, if it be the design of Providence to extirpate these savages, in order to make room for the cultivators of the earth, it seems not impossible that rum may be the appointed means. It has already annihilated all the tribes who formerly inhabited the seacoast."

When the turn came for the colonists to reply to the Indian demands, the other commissioners turned to Conrad Weiser for a decision as to what could be done to satisfy the western Indians and hold them loyal to Pennsylvania. Weiser decided that only by expending the entire appropriation of 800 pounds immediately could "we expect to hold the Friendship of the Indians."

A significant passage is quoted here—It is from the reply of the commissioners as spoken by Conrad Weiser:

> Be pleased to cast your Eyes towards this Belt, whereon Six Figures delineated holding one another by the Hands. This is a just resemblance of our present Union, the Five first Figures representing the Five Nations to which You belong, as the Sixth does the Government of Pennsylvania, with whom You are linked in a close and firm Union. In whatever Part of the Belt is broke all the Wampum runs off and renders the Whole of no Strength or Consistency. In like manner, should you break Faith with one another or with the Government, the Union is dissolved. We would, therefore, hereby place before You the Necessity of preserving your Faith entire to one another as well as to this Government. Do not separate. Do not part on any Score. Let no Differences nor Jealousies subsist a Moment between Nation and Nation, but join all together as one man sincerely and heartily. We on our Part shall always perform our Engagements to every one of You. In Testimony whereof We present You with this Belt.

Goods were brought as soon as the commissioners returned to the settlements. For the moment, at least, the western tribes were kept in the Pennsylvania interest.

Virginia governor Robert Dinwiddie

Benjamin Franklin was present for the Treaty of Carlisle.

CHAPTER XIV

Inter-Colony Quarrels

SEA TO SEA CHARTERS

In October 1753, Governor Dinwiddie of Virginia sent the young surveyor George Washington to warn the French against trespassing in the Ohio country. Accompanied by Christopher Gist and several friendly Indians, the young Virginia agent reached the French fort at Venango, near present-day Franklin, Pennsylvania. There he was treated with perfunctory courtesy, but his eyes were not blinded to the serious warlike preparations of the French. He reported to Dinwiddie that a French invasion was imminent.

Conrad Weiser expressed the same opinion. In a fragment of a letter, no date, Weiser made the following astonishing assertions: "If the French are suffered by the English to take and keep possession of the Ohio as they now have part to which about 100 miles above Loggstown . . . they will be very troublesome neighbors to us as they will get Settlers out of Pennsylvania in great numbers for here are a great many of the king of French subjects out of Elsace and Lorain (Alsace and Lorraine) and a good many of them would never yet naturalize unter the Crown of England and our people connives at them. If they should hear that the french king would give them Land in Ohio for a little or nothing and tolerate them in their religious Persuasion it is my opinion several hundred if not thousands would steal away (which they can very easily do) to the French to Ohio and provide them with cows and horses and Plowmen to say nothing of Roques and Villains that would fly from Justice . . ."[1]

As the Ohio situation crystallized Weiser lost all faith in Andrew Montour. It appears that the French-Indian agent in the employ of Virginia was playing the interests of his employers against advantages he could gain for himself in the councils of the Ohio Indians. It will be remembered that at the Treaty of Lancaster in 1744 the Six Nations sold their lands to Virginia "west of the setting sun." The Virginians understood this figurative phrase to mean from sea to sea, thereby including the Ohio lands beyond the Appalachian Mountains. Montour told the western Indians that Weiser had imposed upon them in interpreting the treaty terms to Virginia. In the presence of the Pennsylvania commissioners at Carlisle in 1753, Weiser called Montour to account for this statement and "told him in plain words that he was an impudent Fellow to say so, in short he wants your Governor to pay for the Land from the Ohio Indians and yet not settled it. I am so sorry that I ever recommended him."[2]

WHO SHALL PROTECT THE KING'S DOMAIN?

Facing the imminent outbreak of war with the French, it became more and more urgent to gain the active support of the Ohio tribes. Dinwiddie begged, goaded, and threatened his assembly into granting ten thousand pounds for a military expedition and then dashed off reams of letters to the governors of the other colonies to furnish additional aid. Governor Hamilton of Pennsylvania lost his temper several times when his urgent calls for aid were either ignored by the Quaker legislatures, answered by specious arguments, or delayed by sudden adjournments. When Dinwiddie offered land grants in the Ohio Valley as an inducement to secure recruits, the Pennsylvanians charged him with giving away land belonging to the Penns. The Quakers were unwilling to defend the land; unwilling to permit settlements there; unwilling to build

---
1. Weiser MSS, 2:2.
2. Colonial Records, 5:670–680.

forts; and as one writer put it "they would not permit anyone to enjoy it except the French."

The best that the Assembly could do was to suggest to the Indians that the land be sold to the English in exchange for the cancellation of debts owed to the English traders. When Conrad Weiser carried this proposal to John Shikellamy at Shamokin, the astute son of Weiser's old friend asked, "Will my dets be cancelled too?" to which Conrad was forced to give the weak reply that he did not know.[3]

While Hamilton was trying to cajole the assembly into voting money to fight against the French, Weiser wrote to him urging that two thousand men should be raised (Virginia had recruited only four hundred) and to take a firm stand on the Ohio. In characteristic language, he urged that they should "knock every Frenchmen on the Ohio that won't run on the head and if we don't do it now we never again shall be able to do it and our Posterity will condemn us for our Neglect."[4] While Hamilton must have welcomed Weiser's sentiments, they had no force with the lawmakers who controlled the purse strings of the province.

It is not necessary to recount the experiences of the Virginia military expedition led by George Washington in 1754. The sparks that flew from Fort Necessity in the wilderness of western Pennsylvania set off a martial magazine that finally plunged the civilized world into the Seven Years War. The financial obligations contracted during that period remain unpaid to this day. The struggle for empire had begun!

THE LONG ARM OF CONNECTICUT

Meanwhile, Pennsylvania was beset with Indian problems nearer home. The Wyoming lands on the Susquehanna had never been purchased from any other tribes. These lands were cherished by the Indians and in all previous negotiations, they had steadfastly refused to part with them. Equally insistent were the Indians that no settlers should squat on these domains. Pennsylvania had always respected the position of the Indians and officials used their best efforts to keep their people from trespassing.

---
3. Weiser to Peters, from Lancaster, February 7, 1754, Weiser MSS, 2:55.
4. Weiser MSS, 2:25. A fragment, n.d.

Late in 1753, came the disturbing news that settlers from the province of Connecticut were staking out claims for the Wyoming lands in Penn's province. Invoking the nebulous terms of her sea to sea charter some enterprising New Englanders were planning a migration westward along the parallels established in the ancient document. There is no evidence that the project had the official sanction of the governor of Connecticut, but persons of considerable prominence were involved in the scheme, among them William Ogilvie, a missionary among the Stockbridge Indians of New England.

When Ogilvie first came to Wyoming, it was believed that his purpose was purely charitable. The first plans of Pennsylvania were dealing with this new problem called for sending Moravian missionaries to Wyoming to counteract the influence of the "Scotch Religion" as Ogilvie's professed faith was known to Pennsylvanians. Weiser recommended that Moravians be encouraged at Wyoming and he wrote to Reverend Peter Boehler, at Bethlehem, to this point.[5]

The invasion of the Connecticut people took on a far more serious aspect when it was learned that the New Englanders were trying to negotiate a treaty of purchase of these lands from the Mohawk Indians. They were using Colonel Johnson and Henry Lydius, Albany people, to carry on the transaction.

The terms of the alliance between Pennsylvania and the Six Nations were clear and definite in the provision that Penn would never buy land through any tribe other than the deputies of the Six Nations. Although the Mohawks formed one of the Six Nations, they were not empowered to act individually, in fact, this tribe never shared in the distribution of goods received by the Six Nations at the time of the sale.

This new complication would certainly provoke discord among the Indian allies of the British colonies at a time when one of them could risk such a breach. The Indians residing at Wyoming would resent the encroachment of the New Englanders and doubtlessly would look to Pennsylvania to evict them by force, if necessary.

Governor Hamilton handled this problem judiciously by making several concurrent moves, all of which proved, on the surface

---

5. Berks and Montgomery County MSS, 55.

at least, to be wise and prudent. He wrote to Colonel Johnson,[6] asking him to refrain from selling any lands in Pennsylvania to Governor Roger Wolcott of Connecticut, pointing out that such settlements would trespass on Penn's lands, and on April 6, 1754, he sent Conrad Weiser to Wyoming, by way of Shamokin, to investigate the state of affairs and assure the Indians his interest "to see Justice done."[7]

Weiser and his son Sammy set out for Wyoming on horseback, traveling by way of John Harris (Harrisburg) "being afraid of the two high mountains."[8] By this phrase, Weiser meant that he did not follow the Shamokin Trail over the Blue Mountain near present-day Bethel, Berks County, and Second Mountain, north of present-day Pine Grove, Schuylkill County. At Shamokin, the Weisers met with some delays. Conrad "thought fit" to send Sammy and the two sons of Shikellamy to Wyoming, while he investigated matters in Shamokin and along the northwest branch of the Susquehanna. Samuel Weiser had been taught the Mohawk language during the previous year and now he had a chance to use it. In addressing the Delawares, Sammy spoke in Mohawk which James Logan, one of Shikellamy's sons, relayed in Delaware.

Weiser reported that he and Sammy had learned that the Indians at Wyoming had observed some "New England Men that came as Spies last Fall; and they saw them making Draughts of the Land and Rivers and are much offended about it."[9]

Before the Weisers set out for Wyoming, Governor Hamilton had a reply from Governor Wolcott, declaring that Connecticut had no designs upon lands belonging to Pennsylvania and that any persons who moved to Wyoming had done so without his consent. When the Indians complained to Weiser therefore, he was able to say that the "spies" had come "against the Advice of their Superiors as a parcel of headstrong men and Disturbers of the Peace." The Indians replied that they were glad it was so.

Colonel William Johnson assured Governor Hamilton that he would have nothing to do with land transactions in Pennsylvania.

---

6. Colonial Records, 5:775–777.
7. Ibid., 6:24.
8. Weiser to Peters, April 17, 1754, Berks and Montgomery County MSS, 59.
9. Penn Papers, Indian Affairs, 2:9. Also Colonial Records, 6:34–38. His Journal.

Thus, for the moment, at least, a dangerous issue was avoided but it was destined to rise again.

Weiser's inquiries at Shamokin extended far beyond the problem of the Connecticut squatters. The Delawares were alarmed at the reports of French incursions. Many Delawares and Shawnees had moved to the Ohio country and their relatives along the Susquehanna had news of their fears. Weiser reported that the western Delawares had sent an urgent appeal to Onondaga couched in the following words: "Uncles of the United Nations, We expect to be killed by the French your Father; We desire, therefore, that You will take off our Petticoat that we may fight for ourselves, our Wives and Children." The term "petticoat" was a term of derision, which the Iroquois used to designate vassal tribes. Conquered people were women and not allowed to engage in warfare. Many other details were reported by Weiser in his journal of the Wyoming journey of 1754. In reporting to the Assembly, Hamilton declared: "Mr. Weiser's journey answered my Purposes."

INTERCOLONIAL CONFERENCE AT ALBANY, 1754

The modified state of Indian affairs in the American colonies convinced the London Board of Trade that His Majesty's government must now take a hand to bring about more unified action in all English possessions in North America. Accordingly, a conference of all colonies was summoned to meet in Albany in the summer of 1754. James DeLancey, replacing Clinton as governor of New York, issued the call and in his letter to Governor Hamilton he begged "to let Mr. Weiser accompany your commissioners to Albany." He complained, "Where I shall find an able Interpreter in this Country I know not, nor have been able to learn, the one we have is very unequal to the Service." He asked for Weiser "that we may have his Assistance, or else WE shall be at some Difficulty to understand the Indians or they us."[10]

When Conrad Weiser was informed of Governor DeLancey's question that he should act as chief interpreter at the Albany

---
10. James DeLancey to Governor Hamilton, April 1, 1754, Colonial Records, 6:15.

intercolonial Conference of 1754, he accepted the assignment hesitatingly.[11] He was willing to accompany the Pennsylvania commission but, pleaded Weiser, he had lost his fluency in the Mohawk tongue. This assertion of Weiser's is difficult to understand when we bear in mind that less than one year earlier Conrad had amazed the Mohawk squaw Susanna with his expertness in speaking the Indian language.[12]

We must conclude that Weiser had other reasons for his reluctance than the one he expressed. In his letter of February 7, 1754, Weiser wrote to Peters: "I don't like the request of the Board of Trade that all these governments should treat with the Indians at Albany. It will not turn out to the best of us and other governments besides New York. Such has been the New Yorkers' aim for several years and they will no doubt not rest there, but they will serve us also as managers for us and pay themselves out of your stock if they can." In this statement, Weiser may have referred to reported plans to make Colonel William Johnson master of all Indian affairs in North America as a deputy from the King of England.

His reluctance to serve as chief interpreter may have been due to Weiser's intimate knowledge of New York provincial politics. William Johnson and James DeLancey were political foes. Former Governor Clinton had been Johnson's sponsor, while Lieutenant Governor DeLancey quarreled bitterly with the white friend of the Mohawks. In 1753 Governor Clinton, weary of colonial problems, sailed for England in retirement. The man named to succeed him, Sir Danvers Osborne, committed suicide soon after his arrival in America and Lieutenant Governor DeLancey was promoted to the vacant position. In seeking an explanation of Weiser's sudden deficiency in the Mohawk tongue we may toy with the conjecture that he felt that DeLancey was using him to eliminate Johnson or Johnson's men from the Albany Conference of 1754. Such reasoning on Weiser's part would not be magnanimity but a calculated gesture to avoid giving offense to Johnson's Indian wards of Mohawk's Castles, or to Johnson himself.

Then, too, Weiser's objections may have grown out of the problems presented by the Connecticut encroachments on

---
11. Peters MSS, 3:99.
12. Colonial Records, 6:49.

Pennsylvania soil. A new purchase of Indian lands in Pennsylvania was being urged by the provincial authorities and there were some suggestions made that such a purchase should be negotiated at Albany during the forthcoming conference. Weiser disapproved strongly of treating for lands in Albany "because I know that there is people that will oppose us and do us mischief and have already done it . . . I cannot force things to go as I will, but must submit to accidents." This expression forms a part of the same letter quoted earlier in which Weiser demurred against the wisdom of an intercolonial Indian conference to be held in Albany. He goes on to suggest to Peters that the restrictions against squatters be abandoned, allowing whites to settle on the unpurchased lands and then arranging a purchase once the lands are occupied. "What can they (the Indians) say?" asks Weiser "The people of Pennsylvania are their Brethren according to the Treaties subsisting." Had Weiser joined the land-hungry wolves who were evicting the natives by fair means or foul? His recommendation of February 1754 and some of his subsequent actions might lead the observer to such a conclusion.

On May 24, 1754, Weiser received instructions to come to Philadelphia one week later and confer with the governor, preparatory to setting out with the commissioners to Albany. Sammy Weiser was ordered to join with his father in the journey northward. Governor Hamilton appointed the following persons as Pennsylvania's commissioners at the Albany Conference: John Penn, Richard Peters, Isaac Norris, and Benjamin Franklin.

On June 3, the travelers reached Trenton and on the next day came to Brunswick. Two days later, in New York, Weiser advised the commissioners on the purchase of Indian treaty goods. The Pennsylvania Assembly had not hesitated in providing money for the Albany Conference. On the following day, Friday, June 7, Weiser and Benjamin Franklin helped the Maryland commissioners select their presents for delivery to the Indians at Albany. In his diary of the journey, Franklin refers to Conrad as Mr. Weiser. The Pennsylvania party boarded a sloop to sail up the Hudson and on June 12, they "came to anchor near Albany," as Franklin puts it.[13]

---

13. Benjamin Franklin's account of journey to Albany, 1754, Pennsylvania Archives, 2:145.

Every American school child has learned that Benjamin Franklin was the author of a Plan of Union of the American colonies, as proposed at the Albany Conference of 1754. Certain it is that the plan grew out of the realization disunited colonies dissipated their strength in dealing with Indian affairs individually. Our purpose, here, however, is to follow the services of Conrad Weiser as he dealt with problems which arose during the historic conference.

Days intervening between the arrival of the commissioners and the opening of the treaty on July 3 were consumed in waiting for the tardy representatives of some colonies and some Indian Nations. Robert Proud, the earliest Pennsylvania historian, writing during the Revolutionary War period, stated that DeLancey's speech was "probably prepared by Conrad Weiser." A portion of the speech declared "It is fortunate that Mr. Weiser, who transacts the publick business of Virginia with your (Six) Nations, and is one of your Council and knows these matters well, is now present. Hear the account he gives."[14]

FACING FACTS

Weiser then spoke directly to the Indians, explaining the chain of events which led to the outbreak of hostilities in Ohio. He told them very frankly the circumstances which led to the capture of 44 Virginians under Captain William Trent while the men were engaged in constructing a fort on the spot which later became Fort Duquesne under French control. Weiser could not know that at the very moment he was framing his speech in Albany, George Washington was losing Fort Necessity to the invaders, July 3, 1754. Bluntly Weiser told the Six Nations "As to Pennsylvania, they have never sent a Warrior or built a Fort at Ohio."

On July 5, the Indians replied to Weiser's remarks: "We thank the Governor of Virginia for assisting the Indians of Ohio, who are our Relations and Allies; and we approve of the Governor of Pennsylvania not having yet intermeddled in the affair. He is a wise, prudent Man, and will know his own Time." How Governor Hamilton must have chafed and his Quaker Assembly chortled when they read this utterly insincere statement of the Indians.

---

14. Colonial Records, 6:84–85.

In stating Pennsylvania's case before the New York Indians, Weiser was acting in accordance with an Indian policy which he had always recommended to the Pennsylvania authorities. This policy was based upon the assumption that all Indian affairs were centralized in the Councils of the Six Nations, with Onondaga (Syracuse) as the capital of the Confederacy. All other tribes were vassals to the Mingoes; wearers of "petticoats" if conquered and merely "cousins" if tribes were too weak to resist aggression from powerful neighbors. For more than a score of years this policy had served Pennsylvania well, but when Iroquois authority tried to extend itself into the Ohio, it was not the strong hand that lay upon such inferior tribes as the Conestogas, Nescopecks, and other Pennsylvania Indians.

In confronting a powerful enemy such as the French, the political organization of the Six Nations was unequal to the task of offering effectual aid to their distant "cousins" in Ohio. Even the Onondaga Councils were divided in their loyalty to the English cause. In the light of these circumstances we can look back today and conclude that Weiser's efforts at Albany were in vain, but ours is second sight and Weiser, in his day, could not be expected to be aware of all the great changes which forest diplomacy had undergone between 1748, when he made his first journey to Ohio, and 1754, when French soldiers were sweeping on to victory over the Virginians and the friendly Ohio Indians.

THE ALBANY PURCHASE, 1754

Despite Conrad Weiser's advice against attempting to effect land purchased during the Albany Conference, the Penn Proprietors had instructed their commissioners to try to negotiate two purchases. One parcel of land desired by the Penns was the vast, unsurveyed tract of land extending through the Juniata Valley, northwestward to some undefined limits fixed by Penn's original grant from King Charles II. The other lands to be granted were the Shamokin and Wyoming lands along the northeast branch of the Susquehanna.

The purchase of the Juniata lands seemed to be the best way of solving the problem of trespassing settlers upon those lands. In

1750 the authorities, led by Conrad Weiser and Richard Peters, had attempted to evict the squatters from that area, but the arm of the law was unequal to the task of keeping settlers from building their frontier homes on the Indians' lands. Frankly confessing their inability to live up to their treaty pledges on this count, the Pennsylvania authorities asked for the deeding of the Juniata as the best solution to the problem. Prior to joining the commissioners on their journey to the intercolonial conference at Albany in 1754, Weiser had dispatched John Shikellamy to Onondaga with orders to find out how the Six Nations felt about parting with the lands drained by the Juniata.

The desire to purchase the lands east of the Susquehanna grew out of the aggressive moves of Connecticut people in the Wyoming Valley. Even though the matter appeared to have been settled satisfactorily after Weiser's visit to Wyoming in 1753, it was learned that the New Englanders had formed a stock company knows as the Susquehanna Company and that they were conniving with the Mohawks to gain an Indian title to the lands.

From the earliest days of William Penn and his famous treaty under an elm tree, it had been the policy of the Penns to conduct all Indian treaties publicly and in open Council. Weiser had always adhered to this policy and it is probable that he foresaw difficulties growing out of a treaty purchase staged in New York province, where the procedures would be determined by New York practice of private dealing rather than open covenants, openly negotiated.

When the matter of land purchases by Pennsylvania was broached in the conference, Governor DeLancey first satisfied himself that no New York lands were involved in the contemplated sale and then promptly forbade the Pennsylvanians to treat with the Six Nations as a part of the public proceedings. References to Pennsylvania's land interests were ordered struck from the minutes of the conference if alluded to by the Indians and all transactions had to be carried on in the "Indians' Lodgings" in Albany. The Pennsylvania commissioners, John Penn, Richard Peters, Isaac Norris, and Benjamin Franklin, protested this ruling, but it availed them nothing. The Albany Purchase was effected at the private home of James Stevenson of Albany.

NEGOTIATING THE PURCHASE

On the 19th of June, John Shikellamy came to Albany to report on his mission to Onondaga, bringing with him several Oneidas and Cayugas.[15] The tribes were most concerned in the Juniata lands because they had won them by conquest. The tribes were willing to sell the western lands, reported Shikellamy's son. He was ably supported by Gachradoda, the Cayuga orator who had figured in the Lancaster Treaty of 1744. "Gachradoda, in particular, was very hearty for the Proprietaries."

The Cayuga Chieftain, in company with several Oneidas and Tuscaroras, made a friendly visit to his old friend Conrad Weiser in the latter's rented quarters. Weiser won the complete support of Gachradoda "by a Reward to serve as his private Counsellor and direct him in what measures to take to engage the Indians for a Sale, either of the whole Province or so much of it as to take in the Western Branch of Susquehannah called in their Language Senaxsee." Gachradoda set himself to the task of bringing the Six Nations representatives already at Albany into line with these proposals.

The "Counsellor" reported to Weiser that all tribes were agreed to the sale except the Oneidas, who insisted that no action be taken without consulting the Mohawks. Here was the first sign of trouble. The Mohawks led by Hendricks were conniving with the Connecticut people to block the sale of the Wyoming lands and Hendricks, the orator of Mohawk's Castles, held great sway in Indian Councils. When the Mohawks were consulted by the Oneidas on the matter of the sale of western lands in Pennsylvania, Hendricks, the Mohawk Chieftain, was given the management of the transaction and Weiser's "Counsellor" Gachradoda was effaced. Hendricks prevailed upon the Six Nations to refuse to sell any lands west of the Allegheny Hills and any lands which drained into the northwest branch of the Susquehanna.

When the commissioners made their proposal to seventy chiefs of the Six Nations, interpreted by Weiser, it was soon noticed that the Indians were divided in opinion. They formed a circle in

---

15. Weiser had sent John Shikellimy to sound out the Six Nations about further purchases by Pennsylvania. Colonial Records, 6:110–113.

a room in the Stevenson house and carried on heated debates among themselves. Chief Hendricks, observing Weiser standing near the circle, asked the interpreter to leave them to themselves and Conrad obliged by withdrawing. Sometime later they sent for him again and stated that they were ready to answer.

They were willing, declared Hendricks, to sell some land west of the Susquehanna, but the lands at Shamokin and Wyoming "we will never part with . . . Our Bones are scattered there . . . We reserve it to settle such of our Nations as shall return from Ohio." In speaking about the claims of the New Englander, Hendricks averred "neither of you shall have it. We will not part with it to either of you." It was evident that the Mohawks, although not empowered to sell the Wyoming Valley to Connecticut, were determined to prevent Pennsylvania from acquiring possession.

Hendricks' plan to limit the sale of the Juniata lands to the crest of the Alleghenies dismayed the Pennsylvania commissioners. One objective in making the purchase was to establish the Penn claim to the western limits of Penn's grant and it was believed that the grant extended into the Ohio country, perhaps as far as the shores of Lake Erie.

After Hendricks made his speech, Weiser observed that "high Dissensions arose among the Indians." He reported this to the commissioners, saying that he did not know "the Issue of their Consultations." Advised "not to truckle" or to attend these debates, Weiser joined in the deliberations of the commissioners. The result of their conference was a bold stroke in Indian diplomacy. Weiser was instructed to charge the Six Nations with disloyalty to the English in refusing to sell lands beyond the Allegheny Hills; that the Six Nations were in league with the French, secretly selling them the Ohio lands which belonged to Penn. This accusation had the desired effect upon the Indians and soon thereafter they came penitently and offered to sell western lands in Pennsylvania south of the west branch of the Susquehanna, no matter how far they extended into the Ohio country. The Indians called Weiser into their Council and told him that they were resolved "not to suffer the commissioners to depart in Anger."

The terms of the sale agreed upon by Weiser and the Indians were as follows: From the Blue Mountains on the Susquehanna north to present-day Penn's Creek, Snyder County, and then northwest by a line to be run at some later time to the western limits of the province, wherever that might be. These terms were agreed upon while consulting Lewis Evans' map, taking for granted that the lands sold would embrace the entire area drained by the Juniata.

When Hendricks faced the commissioners to present the new plan he announced the terms, concluding by saying tersely, "Make out your Deed and be long about it."

"The Wyoming lands were not for sale," reiterated Hendricks. "If colonists settled there, be they sons of Onas or New Englanders, we will come ourselves and turn them all off." And that settled the matter!

Chief Hendricks had made it very plain that the Indians would not sell the Wyoming lands to Pennsylvania. All that the Penn commissioners could try to do was to prevent the Mohawks from selling these lands to the Connecticut people, and after the signing of the treaty, purchasing the western lands, Weiser was instructed to see what he could do to convince both the Indians and the Connecticut agents that the Mohawks had no right to sell.

Several weeks before the commissioners had set out for Albany, Weiser wrote to Richard Peters from Tulpehocken suggesting that the governor's secretary make a search for the Indian deed of 1736 negotiated at Weiser's house in the days of James Logan before Peters came upon the scene in his official capacity. Peters found the treaty of 1735 and brought it to the Albany Conference.

Weiser summoned the chiefs of the Six Nations, including Hendricks, showed them the signatures of their departed chiefs and received grunts of agreement from the sachems as he translated its terms. Next, the deeds were shown to the Connecticut agents, Woodbridge and Williams, who agreed that Pennsylvania had prior rights in all land purchases. Both men agreed that they would not press the Connecticut claims. For the moment, at least, Weiser's foresight in resurrecting the 18-year-old treaty had served a good purpose.

THE AUGHWICK MISSION

Soon after his return from the Albany Conference of 1754, Conrad Weiser was entrusted with a difficult mission to George Croghan's plantation at Aughwick, near present-day Shirleysburg in Huntingdon County, Pennsylvania. A veteran of many critical conferences in forest diplomacy though he was, Weiser, aged fifty-eight, faced a situation that called for all his gifts in diplomacy; his skill in turning phrases to soothe injured pride; his adroitness in promising much with little to offer; and his patience and forbearance with human frailties. That he realized the broad and ominous implications of the events connected with that mission is evident from the precise and detailed accounts of the journey as he recorded them for his superiors, and for posterity.

The chain of events which led to the mission fell suddenly into the lap of Governor James Hamilton while that worthy gentleman was contemplating the ease which would soon be his when the newly appointed deputy governor, Robert Hunter Morris, would assume his office. When the first signs of trouble came to Hamilton's attention, he was without counselors to help him. Peters, Franklin, Norris, Penn, and Weiser were at Albany in July 1754, when a letter from Andrew Montour, sent from Winchester, in Virginia, informed Pennsylvania that the Half-King, the Six Nations vice-regent to Ohio, had left Virginia to settle in Aughwick, Pennsylvania.

The Half-King, Tanacharisson, was an ally of Colonel George Washington, the Virginia commander of the expedition against the French. The presence of the Half-King and Scarroday, known as Monckatootha, an Oneida, had served to keep the Indians in Ohio loyal to the English cause. Washington had been defeated at Fort Necessity and the two representatives of the Six Nations had parted company with him, seeking refuge in the Pennsylvania government. They had brought their families with them and, according to Montour, were planning to have the Delawares and Shawnees join them.

A second letter, this one from George Croghan, written from Aughwick, arrived after the Pennsylvania delegation, including

Weiser, had returned from Albany. Croghan was surrounded by Indians seeking refuge on his plantation. The late-comers brought word that the French were spreading a report that the Half-King and his Six Nations adherents had been slaughtered by his Catawbas Indians. They expressed their impatience with the English for failing to come to their aid. Croghan urged that Pennsylvania should send a representative of the governor to reassure his unwelcome guests of aid in the days to come.

The third letter from Fort Duquesne written by Captain Robert Stobo urged aggressive action in attacking the French invaders.[16]

When these matters were presented to the provincial council, that body decided that "Conrad Weiser should be immediately sent with a Sum of money and proper Instructions to Aughwick." There was no time to wait for the assembly to vote a sum of money, but it was hoped that "if the Letter (Croghan's) should be laid before such of the Members as lived in Town they would readily supply the Money."

Hamilton wrote to Croghan informing him of Council's action and stating that "Mr. Weiser, who was fortunately in Town" would set out for Aughwick immediately. Croghan was asked to give Weiser every possible assistance in carrying out the Governor's instructions. The continued loyalty of the western Indians was at stake.

Conrad Weiser was given a set of specific instructions. He was to study the situation at Aughwick, to learn the intentions of the various western tribes; to find out what part the Onondaga council had in their deliberations, and particularly the disposition of the Senecas. In the name of the governor, Weiser was to welcome all of them as wards of the province. He was to explain the delay in furnishing aid by telling the Indians that Hamilton's term "draws to a Period" and that the new governor would effect plans to drive out the French.[17] A very pointed instruction was added, charging Weiser to destroy all liquor found at Aughwick. Three hundred pounds had been raised to be placed at Weiser's disposal, to be spent to the best advantage.

---

16. These letters are reproduced in the Colonial Records, vol. 6.
17. Instructions to Weiser, Ibid., 143.

Weiser received his instructions on August 24, 1754, and returned to his home in Heidelberg, now Berks County. There he rested for one day "the weather being excessive hot" and then, on the 29th, he and Sammy set out upon his 180-mile journey westward. When he reached Harris Ferry (Harrisburg) on the Susquehanna, he learned that the Half-King was at a trader's house nearby. Sammy Weiser was sent to invite the Half-King, who was then "a little in Liquor" to join the Weiser party to Aughwick. The invitation was accepted promptly and soon there was heard a "hallo" from the west bank of the Susquehanna. It was Andrew Montour and a party of Indians. This group decided to join Weiser and the Half-King on their journey westward to George Croghan's farm.[18]

The route by which Weiser and his companions traveled led to Andrew Montour's farm. Fifteen Indians greeted Weiser, and the Half-King when they reached Montour's. Andrew's wife had killed a sheep for them and the hungry natives made free use of the ripening corn. Weiser expended ten pounds "of the Government's money" to compensate the Montours.

AN INDIAN'S OPINION OF GEORGE WASHINGTON

As they rode on toward Aughwick, Weiser and the Half-King discussed the Virginia disaster at the Meadows and the Half-King confided to Weiser his opinion of Colonel George Washington. Weiser recorded these remarks and therefore we have a unique appraisal of George Washington made by an Indian contemporary. The Half-King complained that the young colonel treated the Indians as slaves; he would "by no means take Advice from the Indians; he dallied too long and failed to build the proper fortification; the English had acted 'as Fools' at Fort Necessity." On the whole, however, the Half-King opined that Colonel Washington "was a good-natured man, but had no Experience."

At noon on September 3, Weiser and his party reached Aughwick. They were greeted by the firing of many guns.

---

18. Weiser's Journal of Journey to Aughwick, Ibid., 150–160.

When the conferences began the Delawares and Shawnees explained that they had come to Aughwick in compliance with the terms of the Carlisle Treaty of the previous year. At that treaty, they stated they were asked by Pennsylvania and the Six Nations to refrain from fighting and to report any news they learned. They had lost some of their chiefs and needed to have their tears wiped away. This Weiser proceeded to do by purchasing presents from Croghan's stock.

In delivering the governor's message, Weiser explained that Hamilton's term was ending; that the new governor would "doubtless bring the King's Order to all" concerning what steps should be taken to deal with the French invaders. "Make yourselves quiet and easy . . . till you see Us first stir," he counseled. He asked the Delawares and Shawnees to stay in Pennsylvania until the new governor arrived.

The conferences at Aughwick proceeded without complications through the early discussions. These were the customary ceremonials and flattering speeches. On September 4, the Beaver, speaking for the Delawares, reminded the Governor of the ancient pledges of William Penn. To this Weiser replied, "I am too mean a man" to answer so "weighty a Matter." To this, the Indians shouted Yoh-ha, the cry of approval.

WEISER REPORTS THE ALBANY PURCHASE

On September 5, a very delicate subject was broached. The Indians asked Weiser what business was transacted at Albany. Confronted by the Chiefs whose lands had been sold from under them by their "uncles," the Six Nations, Weiser told them frankly that a large purchase had been made west of the Susquehanna. This was indeed a difficult situation. Some writers have charged Conrad Weiser with the responsibility of alienating the Delawares and Shawnees and insofar as he was directly responsible for shaping the Indian policy of Pennsylvania in general, the charge can be sustained. Certainly, it was Weiser who urged that all Indian matters in Pennsylvania should be negotiated through the

Six Nations, instead of dealing directly through the Council of the Delawares.

In taking such a position, Weiser was acting and advising in accordance with his best knowledge of Indian affairs, knowledge gained during his boyhood life with the Indians and forty years of experience. The Six Nations looked upon all peoples whom they had conquered as vassal tribes; they scornfully called them "cousins" and neutralized their councils by declaring them to be women, figuratively wearing "petticoats." According to Indian psychology, Weiser knew that "cousins" in "petticoats" had no sovereign power to make treaties.

Here it must be pointed out, too, that so long as Weiser's hand was free, before the advent of Colonel William Johnson, this policy had always worked.

While it is true that the Albany Purchase of 1754 was the most vital link in the chain of circumstances which finally brought about the desertion of the Delawares and their allies to the French, and consequently brought the tomahawk and firebrand into Pennsylvania in 1755, drenching the frontiers in blood, this act cannot be charged to Weiser. It will be remembered that Conrad had advised against land purchases at Albany, urging that such treaties be made in Pennsylvania, where the treaty goods could be divided properly. It will be remembered, also, that Weiser disapproved of the Albany conference in general, even to the point of pleading that he had lost his fluency in the Mohawk tongue. It will be shown that the overt act which brought on the bloody Indian massacres beginning in 1755 was something entirely disassociated from Weiser's activities.

When the Indians at Aughwick learned of the sale of their hunting grounds, "they seemed not to be very well pleased," wrote Weiser. Yet, when he explained the "Design" of the Connecticut people to buy the Wyoming lands and dwelt upon French methods of securing Lands, the Delawares were appeased "but would have been more so (content) if they had received a Part of the Consideration."

The Indians at Croghan's farm did not realize the full significance of the Albany Purchase yet. The treaty line to the northwest had not yet been run and it is doubtful whether Weiser himself envisioned the vast territory embraced in the terms of the Albany Purchase. Certainly, the Indians did not, for as John Shikellamy remarked when he first heard of the terms of the treaty: "Indians do not know the Points of the Compass."

The formal conference ended on September 6. That evening the Indians "got Liquor and all got drunk." Weiser had planned to set out upon his homeward journey on the following day, but Tanacharisson, the Half-King, a Seneca, and Scarroday, an Oneida, implored him to stay to discuss some other business of grave concern. But these chiefs became drunk soon after making their request and Weiser was forced to linger at Aughwick until the two sachems became sober once more.

Scarroday and the Half-King represented the Six Nations at the Indian conference at Aughwick in September 1754. Both chiefs were zealous in the cause of the English and earnestly tried everything in their power to resist the French invasion of the Ohio country. The other Indians, Delawares, Shawnees, Wyandots, and Miamis, deferred to these two, the Half-King, a Seneca, and Scarroday, an Oneida. In public address, they were "uncles" to the subordinate tribes.

CONCERN FOR INDIAN WELFARE

Weiser reported to Governor Hamilton that at least two hundred Indians were encamped on Croghan's farm at Aughwick "and a great many more scattered thereabouts." This great company of natives made inroads into Croghan's store of supplies. A twenty-five-acre field of ripening corn was being denuded to secure roasting ears and petty thievery robbed the master of the plantation of milk, butter, and other edibles on hand. The "Bloody Flux" attacked some of the host of Indians. And to make matters worse, Lewis Montour, Andrew's brother, brought liquor and hid it in the woods, beyond the power of Weiser to stave the casks. The Indians sneaked into the woods and in Weiser's words "drink their Clothing and so come back to Croghan's drunk and naked." When Lewis Montour was charged with the blame he took the position "that his Wife, which is an ugly Indian Squa(w), does it."

It will be remembered that Weiser's instructions for the Aughwick mission ordered him to put a stop to the liquor traffic. In reporting to the governor, Weiser charged that the magistrates of Cumberland County were, themselves, the worst offenders in the illicit trade. One magistrate named Smith came to Aughwick while Weiser was there, "He is an old Hypocrite," declared Conrad in reporting this visit. The magistrate came ostensibly to Weiser to protect liquor violations, but his real purpose was to collect for whiskey he had sent in advance. When Smith blamed the governor for failing to put an end to the traffic in strong liquor, Weiser countered by asking Smith whether he wanted "the Governor to come up with his Sword and Pistol to prevent it." Smith said, "No." "Well, then, says I," Weiser clinched his point, "there is no other way for the governor then to break you all and put others in Commission (magistrates) that are no Whiskey Traders."

It was Weiser's duty to do what he could to relieve the distress of the wards of the province who had cast themselves upon the hospitality of George Croghan. Some of the provincial funds were spent to buy lead and powder so that the Indians could hunt for their own food. Other sums were spent to distribute gifts purchased in Croghan's trading house and to compensate Croghan for the losses he suffered and probably would continue to suffer for some time to come if the Indians heeded the governor's request that they should remain there until the new governor gave the signal for action.

Weiser's instructions were emphatic on the point that he should inquire about the state of Indian affairs at Onondaga and Ohio. Such information could be had from the two leading Six Nations Indians, the Half-King and Scarroday, both drunk after the formal discussions ended. Weiser always depended upon private conversations to learn the true state of affairs, in this way getting at the roots of generalities expressed in open Council. When the two sachems recovered from their stupor, Weiser engaged them in conversation and learned a few things which he deemed important enough to transmit to the governor.

Among other things, he had learned that the Senecas had given their wards in Ohio orders not to meddle with the French; that the Twightwees (Miamis) had urged the Shawnees to take up the hatchet in vengeance and that the Shawnees had sent the Miami deputies home with orders to get out of the village immediately lest the French strike while they were there; that at least three of the Six Nations could be depended upon to help the English in a war against the French, namely the Oneidas, Tuscaroras, and Mohawks; that Scarroday was going to the Six Nations council to plead with them for complete cooperation with the English.

Perhaps the most significant item of information, in the light of subsequent events, was the intelligence that the French had made large presents to the Delawares and Shawnees, urging them to join the enemies of the English. The two nations had not committed themselves to any side of the issue but instead had come to Aughwick to see what the English had to offer.

Throughout the conference, Weiser had the complete cooperation of the trader, George Croghan, at whose farm the motley assemblage of natives were camped. It was to Croghan's interest to support Weiser because his reimbursement for expenditures depended upon Weiser's recommendations to the Governor and the Council.

TROUBLE WITH ANDREW MONTOUR

In his dealings with the other non-native at Aughwick, Andrew Montour, Weiser was not so fortunate. The half-breed caused trouble in many ways. He was drunk most of the time and when intoxicated he fell to abusing Weiser in vile language. He damned Weiser, the Governor, and Richard Peters; he stirred up the Indians against the Albany Purchase, saying "he was a Warrior—how could he suffer the Irish to encroach upon him he would now kill some of them."

Weiser reprimanded Montour when he became sober, but as soon as he became drunk again the half-breed, agent of Virginia, repeated his threats, his cursing, and his blessings. Realizing that Montour might do a great deal of harm among the Indians, Weiser invited, urged, cajoled him to return to the settlements in his company. Montour refused and Weiser left the drunken interpreter at Croghan's with "a shoe on one leg that had no stocking on the other leg that wore no shoe." Repenting when he became sober, Montour hastened to follow Weiser to beg his pardon and some pocket money. In a few days, the penitent half-breed caught up with Weiser at Carlisle and asked for forgiveness and forty shillings. Weiser granted both requests and Montour set out for Virginia. The magnanimous Conrad, in reporting these human frailties, observed, "I don't take him to be in himself an ill-natured Fellow, but it is rather a Habit he took from the Indians and Indian Traders. He is always Extremely good-natured to me when he is sober." In weighing this utterance of Weiser, it is well to bear in mind that the Indian never held a man responsible for acts committed while intoxicated. They make a naïve distinction there, declaring that the evil deeds were performed by the evil spirits in spiritous liquor and not committed by the man himself. Note Weiser's use of the phrase, "to be in himself."

Weiser returned to his home on September 13, 1754. At Aughwick, Croghan was having his troubles with the Indians, as he reported to the governor under several heads introduced by the words, "Since Mr. Weiser left."[19]

Early in October, Weiser received an urgent message to come to Harris Ferry. The Half-King had died and was to be buried there. The Indians declared that the French had bewitched their leader. Weiser attended the funeral and saw the Seneca chieftain lowered into a grave near the last resting place of the first John Harris.[20] The Half-King's grave is probably within the present enclosure which marks the tomb of the founder at Harrisburg. The Indians at Aughwick requested that their leader should be buried according to the customs of the white men. The death of the Half-King was a severe blow to the English cause.

On the same day that the leader of the Indians died, October 1, 1754, a new leader of the white men of Pennsylvania arrived in Philadelphia. Robert Hunter Morris, formerly a judge in New Jersey, arrived in Philadelphia to assume his duties as governor in place of James Hamilton, retired.

Soon after the new governor had assumed his duties, Conrad Weiser reminded him of the pledges made at Aughwick a month earlier. Morris sent a message to the Indians, assuring them of

---
19. Croghan to Hamilton, Sept. 27, 1754, Pennsylvania Archives, 2:173.
20. Notes and Queries, *Pennsylvania Magazine of History and Biography*, 4:251–252.

the friendship and ratifying Weiser's speeches to them. "Consider always there is your Home," he urged. The message was written by Conrad Weiser and signed by the governor. This message was sent to Aughwick, Andrew Montour acting as messenger.

Scarroday had assumed the vice-regency of the Six Nations after the Half-King's death. In December, he came to Philadelphia to plead the cause of the Indians before the Council of the province. In impassioned terms, he painted a melancholy picture of the state of affairs. "I am revolving in my Breast the Fate of our Forefathers. Multitudes of Sculls, some of our Forefathers, some of our Brethren, lye on Heaps before my Eyes. I see large Quantities of dry Bones; those who animated them were all destroyed by our Enemies." He begged that the English should bestir themselves. He was on his way to Onondaga to raise the war-cry in the Councils of the Six Nations. What could he promise for Onas, for Pennsylvania? The Indians would strike if the white men would give them a signal.

The best answer that the governor and council could give to this ardent plea was a promise to refer it to the assembly, an assembly hostile to the governor and committed to a pacifist policy. Scarroday's tears availed him nothing, as he departed to plead with his own people.

In the meantime, hundreds of Indians were fastened upon the farm of Croghan at Aughwick, consuming the provisions that this plantation offered. Weiser had left a sum of money with Croghan for the purchase of 500 bushels of wheat, assuring the trader that more money would be sent if needed. On December 2 a letter from Croghan to Peters complained that no additional funds or supplies had arrived, which made the writer conclude "that those Indians was taken no Notice of" and the Indians were "always teasing me for those promises." Three days later, Croghan informed Peters that the Shawnees had tired of waiting and had gone into the woods. As a partial solution to the vexing problems confronting him, Croghan suggested that the remaining Indians he quartered nearer to the settlements.

To the last suggestion, Peters replied that such a course would be out of the question. He urged Croghan to keep the Indians where they were to build a stockade for them and keep on the west of the "Blue Hills." Late in December, a sum of money was sent to him to make good Weiser's promises. Croghan was left to devise means of protecting the hundreds of natives in his custody as the year 1754 moved into the bloody record of 1755.

DEEDS AND MISDEEDS

Christopher Sauer, the German publisher of Philadelphia, used the columns of his newspaper to assail the Albany Purchase of 1754 as an act of greedy men defrauding the Indians and sowing the seeds of war on the frontiers of Pennsylvania.[21] Soon after the news of the purchase was made public, settlers began to pour into the valleys north of the Juniata and Sherman's Creek, creating their homes in present-day Snyder County. Just as promptly, the squatters were given orders by the Indians to clear out of these lands. It became evident that the Pennsylvania Indians, either refused to honor the deed which their "uncles," the Six Nations had given at Albany, or else they did not know its terms. It is certain that they did not comprehend the full significance of the sale which gave the proprietaries seven hundred thousand acres west of the Susquehanna or more than twice the area purchased by any previous treaty.

The Indians were within their rights in evicting settlers who arrived before the boundary lines were determined. Realizing the need to establish such boundaries the provincial authorities ordered Conrad Weiser to "run" the northwest boundary lines, establishing the limits of the purchase. It will be remembered that the Albany deed granted the Penns the entire basin of the west branches of the Susquehanna, on both sides of the river, beginning at a point on the west bank of the river opposite the Blue mountains, near the present-day Penn's Creek, and then by a line northwest to the western limits of the province.

In attempting to carry out this assignment in October 1754, Weiser combined several other missions. We have seen that he attended the funeral services of the Half-King, assassin of the French officer Joseph Coulon de Jumonville, at Harris Ferry. At Shamokin, he lingered to build a log house for the Shikellamy

---
21. *Berichte*, September 16, 1754.

family. Earlier that year, one of the great chieftain's daughters had trudged to Weiser's home in Heidelberg and poured a tale of woe into Conrad's sympathetic ear. Things were going badly for the Shikellamys. The complainant's husband had died of smallpox; a son and a nephew had been slain by the Catawbas. John Petty, the youngest of Shikellamy's sons, had prevailed upon her son to take the warpath against the mother's protests. She was "perplexed and ashamed" records Weiser. At the time of her appeal, Conrad offered her little spiritual consolation. "I told her that it was the Hand of the Most High that fights now against those that went against the Catawbas after they had made a public and firm peace with them."

But out of human sympathy and perhaps with an eye to securing goodwill, Weiser undertook to ease the road for the Shikellamys by building them a house before winter set in. He employed six men to assist him. These deeds of charity were combined with the mission to determine the line of the Albany Purchase. On October 12 Weiser informed Richard Peters "I have also run the Boundary Line and made the Corner between the Honourable Proprietors and the Indians' Land a mile or two above the mouth of the Cayaunta and run near two miles Northwest by west." But Weiser did not survey the line. The Indians helping him, two Shikellamys, refused to carry the chain saying that the course "was not according to the Bargain." The Indians argued that they understood that the purchase did not involve the lands drained by the west branch of the Susquehanna and that it did not include Big Island, near present-day Lock Haven.

In his letter to Peters, Weiser supported this claim of the Indians, reminding Peters that the commissioners at Albany had assured the Indians that the Big Island would not be contained in the purchase. Weiser reminded Peters that Lewis Evans' map had been consulted at the treaty in Albany and that the map was shown to the Indians then as evidence that the Susquehanna basin was not involved in the sale. "But I saw plain," wrote Weiser in October, "that that Course would cross the Zinzchsa (West Branch) about Canasorgo (Muncy)."

In the light of this development, Weiser urged that the Proprietors should not stop at killing any settlers who ventured to settle in the disputed areas. John Shikellamy, who helped to carry the chain in October, had been present at Albany during the treaty purchase, even to the extent of urging the Six Nations to agree to it.

Because of the attitude of the Indians, Weiser did not conclude his task of "running the line." Later events proved that this was a very wise decision because other complications were developing east of the Susquehanna. Because of Weiser's patience in the matter of determining the limits of the Albany Purchase, the Delawares and Shawnees were disposed to listen to Hendricks, who urged them to honor the Albany treaty and not molest settlers. Also, because the problems west of the Susquehanna the province of Pennsylvania could deal with the new problem in Wyoming with clean hands.

"This dark Affair," wrote John Penn and Richard Peters, in referring to the schemes of the Connecticut people to secure a Mohawk deed for the Wyoming lands in Pennsylvania. Despite pious phrases and assurances to the contrary, the Connecticut commissioners left the Intercolonial Conference at Albany with an Indian deed to the Susquehanna Company, a group of more than four hundred and fifty New England people who planned to speculate in lands claimed under Connecticut's ancient sea to sea charter. These lands lay within William Penn's grant of land, but Yankee cupidity outweighed such consideration and they had no scruples against negotiating with Indians who had no right to sell for lands which the Susquehanna Company had no right to claim. Conniving with the New York agent, John Lydius, of doubted integrity, and Abraham Peters, wily Mohawk chieftain, the Connecticut commissioners boldly violated promises given to the Pennsylvania people but a day or two before the evil deed was done.

Having secured the signatures of some Indians present at Albany, the villainous Lydius rode among the Indian villages of the backcountry in New York, prevailing upon drunken Indians to affix their marks to the deed. In this way, he secured the signatures of some chiefs other than the Mohawks, which tribe had no rights to contract an individual sale without the approval of others of the Six Nations. Lydius had the audacity to induce one of Colonel William Johnson's Indian "guests" to sign. For this, he was severely upbraided by Johnson who, true to his promise to Pennsylvania, refused to be a party to Connecticut's nefarious schemes.

One day after Weiser returned to his home after spending two weeks in Shamokin trying to determine the Albany Purchase limits, he received a packet of letters apprising him of the perfidy of Lydius and the Connecticut people. His counsel was asked on how to proceed.

Through Indian channels, Weiser had learned of the Mohawk deed as early as September 23. At Shamokin, he learned from the Indians living there that the Indians would never permit the deed to stand. Conrad expressed his opinion that if colonists should attempt to settle in Wyoming lands "there will be Bloodshed and a great Deal of Mischief done."

In response to the request for suggestions, Weiser advised that some of the leaders of the Six Nations should be invited to Philadelphia to get them to deny the deed. If they would not come to Philadelphia, then Wyoming would be the proper place to confer. Also, advised Weiser, a special effort should be made to have the Cayugas represented because Lydius had not secured a single signature from that nation, as Weiser noted.

In a letter written October 27, Weiser advised further that a diligent search should be made in advance of a conference to determine whether Old Hendricks had been a party in the Mohawk deed. "If he has not, we will succeed without Doubt," he averred. If Hendricks refused to come into Pennsylvania, then we must send to Onondaga next Spring."[22]

Early in January 1755, Hendricks and several Mohawks came to Philadelphia and appeared before the Council. Weiser acted as interpreter.

Without quibbling, Hendricks came to the point very quickly, declaring, "Brother: WE have considered what you have said to Us about the deceitful Deed that John Lydius inveigled some of Us to sign."

We agree that the Deed should be destroyed. We agree with you "that it is a false Proceeding."

He advised that the whole matter be laid before the Six Nations for the final denunciation of the transaction.

---

22. Weiser to Peters, Dreer Collection, Historical Society of Pennsylvania, 62.

In presenting some of Hendricks' own words, we try to convey to the reader the brusque character of the Mohawk chieftain. He did not indulge in circuitous language and he sent his verbal shafts flashing to their destinations. At one point of the conference, Weiser informed the governor that Hendricks was making "Complaints against a Neighboring Province and therefore he deemed it best not to interpret these remarks into the record." Governor Morris agreed to this and directed that Weiser and Peters should take up such matters in private conversations.[23]

The bitter complaints were against New York and do not, directly, concern us here. But out of private discussions with the Mohawks, Weiser and Peters agreed upon a plan by which the deed to Connecticut could be invalidated.

The vexing problem of Connecticut claims did not end with the Mohawks' renunciation of the deed, but the part played by Conrad Weiser did end with this achievement.

It must be clear that Weiser had played a judicious part in trying to ward off the evil days that came in the autumn of 1755. He knew the temper of the Indians better than anyone then living.

---

23. Colonial Records, 6:243–249.

A young George Washington

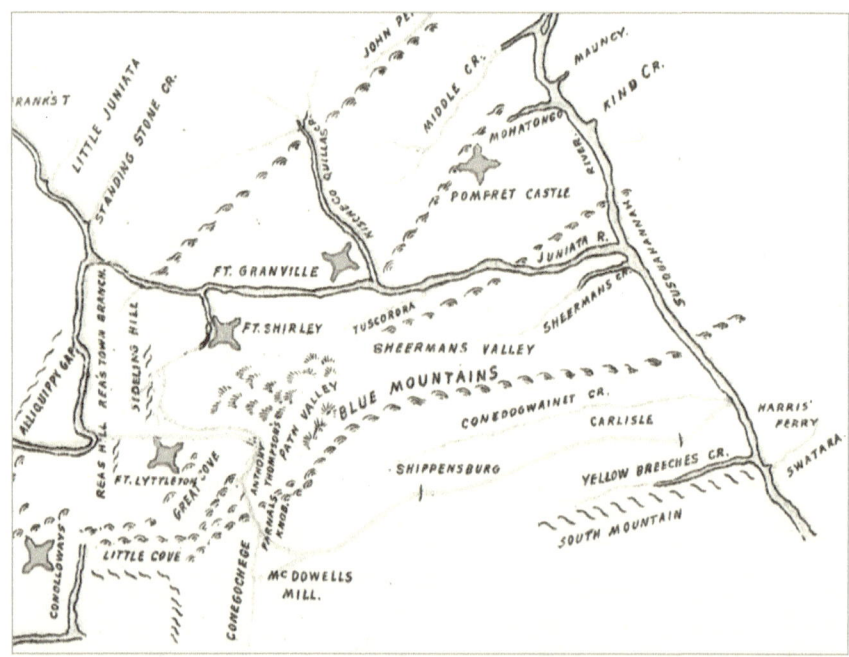

Detail from Darlington's 1755 Map. Croghan's Aughwick was near Fort Shirley, left of center.

CHAPTER XV

The Founder of Institutions

During the years 1748 to 1755, Conrad Weiser took an active part in establishing the institutions of civilization. He was one of the leaders in the building of the city of Reading; first president-judge of Berks County; a trustee of the Charity Schools and a leader in the establishment of the first Lutheran Church in Reading.

THE FOUNDING OF READING

Pocketed between the towering hills of the Neversink and Penn to the north and the serrated skyline formed by the Flying Hills to the southward, the city of Reading forms on the eastern bank of the Schuylkill River on a gently rising slope to the eastward. In early colonial days, the keen eyes of land speculators had marked this area as a desirable location for a city that was to grow in the huge bowl-shaped valley near the confluence of the Tulpehocken and Schuylkill. The original owners of this land were Richard Hockley, treasurer of the Penns; Thomas Lawrence, a member of the Executive Council of the province; Samuel Finney, a friend of William Penn, and a tract of 126 acres which remained as the property of Thomas and John Penn, sons of the Proprietor.

During the years that intervened between the original grants of patents and the surveys for planning a town, some of this land had changed ownership. Some of the Proprietary tracts had been sold to Francis Parvin, a Quaker, and to Peter Bingaman, a

German settler. Samuel Finney's tract was owned by his grandson's widow. In some of the earliest records, the town we know as Reading was referred to as "Widow Finney's Town."

In 1748, William Parsons, surveyor of the Penns, drew the plans for building lots and named the streets of Readingtown. In choosing names for streets the dutiful Parsons tried hard to flatter his employers, the Penns. The chief thoroughfare was named for the Penn family and the main intersecting street was named Callowhill (now Fifth Street) in honor of Hannah Callowhill, William Penn's second wife. Present-day Franklin Street was named Richard Street and Thomas Street was the present Washington Street, both early names honoring sons of the founder. Walnut Street was originally Margaret Street, in honor of one of Penn's daughters. Other streets were named in honor of Penn's friends in England.[1] The present-day numbered streets bore regal names, such as King, Queen, Prince, and Duke. In 1833 the Town Council of Reading abolished these names, excepting Penn Street, the main thoroughfare.

In February 1749, three commissioners were appointed to sell the lots upon which a city was to be built. These commissioners were Francis Parvin, William Hartley, and Conrad Weiser. A few houses already were constructed in the area and other lands were fenced in by renters, but for the most part, the site was open country in 1749 when the commissioners appointed the day of June 15, 1749, for the opening of the sale of lots.[2]

The area included in Parsons' plan embraced the present section of the Hampden Reservoir. The proprietors believed this to be thickly wooded and therefore promising an abundance of building timber, and it was believed that the building stone was plentiful. These materials would be needed by builders, for most of the remainder of the designated lots were lacking in both resources. By some means, unknown to us now, Francis Parvin of Maidencreek, one of the commissioners, had secured a warrant to this tract before the sale of lots was opened to the public. Penn's agents were infuriated when they learned of the transaction. They

---

1. Berks and Montgomery County MSS Collection, Historical Society of Pennsylvania, 48–49.
2. Ibid., 17. Also in Sauer's *Berichte* of July 1, 1749, announcing that "100 lots are laid out in Bershire Counti." The county of Berks was not formed until 1752, three years later.

realized that their town-building project would serve to enrich others than the Proprietors. Richard Peters asked Conrad Weiser to act as a mediator in the quarrel that ensued between Parvin and the Penn agents in Philadelphia.[3]

"To make the Story short," wrote Weiser, "I took Horseback with him (Parvin) and went to the very spot and followed the Lines all around the whole tracts (in Dispute) and I can safely say that I wondered as much at your disputing the thing or delaying the fulfilling of your promise to Francis as I did at the obstinacy and Stiffneckedness of Francis, for there is not one single Timber tree upon the whole Tract. Not one Foot of water, but a small or little spring of water under the Foot of the Hill not in Dispute. Not one Foot of medow can be made—Never a Stone will be fetch'd from there to build the town if it was to be so big as Philadelphia for there is Stones much nearer on the Proprietor's and Mr. Hockley's Lands—It is true forty acres or thereabouts may be fit for outlots for very poor ones and there may be some Rafters had for small building. As to the Distance from the Town (you know better than I) it is far enough. It is so far however in my humble opinion that he will never have nor his Posterity after him any Lots to sell or to build upon (as in the Town of Reading) but what he has from the Proprietors. I did all whatever I could to persuade Francis to drop the thing and take some other consideration for it but to no purpose. 'No,' says Francis, 'I will not give it u so why may not i have it as well as some others. The proprietors will never have or take it from me. It is some others that want it.(I suppose he reflects upon Mr. Hockley) and the proprietors should know of it.'"

Richard Peters relayed Weiser's message to Thomas Penn in England. The proprietor replied that he was displeased with Weiser that he (Weiser) could "think it possible that a piece of vacant land . . . should be surveyed without my express order." As one of the three commissioners, Weiser was partially responsible for this transaction warranting the land to Parvin.

Weiser incurred the displeasure of Thomas Penn on another score, the overt act coming at the same time as the Parvin affair. In his earlier years of service to the Penns, he had received

---

3. Penn Official Correspondence, 219. Also Bennett, Nolan J., *The Foundation of the Town of Reading, Pennsylvania*, 60.

payment for his services in cash, in some varying forms thirty to sixty pounds for services. After 1745, he preferred to accept his payments in the form of land grants. In 1748, Weiser acquired a self-appropriated "gift" of lands fronting along the Susquehanna near present-day Selinsgrove. When Thomas Penn learned of this transaction, he was exasperated. On February 13, 1749, Penn wrote to Peters:

> London, February 13, 1749
> Conrad by a pretended gift and in a manner very improper has acquired about three miles of the Susquehanna riverfront at Shamokin. This gratuity is much too large for his services. When we pay him money we know what we pay but we cannot estimate the value of this land. Though William Parsons writes Conrad must not be disobliged, I desire you to acquaint him that I am not well pleased with his action. Eight hundred acres is too much pay for his services. I think Conrad has been a serviceable man but I think he has been well paid for a man in his station. In the last Indian purchase, he will have been paid more than three times the value of what he should have for coming down with them. In the future, he should do as he is instructed for I will not have any more of his 'great services'.[4]

It is fortunate that Conrad Weiser did not know the contents of the Penn letter. The snobbery implied in the phrase, "For a man of his station" would have dampened his ardor for serving the Penns. As to the implied charge that Weiser had acted without permission Thomas Penn's pique got the better of his memory, for in May 1748 Richard Peters had informed the proprietor of the warrant granted Weiser to survey lands for himself. Of course, it is impossible to state with certainty what is in a man's mind; but from Richard Peters' letters of 1748, it appears that he was preparing his employer for the shock of a large grant to Weiser. Early in that year, he wrote, "We should train someone to succeed

---
4. Thomas Penn to Richard Peters, February 13, 1749, Penn Letter Book, 2:299. Also Nolan, supra, 65.

Mr. Weiser as interpreter as the Province will be in a dreadful condition in case of his death." Later, in May, he wrote, "Poor Conrad Weiser had like to have died a week or two ago and if he had what would have become of Indian affairs. I have given Mr. Weiser a warrant to accept the survey of some acres, all miserable stuff . . . and have told him it is a present from the Proprietors. He is exceedingly thankful and it is a great honor to him as the World must think that the Proprietors have a great regard for him or they would not at this Distance think of him and the accommodation of his little country affairs."

But Weiser knew nothing of these patronizing statements by Peters or the scornful imputations of Penn. He went about his duties as a commissioner for the sale of Reading lots, acquiring some choice locations for himself and his sons. He acted as the agent of the Lutheran clergymen Brunnholz, Muhlenberg, and Kurtz, in a plan to acquire several lots on which to build a church . . . "Some convenient backlots," as Weiser suggested to Peters.

William Parsons advertised the lots which the Proprietors had for sale in Reading. Quit rents of seven shillings sterling for frontage of sixty feet on Penn Street was the price fixed upon them. They would be offered at this price until March 1, 1750. The commissioners were to see to it that purchasers would construct a brick or stone building before March 1 of the next year after purchase. Stones could be quarried on nearby proprietary lands. Tanners who applied were to be sold lots at places where their establishment would not "be offensive."

Especial terms were laid down for the building of the center square of Callowhill (Fifth) and Penn Streets. The commissioners were instructed to see to it that all the space in the square was built upon within one year after March 1, 1750. Conrad Weiser interpreted this ruling to mean that the sixty-foot frontage would have to be built solidly. There were many prospective purchasers who balked at the obligation to build such large structures, whereupon Peters ruled that "If Mr. Weiser did not engage to each a 60-foot lot then on the dividing the lots into 2 equal Parts there may be Room for four or five more people in the center square."

While the proprietors were insisting that all the lots in the square be sold and built upon, they held out that each fourth lot on Penn Street remain their property. In this way, they insured to themselves the unearned increment of future "socially created values."

In the sale of Reading lots, Weiser acquired lot number 120 on Penn Street above Fifth. The original survey reads "East and West 60 feet and in length, 270 feet, Bounded northward by Penn Street and westward by Prince Street, Southward with a 20 ft. alley and Eastward with lot number 119." On this site, Weiser erected the first business establishment in Reading. In 1750, he built a general merchandise store. In 1769, this property passed into the ownership of Nicholas Keim, whose family conducted a hardware store in the building for seventy years. Then the property was sold to the Stichters, who have continued in the hardware business on the site to the present writing.

On May 4, 1750, Weiser wrote to Governor Hamilton, informing him that "we got water at 52 or 53 feet" in digging. A week later Richard Peters informed the proprietor that "Mr. Weiser has laid the foundation of a house of twenty-three feet in front." Others were then digging their cellars. Amid these activities connected with building a new town, William Hartley, one of the three commissioners, died. Hartley was the only commissioner whose home was on the spot. He had been the tenant living in the Widow Finney's farmhouse and was trusted by his employers. The vacancy created by his death was not filled and all the duties fell upon Francis Parvin and Conrad Weiser, the surviving commissioners.[5]

The real sport of building activity began in 1752. Conrad Weiser was diligent in duty in seeing to it that owners of lots met the terms of their bargains and constructed houses as they had agreed to do. His methods in achieving his ends were not always tactful but they got results. On March 16, 1752, Peters informed Penn, "It was very lucky that I gave the management of that town (Reading) to Conrad, whose imperiousness has been of great service, for they build regularly, or if they don't, or are in any way abusing, Conrad deals about his blows without any ceremony and down drops the man who shares to resist his ponderous

---

5. Pennsylvania Archives, 2:44–45.

arms. But with all, I must say that it is guided by good sense and a necessary fortitude."⁶

Along this line, it is interesting to observe one of Weiser's statements, which reveals his methods. Two men, Jacob Heller, and Michael Greter, both applied for Lot number 310. "I gave Jacob Heller the return," says Weiser in a letter to Peters, "and ordered him to go and get a patent or be kicked which he would. I was then quite out of humor." Decidedly!⁷

The incidents growing out of Weiser's activities in the founding of Reading serve to give us a light upon his character, which is lacking in the accounts of his transactions with the Indians or with the provincial authorities. In Reading, he was dealing with his own people and he dealt "imperiously" and none too gentle.

In the performance of his duties as a commissioner of Reading, Weiser encountered many difficulties. His rather high-handed methods in dealing with the settlers earned him the abuse of his fellow townsmen. Reports of his disaffection of the homebuilders of Reading reached the ears of Governor Hamilton, whose secretary wrote to Weiser as follows: "I hear that there are some People underhand making observations on your Conduct, and that they intend, one and all (I suppose it the mad disappointed People) to throw together an Abundance of Aspersions against you and lay the Paper before the Governor. Poor People, they will not, nor cannot do anything themselves and yet are extremely angry that there is a man of better Sense and more Spirit than themselves."

BERKS COUNTY

With the building of a large town on the Schuylkill, there developed renewed agitators for the creation of a separate county. As early as 1738, some persons in the upper end of Philadelphia County had petitioned for the erection of a new county and Conrad Weiser was their spokesman. But the provincial assembly paid little attention to the request until 1752 when it passed a bill creating the county of Berks. Three years earlier, Christopher Sauer had referred to the plans for building a town in "Berkshire County."

---
6. Peters Letter Book, 3:219.
7. Ibid., 69. Thomas Penn did not approve of Weiser's method of enforcing his orders. See Penn Letter Book, 3:138.

In a letter to Thomas Penn, Richard Peters declared, "It is my opinion that Conrad Weiser has teased the Assembly into the erection of the county of Berks."[8]

At the time of its creation, the estimated population of the county was 12,000 and although the boundaries extended northwest to the Susquehanna River, almost all the inhabitants dwelled south of the Blue Mountains. In the creation of Berks, the portion of Lancaster County in which Weiser resided was added to Berks. Henceforth, his letters were no longer dated from Tulpehocken, Lancaster County, but from Heidelberg, Berks County, the same county in which Reading was located.

TRUSTEE OF THE CHARITY SCHOOLS

Thousands of German immigrants sought the shelter of Pennsylvania each year during the middle decades of the 18th Century. Their numbers were so great that Englishmen feared that Pennsylvania was rapidly becoming a German colony. In 1751, Benjamin Franklin wrote an essay "Observations on the Increase of Mankind." "Why should Pennsylvania, founded by the English, become a Colony of Aliens who will shortly be so numerous as to Germanize us instead of Anglicizing them . . . ?" Other persons, minded as was Franklin, set themselves to the task of converting these immigrants to the English way of life.

Prominent among those who organized the Charity Schools of Pennsylvania was Dr. William Smith, later the provost of the University of Pennsylvania. In cooperation with the London Society for the Propagation of the Gospel, he organized a school system in colonial Pennsylvania dedicated to the purpose of anglicizing the German youth. Smith wrote many letters to London depicting the sorry conditions on the Pennsylvania frontier and prevailed upon the Society to sponsor an educational program.[9]

On March 15th, 1754, the Secretary of the London Society sent a letter outlining the plans for such schools. The letter was addressed to the following persons: To the Honorable James Hamilton, Esq., Lieutenant Governor of Pennsylvania; William

---
8. Peters Letter Book, supra.
9. Smith, Horace Wemyss, *Life and Correspondence of Reverend William Smith, D.D.*, 1:30–40 passim.

Allen, Esq., Chief Justice; Richard Peters, Esq., Secretary of Pennsylvania; Benjamin Franklin, Esq., Postmaster General; Conrad Weiser, Esq., Interpreter; and the Reverend William Smith.

Space here will not permit us to give a detailed account of the plans for organizing the Charity Schools. To the point for us is the stipulation that the Reverend Michael Schlatter, Reformed church clergyman, was to be the "supervisor and visitor of all these schools." The London Society directed that the buildings be erected in Reading, York, Easton, Lancaster, Skippack, and Hanover; that the teachers employed should know both English and German and that the trustees should seek the advice of the German ministers in selecting the proper instructors.[10]

When the Society's letter reached Philadelphia in May 1754, all the persons to whom it was addressed had gone to the intercolonial Conference at Albany, excepting the Governor, Judge Allen, and Reverend Smith. "We cannot, therefore, do anything in the business," wrote Reverend Smith on May 26th, "until their return, especially as Mr. Weiser attends them." In this same letter, Smith warns Secretary Samuel Chandler of the Society that the French in Ohio may strive to coax the Germans to settle there. Very strikingly he uses almost the same phrases that Weiser used in his letter to Governor Hamilton on this point. (See Chapter XIV) Smith declared that the French hope to draw American-born Germans to their side "as they are entirely ignorant, and have not the same notions of the French government that their European parents had."[11]

The internal evidence of the undated Weiser letter would seem to show it to have been written in the autumn of 1753, a half year before Smith expressed similar views in the Society for the Propagation of the Gospel.[12]

On August 10, 1754, Governor Hamilton called a meeting of the trustees of the Charity Schools at the home of Judge William Allen in Mount Airy. Weiser did not attend the first meeting of the Board. After the Albany Conference, he went directly to his home in Berks County. At this first meeting, the trustees were greatly

---
10. Harbaugh, Henry, *The Life of Reverend Michael Schlatter: With a full account of His Travels and Labors Among the Germans in Pennsylvania, New Jersey, Maryland and Virginia*, 258–310.
11. Smith, William, *A Brief State of the Province Pennsylvania*, London, 1755.
12. Weiser MSS, 2:25.

disturbed by the violent opposition on the plan as expressed in the columns of Christopher Sauer's German newspaper. Sauer charged that the plan to educate the German was a nefarious scheme to undermine their thrift and industry. On the other hand, a letter written by Reverend Henry Melchior Muhlenberg "rejoiced" that such an undertaking was being planned and sponsored.

The second meeting of the Trustees was held at the home of Governor Hamilton at Bushkill. Weiser was present at this meeting. That is why he was "fortunately in town" when the urgent messages came from George Croghan at Aughwick in August 1754. At the second meeting of the trustees, two petitions were read. They came from Pastor Muhlenberg's churches at Trappe and New Hanover. Schools were to be opened there, "provided the German Calvinists' (Reformed) congregations in the same township signify their approbation."

The next order of business called for appointing deputy trustees for the six districts designated by the London Society. In selecting deputy trustees the members of the central body named persons known to themselves, "many of them being personally known to the Governor and the Secretary, Mr. Peters, and almost all of them to Mr. Conrad Weiser."[13] Care was taken to have all ethnic and religious groups represented on each local board. The following persons were appointed:

DEPUTY TRUSTEES FOR CHARITY SCHOOLS

Lancaster—English: Edward Shippen, James Wright; German: Adam Kuhn, Philip Otterbein, John Baer; Lutheran: Mr. Gera; Calvinist: Sebastian Graeff.

Providence and Skippack—English: John Coplin, Robert White, Henry Pawling; German: Abram Sahler, John Schrack; Lutheran: Nicholas Kuster; Calvinist: John Dreiner.

Reading—English: James Read, Francis Parvin, James Seely; German: Sebastian Zimmerman, Isaac Levan; Lutheran: Martin Gerick, Jacob Levan; Calvinist: Samuel High.

---

13. Eine Kurtze Nachricht.

Easton—English: William Parsons, Lewis Gordon, John Chapman; German: Peter Trexler; Lutheran: ----------; Calvinist: John Lefevre.

New Hanover—English: John Potts, William Maugridge; German: Henry Antes, Andrew Kepner; Lutheran: Henry Krebs; Calvinist: John Reifsnyder.

York—Nobody was yet recommended, but Mr. Weiser agreed on his journey to the frontiers (to Aughwick) in the service of the governor, to converse with the proper persons regarding the school to be fixed at York.

The trustees discussed the advisability of inviting a Lutheran and a Reformed clergyman to be a member of each local board. Conrad Weiser spoke against this proposal, pointing out that, for the present at least, jealousies between the two denominations were too keen to make such a plan work. It was argued by other trustees that one of the purposes of the Charity Schools was to eradicate such prejudice "without which there was little possibility of rendering them peaceable, industrious and governable subjects." While this observation is not definitely credited to Franklin, who attended this meeting at Hamilton's home, it sounds very much like some of his other statements along this line. However, Weiser won the debate and clergymen were not made deputy trustees.

Although clergymen were not named to the local boards, Reverend Smith made a point of writing to some of the outstanding Reformed pastors, trying to enlist their aid in establishing the schools. He already had the support of the Lutherans through Muhlenberg and Weiser. Reverend John Philip Leidig, the Reformed pastor at Providence, had joined with the original petitioners. Smith wrote to Reverend William Stoy of Tulpehocken and Reverend John Bartholomaus Rieger, Reformed clergymen in Lancaster. In a joint reply, these two Calvinist pastors stated that they would consult with Reverend Michael Schlatter on the matter but they were well-disposed regarding the venture.

Several steps were taken to counteract the influence of Sauer's opposition to the schools. Benjamin Franklin offered to sell his old German press to the Society for a nominal sum in order that the trustees might have an agency of their own through which to appeal to the German residents. Then the problem arose as to how to secure the services of someone who could set German type. When Franklin found a properly qualified typesetter, the man insisted that he would purchase the press as an independent venture and serve the purpose of the trustees at the same time at such rates as were proper. The trustees refused to adopt this plan. They wanted a medium of their own.

The next step of the trustees was to publish a pamphlet in both languages, entitled, in English, "A Brief History of the Rise and Progress of the Scheme carrying on for the Instruction of Poor Germans and their Descendants." In abbreviated form, the German version was known as "Eine Kurze Nachricht."

A third meeting of the Trustees was held on December 10, 1754. Those present were Judge Allen, Secretary Peters, Conrad Weiser, Reverend William Smith, and Reverend Michael Schlatter, the supervisor of the schools. It was decided to distribute 800 English copies of the memorial to the Germans: 1000 German copies and five hundred printed in both languages. Schlatter received 325 German copies and Weiser was given 275 copies to distribute among the Lutherans. At the December 10th session of the Trustees, it was decided to open a school at Reading.

On January 15th, 1755, the Trustees met again. (Weiser probably attended this meeting. He was in Philadelphia on that date, acting as Interpreter for the Mohawks.) This time they considered, among other things, whether a school should be erected in Weiser's own district of Tulpehocken and Heidelberg in Lancaster and Berks. But it was felt that the folks in those townships were at odds with each other on the matter of the location of the school and therefore the petition was denied for the time. A few months later, on April 1, 1755, Conrad Weiser opened a school in Tulpehocken, Berks County, employing John Davis as a teacher at thirty pounds per annum.

After the initial stages of planning for the Charity schools, Weiser dropped out of active participation as a trustee of the central board. Governor Hamilton also surrendered his position to the new governor, Robert Hunter Morris. Opposition to the schools became very keen as the year 1755 saw the buildings erected and in operation in eight scattered districts of the province. Lutheran pastors John Frederick Handschuh and Peter Brunnholtz were added to the Board of Trustees and they served to represent the German interest. Reverend Gilbert Tennant, the Presbyterian clergyman, too, was added to the Board in that year.

In September 1755, after most of these schools had been in operation for six months or more, Christopher Sauer wrote to Weiser, virulently condemning the motives of the incumbent trustees. He charged that Schlatter, Peters, Franklin, and others were trying to "establish the thraldom of the Germans, so that each of them may secure his propos grandeur, or own private interest."[14]

We cannot determine to what extent, if any, Weiser shared the views of the Germantown publisher.

The Charity Schools struggled on for a few years and then capitulated to the forces opposed to them.

Weiser's interest in formal education was aroused by his service as a trustee. In May 1755, he sent two Mohawk Indian boys to Philadelphia to be enrolled in the Academy. They were the two sons of Jonathan the Mohawk, one named Jonathan and the other Philip. "Jonathan," declared Weiser, "is a very Intelligiable Boy, and good-natured, the other is not so, but more of an Indian, and something cross, as his Father says." Governor Morris assured Weiser that the boys would be well cared for. He had sent them to Mr. Franklin and Mr. Allen. The boys failed to make an impressive record in the school.[15]

THE FIRST CHURCH OF READING

Even though affairs of state demanded much of his time in the year 1751, Weiser found renewed zeal in his religious interests. At Easter time he acted as host and guide to those devout men of God who planted the Lutheran Church firmly in American soil. Reverends Brunnholz, Handschuh, and Tobias Wagner tarried at this home and his son-in-law, Muhlenberg, joined the entire group in an early morning climb to the top of South Mountain, where

---

14. For Sauer's letter to Weiser, see Graeff: op. cit., 47–48.
15. The two Indian boys were the sons of Jonathon, whose Indian name was Cayenguilagoa. *Notes and Queries*, 8:494. Also Weiser to Peters, May 19, 1755, Pennsylvania Archives, 2:318–319. Also Morris to Weiser, May 23, 1755, Peters MSS, 4:15.

the youthful clergymen were inspired to the pastoral scenes they observed below. The flight of some eagles reminded Muhlenberg of some familiar scenes at Halle and then he named the spot "Adler's Kopf" or Eagles' Peak.

Weiser aided these clergymen in securing lands upon which to build the first Lutheran church in Reading and in that same year he wrote the hymn of dedication (June 17, 1753) for that congregation, a majestic paean of praise, which the choir of Trinity Lutheran Church of Reading, heir of the first church, still sings on memorial occasions.

CONRAD WEISER'S HYMN
EINWEIHUNGS-LIED

Jehovah, Herr and Majestät!
Hör unser kindlich Flehen;
Neig' deine Ohren zum Gebet
Der Schaaren, die da stehen
Vor deinem heiligen Angesicht;
Verschmähe unsere Bitte nicht,
Um deines Namens willen.

Dies Haus wird heume eingeweilht
Von deinem Bundes-Volke;
Lass uns, Herr, deine Herrlichkeit
Hernieder in der Wolke.
Dass sie erfülle dieses Haus
Und treibe alles Böse aus,
Um deines Namens willen.

Es haite Niemand das gemein,
Was du für rein erkläret;
Dies Haus soll eine Wohnung sein,
Worin man dich verehret.
Es bleibe stets ein Hellingthun
Fü's reine Evangelium!
Unt deines Namens willen!

Verleihe, dass es nie gebricht
An treuen Kirchen-Räthen,
Die nach Gewissen, Amt und Pflicht,
Für sich und Andere beten,
Damit durch ihren Dienst und Treu
Der Kirche wohlgerathen sei,
Um deines Namens willen!

O Majestät, erzürne nicht,
Dass wir uns unterwinden,
Zu bitten, dass dein Recht und Licht
Hier stetig sei zu finden!
Drum gibe uns Lehrer, die erfüllt
Mir deinem Geist und Ebenbild,
Um deines Namens willen!

Wenn deine treuen Knechte hier
In deinem Namen lehren,
Wenn sie erhöffne dein Panier,
Dann lass dein Volk so hören,
Dass sich eröffne ihr Verstand,
Ihr Wille werde umgewandt
Um deines Namens willen!

Hier öffne sich der Boten Mund,
Und triefe recht vom Fette!
Erm ache Fluch und Segen kund,
Und ringe um die Wette
Mit Gott und seines Geistes Kraft,
Die ihm den Weg zum Herzen schafft,
Um Jesu Christi Willen!

Lass, Jesu, diese Quelle sein
Ein reines Meer der Gnaden,
Darinnen unsera Kindelein
Von Erb- und Sünden-Schaden
Durch dein Verdienst, Blut, Schweiss und Tod,

Erretter warden aus der Noth,
Um deines Namens willen!

Lass, Majestät, auf diesem Platz
Die reinste Lehre bleiben,
Und deine Knechte solchen Schatz
Nach deinem Willen treiben.
Behüte uns vor Zänkerei,
Vor Sicherheit und Heuchelei,
Um deines Namens willen!

Das ist und bleiber ewig wahr,
Was Christi Mund gesprochen;
Wer ab-und zuthut, hat ganz klar
Des Mittlers Wort gebrochen.
Drum irret nicht, Gott lässet sich
In solcher Sach' absonderlich
Nicht in die Länge spotten!

Lass dieses Hans die Werkstatt sein
Worinn viel tausend Seelen
In Buss und Glauben nur allien
Mit Jesu sich vermälen
Dutch deines Wortes Lebens-Saft
Und deiner Sacramenten Kraft
Um deines Names willen!

Gieb endlich, höchste Majestät
Des Himmels und der Erden
Dass Fürbitt, Dank, Preis und Gebet
Mag hier geopfert warden
Für jeden Stand der Christenheit,
Damit in alle Ewigkeit
Dein Nam' geehret wede!

Vor Feuer, Krieg und Wassers-Noth
Wollst due dies Haus bewahren!

Damit nach sel'gem Tod
Die Nachkommen erfahren
Dass wir ditch, wahren Gott, geliebt
Und uns in delnem Wort geübt,
Um deines Namens willen!

OTHER INTERESTS

The expanding activities of the farmer of Heidelberg included ventures into merchandising as he built the first store in Reading; built a tannery on his farm near Womelsdorf; and acquired real estate in widely scattered portions of the province. The landholdings were principally in Bethel, Pine Grove, and Selinsgrove. The lands patented to him beyond the Susquehanna were not surveyed during his lifetime.

In 1751, as one of the magistrates, he was involved in the trial of George Boone, grandfather of Daniel Boone, of Kentucky fame. As magistrate more and more cases came under his jurisdiction because of the greatly accelerated growth of the province which grew out of the ever-increasing immigration of his former countrymen from the south German states.[16]

Thus, the many-sided Weiser gave much of his time and substance to establish the foundation of a lasting culture in the community in which he lived, at the same time that he was serving his province and his king in founding an empire in the New World.

---

16. Peters MSS, 3:33–38 passim.

Sketch of Conrad Weiser's store on the square in Reading.

Detail of the diorama of colonial Reading at the Berks History Center. Weiser's store is left of center.

Portrait sketch of an elderly Weiser.

The signature of Conrad Weiser would have appeared on many deeds in the area.

Weiser as an older gentleman, perhaps when he was supervising in Reading.

Reverend Michael Schlatter

Dr. William Smith who pressed for schools to Anglicize the German children.

CHAPTER XVI

The Storm

The year 1755 was an eventful one in the colonial history of Pennsylvania and a very busy one for Conrad Weiser, whose many interests crowded each other clamoring for attention. It was this year of Braddock's expedition; Dunbar's retreat and the outbreak of Indian hostilities in the outer settlements of the province. The horrors of Indian war did not strike the eastern settlements of the province until late autumn of 1755. We shall see how, during the earlier portion of that momentous year, Weiser and his associates tried to avert the gathering storm.

In January, Weiser was summoned to Philadelphia to meet with Hendricks and the Mohawks. We have seen how that conference was successfully terminated. Once that business was transacted, the Indians became drunk and the new Governor, Robert Hunter Morris, meeting this problem for the first time appealed to Weiser to stay in the city until they became sober, and then to escort the troublesome guests as far as Germantown. This was on Conrad's homeward route and on January 22, he accompanied the Mohawks part of the way. On the following day, from his home in Heidelberg, he wrote a letter to Colonel William Johnson, informing him of the action taken by Hendricks in renouncing the Mohawks deed to the Connecticut people.[1]

Four days later, Weiser wrote to Governor Morris, informing him that several groups of Indians, mostly Shawnees, had come to his house to inform him and the governor that they planned

---
1. Weiser to Colonel Johnson, January 23, 1755, Colonial Records, 6:291–292.

to build a village for themselves next spring, within the territory acquired by the Albany Purchase. They sent a string of Wampum to confirm their announcement and asked that someone be sent to their new settlement "to fence in a Small piece of ground for a Cornfield."[2] Morris replied, instructing Weiser to inform the Indians that he was pleased to learn of their plans and designating Weiser as the proper person to go to their new village and build the fences. This Conrad did early in June.

Meanwhile, Weiser's son Philip was in Shamokin, staking out land claims for himself and his father in the new purchase, along John Penn's Creek, present-day Snyder County. While he was there he learned that other persons had already staked out claims for themselves, marking the tracts with the names of Conrad Weiser and Richard Peters. This information Weiser conveyed to Peters in a letter dated March 11, 1755. In reply, a vexed Peters declared that he was "thereby thrown into more confusion than ever I was in my life." It appears that Weiser and Peters had some private understanding about the division of some of their lands, but now Peters wished to be removed from participation in all these transactions. "I will not hold lands where any man has the least pretensions," he wrote. But "now that my name is published I have thought it better and more consistent to put my name in the Warrant along with yours that all may know I am concerned any that be no Room for any charge of Hypocricy or double dealing which I abhor."[3]

Philip and Sammy Weiser had carried their father's letter to Philadelphia. Through it, Peters learned that a group of frontier settlers had already formed a "combination" to secure the choice lands along Penn's Creek. Peters believed the combination should be broken for the public good.

On the same day that Peters answered Weiser's letter, Governor Morris directed a letter to the Interpreter. Among other things, Morris informed Weiser that his nephew Captain Morris would accompany Philip and Samuel on their return trip to Reading. Captain Morris was commissioned by Governor Shirley of Massachusetts to raise a regiment of soldiers to join in the spring

---

2. Weiser to Governor Morris, January 27, 1755, Pennsylvania Archives, 2:259.
3. Weiser to Peters, March 11, 1755, Peters MSS, 4:7.

campaign against the French at Fort Duquesne. "I have a great dependence upon our assistance in the thing," he wrote. Captain Morris would go from Reading to Lancaster and then westward to join the British forces that were gathering at Wills Creek, Cumberland, Maryland.[4]

In May, Weiser received a petition from the Susquehanna Indians. They needed food and supplies. He turned the petition over to Governor Morris, who committed the assembly and then sent Weiser fifty pounds "to dispose of in the best Manner you can . . . to send an Account of the number of these Indians . . . and your option as to the best method of providing for them in the future."[5]

Everything was being done that could be done to appease the Pennsylvania Indians.

EQUIPPING BRADDOCK'S ARMY

On the banks of the Potomac, in Alexandria, Virginia, General Edward Braddock, in command of a large force of British soldiers, was growling at the delay caused by the lack of horses and wagons to transport his army to his objective, the French Fort Duquesne. Virginia and Maryland had promised to supply the teams and provender, but, alas, there were no animals equal to the task; no wagons and only putrid beef, awaiting him when he disembarked. In dismay, he called a conference of the governors of all neighboring provinces to secure their advice. Benjamin Franklin, postmaster-general of the colonies, went to Alexandria and offered a ray of hope to the perplexed Braddock.

Pennsylvania could furnish the teams and necessary provisions. Braddock clutched at Franklin's idea like a drowning man reaching for a straw. Franklin had his way and Pennsylvania farmers supplied the necessary teams for the expedition, Conrad Weiser assisting the local magistrates in collecting them.

On March 31, Scarroday returned from his journey to Onondaga and Weiser was summoned to Philadelphia to act as an interpreter. The Oneida Chieftain reported that only four Nations had met with him in Council, these declaring that they were

---
4. Morris to Weiser, March 15, 1755, Ibid., 8.
5. Morris to Weaver, May 15, 1755, Ibid., 9. The letter is in Peter's hand, though Morris signed it.

opposed to the French occupation of the Ohio, but that they were obeying instructions to remain inactive in the controversy. He, Scarroday, had presented an invitation from the governors of Pennsylvania, Maryland, and Virginia, to come to Winchester in Virginia to receive presents. The matter would have to be presented to a general council for the final decision. Scarroday believed that the Indians would come.

Plans were organized to negotiate another Indian purchase in the hope of further appeasing the Indians and opening new lands for settlement. At the conference of Alexandria, General Braddock had appointed Colonel William Johnson of New York as His Majesty's Deputy in sole charge of Indian affairs in the Colonies. Any new purchase would, therefore, have to be made with full knowledge and sanction of Johnson. A delicate situation developed here. Thomas Penn, writing from London, stated that he would prefer Weiser negotiate the treaty in preference to Johnson. The new Deputy ignored Weiser's position as the chief interpreter and agent for Pennsylvania. One of the first acts under his new commission was to consult George Croghan on the state of affairs. In June, Weiser returned from the fence-building expedition in Otatuaky, the new Shawnee village, forty-five miles north of Shamokin. There he had found a deserted village. A severe drought had killed all the young Indian corn and there was no chance of realizing a yield. Weiser left some provisions to tide the Indians in neighboring villages over the immediate food scarcity and when he returned to his home in Berks purchased large quantities of flour from mills in Tulpehocken. He had promised the Indians that he would see to it that provisions would be sent to Harris Ferry, where they might come in canoes and get them.

In reporting to the Governor, Weiser relayed several reports that he had learned from the Indians as he passed through their villages. The Indians were pleased to know that the English king had sent General Braddock and many soldiers to drive away the French. A Shawnee Indian, returning from Ohio, reported that the French were weak at Fort Duquesne, having only 150 men and a few praying Indians to help them.[6]

---

6. Penn to Peters, May 29, 1755, Ibid., 17.

DISASTER IN THE OHIO COUNTRY

Ominous news reached Weiser on June 30 when John Harris, writing from Paxtang, informed him that some of the settlers near Wills Creek, in Maryland, had been killed and scalped by the Indians, adding "Our own Indians are strongly suspected." The Pennsylvania Indians attached to Braddock's army were deserting and English goods were found on the one Indian that was killed by the settlers during the raid. "Upwards of twenty" people had been killed or captured.

This report was merely a prelude to the consternating news which came a few weeks later when it was learned that the British forces had met with complete disaster, after being ambushed by the French and Indians at Turtle Creek, near Fort Duquesne. General Braddock had been killed and his army was in full retreat, under the command of Colonel Thomas Dunbar. On the day that this defeat took place, Conrad Weiser wrote from Harris' Ferry, offering to join the forces at Wills Creek. He had come to the Susquehanna to distribute food among the families of Indians whose sons had gone off to fight; on which side they fought was uncertain. In reporting his visit, Weiser stated: "Our people are very malicious against our Indians; they curse and damn'em to their Faces and say, must we feed You and our Husbands fight in the mean time for the French."

UGLY REMORSE

Public indignation was great when the defeat of Braddock became known. In seeking to vent their anger upon someone, the citizens of Berks, in a sort of hysteria, charged that the Catholic church at Goshenhoppen (Bally) was a nest of French spies and its building an arsenal in which guns and ammunition were stored. The Justices of Berks County, five of them, including Conrad Weiser, warned the Governor and his council by a joint letter, dated July 23, 1755. Among other things, it was charged that the brothers at the Catholic church staged a parade to celebrate the French victory at Fort Duquesne.[7] Today we know that the "pa-

---
7. Colonial Records, 6:593–594.

rade" was the Corpus Christi procession, observed in July during colonial times. But to men of warped minds, the most harmless acts of persons who differ with them on some points are suspect on all points.

Some persons have pointed to the fact that Weiser's signature was attached to the letter warning the governor, to prove that the first Justice of Berks County was bitterly anti-Catholic. Nothing could be farther from the truth. While it is true that the letter was sent from Weiser's home and his signature is the last of the five judges: Henry Harvey, James Read, William Bird, Jonas Seely, and himself, it must be pointed out that Weiser was merely acting in what was line of duty. To neglect to send a warning might have proven disastrous if the reports were true.

The Governor's council decided to consult Weiser directly on the matter and when that was done, Weiser assured the authorities that the reports were false.

We have further proof of Weiser's fair-minded attitude toward people of the Catholic faith. In 1754, his daughter, Margaret, married a young Lutheran clergyman named J.D.M. Heintzelman. Soon thereafter the young husband died. When Margaret remarried, she married a man named Anthony Fricker, a Catholic. In his will, 1760, Conrad Weiser stipulated very carefully, that his daughter, Margaret should not be discriminated against because of her marriage to a Catholic.

ALARMS

In July 1755, the remnants of Braddock's defeated army were scurrying through Pennsylvania woodlands toward Pennsylvania, seeking the shelter of brick-walled houses. Yelping warriors, breathing murderous oaths barked at the heels of the retreating soldiers, their firebrands waved in one hand and bloodstained tomahawks clutched in the other. The war cry was sounded in the mountains. Nearer and nearer to the eastern settlements came the natives wreaking scarlet vengeance for their real and fancied wrongs.

Conrad Weiser had foreseen the gathering storm. Even as late as August and September of that fateful year he was striving to avert the full force of the horrible assault upon the frontier settlers. After nearly three decades of successful efforts at making peace he still hoped, even against hope, that hostilities could be avoided. Most of the months of July and August he was on duty in Philadelphia, acting as interpreter for bands of friendly Indians that came to plead for aid. He served as chief advisor for Governor Morris when the Wyandots humbled themselves in July and when Scarroday made his tearful plea in August.

Early in September, Weiser traveled to Harris' Ferry, carrying flour and provisions for the friendly Indians at Shamokin. In October, he sent two of his sons, Sammy and Frederick, to Shamokin to try to reassure the Indians there. The Weiser boys brought appeals for ammunition with which to fight against the French. Again, late in October, the two Weiser sons were dispatched on a similar mission. They brought gloomy news.

Settlers north and west of Blue Hills were abandoning their plantations, the Indians were in "the utmost confusion." From Cumberland, from the "Big Island"; from Penn's and Sherman's creeks came reports of Indian massacres.

On October 26, Weiser wrote to Justice James Read of Reading, "for God's sake let us stand together and do what we can, and trust to the hand of Providence." He informed Read that he was "sending armed men to the Susquehanna or as far as they can go for Intelligence."

In reply to a letter from Weiser, appealing for arms and ammunition, Governor Morris promised to lay the matter before the assembly but regretted that he had neither at his immediate disposal.

"THE TULPEHOCKEN WATCH"

The Indian atrocities were increasing late in October. Families were wiped out near Hunter's Mills, east of the Susquehanna. When Weiser learned of the attack east of the river he sent his servants and sons to sound the alarm in Tulpehocken and Heidelberg. His neighbors rallied at the Weiser house and volunteered to follow him on an expedition against the rampant warriors.

Accepting the responsibility of leadership, Weiser directed the volunteers to hurry to their homes, there to equip themselves with "Arms, whether Guns, Swords, pitchforks, axes or whatever might be of use . . . and for three days Provisions in the Knapsacks and meet me at Benjamin Spicker's."[8]

Most of the farmers who responded at the Weiser house were Heidelberg men. Weiser issued orders to the Tulpehocken people to assemble at the Spyker home, six miles west. There he found a hundred Tulpehocken settlers waiting for instructions. Weiser suggested that the two groups unite under a joint command. The Heidelberg and Tulpehocken men agreed to this arrangement and proceeded to organize themselves into military companies.

While the men were completing their organization, Weiser sent for Reverend John Kurtz, the Lutheran pastor at Christ (Long's) Church. The pastor "gave an Exhortation to the men and made a Prayer suitable to the time."

The volunteers were marched westward toward the Susquehanna; fifty were sent north to guard the Swatara Gap in the Blue Mountains. Three hundred and twenty men marched with the main body of volunteers. Resolutely they pledged each other to "die together and engage the Enemy wherever they should meet with them."

These brave resolves cooled the next day when it was learned that the Irish settlement at Paxton had been attacked by black-faced Delawares. The Tulpehocken Guards, as they called themselves, held a consultation and agreed that "as we did not come up to serve as guards to Paxton people but to fight the Enemy if they came so far as we first hear, we thought it best to return and take care of our own Township."

During the homeward march, the Guard heard an alarming report that 500 Indians had crossed the mountains at Tolheo.[9] Investigation proved this rumor false. The fifty guards detached from Weiser's command had fired off their pieces to keep their barrels dry and the volley had thrown settlers into a panic.

Governor Morris commended Weiser for his "conduct and Zeal"; expressed the hope that he would continue to act with "Vigour and Caution" and appointed him "a Colonel by a Commission herewith."

---

8. The Spicker (Spyker) residence still stands in Stouchburg, Berks County.
9. Bethel and Rehrersburg, Berks County.

THE CLOUDS HANG HEAVY

Weiser's commission as colonel gave him wide discretionary powers, including the power to offer rewards and the right to distribute provincial goods designed for the [10]Shamokin Indians "in any manner for the Service of the Publick that you shall think best." Weiser had stopped the delivery of flour to Shamokin. It was suspected that the Pennsylvania Indians had joined the French.

On November 2, 1755, Weiser joined with the other magistrates of Berks in addressing a strong appeal to the Governor, "we are all in uproar, all in Disorder, all willing to do and have little in our Power." If their "Friends" in Philadelphia failed to send them aid "we are determined to go down with all that will follow us to Philadelphia and quarter ourselves on its Inhabitants and wait our Fate with them.

Murders, horrible butcheries, were being committed along the foothills of the Blue Mountains at the time the Tulpehocken Guards were marching. Men, women, and children were found cruelly murdered, their skulls split by blows from Indian hatchets; their bodies horribly mutilated and their sex organs subjected to crass indignities. Fury was raging in the Blue Hills that sheltered the eastern settlements of Pennsylvania. Adam Read, William Parsons, George Croghan, George Stevenson, and other magistrates from neighboring counties, were sending reports of death and pillage during the final days of October and the first days of November.

On November 6, three Indians and Andrew Montour came to Weiser's home in Berks. They brought news about the events which were happening in the forest councils of Indians. Scarroday and his son, the drunken Zigera, Montour, and Weiser set out for Philadelphia. From Germantown, Weiser wrote to Morris, announcing his party's approach and expressing the belief that the Indians on the Susquehanna were still friends. "the Question is whether we are theirs" observed Weiser, referring to the stoppage of provisions on the strength of the suspicion that the Shamokin Indians had joined the French.[11]

---

10. In a letter to William Parsons, dated November 1, 1744, Weiser expressed the hope that he and Parson might meet, "It may be for the last time." Timothy Horsfield MSS, American Philosophical Society, 35.
11. Colonial Records, 6:681.

On Saturday, November 8, 1755, Governor Morris was reporting in his council that the assembly had refused to vote funds for the protection of the province, speciously arguing that such funds should be raised by taxing the Proprietary estates, a measure which no deputy governor could ever condone. The council was helping the governor to draw up a reply to the Assembly when Conrad Weiser, Montour, and the three Indians entered the council chamber. Scarroday announced that he had something to say of "great Consequence," as indeed he did.

The Delaware Indians from Ohio had come to the villages on the Susquehanna, urging their brethren to join in a way to exterminate the English. The Pennsylvania Indians refused. The Delaware messengers reported that their nation had declared war against the English. "when Washington was defeated, we, the Delawares, were blamed as the Cause of it. We will now kill. We will not be blamed without a Cause."

Three warring parties had been formed by the Delaware allies of the French. Spreading out from Fort Duquesne these parties were deployed as follows: "One party will go against Carlisle, one down the Susquehanna and I myself (the Delaware spokesman) will go against Tulpehocken to Conrad Weiser. And we shall be followed by a thousand French and Indians, Ottawas, Twightwees, Shawanese, and other Delawares. Scarroday was quoting the Delaware messengers.

Weiser and his party attended the morning session of the Council. The import of Scarroday's message was fraught with so much gravity that the governor and the Council decided to invite the members of the assembly and several city officials to a special session in the afternoon of Saturday, November 8th. The invited members of the assembly took their seats when the conference was resumed. Scarroday was making his last appeal to the white men. He had traveled up and down the province, trying to enlist the aid of Nanticokes, Nescopecks, and other Indians, to resist the traitorous Delawares, who had warned that they would kill any Indians who remained loyal to the English.

Scarroday's final speech bears repetition here:

"Brethren: I must deal plainly with you, and tell you if you will not fight with us we will go somewhere else. We never can nor ever will put up with the affront. If we cannot be safe where we are we will go somewhere else for protection and take care of ourselves.

"We are charged with having been concerned in a late Engagement that the Enemy had with your people. We absolutely deny it. We hate Onontio as much as you do . . ." He produced the scalp of a French Indian to prove that his people were loyal.

Governor Robert Hunter Morris grasped the full significance of Scarroday's words. Turning to the members of the Assembly he challenged:

"You have heard what the Indians have said. Without your aid, I cannot make a proper answer to what they now propose . . . strengthen my Hands and enable me to give them a full and proper Answer."

The Governor and his Council met in special sessions on Saturday night and again on Sunday, but the Assembly made no move until the following Tuesday, and then it refused to accede to the governor's demands.[12]

Scarroday and his companions left the City of Brotherly Love with heavy hearts.

COLONEL CONRAD WEISER

While Governor Morris wrangled with his lawmakers, urging them to pass a militia act to defend the province, the Indian war whoop was echoing through the valley of the Tulpehocken. Conrad Weiser, Colonel of the Guard, was in Philadelphia, waiting for the Assembly to do something to strengthen the governor's hand. He and his Indian companions were forced to wait in idleness, while the provincial authorities indulged in the pleasures of acrimonious debates. William Logan, son of James Logan, availed himself of Weiser's presence in the city to adjust some land claims regarding the Durham Iron Works in Bucks County. In his final reply to the Indians, Morris was forced to resort to the ruse of sending them to Onondaga with a message and urging them, in the future, to make their appeals to Conrad Weiser.

Precious hours were being wasted. Back in Heidelberg and Tulpehocken, Weiser's deputy, Peter Spyker, was trying to stem

---

12. Full account of the conference with Scarroday in the Colonial Records, 6:682–688.

the tide as family after family felt the keen edge of the tomahawks and scalping knives or stood upon some distant peak to see their barns and homesteads go up in flames. Filled with despair, Spyker sent a letter to Weiser in Philadelphia. "The Assembly can see by this work how good and fine friends the Indians are to us and we hope their eyes will go open."

Weiser was needed in Tulpehocken. Escorting his disappointed Indian companions northward, he left Philadelphia without securing any definite assurances of aid. At his home in Heidelberg, he quickly attended to equipping the Indians for their journey to Onondaga, gave them letters of introductions to white traders along the northern paths and sent them on their way to make one final appeal to the sachems of the Six Nations. Weiser was forced to escort the Indians through Tulpehocken lest irate settlers kill them. In leading his charges westward Colonel Weiser encountered his own soldiers of the Guard, massed along the road near Spyker's in Tulpehocken. They numbered four or five hundred men. "Why must we be killed by the Indians and we not kill them?" shouted someone as Weiser and his native companions rode along. Fearing that some harm might be done, Weiser hurried his charges to Spyker's house, treated them to a dram of whiskey and then set out to detach Captain Dieffenbach and five guards to conduct the Indians to the Susquehanna.

"Oh, my Country! My bleeding Country!" prayed Edward Biddle in a letter written from Reading on November 16, 1755. "Oh God! Be merciful and help us. God save our Land" was the misery prayer of the hapless, helpless victims of neglect, as reported in the *Philadelphia Zeitung* of November 27, 1755.

BLUE MOUNTAIN MASSACRES

Soon after Weiser reached his home on November 17, two of his sons, Philip and Frederick, returned from an expedition against the Indians. The boys furnished their father with a lurid account of the horrors they had seen, the gory details of which Weiser related in a series of letters to the provincial authorities. During his absence Weiser's sons had taken the liberty to distribute the guns and ammunition which was stored at Weiser's home, awaiting delivery to the Shamokin Indians, but these weapons were inadequate. "I pray Your Honor," wrote Weiser to Morris, "if it lies to your Power to send us up a Quantity upon any Condition. I must stand my Ground or my Neighbors will go away."

His Neighbors . . . "a prophet is not without Honor save in his own country" . . . In a council of the militia, following the departure of the Indians under escort, Weiser faced his disgruntled countrymen in Peter Spyker's home. "They begun, some to Curse the governor," he records, "some the Assembly; called me a Traitor of the Country who held with the Indians." Seated near a window in the Spyker stone house, Weiser heard his own men condemn him. Some friends urged him to change his seat lest some hotheads make good a threat to shoot him from outside of the house. The colonel was a prisoner in his own fort! Undaunted by threats, dismayed by the hoots of his own neighbors, Weiser offered to go before the whole guard, first to try to "passify" them by oratory, and if that failed to "make the King's Proclamation," the reading of the eighteenth-century Riot Act, which when read to a mob by a magistrate made any continuing offender a criminal. But Weiser's fellow officers prevailed upon him to remain in the house.[13]

The guards demanded that Weiser should fix a reward for Indian scalps, whether the Indians were enemies or not made no difference to their thinking. The pay of the guards was too small they grumbled, and he, Weiser, was pocketing the difference between their pay and the amount due them, they charged. "The Land was betrayed and sold" was the general cry. "I was in Danger of being shot to Death."

Smoke! Black, curling smoke, rose like a funnel from the distant mountains. The common danger became uppermost in the minds of the angry farmers who were gathered at Tulpehocken. Alarm! A raid on the Mill Creek[14] was reported. Weiser's worst detractors were the people from the southwest; it was their territory that was endangered. The guards took to their heels and those who had horses rode as fast as they could. To the scene of the

---

13. The various letters from which extracts are quoted can be found in the Colonial Records, or Minutes of the Provincial Council, vol. 6.
14. Near present-day Newmanstown, Lebanon County.

supposed disaster? No, to their own homes. They had not waited for orders from their colonel.

His immediate danger vanished by a stroke of providence, for the alarms were false. Weiser availed himself of the opportunity to mount his own horse and ride six miles eastward to his own home, "where I intend to stay, and defend my own House as long as I can. There is no Doings with People without a Law or Regulation."

Five days later Weiser joined with several Lancaster County subscribers in an urgent appeal to the Governor. Bethel Township in Berks was completely deserted, most of the residents of Tulpehocken had fled and the farmers of Heidelberg were moving their personal property to places of greater safety. With guns cocked, the members of the "watch," as the Tulpehocken Guard was called, demanded that rewards be offered for Indian scalps. The incensed settlers threatened to march on Philadelphia and demand a militia act. In the opinion of the subscribers, it was feared that such a mob would "commit the vilest Outrages." The men declared that they would "rather be hanged than be butchered by Indians."

On November 23, Weiser and his officers made some arrangements with the volunteers, including an offer of a reward of four pistols for every Indian man they might kill.

In recounting the story of the Indian raids along the Blue Mountains, the disaster which befell the Kobel family will serve as an example of many similar atrocities. Frederick Kobel and his wife had migrated to Pennsylvania from the Schoharie. He as a miller by trade and his mill stood on the Tulpehocken Creek between the present-day Womelsdorf and Charming Forge.

THE KOBEL TRAGEDY

Kobel with his wife and family of eight small children had abandoned their home and were running from the native warriors who pursued them. The mother carried a fourteen-day-old daughter in her arms as she ran, while the father carried another child and a gun that was not in condition for use. While they ran two Indians fired upon the father, who fell wounded. With tomahawks, they stunned the mother. But the wounded Frederick

Kobel managed to hold the Indians at bay by pointing his worthless gun at them menacingly. The mother regained consciousness and struggled to a tree stump, where she seated herself and began to nurse her infant. The Indians spoke to the group, as Weiser reported, "in High Dutch," assuring them that they meant no further harm. Suddenly one of the fiends drove his tomahawk through the mother's skull. She fell, face-downward, her body shielding the baby she held in her arms. Cruelly the murderer placed his foot upon the woman's neck and tore off the scalp. The children ran for safety, four were captured and scalped, but two of these survived the horrible ordeal. The father was killed. The story was related to Weiser by one of the scalped children, aged eleven. When searchers overturned the body of the mother, they found the little child alive and well. She was Barbara Kobel, who later became the wife of Peter Deppen and one of the progenitors of a long line of descendants.[15]

THE MARCH ON PHILADELPHIA

The irate settlers made good their threat to invade the city of Philadelphia to force the Assembly to pass a militia act. As gruesome evidence of the horrors they experienced, they brought with them a wagon-load of the hacked corpses of friends and relatives. Confronting the Governor with their demands, they stormed his home and extracted from him a pledge to compromise his differences with the assembly and on November 26 a militia act was passed granting 60,000 pounds for the protection of the province.[16]

Weiser did not accompany the angry settlers on their march to Philadelphia. On November 27, Richard Peters informed the newly appointed Colonel that the militia bill was passed and instructed Weiser to secure from Benjamin Franklin or James Hamilton whatever was needed to protect the province. The governor would not be in Philadelphia, because he was planning a tour of the frontiers. Peters concluded his letter saying, "God Bless You."

---

15. Deppen, E. E. and M. L., *Counting Kindred*, 105–106. The data was found by the authors in the records of St. Daniel's (Corner) Church, near Robesonia.
16. Graeff, Arthur D. *The Relations between the Pennsylvania Germans and the British Authorities*, Pennsylvania German Society, chap. 7, 109–125.

A small quantity of arms and ammunition was sent immediately to colonial officers in various parts of the province. Two wagoners, Lesh and Bricker, carried one hundred pounds of lead to Weiser's home. Later Nicholas Kintzer's wagon brought pistols and muskets for Weiser's men.[17]

Early in December, Weiser and other provincial leaders were summoned to Philadelphia by acting governor James Hamilton for advising the proper steps that should be taken to protect the province. Weiser signed commissions for his officers, giving Captain's rank to John Lesher, of Oley, and several minor appointments were made, as well as recommendations for commissions for James Seely and Dr. Christian Busse of Reading.

Plans were laid to raise an army of volunteers.

"OUR TROUBLES MULTIPLY APACE"

On New Year's Day, 1756, George Washington wrote to Governor Morris of Pennsylvania, stating that he was pleased to learn that "your—Martial Assembly" had voted a sum for the protection of the province, "which with your judicious application will turn out to the general Good." When Washington wrote that letter, Governor Morris was in Reading, consulting with Conrad Weiser on matters relating to military preparedness and the possibility of regaining the support of some of the Pennsylvania Indians.

Morris planned to meet with the Indians at some place in the interior of the province. Weiser was asked whether Harris' Ferry would serve as a proper treating place. No, thought Weiser, too few Indians remained east of the Susquehanna. To his knowledge, only Old Belt and the Broken Thigh had remained at John Harris' place. All the other Indians had fled to Croghan's at Aughwick. Carlisle would be much better in Weiser's opinion. Governor Morris decided that he would go to Carlisle by way of Harris' Ferry and accordingly gave orders to Captain James McLaughlin that 20 men should be detached from his company and "taking the road by Conrad Weiser's" send them to Harris' Ferry.

On January 5, while Morris was still in Reading, Weiser penned a letter from his home in Heidelberg, informing the governor of

---

17. The list of names of those who secured weapons from Kinzer's wagon is found in the Weiser Correspondence, Weiser MSS, 2:17.

some of his precautionary measures taken when the first reports of the massacres had occurred. He had employed George Gabriels, the last remaining settler near Shamokin, to bring some Delaware chiefs to Heidelberg for interview.[18]

GOVERNOR MORRIS TOURS THE PROVINCE

Shortly after receiving this account, Morris and his commissioners visited Weiser at his home and together they set out for Harris' Ferry. At the home of John Harris, an Indian conference was called. Among those present was the former governor, James Hamilton, Richard Peters, and Joseph Fox. Only "The Belt of Wampum," Old Belt, a Seneca, and a Mohawk named Broken Thigh, represented the Indians. Morris thanked the two chieftains for their loyalty and invited them to accompany his party to Carlisle. Old Belt made a speech, interpreted by Conrad Weiser, accepting the invitation and declaring, "the sky is dark all around us. The Mischiefs done to you I consider as done to the Six Nations." Here was a ray of hope! The Six Nations had not deserted the English cause entirely, especially if the Belt spoke for the Senecas, the most questionable nation of the six.[19]

When the governor and his party reached Carlisle, they found Croghan and seven Indians awaiting their arrival. Before calling a general conference, the commissioners engaged Croghan in a private conference to learn the exact status of Indian affairs west of the Susquehanna. Croghan painted an alarming picture, but, according to him, not all the Delawares had agreed to war against Pennsylvania. "Mr. Weiser was then sent for and it was taken into Consideration what should be said to the Indians."

One of the Indians at Carlisle was Aroas, known to the English as Silver Heels. He reported that in November 1755 he had visited Shamokin and found no Indians there. Then he had followed the Susquehanna to Nescopeck, where he found 140 Indians dancing the war dance, preparing an expedition against the settlers. An uncle of Silver Heels told him that the French had prevailed upon the Delawares and Shawnees to take up the hatchet.

---
18. Weiser to Morris, January 5, 1756, Weiser MSS, 1:63.
19. Colonial Records, 6:756.

When asked by the commissioners why the Delawares did not come to Croghan on his earlier invitation, Aroas explained that the Delawares were angry at the Old Belt and other Six Nations Indians, because of the political feud growing out of the election of succession of the Half-King.

The governor spoke to the Indians at Carlisle, deploring the "rift" which had occurred and asking those present to act as his messengers in trying to heal the breaches which had occurred. Then the Old Belt made a speech in which he charged that the Delawares and Shawnees had been in secret alliance with the French for some time past. The Shawnees, he said, found their grievance in the imprisonment of some of their braves in South Carolina, "but we look upon that as mere pretense." The imprisoned Shawnees had been released through the intercession of Conrad Weiser. The Old Belt advised that no steps should be taken until Scarroday and Zigera returned from their mission to the Six Nations.[20]

One of the results of the Governor's visit to Carlisle was to lead him to believe that Nescopeck was the headquarters of the French and Indian marauders. At Carlisle, on January 19, the governor drew a set of instructions to Weiser, ordering him to undertake a journey to Nescopeck in company with two Indians, there to learn all that could be learned about the strength of the enemy.[21] This information would be of especial value because the province planned to erect a fort at Shamokin.[22]

AT HARRIS' FERRY

Weiser returned to his house after the Carlisle meeting and on January 29, he set out with one of his hired men. In the Old Belt's cabin at Harris' Ferry, he announced the purpose of his mission. Silver Heels and David, a Mohawk, agreed to act as his messengers. These loyal Indians were engaged to carry peace tokens to the Shikellamys if they could be found. "The Old Belt gave the young messengers a long lesson," reported Weiser and Silver

---
20. For Proceedings of Carlisle Counsel see Colonial Records, 6:783; also 7:1-6.
21. Instructions to Weiser, Pennsylvania Archives, 2:551.
22. Later Fort Augusta, in present-day Sunbury.

Heels pledged that he would return in ten days, if not in fifteen, then it could be assumed that he was dead.

While Weiser waited at Harris' Ferry, many other matters arose to claim his presence and attention. There was a report that fifteen armed settlers were on their way to kill any friendly Indians they might find along the Susquehanna. Weiser sent a letter to the magistrates and the citizens of Cumberland County, warning them of the evil consequences of "such imprudent behavior." He sent several Indians to Carlisle, urging the friendly Indians who lived there to place themselves closer to the protecting arm of the province by coming to Harris' Ferry, instructing his agents to hire a wagon to transport the wards of the province, if necessary to do so.

Weiser tried to withhold the news of the alarm from the Indians at Harris' Ferry, but they learned of it despite his precautions and "I had a great deal of trouble to quiet their Minds (if I did at all)." One of the Indians, Newcastle by name, became drunk and made threats, and on the following morning, he was missing. Weiser warned the countryside that Newcastle was at large.

In urging that all friendly Indians be brought closer to the provincial settlements, Weiser warned that "our foolish people" might alienate the goodwill of all Indians. He signed his report as follows: "Submitted to his Honour, the Governor, his Council, and the Assembly, By their faithful Indian Interpreter, Conrad Weiser."

Urgent matters called Weiser from Harris' Ferry early in February 1756. After the return of the governor to Philadelphia, elaborate plans were laid to build a chain of forts along the Blue Mountains and Weiser, as colonel of Berks, was commissioned to superintend the erecting of the forts extending from the Schuylkill to the Susquehanna.

SORROW

Weiser was confronted with a terrible disaster that struck his own household. In 1748, his second daughter, Margaret, had married a young Lutheran clergyman, Reverend J.D.M. Heintzelman, assistant pastor to Reverend Brunnholz in Philadelphia. Early in

1756, the young man became ill. His wife was expecting the birth of a child. Mrs. Conrad Weiser had left her home in Heidelberg to go to Philadelphia to assist in running the household.

On February 9, Reverend Heintzelman died. One day later a son was born to the young widow. Weiser came to Philadelphia to attend the funeral. Among the condolences which he received was a letter from Richard Peters.[23]

> February 9, 1756
> My Dear Friend:
> Our Troubles multiply apace. I heard nothing of M. Heinselman's Illness, so that your kind letter is as a Flash of Lightening from Heaven. God grant you & Mrs. Weiser fortitude to bear your heavy affliction. I very heartily condole with you both, and—particularly with Mrs. Heinselman whose distress is still greater. I wish it was in my power to administer Consolation, it should not be wanting. I thank you for your kind note & am always . . .
> Richard Peters

A description of the melancholy event is best supplied by reproducing portions of a letter which Weiser wrote to William Parsons on February 13, 1756:

> but my good friend I must acquaint you now with another piece of news which gives me and my old womin a great deal of trouble, to witt my dear Sonilaw Mr. Hentselman the younger lutherian minister in this town departed this life last Sunday and is very much lamented by his Congregation, neighbours and by all most everybody that knew him—yesterday he was Buried, the day before yesterday his widow was delivered of a healthy and well Shaped son, you can think how moving it was to me and my wife (She has ben here this 4 weeks) to see the poor orphan & his dead father and the mother Sheding tears over both. However all this said a great many more

---
23. Peters to Weiser, February 9, 1756, Peters MSS, 4:48.

affliction comes from the hand of a Mercyful god, and I will bear with it. I worship him and pray that he would be pleased for his great names Saik to grant our Bleeding Country peace again, and in the meantime Comfort the fatherless, the wounded, the dieing, and teach our hands to fight Such a Cruel and Enemy, & would the people of pensilvania obey him he would root out Enemy Soon.[24]

When a man is deeply moved, his emotions reveal his character. During all his own grief, Weiser could still pray for suffering victims of the Indian raids and his faith in God was reinforced in moments of great trial and bereavement.

WAR DECLARED

It will be remembered that Weiser had dispatched two sets of Indian messengers to learn what was really happening in the Indian villages west and north of the Pennsylvania frontiers. Late in December, he had escorted the vice-regent of the Six Nations, Scarroday, and Andrew Montour, through the hostile ranks of the armed guards at Tulpehocken, sending them north along the Susquehanna to the councils of the Six Nations. Late in January of the next year, 1756, he had sent Silver Heels and David the Mohawk to Nescopeck, a village suspected to be the headquarters of the murdering Indians.

Governor Morris and his Indian commissioners were anxiously awaiting the return of the first messengers. The future actions of the province would depend on the report Scarroday and Montour would bring from New York.

Weiser was anxious to learn what had become of the three sons and one daughter of his old friend Shikellamy, and of Indian boys he had sent to Philadelphia in 1754 to be educated in the white men's school. These men and their families could certainly be depended upon to remain true to the English and if they could be found they might be in possession of valuable information.

Silver Heels and David found John Shikellamy at Wyoming and had prevailed upon him to accompany them to Philadelphia.

---

24. Horsfield MSS, 1:103.

The instructions were that the messenger should proceed from the Susquehanna to Conrad Weiser's home, but Shikellamy and his guides refused to travel through Tulpehocken "apprehensive that the Dutch would fall upon them." Instead, they came to Philadelphia by way of Lancaster, the Belt and other Indians joining them at Harris' Ferry. Conrad Weiser was in Philadelphia when they arrived on February 21. He had come to the city to attend the funeral of his son-in-law. The Belt was the spokesman for the messengers. Weiser and John Davison acted as interpreters. In open council, the Belt related that the messengers had found Nescopeck completely deserted and then went on to the Delaware town of Wyoming. Fearing to enter the hostile village they induced some Indians living nearby to carry a message to Paxinosa, the Shawnee chief, at Wyoming. Paxinosa called a meeting of his own people and sent his reply, declaring that it was useless to try to reason with the Delawares. Scarroday had been at Wyoming on his way to New York and the Delawares refused to listen to him "and gave him ill Language."[25]

The two interpreters, Weiser and Davison differed in translating a portion of the Belt's speech. The difference grew out of the turning of a phrase and the addition of a statement by Davison to the effect that two Delawares had gone to fight the English.

The Old Belt turned to his son-in-law Silver Heels and asked for confirmation of a point before proceeding. Then he related that a Delaware named Cut-Fingered-Peter had gone from Nescopeck to the Seneca country, carrying an English scalp to prove that the Delawares had avenged themselves on the people of Pennsylvania.

All of this was confusing. The council adjourned for two days and during that interval, Conrad Weiser secured "the true Interpretation of what was said by the Belt." Inviting John Shikellamy and his wife to breakfast, Weiser engaged the son of his deceased friend in a lengthy interview which Weiser wrote in the form of a report and submitted to Davison for checking before it was read in Council on February 26.

When the Delawares from the Ohio proclaimed war against the English, a Council was held at Shamokin. There it was determined to evacuate the village and move to Nescopeck, farther

---
25. "Narrative of a private conversation with an Indian," Penn Papers on Indian Affairs, 2:73.

up the Susquehanna. The Shikellamys planned to seek shelter at Weiser's home in Heidelberg, but the Delawares would not permit them to do so. At Nescopeck, Shikellamy found that all Indians there were in the French interest. When the scalps of white men were being brought to Nescopeck by Delaware warriors, the Shikellamys went to Wyoming and gathered a group of 30 warriors about them, mostly Shawnees, Chickasaws, and Mohicans, friendly to the English.

Nescopeck was deserted when a rumor reached the Delawares that Conrad Weiser was on his way north at the head of a large body of soldiers, the Delawares fleeing as far north as Tioga.

"Are there any white people amongst them?" asked Weiser.

"Yes," was the reply, "several deserters from Fort Oswego who paint their faces black and several white prisoners."

"What of James Shikellamy and John Petty?" "His two brothers," replied John Shikellamy, "had joined several Delawares in a search for food on the Delaware River. James, the Lame One, could not go the entire distance, but John Petty had witnessed a skirmish between Indians and whites near the Delaware River. He had not participated in the fight and came home empty-handed. The sister, Diana Logan, was living with the Conestoga Indians on the lower Susquehanna."

"How did Scarroday fare when he visited the Delawares?" Weiser asked. "He was in danger constantly. Even in council, the younger braves had shouted, 'kill the Rogue'."

After the reading of Weiser's written account, the Old Belt delivered another oration, the length and circumlocution of which taxed the patience of Council and Benjamin Franklin, who was present. The only pointed remarks of his speech were to repeat the advice he had given at Carlisle, to build a fort at Shamokin, and an offer to carry the hatchet for the English if called to do so.

Governor Morris thanked the Indians for their consideration and stated that his future actions would depend upon reports which were daily expected from Scarroday and Montour.[26]

Before leaving Philadelphia, the Old Belt complained that he had lost one "of his Ears." By this, he meant one of his interpreters was missing. John Davison had been imprisoned for debt.

---

26. Colonial Records, 7:46–50.

Meanwhile, Conrad Weiser had returned to the frontiers. There were many problems connected with provisioning the men who were stationed at strategic points in the gaps of the mountains; problems connected with the building of the chain of forts and recurring alarms and reports of cruel Indian massacres all along the foothills of the Blue Mountains. Because he was occupied elsewhere, Weiser was not in Philadelphia when Scarroday and Montour returned from their mission to the Six Nations. Daniel Claus and George Croghan acted as interpreters during the early interviews, but Weiser was called into the conference before the weighty matters growing out of them were concluded.

The messengers had an interesting story to relate. They brought with them Jonathan, the Academy student, and Newcastle, who had left Harris' Ferry under suspicious circumstances, as well as Silver Heels, the Old Belt, Moses, Seneca George, Jagrea, the Broken Thigh, the Fire Poker, and The Thick Leg. They had found Jonathan near Shamokin, hunting in the woods. It was planned to send the "educated" Indian back to Philadelphia with news of their progress, but circumstances made it too dangerous to do so.

At Wyoming, Scarroday saw the three sons of Shikellamy lined up with a party of Delawares, about to set out on a raid against the settlements. He called John aside and pleaded with him to be loyal. He protested that he was afraid to refuse the demands of the Delawares. The warriors at Wyoming declared that the hatchet had been sent to them from their uncles, the Six Nations. Scarroday refused to believe this. They spurned a belt of wampum he offered in council, pushing it aside with a stick, and the Pennsylvania emissaries set out northward in fear that they would be pursued and killed.

In all the Indian villages in the north, they found the war spirit high. At Chinkanning they saw a Dutch woman and her child as prisoners. There, too, they saw Teedyuscung, the new King of the Delawares. The King told them that he had recently sent three English scalps to some of the Six Nations. Cut-Fingered-Peter had delivered some of those scalps. But thus far no reply had come from the Six Nations. "I will send again," said Teedyuscung and "if they send an answer, well and good; if they do not, I shall know what to do." Here was evidence that the Indians at Wyoming had not received the hatchet from their masters, the Six Nations.

At Onondaga, Colonel William Johnson had reported the "unbrotherly Behavior" of the nephews toward the people of Pennsylvania. The Sachems declared that the Delawares "were drunk and should have their heads shaked until they were sober" and that the Hole of their Ears was very small so that they could not hear the commands of heir uncles, "but they were determined to bore a larger (hole) in their Ears and make them hear." Everything that Scarroday reported from the Six Nations indicated that the powerful confederacy was still loyal to the English interest.

Weiser was summoned to Philadelphia early in April. The Governor and his council were deliberating upon the reply that should be made to the Indians. Ever since January, Morris had avoided making any definite commitments to Old Belt and his companions, pending the report of his messengers to Onondaga. Now that report was at hand and all the Belt's associates had heard it.

The five Indian commissioners advised that the governor should declare war against the Delawares. When Morris broached this matter to his council, it met with the favor of all members except William Logan, the Quaker son of James Logan.

The announcement was made to the Indians by Conrad Weiser, speaking for the Governor, "I, therefore, by this belt, declare war against the Delawares . . . I offer you the Hatchet." A reward was promised for enemy prisoners and a somewhat smaller sum for Indian scalps. "I am now going to build a fort at Shamokin."

On Saturday, April 12, the Indians made their reply. The council chamber was filled with onlookers. Scarroday was the spokesman. "We heartily approve of your Resolutions," he declared as Weiser translated. "Awake, shake off your Lethargy; Stand up with your Hatchet in your Hand and use it manfully. Show them that you are men . . ." and then the floor of the council chamber shook as all of the Indians present joined in a war dance, the Old Belt chanting the falsetto notes to prove the cadence, while he waved a belt of wampum in his hand.[27]

---
27. Ibid., 78–83.

Stern Quakers shook their heads as they beheld the scene. The arm of the flesh had triumphed.

THE ASSOCIATION OF FRIENDS

"We humbly subscribe to the infinite Wisdom and Goodness of God" and to "the Angelic Acclamation of 'Glory to God in the Highest, Peace on Earth and Good Will to Men.'" Thus, in part, a group of Quakers addressed Governor Morris, protesting the declaration of war against the Delaware Indians in April 1756. The address was presented while the governor and his council were trying the exact wording of the declaration before publishing it. Great care had to be exercised to exempt all friendly Indians from the ban. Weiser was asked to consult Scarroday on this point.

The vice-regent of the Six Nations could not be consulted. Weiser reported that Scarroday was drunk. The Quaker petition, read before a special evening session of a fully attended council gave the governor pause. The Society of Friends urged that further steps should be taken to reconcile the disaffected Indians, declaring the proposed Declaration to be "hasty." At the meeting of council, the governor posed the question of delaying the proclamation. The vote of his council was nine to one in favor of proceeding as originally planned. The dissenting voice was that of William Logan, the Quaker member. Two days later, on April 14, the official declaration of war was published at the Court House. It included a reward for scalps and tried to exempt the friendly Indians by fixing boundaries of operations. The reading of the proclamation was done with great ceremony and before a great concourse of people.

After the reading of the declaration, Scarroday and the Indians called upon the governor and asked that Conrad Weiser be summoned. The minutes of the provincial council record that he came "with Reluctance." Some dissensions had arisen between the Indians and both Weiser and the governor were puzzled as to the cause. Scarroday peremptorily announced that he was going to leave Philadelphia within a few days and take all the Indians and their wives with him to the Six Nations, except for Silver Heels, Newcastle, and Seneca George. He promised that he would bring some warriors with him when he learned that the fort at Shamokin was built.

Morris asked Weiser's advice, before answering Scarroday. The interpreter had no explanation to offer to account for the sudden turn of events. He merely advised Morris to tell the Indians that they would be sent for when everything was in readiness. The governor then instructed Weiser to find out what lay at the bottom of what appeared to be dissension among the Indians. Later Conrad reported that the Indians expected gifts and included in his report the exact rewards which should be made to prevent jealousies from arising. When these matters were carried out, the Indians changed their minds about leaving immediately.

Meanwhile, the Quakers did not rest with their address to the governor. Soon after war was declared, Israel Pemberton, an outstanding leader among the Society of Friends, asked Governor Morris whether he and his associates would be permitted to invite the Indians to a banquet. The purpose was to suggest that a message should be sent to the Delawares, urging them to sue for peace. The venture was to be undertaken as a private enterprise financed by a group of Quakers who came to be known as the Friendly Association.

Morris gave his permission to invite the Indians to a banquet on the one definite condition "that nothing be said to them but by Mr. Weiser and that all that should pass should be faithfully related to him (Morris) for his farther consent."

The banquet was held and Weiser, in company with Pemberton, reported to the Governor that the Quakers had offered to act as a mediator between the Delawares and Pennsylvania. The Friends; offered to finance a journey to the Indian villages for their purpose. Scarroday was well pleased with the proposal and offered to help.[28]

The Indians' conferences with the members of the Friendly Association were conducted at the home of Israel Pemberton, extending through April 19 to April 25, 1756. Weiser attended these conferences and acted as the governor's unofficial observer.

On April 25, the Association and Indians agreed that Scarroday should send a message in the name of the Six Nations,

---

28. Etting Papers, Miscellaneous MSS, Historical Society of Pennsylvania, 1:84–86.

setting for the aims of the Quakers, urging the Delawares to cease their warfare and offering a pardon for those who had offended.[29]

Governor Morris asked his council whether in their opinion he should give official countenance to the message. "No," said Council, "the matter should be left entirely to the Quakers." They did suggest, however, that it might be well to send a personal message of assurance to each friendly Indians as Chief Paxinosa and others.

A MESSAGE TO WYOMING

Difficulties arose, however, when Newcastle, Jagrea, and a Delaware named William Laquis came to the governor to complain against Scarroday. The vice-regent had appointed these three to carry the message to Wyoming. Now, they declared, they would refuse to go. Scarroday had not consulted them in making the assignment. "We are not his Vassals," but if the Governor of Pennsylvania should order them to go, they would gladly, "but we will not go on Scarroday's Errands." The governor explained that the proposed journey was not a government matter. If the three Indians refused to go, he had "no Power," that the proposed journey to Wyoming was of grave concern to the province. Two days later he was glad to avail himself of the services of the three messengers, officially.

A letter from Sir Charles Hardy, governor of New York, informed Morris that Colonel William Johnson had held a conference of Six Nations Indians at Otsiningo, at which 300 Delawares attended. There the Six Nations upbraided their vassals for taking up arms against the English and ordered them to make peace immediately. The Delawares had agreed "to strike no more." Perhaps, admitted Morris, he had been too hasty in declaring war and perhaps he should proclaim a suspension of hostilities. Weiser was summoned and apprised of the news. He, in turn, relayed the information to some of the Indians and sought their advice. In submitting his opinion to the council, Weiser counseled "that for the present it might not be proper to take any publick notice of it."

---

29. For a more complete account of the activities of the Friendly Association see Coates Papers, recently acquired by the Historical Society of Pennsylvania.

The declaration should remain in effect as a disciplinary measure to force the Delawares to sue Pennsylvania for peace.

Weiser then reported lengthy conversations he had had with the Indians before war was declared. All the Indians had agreed that such a step was necessary to bring the Delawares to their senses. Scarroday had assured him that the Six Nations would not "take it amiss that rewards were offered for the Scalps of the Delawares." He did advise, however, that Newcastle and his two companions should be sent to Wyoming to inform the Indians there on what had taken place in New York province. Council agreed that such a message should be sent and the three messengers were duly instructed by Weiser as to what they should say to the enemy Indians at Wyoming.

Bishop Spangenberg, who attended the meeting of Council on April 26, offered to act as host of the messengers as far as Bethlehem and there he would furnish other Indians to accompany the messengers. Weiser and the governor left Philadelphia for a tour of the newly constructed forts. Weiser accompanied the Governor's party as far as Harris' Ferry and then returned to his home in Heidelberg, while Morris went on to Shamokin to inspect the work in the construction of Fort Augusta at the confluence of the two branches of the Susquehanna.

The month of May 1756, passed. Weiser was busy giving direction to his subordinate officers stationed along the base of the mountains. The number of Indian raids diminished markedly in the early spring of 1756 and became infrequent as the summer approached. Many settlers who had fled during the previous winter returned to their plantations and resumed their cultivation of the land.

Later in May came the summons to Weiser to return to Philadelphia. Newcastle and his companions had returned from Wyoming and the interpreter's services were needed. In Council, June 3, 1756, Jagrea turned to Weiser and stated that since not one of the three was an orator, they would relate their stories to Weiser, who should write their answers and read the document to the counselors. Weiser agreed to this and accordingly read a lengthy memorandum which he had taken from the words of the Indians on May 31.

The messenger reported some early difficulties they encountered and then went on to report the essence of their conferences. There were speeches by the heads of many nations; the most significant one was made by Teedyuscung, the King of the Delawares.

"We rejoice," said he, "that Brother Onas is willing to renew the old good Understanding . . . We take hold of them by Treaties with both our hands . . . we on our side will certainly do it . . . look upon us with Eyes of Mercy. Pity us." Speaking only for those Delawares who lived on the Susquehanna, Teedyuscung agreed to abide by the directions of the Six Nations; the young braves were instructed to obey; but Onas must be careful not to blame the Pennsylvania Delawares for crimes committed by those Delawares who had joined the French on the Ohio.

A TRUCE

The governor and his Council pondered for a time after hearing this very welcome message. After the Indians left the chamber, they constructed a draft of a Suspension of Hostilities for thirty days. It was engrossed and then the Governor and his Council went to the courthouse, where the proclamation of the Suspension was published before a large group of people.

On June 8th, the Indian messengers begged permission to return to Tioga, where they had held their conferences. They feared that their absence might give the Indians there cause for alarm. Morris, through Weiser, informed the messengers that he had still another for them to take back to their friends at Tioga. Then Weiser instructed Jagrea and Newcastle to report the proclamation of suspension of hostilities and to invite Teedyuscung and the Delawares to a treaty to iron out their differences. "I now kindle a Council Fire at the House of Conrad Weiser," the governor declared. Weiser informed Morris, however, that the treaty place must be left to the choice of the Indians. Newcastle believed they would choose Minisinks, the Forks of the Delaware.

As the three messengers set out upon their second journey northwest, it appeared that the program initiated by the Society of Quakers had borne fruit.[30]

---

30. Account of this Indian conference in Colonial Records, 7:137–141.

LIEUTENANT-COLONEL WEISER

From Hunter's Mills on the Susquehanna to the Minisinks on the Delaware, the Blue Mountains, in 1756, formed a natural wall between the settled portions of Pennsylvania and the domains of Indians. At frequent intervals there are deep gaps in these mountains, permitting groups of men on foot or on horseback to travel from the English to the Indian's land. It was through these gaps Swatara, Schubert's, Manada, and other mountain passes, that marauding Indians had poured to wreak death and destruction in the autumn of 1755, inaugurating a reign of terror now commonly known as the Blue Mountain Massacres.

In November 1756, the provincial assembly passed a militia act granting 60,000 pounds to protect the province. To the military men in Philadelphia, it appeared that the strategic thing to do was to build a chain of forts and block-houses on the southern foothills of the mountains, locating these establishments near the gaps and rivers that cut through the high hills.

BUILDING A CHAIN OF FORTS

Provision was made, also, to construct a continuation of the chain of forts southward from the Susquehanna, through Cumberland County to the Maryland line. We are concerned primarily with the Blue Mountain forts. Conrad Weiser and Benjamin Franklin were commissioned to build them in that district and Lieutenant-Colonel Weiser was directed to garrison all of them with detachments from the First Pennsylvania Regiment of Volunteers.[31]

Franklin and Weiser divided the line assigned to them, Franklin superintending the construction of forts east of Allemängel (Albany, Berks County) and Weiser assuming the responsibility for the building westward from Allemängel to Hunter's Mills on the Susquehanna. The first fort to be built was named Fort Allen, in honor of Judge William Allen. It stood where Weissport, Carbon County, now stands, not far from the unhappy ruins of the Moravian settlements of Gnadenhutten. Franklin personally supervised the work of building this fort, hearing the title "General" bestowed

---

31. Date of the Commission was May 5, 1756, Pennsylvania Archives, 5th ser., 1:76.

upon him by Moravians in the neighborhood. Sometimes they addressed him as Lieutenant General to distinguish his military office from that of Postmaster General of the colonies, an office he held concurrently. Franklin did not hold a military commission.

Fort Allen was built early in January 1756, and soon thereafter Fort Norris was erected by Captain Jacob Arndt under Franklin's direction.[32] Fort Norris stood near the present village of Kresgeville.

Meanwhile, Weiser was busy directing the construction of forts westward to the Susquehanna. Fort Lebanon, near present-day Port Clinton, Fort Northkill near Strausstown, Fort Henry along the Shamokin Trail near Bethel, Forts Swatara, Manada, and Hunter, were the bulwarks raised against Indian incursions.

Sometimes block-houses had to be built in addition to the garrisoned forts. Some of these were Dietrich Sixes on the Blue Mountain, north of Bethel. Others were Brown's, near Manada Gap, and Harris', in Paxton. Sometimes strong houses served as shelters to which settlers could scurry if the Indians made a warpath toward their homes. In this class was Fort Zeller, near Newmanstown, still standing today.

The construction of the forts followed a pattern. Almost all of them were composed of a heavy stockade of heavy planks enclosing a space of ground on which were built from one to four blockhouses pierced with loopholes for muskets. Members of the garrison lived in these houses and, on occasion, settlers fled to them when the alarm was raised. The sites of these forts have been marked by historical commissions, but only a few vestiges of the battlements remain. In 1926, a visit on the site of Fort Northkill revealed a depression in the earth which once was the cellar of a blockhouse, but even that faint reminder of the past is rapidly becoming indistinct as forest, leaves, and debris are filling in the crater.[33]

A PROBLEM OF LOGISTICS

In June 1756, the work of building the forts was completed. The task of garrisoning all the forts east of the Susquehanna was committed to Lieutenant-Colonel Conrad Weiser. Fort Henry, on

---
32. *Berichte*, February 1, 1756.
33. For detailed account of the building of the Blue Mountain forts see *Frontier Forts of Colonial Pennsylvania*, vol. 1, Report of the Pennsylvania Historical Commission.

the road which Weiser had taken many times on his journey to the Indian capital at Shamokin, was closest to Weiser's home in Heidelberg. Therefore, this fort served as a distributing center for the commands of the colonel and for supplies. In command at Fort Henry was Captain Christian Busse, a Reading physician who turned soldier during the Indian uprisings. Busse wrote letters in German to his "Ober-Amt" officer, reporting the news brought to Fort Henry by scouts and rangers. Indian forays and occasional attacks upon settlers were reported in detail. A year before his death in 1941, Dr. George Wheeler of Philadelphia had most of Busse's letters translated into English, thus enabling us to study detailed accounts shedding light upon the events and times. Benjamin Franklin wrote his autobiography in English thereby, enabling all American historians to learn the story of his fort-building career. The letters from Busse to Weiser, and from Weiser to Hauptmann Busse, have remained a mystery until recent times because very few could read them. They tell of the deployment of troops of men sent to stand guard while farmers reaped their harvests; of messages from Colonels James Burd and William Clapham, commanders in the north (Augusta) and western fronts. A muster roll of enlisted men reveals the names and records of the members of the garrison.[34] Many of these names can be traced to the Palatine Subsistence records and the ship lists of Pennsylvania German pioneers, published by the Pennsylvania German Society.

A PROBLEM OF MORALE

Wagons carrying arms, ammunition, and supplies were dispatched from Weiser's to Fort Henry. One of Weiser's older sons, either Frederick or Philip, accompanied the wagons and delivered the goods to Busse, whose rangers saw to it that a proper distribution was made to the garrisons east and west of Fort Henry.

Busse's reports contain some accounts of disciplinary measures taken from time to time, but the Berks-Lebanon chain of

---

34. Some soldiers stationed at Reading in May 1756, surnames are Fichthorn, Wolf, Rosh, Retchmeyer, Geisler, Brendlinger, Arenstein, Shock, Riem, and Sanerberg. At Fort Henry in September 1756: Mauer, Adelman, Albert, Andre, Antes, Bauer, Breitenbaugh, Diem, Eisenbets, Ehrman, Gutterman, Kreischer, Loch, Marks, Rabold, Ruppert, Weis, Zeit, and others. Nearly all of the names are clearly German.

forts did not create the vexing problems of discipline that crowded Weiser's desk from the Lehigh-Northampton district. There Timothy Horsfield, Jacob Arndt, and William Parsons tried to coordinate the military measures under Weiser's general directions. Horsfield's letters are now deposited in the Archives of the American Philosophical Society and the tomes of Northampton County Manuscripts in the Historical Society of Pennsylvania. Some of the incidents of garrison life recorded there, in letters to Weiser, make sordid reading. Lewdness, putrid disease, wantonness, and drunken Indians are mixed with stories of inefficiency; bribery; and neglect of duty. Unfortunately, we have very little from Weiser's own pen to reveal the way he dealt with these problems. He must have welcomed the arrival of Captain John Schlosser's Company of Royal Americans, regular troops, in Easton during the summer of 1756.

It is difficult to take the measure of Weiser as a soldier. Difficult partly, because few of his military orders are extant. There are many copies of letters, which subordinates wrote to him, complaining, demanding, pleading for some provisions and more men. In these letters, it is discernible that his fellow-officers, many of whom were career-men in military service, showed him every deference due to his rank and there is evidence, too, that the strategist in Philadelphia deferred to Weiser's judgment on matters purely military as they did in Indian diplomacy. In the absence of documentary evidence, It is assumed that Weiser gave his commands orally, through messengers. It must be remembered that the soldiers and most of the officers were Pennsylvania Germans, who from time immemorial have preferred to speak their minds rather than write them.

THE SWORD AND OLIVE BRANCH

Another circumstance which makes it difficult to appraise Weiser's skill as a soldier is the incongruous position which he held as peacemaker and war leader, for and against the friend-enemy, the Indian. At that same time that he was delivering lead, powder, and muskets to soldiers sent against Indians, he was the agent of the Friendly Association of Quakers planning a peace parley at Easton, the agent of Pennsylvania in charge of treaties, and one-half of him, as Shikellamy once said, "belonged to the Indians." Therefore, if Conrad became too active as a warrior, he lost all chance to become a peacemaker. Perhaps he was confronted with the choice of profession and being a Christian, chose the less glamorous role of as the channel through which to pour his efforts.

The frontier forts served as a barrier against any largescale Indian invasions from the forest-world north of the Blue Mountain. The rangers from the forts patrolled the woods, deploying themselves several miles east and west of their bases until they met with rangers from neighboring forts. In this way, the foothills of the mountains were thoroughly scouted. While these forts gave security to the towns and cities of eastern Pennsylvania, they could not give complete protection to the settlers near the mountains. Occasional Indian marauding parties sneaked through the defenses and fell upon remote settlers in the partly cleared farmsteads near the frontiers.

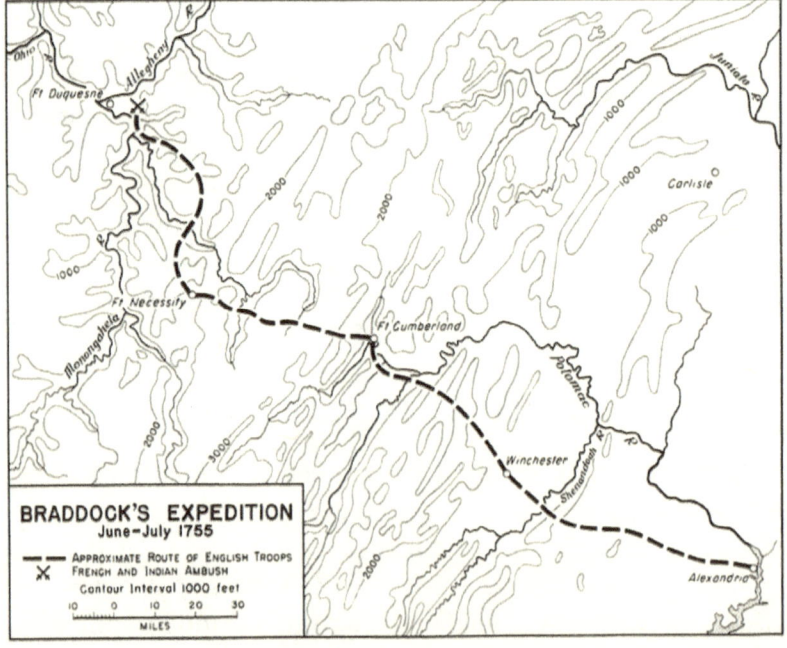

Map of General Braddock's route.

General Braddock falls in battle.

General Braddock, dying, as the British army retreats. Braddock died on the road and was buried under it in order to hide his body.

Delaware chief Teedyuscung

CHAPTER XVII

Treaties of Easton

Jagrea and Newcastle, the Indian messengers dispatched by Weiser under the auspice of the Association of Friends, returned from Tioga with news that he Six Nations would permit the Delawares to treat with Pennsylvania. Governor Morris and his staff had hoped that the Indians would select Weiser's home in Heidelberg as the meeting place, but the Delawares preferred the Minisink, on the Delaware, or the town of Easton. One of the conditions imposed upon the enemy, Delawares, was that they must bring their "English" prisoners to the treaty.

Great preparations were made to provide a military setting for the Easton conference.[1] The company of Royal Americans stationed at Bethlehem was ordered to escort Teedyuscung, King of the Delawares to Easton, and Lt. Colonel Conrad Weiser was instructed to furnish a military guard of honor for Governor Morris and his party. These trappings were altogether out of proportion to the importance of the conference and we cannot refrain from wondering how the good Quakers representing the Friendly Association must have felt in their military surroundings.

Weiser received his orders to attend the governor's party in mid-July. Summoning detachments from the frontier forts under his supervision and in company with Captain Christian Busse, commandant at Fort Henry, Weiser marched his men through Reading, Maxatawny (Kutztown) to Bethlehem Inn, arriving on July 27, one day late.[2]

---
1. Timothy Horsfield to Governor Morris, Horsfield MSS, 255.
2. Weiser MSS, 1:78.

KING TEEDYUSCUNG

The Easton conference was scheduled to open on July 26th, but Morris informed Teedyuscung that it would not be proper to do business until Mr. Weiser was there. The Delaware King was impatient, saying that "time was precious," but when Morris explained that Weiser held the dual position of Provincial interpreter and membership in the Council of the Six Nations, the King agreed that his "Uncles would be better satisfied to have Mr. Weiser present." On the following day, Weiser and his soldiers arrived. Now it was Weiser who asked for delay.[3]

Declaring that he did not know the Delaware King personally, Conrad asked that the formal sessions be postponed for one day longer in order that he might talk to Teedyuscung and learn something of his character and history before appearing in a public meeting. The wisdom of this decision on Weiser's part is another evidence of his great skill in dealing with Indians, for this Teedyuscung was a man apart from his fellows in personality traits. Richard Peters described him as follows: "He (Teedyuscung) is a lusty, raw bon'd man, haughty and very desirous of Respect and Command, he can drink three Quarts or a Gallon of Rum a Day without being drunk." The King was an egomaniac, declaring that he had it in his power to decide the issues of the war between the French and English. One minute he would declare that he would force the English to pay him well and the next he would declare in self-righteousness that he had no material interests, but was the Great Spirit's agent to bring everlasting peace to the world. Boasting that he was the King of Ten Nations, he declared that he could whip either the French or English, according to his whims. When asked to name the Ten Nations, he added the Delawares, Shawnees, Mohicans, and Muncies to the Six Nations of the Iroquois Confederacy. With such a man Weiser and Morris had to deal at Easton in July 1756.

Fourteen chiefs accompanied the Delaware King to Easton. These, together with three of Teedyuscung's sons, several squaws, and a few Indian wards of the Moravian settlement, comprised the

---
3. Pennsylvania Archives, 2:726.

Indians' delegation to Easton. For Pennsylvania, there were many representatives: the governor and four members of his Council; the three Indian commissions for the province; thirty Quakers from Philadelphia, guarding the presents they had brought with them at the instance of the Friendly Association; many officers in uniform, those of the Royal American Regiment and Weiser's Provincial troops; together with many magistrates from Pennsylvania and New Jersey. Lt. Colonel Conrad Weiser, at war with the Delawares, was the chief interpreter in open council and Governor Morris's private counsel in his lodgings. Weiser advised that Teedyuscung should be invited to make the first speech in the assemblage and the King readily accepted the assignment.

In a series of metaphorical expressions, the orator addressed the audience. Most of his remarks were merely glittering generalities which brought no issue to the surface. When he concluded his remarks, the King placed one hand upon his chest and declared that he had now said all he had to say except "that which is still in my Breast,"—and then came the word "Whish-Shiksy." With this word he threw a lot of consternation into the assemblage. Weiser was puzzled about its meaning. Could it be of evil portent? But when Conrad learned from Teedyuscung that "Whish-Shikey" in the Mohawk was rendered "Jago," all fears were allayed as Weiser interpreted it as a meaning strength to be gained through cooperation. Teedyuscung was prodding the English to unite with the Indians against the French.

"Whish-Shikey" became the keynote of the Easton Conference of July. Governor Morris took up this note in his reply to the Delawares. Teedyuscung's full cooperation was promised to round up representatives of the "Ten Nations" to reassemble in Easton later in 1756, probably two months later, after the King could send messages summoning the tribal chieftains. Newcastle and Teedyuscung were commissioned by Pennsylvania to invite all the tribes in a peace effort.

Inflated by his new-found importance and as a gesture of earnestness of purpose, Teedyuscung turned upon the Delawares present at the conference and gave them severe chastisement: "Cousins, the Delaware Indians: You will remember that you are our women; our forefathers made you so and put a petticoat on you and charged you to be true to us and lie with no other man. But of late you have suffered the String that tied your Petticoat to be cut loose by the French, and you lay with them and so become a common Bawd—in which you did very wrong and deserved Chastisement, but notwithstanding this we will still Esteem you and as you have thrown off the Cover of your Modesty and become Stark naked, which is a shame for a woman. We now give you a little Power and put it into your private Parts, so let it grow there until you have become a complete man."[4]

After the conference, the governor distributed the presents which the Friendly Association had brought to Easton. Weiser's advice was asked about the opening of the sessions, giving four to Governor Morris: one to brush the thorns from the governor's leg; another to rub the dust out of his eyes to help him see clearly; another to open his ears to hear the Indians patiently; and the fourth to clear his throat that he might speak plainly. During the conference he presented a large belt which was sent by the Six Nations. This belt had symbols woven into the beads. Teedyuscung had explained: "You see a square in the middle meaning the Lands of the Indians and at one end the figure of a man, indicating the English and at the other end another, meaning the French; our Uncles told us that both these covered our lands."

When the Conference was ended, Weiser advised that Newcastle and Teedyuscung should be given ample supplies of wampum. If they were to prevail upon all scattered tribes to join in a peace effort they would need beads and strings to seal many pledges. He advised that the large belt, sent by the Six Nations, should be returned to the Delawares, to whom it was originally sent. All additional wampum belts should be put into Teedyuscung's hands. Secretary Peters had brought fifteen strings and belts to Easton. There were 7000 pieces of black wampum, strung on these strings. While beads would be needed to construct a symbolic design.

---

4. For account of the Easton Conference of July 1756 see Colonial Records, 7:204–220. The account of the conference published by Benjamin Franklin differs from that which was spread on the Minutes of the Executive Council. We have used Franklin's rendition in quoting the line preceding this reference in the text.

BLACK WAMPUM

Accordingly, a messenger was sent to Bethlehem where 5000 white beads were obtained. The Indian squaws attending the conference were employed to string the beads into a belt one fathom long and sixteen beads wide. The designs to be incorporated in white beads went to show a man, the central figure, depicting the Governor of Pennsylvania and five figures of men on each side of him, symbolizing Teedyuscung's "Ten Nations."

While Morris, through Weiser as interpreter was explaining the assignment to the Indian women, Teedyuscung burst into the room angrily demanding to know why Morris was holding secret conferences with the women of his nation. Weiser translated as Morris explained the purpose of the meeting and Teedyuscung's wrath subsided.

The task of stringing the new belt of wampum was not completed when Teedyuscung and his party left Easton. The governor suggested that the Indian women could work at it "on rainy days" while they were away from Easton.

On August 1, Weiser and his company of soldiers left Easton to resume their duties in the frontier forts. He paid his bill for forty-eight men at "Bethlehem's Inn." There Lieutenant Engle and twelve men separated from Weiser to return to Fort Norris. Thirty-five men had dinner at John Trexler's and on the following day they breakfasted at Daniel Levan's tavern in Maxatawny. On the evening of the 2nd of August, they reached Reading. Only Captain Busse and five men detached from Fort Henry accompanied Weiser to his home in Heidelberg. These men were dined "at Womelsdorf in Heidleberg."[5]

TREATY OF NOVEMBER 1756

If the provincial authorities had any hopes that the boastful Teedyuscung would succeed in effecting an armistice with the warring tribes on Pennsylvania frontiers, they were doomed to disappointment. Massacres and forays commenced anew during

---

5. This is the earliest reference we have found to the name of the Berks borough west of Weiser's home. The town was founded by John Womelsdorff, the official date generally accepted is 1762, six years after Weiser's reference to "Womelsdorff in Heidleberg."

the late summer and early autumn of 1756. Teedyuscung, King of the Delawares, was commissioned as agent for Pennsylvania at the July conference in Easton, but he proved to be a liability to the province instead of an asset. Demanding a military escort from Bethlehem to Fort Allen (Lehighton) he travelled in state and then proceeded to make the colonial fort his headquarters for guzzling firewater.[6]

Conrad Weiser received many complaints of conditions at Fort Allen. On August 6, the soldiers at the fort mutinied against their officers; Captain Reynolds wrote to Colonel Weiser describing some disgusting practices generally ascribed only to degenerates; William Parsons wrote to Governor Morris that he had reason to believe that the soldiers had turned Fort Allen into a "Dram Shop." On August 19, Timothy Horsfield wrote to Parsons, expressing fear that the fort would be captured by the Indians. This alarm was probably superinduced by the news that Fort Granville, one of the forts west of the Susquehanna, had been captured by the French.[7]

These troubles gave Governor Robert Hunter Morris little concern, because his days as governor were rapidly ending. Beyond urging Weiser to restore discipline at Fort Allen, he took no hand in the matter, for on August 21, William Denny, Esquire, the new deputy of the Penns, arrived from England.

One of Denny's first official acts was to order Weiser to go to Bethlehem and "suspend officers if necessary" in order to restore discipline in the fort.[8] To make matters worse, insubordination developed at Fort Norris, near Fort Allen. At the same time, Colonel Burd was asking Weiser to dispatch some soldiers to aid the troops defending the western forts and Colonel Clapham was calling for help at Fort Augusta, built on the site of the Indian village at Shamokin (Sunbury).

Fears were allayed when Colonel Armstrong destroyed the Indian stronghold at Kittanning late in August. But the capture of the village merely served to disperse the Indians and the murders along the Blue Mountains were renewed during September and

---
6. Horsfield MSS, 255.
7. Horsfield to Parsons, August 19, 1756, Ibid., 284.
8. Denny to Weiser, August 21, 1756, Ibid., 292.

October. Weiser tried to solve all the problems by writing letters to the officers giving commands. He could not be at all places at the same time.

In October, Governor Denny urged Weiser to come to Philadelphia, in order that he might be in town whenever either Newcastle or Teedyuscung should bring a message concerning the proposed treaty at Easton, agreed upon in July. Weiser replied that he suffered from "an intermitting Feaver" and therefore could not come to Philadelphia but he would send his son Samuel, who was qualified to act as interpreter, on October 24. Soon afterwards came word that Teedyuscung had returned to Easton and was awaiting the Governor to treat with him at that "Council fire." Conrad Weiser's presence was sorely needed. Newcastle was sent to bring Weiser to the city. The two arrived on October 29, two days after the message from Teedyuscung reached the governor. But Newcastle, the trusted scout, did not live to engage in any treaties. He became ill with smallpox on the same day that he returned with Weiser and quickly succumbed to the disease.[9]

Denny's next move was to dispatch Weiser to Easton, instructing him to urge Teedyuscung to come to Philadelphia for treating on Indian affairs. On November 2, Weiser reached Easton and tried to convince Teedyuscung that Philadelphia would welcome him and his party. In all honesty, Conrad informed the Indians that a mild epidemic of smallpox had claimed Newcastle as a victim, but assured the Indians that their health would be guarded.

"No," declared the King of the Delawares, "the council fires had been kindled in the Minisinks and there the councils must be concluded." These were his spoken words, but we shall see that Teedyuscung had a subtle purpose in insisting upon Easton as the treating place.

Governor Denny, erratic and not mentally equipped to perform the duties of his office, was furious when he learned that Weiser had failed to prevail upon the Indians to come to Philadelphia. He declared that it was ridiculous to humor the Indians. Why should he go to Easton, he asked Richard Peters, when Sir William Johnson had charge of Indian affairs? The new governor had a great

---
9. Colonial Records, 7:307.

deal to learn and his council instructed him to proceed to Easton, notwithstanding his own preferences in the matter.[10]

Accordingly, the Governor wrote to Weiser on November 3, stating that he would come to Easton. For some reason, not clear now, Denny included an order in the letter, instructing Weiser to arrange to have the conference with the Indians behind closed doors. Denny stated that too many people misinterpreted what the Indians were saying, "but I have confidence in your Prudence." One of the cardinal points of Indian diplomacy was "open covenants, openly arrived at" and Weiser knew this very well. His man, Denny, was giving him impossible assignments.

New troubles developed a few days before the scheduled arrival of the governor and his party. On the evening before the Philadelphia group was expected, an alarm was spread through all Northampton that a band of warriors was lying in wait to ambush the governor and murder all the people at Easton. Denny and his party heard the rumor and halted their journey. Weiser sent out some trusted Indian scouts who investigated the cause of the alarm and reported that it was without foundation. Then Weiser and Parsons sent a joint letter, expressed to Denny, assuring him that he and his party could proceed in safety. Weiser promised to meet the governor in person enroute and Teedyuscung dispatched several Indians to join Weiser as an escort of honor to the governor.

For some reason, Weiser did not meet up with the governor on the highway, but this untoward circumstance was repaired magnificently by the panoply and pomp that attended the march of the governor from his quarters to the meeting place. Denny was guarded by a party of Royal Americans in front and on each flank, while Colonel Weiser's Provincial troops followed in the rear of the procession "with Colours flying, Drums beating and Musick playing."

Weiser was directed to invite Teedyuscung to make the first speech when the treaty was begun on November 6. The great orator was not in the best form, perhaps the small audience curbed his talents. Beyond promising to be forthright in all his dealings,

---

10. Denny to Thomas Penn, November 4, 1756, *Pennsylvania Magazine of History and Biography*, 44:106–107.

there was little point to the chieftain's speech on the opening day of the treaty.

On the following morning, Governor Denny addressed the Indians. The meeting was open to the public, as once again Weiser had failed to carry out a Denny command. Instead of Ten Nations, the braggart Teedyuscung had collected representatives of only seven, including the resident Delawares and Moravian Indians. Weiser had taken the measure of the swaggering chief earlier when he wrote to Denny, November 3, that "I am apt to think that Teedyuscung's authority, or influence, is not so great among the Indians as he first gave out or was represented to this government." Twenty Indians had attended the July Conference and now only thirty appeared after all the plans to hold a great peace party for all Indians in Pennsylvania and New Jersey. Denny was disappointed and said, "No."

"IRRWISCH"

The governor urged Teedyuscung to be very frank in stating the case for the Indians and when his turn came to speak, the Delaware King availed himself fully of the opportunity to unburden himself of age-old grudges. His reason for insisting upon Easton as the treating place became apparent when he charged that the very ground he was standing upon had been taken from the Indians by fraud. He was referring to the "Walking Purchase" of 1737. His speech was filled with many analogies and metaphors. Several times Weiser was called upon to explain the figures of speech more fully for the benefit of English ears. In one of his reports on Teedyuscung's speeches Weiser recorded that the King did not wish to follow a "Jack Lanthorn." When this term was not comprehended, he added, "what the Germans call 'Irrwisch'." Evidently, Weiser had not mastered the term "Jack-o-Lantern." It was an odd circumstance by which aboriginal figures of speech had to be translated into German though before they could be intelligible to English ears.

The Delaware's charges fell upon the ears of the peace-planners like a crash of thunder. Not one of the white men present had had anything to do with the trick by which Marshall had run the purchase line in 1737. Hastily a conference was called and Conrad Weiser was asked to advise what answer Denny could give. Weiser replied that few of the Delawares present at the treaty had ever owned any of the land involved in the Walking Purchase; that the complaints of the Delawares had been investigated by the Council of the Six Nations and at the Philadelphia Treaty of 1742, the whole matter had been settled to the satisfaction of the Six Nations.

The governor and his commissioners decided to appease the Delawares by distributing all the presents they had brought with them, even though the number of Indians was not as great as had been anticipated. Teedyuscung was offered money, so that he could distribute it among the disaffected Delawares. But haughtily, the Delaware King refused to accept the coins, but he promised to collect all claimants and bring them to Easton at some future time to make settlement with the governor. The task of approaching Teedyuscung with money had been assigned to Weiser and again he had failed to achieve what Denny desired.[11]

The distribution of presents was left in Weiser's charge, together with the responsibility for getting the Indians out of Easton and Bethlehem to Fort Allen, where the treaty goods was stored. Weiser's journal of this expedition to Fort Allen is filled with annoyances and troubles of may sorts.[12] It is little wonder therefore that when he finally reached the home he had left, despite "Intermittent Feavour," he wrote to Governor Denny, stating, "I am tired of Indian business."[13]

THE FALLEN TREE

"The irregular people I deal with have tired me sufficiently," wrote Weiser wearily on the evening of November 24, 1756, after he returned from Fort Allen. In this letter he told Governor Denny that he hoped to be relieved of all Indian affairs. The use of the word "irregular" by Weiser reveals just what he wished to convey. The interpreter's orderly mind was uneasy because of the turn that public affairs were taking. As a private person he would never

---
11. Account of Easton Treaty of November 1756, Colonial Records, 7:316–336.
12. Weiser's Journal of 1756, Pennsylvania Archives, 3:66–68.
13. Weiser to Denny, November 24, 1756, Pennsylvania Archives, 2nd ser., 7:269.

have participated in the negotiations at Easton, but as an officer under commission from the governor it was his clear duty to obey.

The Easton conferences with Teedyuscung, self-proclaimed King of Ten Nations, were irregular to Weiser, because he always believed in dealing directly with the Six Nations and not with remnant tribes. He had taken the Delaware King's measure and doubted whether any good could result from dealing with him.

The administration of Indian Affairs was not entrusted to Sir William Johnson of New York and Weiser was suspicious of any actions which did not clear through the Mohawk's Castles of Warraghiyagey. Others might have been jealous of the Irishman's preferment over themselves for the King's Indian Commission and some did feel that Weiser had been slighted by the choice of the New York agent, but there is no evidence that Conrad felt any bitterness toward the man who superseded him in the Councils of Albany. Quite to the contrary, the intrepid German settler at Heidelberg was zealous in insisting that Johnson be consulted on major issues relating to the Indians. Whether this conviction grew out of a sense of loyalty to a superior or whether it was the natural consequences of years of dealing with the confederate tribes of the Six Nations, it is not possible to say with certainty. It is probably the latter.

The result of Pennsylvania's altered policy of dealing with separate tribes was a series of "irregular" conferences and so-called treaties during the first of 1747. There were Indian conferences at Harris' Ferry, at Croghan's, and at Fort Frederick in Maryland. The Cherokees, sworn enemies of the Six Nations, came to Pennsylvania to aid the English cause against the French occupation of the Ohio; Teedyuscung was moving through forest paths in northern Pennsylvania, ostensibly searching for Delawares who claimed to have been defrauded of lands at the Minisinks. In April 1757, Indian Nathaniel stopped at Weiser's home on his way to Bethlehem.[14] He had been sent by George Croghan to invite Teedyuscung to a treaty at Harris' Ferry. Later in April, Captain Trent in company with the Mohawks, likewise stopped at Weiser's Heidelberg home. They, too, were on their way to Bethlehem to invite Teedyuscung to a Six Nations treaty in Lancaster.

---
14. Horsfield MSS, 2:371.

Among the Mohawks was Jonathan, the "educated" Indian, erstwhile student of the Philadelphia Academy. Jonathan asked his former sponsor, "Is it true that you have become a Fallen Tree? That you must no more engage in Indian affairs, neither as a Counsellor nor Interpreter? What is the Reason thereof?" Weiser explained that Sir William Johnson now had charge of Indian Affairs for His Majesty. The Indians expressed their dismay and then Jonathan said, "I have heard that you are engaged on another Bottom," meaning that Weiser had become a soldier against the Indians. Weiser then explained the circumstances which had forced him to take up the hatchet. "I," he asked, "take greater Delight in War than in Civil Affairs? I am a man for Peace and I wish there were no war at all."

THE BRIDLED TONGUE

One month before the arrival of the Mohawk messengers, Governor Denny had written to Weiser, urging him to come to Lancaster to interpret during a treaty with representatives of the Six Nations. The first message was delivered orally by Richard Peters while Conrad was visiting Philadelphia in March 1757, but Weiser told Peters that unless Denny would send him orders in writing, he could deem it more prudent to stay at his headquarters at home. Denny sent the necessary letter and Weiser set out for Lancaster early in May, once again concerned about Indian affairs.

In former treaties, Weiser had always played the triple role of interpreter, agent for Pennsylvania, and counsellor for the Six Nations. But at Lancaster, in 1757, his duties were confined to interpreting. George Croghan had been appointed by Sir William Johnson as his deputy agent for Pennsylvania. The deputies of the Six Nations had assembled at Harris' Ferry early in April, almost 200 strong.[15] A preliminary conference was held on the banks of the Susquehanna and a message was sent to Conrad Weiser in Heidelberg apprising him of what had been said and done. All the Six Nations were represented, but the small number of Senecas present did not please the Governor and his commissioners.

---
15. Weiser's Journal, Colonial Records, 7:489.

Some Nanticokes, Conestogas, and Delawares were among those present. Scarroday was the chief spokesman for the Six Nations.

Because Weiser's duties were confined to interpreting, it is not necessary to review the agenda of the Lancaster treaty of 1757, important though it was in the history of colonial Pennsylvania. On several occasions, Weiser was invited to join with Croghan to frame the speeches which Denny was to say to the Indians, but here again we find Weiser's influence waning. When he and Croghan differed on the phrasing of certain passages, it was Croghan's decision that prevailed. It is worth noting that the governor and his commission took frequent occasion to "correct" the draughts submitted by Sir William Johnson's deputy. The main address to the Six Nations, May 6, 1757, is in Weiser's handwriting.[16]

It must not be assumed that Croghan's appointment as deputy to Johnson was dictated by any mean motive on the Baronet's part. After all, Conrad Weiser was the commander-in-chief of the provincial troops of Pennsylvania, at war with the Indians. Weiser's fading glory in council was merely being shadowed by his new importance as a military leader. In this capacity he was being shown the deference due his rank.

Late in May, Weiser enlisted 159 men in Reading; he settled a budding mutiny at Fort Northkill; investigated cases of insubordination at Fort Henry and disbursed large sums of provincial money, paying soldiers and buying provisions.

In June, he was busy deploying men from fort to fort and sending new detachments to Colonels James Burd and John Patterson in the west. At the request of the Governor, he compiled a list of all settlers known to have been killed or captured by the Indians. At one time, he complained about the volume of his correspondence "without a clerk."[17] In July, he set out for Easton, to attend the third conference with Teedyuscung and the Indians he brought with him.

At Lancaster, the Six Nations had approved the scheduled meeting with Teedyuscung and his Indians, and Sir William

---

16. Logan MSS, 11:50. For details of Lancaster Conference see Colonial Records, 7:517–539.
17. For letters of Busse, Arndt, Humphries and other subordinates, see Weiser Manuscripts, Historical Society of Pennsylvania. Also Shippen Papers, Volume II and Burd Papers.

Johnson gave it his blessing. More than 300 Indians, representing all the Ten Nations of Teedyuscung, assembled at the Forks of the Delaware during June and July of 1757 and there awaited the arrival of Governor Denny and the Pennsylvania commissioners. At last, there were genuine prospects of effecting a real peace with Pennsylvania Indians.

Teedyuscung was cordial when Weiser greeted him, but soon became disaffected when Colonel Weiser refused to permit an Indian escort for the Governor. The Delaware King blamed Weiser for this interference with his authority, but he could not have known that the colonel was acting under expressed orders from Denny in refusing to permit it.[18]

In writing to Peters about the prospects of a successful treaty, Weiser averred that things would turn out well "if there won't be too many Cooks, and if Busy Body" would stay at home." Who was the "Busy Body" referred to? Plenty of "Cooks" were at the treaty.[19] George Croghan was there as Johnson's agent; there were members of the governor's council and the provincial assembly. More than a score of Quakers came to Easton in the interests of peace, among them three Pembertons. Weiser suspected that Israel Pemberton was secretly coaching Teedyuscung on what demands he should make. On one occasion, Conrad surprised the two engaged in a whispering session in Adam Yohe's house in Easton.

There were three official interpreters: Captain Thomas McKee, Interpreter for the Crown; Pumpshire an Indian Interpreter for Teedyuscung; and Colonel Conrad Weiser, Interpreter for the province of Pennsylvania.

A RENEWED SPIRIT

Weiser threw himself into the negotiations with much of his old spirit. The fallen tree had rooted once more. His advice was sought and followed on all the major points at issue. When the ominous question of deeds to the Minisinks arose, it was Weiser who was asked to confer privately with Teedyuscung and explain matters to him.

---

18. Weiser Memorandum of Conferences at Easton, July 1757. Pennsylvania Archives, 3:216.
19. Weiser to Peters, July 15, 1757, Pennsylvania Archives, 3:17.

Teedyuscung demanded to see all the deeds that Pennsylvania held to any lands purchased in Pennsylvania. Richard Peters refused to release the deeds from his custody, arguing that only the Proprietors could order him to exhibit them. The Quaker Friendly Association urged that the deeds should be shown to Teedyuscung as a vital gesture toward peace. A compromise was reached when Weiser reported that the Delaware King no longer insisted upon seeing all deeds, but would be satisfied to have copies of deeds relating to Minisink lands. Then Charles Thomson, later of Revolutionary War fame, made copies of deeds that Peters had brought with him.

These deeds were handed to Teedyuscung with a promise on the part of Pennsylvania to pay in full to any Delawares, who after consulting these documents, still felt that they had been defrauded. This turn of events decided the issue of the Conference. The Delawares and other Pennsylvania tribes made peace with Pennsylvania and declared that their only enemies now were the French.

It was realized, however, that the action of the 300 Indians present at Easton in 1757 would not be binding upon those Delawares and Shawnees located in western Pennsylvania, in the shadow of the guns of Fort Duquesne and Venango. Messages were to be sent to the western Delawares, telling them what their uncles in the east had done; that the Six Nations had removed the petticoats of the Delawares and that they were now men, provided they fought only against Frenchmen. The final terms of peace were to be signed the following year, at a fourth Easton Conference.

In order that frontier guard would be able to distinguish between approaching friendly Indians and possible enemy sorties, the treaty arranged that Conrad Weiser should confer with the Delawares present at the treaty and agree upon some signal by which they could always be recognized as friends.[20]

There is a charge that Weiser got Teedyuscung drunk during the Easton treat in 1757. If that is true it is not a difficult task, because the Delaware King was drunk every night during the closing days of the treaty. Perhaps it would be safer to say that

---

20. For account of Easton Conference of 1757 see Colonial Records, 7:649 and 707; also an account of treaty in handwriting of Richard Peters, Weiser MSS, 2:82.

Weiser failed in keeping the Indian from getting drunk. Charles Thomson, later the Secretary of the Second Continental Congress, writing to a friend, stated "On Monday night the king was made drunk by C. Weiser, on Tuesday by G. Croghan and last night at Vernon's."[21]

August 6th, Weiser, Croghan, and McKee noticed that there was a great deal of dissension among the Indians at Easton. Weiser was sent to inquire the cause. He learned that the rank and file of Indians were angry at Teedyuscung "for dwelling so long on the Land Affairs" and neglecting other matters. This attitude seemed to indicate that the Indians themselves were more interested in the terms of a peace settlement than they were about old grievances. An Indian squaw showed Weiser a belt of wampum which she had made, calling his attention to ten white beads woven into the black background. She asked him to explain to white men that the ten beads represented the Ten Nations in friendship with the English. The year 1758 was destined to show the fine fruit that grew from the Easton treaty of 1757.

SOUNDING "THE BIG HALLOO!"

In 1758, Conrad Weiser attained the age of sixty-two; an age at which many men relinquish the strenuous activities of life and consider the major tasks assigned to them to be achieved. For Conrad Weiser, however, his sixty-second year proved to be the climax of a life spent in public service. From the distant day when the seventeen-year old Conrad left his father's house in Schoharie to make his home with the Maquas along the Mohawk, he had been active in Indian affairs. In 1758, the German immigrant who became the greatest peacemaker of colonial times, brought his rich experience of more than two score years of Indian diplomacy to its full fruition.

In January of 1758, Weiser resigned his commission as Lieutenant Colonel of the Pennsylvania Regiment. In his final official letter to Timothy Horsfield, written from Philadelphia, the retiring Colonel announced that his duties would be assumed by Colonel

---

21. *Pennsylvania Magazine of History and Biography*, 22:422.

William Burd. "I have lost the use of my right hand," wrote Weiser, complaining of an attack of palsy.[22]

The relinquishment of his position as a soldier in arms against the Indians restored Weiser to the position of Indian agent. Once again, he could negotiate without brandishing the hatchet; a role which never suited his taste or character. At various times during the two years that he commanded the troops it appeared that Teedyuscung and other Indian leaders were suspicious of Weiser's motives in council and in treaty. In 1758, when he was once more a man of peace, their attitude changed, for they now refused to deal with white men unless their friend, Conrad Weiser was present.

In March, the Interpreter was summoned to Philadelphia to attend a conference between Teedyuscung and the Governor. The King of the Delawares had sounded "the Big Halloo," calling all tribes to take hold of the belt of wampum which symbolized the peace terms of the third Easton treaty of 1757. Together the Indians and whites literally "smoaked a Pipe" and agreed upon many points. The eastern Indians were all inclined toward peace. "We have found," declared Governor Denny, "that whatever Nations smoaked out of it (the pipe) two or three hearty Whiffs, the Clouds that were between us always dispersed." Therefore, the Big Halloo should be shouted to all the Indians, those in Wyoming, New Jersey, Maryland, and especially those wayward Delawares and Shawnees who were consorting with the French on the Ohio River.

The tocsin was sounded through the forests by Teedyuscung and his companions. The Minisinks, Munsies, Conestogas, Conoys, Nanticokes, heard it and some of them sent delegations to Philadelphia to consult with the Governor. Conrad Weiser was summoned repeatedly to act as interpreter and counsellor. Far to the north, the Six Nations heard the Big Halloo and they frowned as they reflected that it was sounded by the Delaware King; they wondered and disapproved this usurpation of power, but Conrad Weiser, their own Tarachawagon, was supporting the plans and he would never fail the Long House of Onondaga. The Six Nations learned also that their ancient enemies, the Cherokees, had entered Pennsylvania to join a military expedition against the French at Fort Duquesne. They would consult Conrad Weiser

---

22. Weiser to Horsfield, January 16, 1758, Horsfield MSS, 2:473.

on that point when they came to Easton once the leaves turned brown in the autumn, 1758.

Remnant tribes heard the Big Halloo in their distant wigwams. The Tuteloes, Chugnuts, Unamies to the west and northwest, and the Pomptons in the Jersies responded to the call with messages of goodwill. Teedyuscung's Ten Nations had become the Eighteen Nations, weary of war and enthusiastic in accepting the Quaker proffers of peace. In one of the conferences, Teedyuscung had asked the governor to send teachers of the Christian religion to the Wyoming Indians "partly because we see that some of our brother Indians who were Wicked before they became Christians, Live better Lives now than they formerly did." The arm of the Lord was proving mightier than the sword!

THE FORBES EXPEDITION

But the arm of the flesh was being wielded on another front. Early in 1758, in the French stronghold at Fort Duquesne. This time the military route was plotted across Pennsylvania instead of following the southern route of the ill-fated Braddock expedition. General John Forbes learned that Conrad Weiser had great influence among the Indians and asked Governor Denny to summon the interpreter to Philadelphia. Several messages were sent to Heidelberg before Weiser could be reached.

Wagons had to be impressed in the eastern counties. Weiser contracted to secure wagons in Berks and late in June he informed the authorities in Philadelphia that the "second division of Wagons," including twenty-six wagons, was on its way. The first division had included thirty-strong wagons. Each team "is completely furnished with four able Horses and an Expert Driver," Weiser reported.

Westward through Pennsylvania rolled the expedition during the summer and early autumn of 1758, along the route which later became the Lincoln Highway. The Cherokee Indians joined the expedition enroute, as did several Six Nations warring parties. It is recorded that on the occasion of friction between these hostile tribes, Forbes warned them that he would report their ill behavior to Conrad Weiser, who would come and devour them.

FALL OF FORT DUQUESNE

The Forbes expedition was delayed by a series of unfortunate circumstances and in October 1758, the general found his army in a sorry condition indeed. An advance party under Major James Grant had suffered a humiliating defeat near the French fort at Duquesne. Winter was approaching, but his wagons were mired, axle-deep, in the mud near Fort Ligonier. Just when it appeared that all hope was gone and that the army was destined to languish through a bitter winter without achieving its purpose; just when Forbes wrote despairing letters from his sick bed, a dull thud rumbled through the leafy overhead. The French at Fort Duquesne had blown up their own fortifications and had abandoned the whole Ohio Valley to the English. A continent had been saved for England!

The Big Halloo had been sounded in the Delaware wigwams under the guns of Fort Duquesne. The Delawares and Shawnees had heard it; heard it from the lips of a German armed with a bible and a crucifix. Christian Frederick Post, a Moravian missionary, had undertaken to carry the message of Easton to the wayward Delawares and Shawnees. Once again, the agent of the Lord had triumphed when the arm of the flesh had failed.

On his westward journey from Bethlehem, Post had visited Conrad Weiser. There he tarried, along with his Indian companion, there he discussed plans and methods with the veteran interpreter. Post had every reason to know of Weiser's power and influence. Had not Conrad interceded for him on a former occasion when Post and a companion had been arrested by New York authorities as suspected spies? Weiser had assured the captors that Moravians were not French priests in disguise and in this way, had secured their release.

While the covered wagons of Forbes' army were stuck in the mud along Ray's Creek the Big Halloo was sounding throughout all the Indian country, summoning bronzed warriors in Easton on the Delaware for the fourth Easton treaty of the French and Indian war period. From all directions the Indians converged upon the Minisinks to smoke the peace pipe. The Oneidas, the Onondagas,

Mohawks, Senecas, and Tuscaroras represented the Six Nations Confederacy among the councils of the Eighteen Nations.

DELICATE DIPLOMACY

The treaty began on October 8 and lasted until the 24th. In such a vast assemblage there was need for many interpreters. In addition to Weiser, there was Henry Montour, interpreter for the Delawares, as well as several Indians who could serve to translate Indian languages which Weiser understood.[23]

The main points at issue had to do with land transactions of past decades and the thorny problem of smoothing the ruffled spirits of the Six Nations who viewed the ascendency of Teedyuscung with disfavor. In meeting these problems, Weiser needed all the tact and diplomacy that he had learned through his fifty-five years of Indian negotiations.

During one heated session of the conference, Weiser refused to translate something Nickas, the Mohawk, was saying about the Delaware chieftain. He saw the clouds in inter-Indian strife arising and his keen understanding of Indian psychology saved a dangerous situation. When it was suggested that Montour do the interpreting that Weiser declined to do, Conrad suggested that the matter by submitted to a private conference.

At first the Iroquois refused, demanding that their charges be heard, but by patient urgings Weiser prevailed and the Six Nations agreed to a private session because Weiser requested it. Shrewdly the veteran of many treaties postponed the private conference until he was sure that the anger of both groups had subsided. In this way he prevented the treaty from breaking on the crags of ancient animosities. When the time came for Governor Denny of Pennsylvania and Governor Sir Francis Bernard of New Jersey to explain why they had elevated Teedyuscung to such an important position in their councils, Weiser put words into the mouths of both governors which succeeded in appeasing the Six Nations.

---

23. Account of Easton Treaty of 1758, Colonial Records, 8:175–219.

THE CLOUDS ARE LIFTED

All the land squabbles were finally settled when the Indians agreed to have Weiser and Peters review all previous purchases and promised to abide by their decisions. Through sixteen days of argument, Weiser's hand was needed to steer the proceedings.

The Eighteen Nations represented at Easton were known as the United Nations. They were united in their efforts to secure peace. Even though the French and Indian War did not end until peace was formally declared five years later, in 1763, the Easton treaty of 1758 provided relief from Indian incursions and the capture of Fort Duquesne proved to be the turning point in the struggle for English dominance of North America.

General John Forbes

CHAPTER XVIII

𝔓osterity 𝔚ill 𝔑ot 𝔉orget

The Easton Treaty of 1758 was the crowning achievement of Conrad Weiser's long service as a peacemaker between Indian tribes and the British colonies of the New World. During the two years that remained to him of life, Weiser lived in virtual retirement, devoting himself principally to the management of personal affairs and to his duties as president judge of the courts of Berks County. The negotiation of treaties was entrusted to younger men, chiefly to Henry Montour and Christian Frederick Post; messages to Indian villages were carried by Weiser's sons Philip and Frederick. Some of Weiser's letters written after 1758 are in the handwriting of someone else, although he's always affixed his own signature. The letters reveal that he himself realized that he was nearing the end of life's journey. In April 1759, he wrote to his friend, Richard Peters, expressing the hope for better times, "if not seen by me, the Posterity may."[1] In March 1760, he wrote, as if it were an afterthought, "Life is uncertain."[2]

Throughout his long service, Weiser had always insisted upon being well paid for his work. By strict account, he always collected his bills for entertaining the Indians and his pay for carrying messages and interpreting at treaty conferences. Not once, in all the years from 1731 to 1756 did the Provincial Assembly or Governor's Council question any item in "Honest Conrad's" account. But in 1756, the administration of Indian affairs was

---
1. Weiser MSS, 2:155.
2. Weiser to Peters, March 18, 1760, Peters MSS, 5:86.

placed in the hands of commissioners who were not so prompt in meeting the financial obligations incurred. In November and December of 1758, Weiser was writing letters to Peters, trying to collect his pay for services at Easton. Because these letters reveal several traits of Weiser's character, it will be interesting to study one of them in its original form:

> To Richard Peters
> Dec. 16, 1758
> Dear Sir:
> I hope by this time my accounts against the Gentlemen of the Provincial Commissioners are settled, some how or other, and as I don't expect much good or favour, nay, even doubt their doing me justice, which they have refused me before now, I don't intent to wait the pleasure any longer if I can help it. I want my pay before it becomes an old debt. I have found by experience that new debts are suffered to grow old ones are never paid, which is poor encouragement for faithful Servants to the Government.
>
> I have served the Government of pensilvania as provincial interpreter Since the year 1731 to the satisfaction of the Governors and Assembly, as much as I know I heard nothing to the contrary till 3 years ago when a Certain set of Gentlemen got the Administration of the purse in their hand, then I could no more please, having been a little too free when the Blood of the Back Inhabitants was spilt like watter and they in a manner unconcerned, they did let me suffer prodigiously and showed their spite openly for me . . . but Truth will prevail at Last.[3]

Several days later, Peters informed Weiser that no money was available to settle the account, but assured that "Your account shall not be an old debt, nor forgotten."[4]

---

3. Weiser MSS, 2:151.
4. Ibid., 143.

Weiser's duties as a justice consumed most of his time during the years from 1758 to his death in 1760. His reports to the Governor deal with such matters as announcing official proclamation, remanding prisoners to jail, land transactions in Swatara and the sale of building lots in Reading.[5]

WAR WEARY

In 1759, Colonel Henri Bouquet led an expedition into western Pennsylvania to guard against Indian uprisings and strengthen the hold of the English on the Ohio country. Most of Bouquet's soldiers were recruited from eastern Pennsylvania and Conrad Weiser was instrumental in securing many enlistments for the ranks and in providing horses and wagons for the expedition. Sammy Weiser was given a commission as a lieutenant in the Pennsylvania Regiment.

In March 1759, Richard Peters informed Weiser that he "had much talk with Colo. Bouquet about Sammy, of whom he (Bouquet) speaks very favorably." But the letters which Sammy sent home from the camp in the Allegheny Mountains gave less cheer to Conrad and Anna Eve. These letters, written in German, told a woeful tale of miserable conditions in camp. Sammy regretted that he had ever accepted a commission and asked his father to arrange for his resignation.

Conrad translated one of Sammy's letters into English and sent it to Richard Peters with a note stating that "I regret that I enlisted so many men and made them miserable." Then Weiser called Peters' attention to the book of Isaiah, Chapter 59, verses 9-15, appending his own lament "but what shall I say or do?"[6]

To this plea, the Reverend Richard Peters replied: "All our affairs run adverse . . . The Proprietors are given up to the will of the commissioners." In stating that Sammy's resignation would be arranged, Peters told his old friend, "I hope I have given you a Comforter in your advanced age."[7]

---

5. Richard Hockley to Weiser, January 7, 1760; Weiser to Denny, February 18, 1760, et. al., Weiser MSS, vol. 2.
6. Sammy Weiser's letter translated, Ibid., 151.
7. Peters to Weiser, May 18, 1759, Ibid., 153.

THE PATRIARCH

Almost apologizing for intruding upon his retirement, the provincial officials frequently consulted Weiser on various matters during the last years of his life. Governor Denny sent copies of Indian treaties for Weiser's perusal and review; Richard Hockley asked his advice on matters relating to the Land Office and Richard Peters never hesitated to call upon his old friend for counsel.[8]

Early in the spring of 1759, the provincial authorities were disturbed by a report that the French had assembled a force of 4000 Indians and 1000 Canadians on the Great Lakes, designing a blow to retake the Ohio country. Weiser was asked what he thought about the item of news. He replied that if such a force were sent against "pitsburg" the English could not hold any territory west of the mountains, but, said he, there could be no basis for the report or else he would have been informed of it through letters from Sammy or others who traveled through the western portions of the province.

What did Weiser's employers really think of him? Logan had called him "Honest Conrad"; the Governors had showered praises upon him for his skill and acumen in dealing with the Indians and Richard Peters, Weiser's most constant correspondent, was always friendly and solicitous for Conrad's welfare. And yet these expressions may have been merely perfunctory in nature, designed to cultivate a very useful man. While it is always impossible to know what is in men's minds, there are several instances in the career of Weiser which would lead the student of his life to suspect that his superiors merely indulged his whims with flattery and insincere words of tribute. Weiser's own letters are devoid of guile or subtlety. Did his associates think of him as a simple farmer who needed a pat on the back occasionally?

The sincerest tribute that one human being can pay to another is asking for advice and then acting upon it. No greater tribute could have been paid to Weiser than Richard Peters paid

---
8. In the latter volumes of Peters' Correspondence, it is noted that the secretary of the province employed an amanuensis to write official letters, and certainly thereby conferred a boon upon historians, but the letters which Peters wrote to Weiser were always in his own handwriting, a monstrosity of calligraphy almost undecipherable.

early in 1759, when he sent Conrad a copy of a pamphlet written by Benjamin Franklin, asking Weiser's thoughts on the contents. It was, Peters said, his only copy and he wished it returned. In his letter to Weiser, Peters complained that he "cannot put certain matters into my letters any longer."

Unfortunately for us today, neither the title of the pamphlet nor Weiser's reply to Peters has been identified or located. Every Indication, however, points in the direction of Franklin's tirade against the proprietors, entitled *Heads of Complaints,* in which Franklin charged the Penns with gross neglect of the King's interest and urged that the Crown convert Pennsylvania into a royal colony by removing all proprietary rights.[9]

We know that Weiser did reply to Peters, giving his views on the matters contained in the pamphlet, because Peters acknowledged receiving such a letter. In July 1759, Peters asked Weiser for suggestions "to answer the pamphlet." In making his request the provincial secretary used the words, "we should answer it." There is no evidence to show who was the other part of the "we."[10] The Penns in England did reply to the *Heads of Complaints.*[11]

THE SHADOWS LENGTHEN

After 1758, the elder Weisers made their home in the growing city of Reading, where Conrad had opened a store near the northeast corner of Fifth and Penn Streets. There he sold supplies to traders who were on the way to Indian villages, to natives of Reading and Berks, and to military contingents stationed or passing through Reading.

His two older sons were married and established plantations of their own. Samuel, the son trained to succeed him, returned from the wars to be Conrad's "Comforter," as Peters said. Benjamin, his youngest son, was at home.[12]

---

9. See Graeff, Arthur D., op cit., chap. 7.
10. Peters to Weiser, July 15, 1759, Weiser MSS, 165.
11. In a letter from Thomas Penn to Richard Peters, December 1758, the writer states that he is enclosing a letter for Conrad Weiser. This letter has not been found. In a letter written from London by Rev. William Smith, July 1759, Smith takes a jibe at Franklin, who is in England to present charges against the Proprietors, stating that "Franklin is mortified at not being called to meetings."
12. Weiser's account of Samuel's expenses to and from Fort Augusta on Indian affairs, Pennsylvania Archives, 3:713. See also Weiser to J. Hamilton, February 18, 1760, Indian Affairs, Gratz Collection, Case 4, Box 9, Colonial Wars, Historical Society of Pennsylvania.

The parents were concerned about Benjamin's education. He had been enrolled as a student at the Philadelphia Academy in 1758 but failed to make a success of his course of study. In 1759, Weiser wrote to Peters, asking advice on what arrangements could be made for Benjamin. Conrad had heard of the new school opened by David Dove in Germantown and sought his old friend's advice. The result was another attempt to master the courses in the Academy.

Another interest in education was manifested by Weiser in 1759 when he wrote to Peters concerning the departure of Dr. William Smith for London. Conrad wondered whether the Society for the Propagation of Christian Knowledge was giving up its efforts to educate the Germans in Pennsylvania. One of his last letters was written in the interest of building a free school at Reading.

As time went on, Weiser became a man of property. In addition to outright money payments, he received vast tracts of land from time to time. He owned many acres in what are now Schuylkill, Northumberland, and Snyder counties. The lands which lay west of the Susquehanna, though deeded to him, were never surveyed during his lifetime. His will provided that these lands should be divided by his children.[13]

Through all his adult life, Weiser suffered from a chronic stomach disorder known as colic. One hot day in July 1760, he left his home in Reading to visit his farm in Heidelberg. There on July 13, 1760, he was seized with a fit of indigestion and never rallied. He died amidst the scenes familiar to him. He lies buried in the orchard near his home, in the center of present-day Weiser Park. His faithful Anna Eve survived him for more than 18 years, joining him in death in 1779, in her 79th year. There is some dispute as to the place of Mrs. Weiser's original burial, but today her headstone stands alongside that of her devoted husband under the shade of a huge apple tree in Conrad Weiser Park. It is thought that her remains were removed from a neighborhood cemetery sometime after internment and then deposited where the headstone now stands.[14]

---

13. For an inventory of Weiser estate see Society Collection, Historical Society of Pennsylvania, Photo D. or Nolan, J. Bennett, *Pennsylvania Magazine of History and Biography*, 56:65–270. For unsurveyed lands see Burd Shippen MSS, 2:9, American Philosophical Society.
14. For speculation concerning the burial of Mrs. Weiser see Richards, Henry Melchior Muhlenberg, *The Weiser Family*, Pennsylvania German Society Proceedings, 32:29–32. In

We search in vain for some obituary tribute to Weiser from his contemporaries. True, most of those he had known best of all had preceded him on the final journey, but Frankly, Denny, Read, Burd, Horsfield, Parsons, Spangenburg, Post, Croghan, Montour, and Richard Peters were still alive. Only from the pen of Peters do we have any note of Weiser's passing, when he wrote to Thomas Penn "Poor Mr. Weiser is no more; he died suddenly last summer and has not left anyone to fill his place as Provincial Interpreter. His son Samuel has almost forgotten what little he knew." To which Penn replied: "Conrad Weiser's loss must have been great . . . there is one fit to be trusted . . . the Confidence both the Indians as well as the Government had in him was a vast addition to his importance."[15]

The only real tribute that came from a contemporary was expressed by Seneca George, an Indian, who, speaking at a Conference in 1761, declared, "We . . . are at a great Loss and sit in Darkness, as well as you, by the Death of Conrad Weiser, as since his death we cannot so well understand one another. By this Belt, we cover his body."

Thirty-three years later, in 1793, George Washington, as first President of the United States, stood at Conrad Weiser's grave and expressed the sentiment, true today as it was then: "Posterity will not forget his services."[16]

Weiser's autobiography, Library of Congress, there is a note written on one of the back pages which states that Mrs. Weiser died in 1781. There is no way of determining which date is correct, 1781, or the one on the tombstone. We accept the explanation offered by Richards.
15. Penn to Peters, October 9, 1761, Penn Letter Book, 7:67–69.
16. For an account of Washington's visit to Berks County in 1794 see Nolan, J. Bennett, *George Washington and the Town of Reading in Pennsylvania.*

The grave of Conrad Weiser in Womelsdorf.

EPILOGUE

The Legacy of Conrad Weiser
by Lawrence Knorr

"That which we do now echoes through eternity."
—Marcus Aurelius, Roman Emperor

It is hard to imagine the world of Conrad Weiser who lived mostly in colonial Pennsylvania decades before the American Revolution. In that time, Pennsylvania, granted to William Penn, was run by the Quakers, a nonviolent pacifist protestant sect. Philadelphia was the primary settlement and the majority of settlers were within the present-day counties of Philadelphia, Bucks, Chester, and Montgomery. In the early 1700s, what are now Berks, Lebanon, Lancaster, Dauphin, and Lehigh counties were the edge of civilization. The aboriginal people, the Native Americans, were numerous and only a short ride away by automobile by today's standards. In those times, only a few days' ride on horseback on ancient trails would take a person to their villages.

In this world, Conrad Weiser, of Germanic heritage, utilized his rare talents to become one of the most influential people in Pennsylvania's, if not our nation's history. Weiser, who was multi-lingual, having lived with natives for a time in New York in his youth, became much more than just an interpreter as he exercised his duties to the Penns. His knowledge and awareness of the customs of the native peoples were just as important as his knowledge of their languages. He was also a strong judge of character and keenly aware of the nuances of human nature. It was Weiser who for many years represented Pennsylvania and sometimes New York, Virginia, and Maryland in negotiations with the native peoples. As more Europeans arrived in Philadelphia, New York, and Baltimore, those pushing west and north into the wilderness became more frequent and numerous. It was Weiser, projecting the Quaker directive of pacifism and peaceful cohabitation that avoided conflict through those years.

This period of relative peace could not have been as easily maintained were it not for the friendship of Weiser and Shikellamy, the chief who lived near Shamokin along the Susquehanna (near present-day Sunbury). The trust established between these two men probably did more to eliminate potential conflict than any other relationship in those times. It was only after Shikellamy's passing in 1748 that things became more difficult. While Weiser continued on for another ten years in his role, the French and Indian War soon followed and Weiser's focus became primarily that of a military defender, establishing frontier forts along the Blue Mountains and leading the militia units in their patrols.

At the time of Weiser's passing in 1760, the natives of eastern Pennsylvania had been largely united in the war against the French and the war was virtually over in the commonwealth. But in the intervening years came Pontiac's War and the Paxton Boys incident, an event that would have been unlikely with a younger Weiser about. Over the subsequent years, the native peoples continued to be pushed west and north and the commonwealth of Pennsylvania was largely empty of them after the American Revolution. Looking back, it is apparent that Weiser helped oversee the peaceful transition of large portions of Pennsylvania from the aboriginal peoples to the English.

So what if Conrad Weiser had not existed? Someone else would have likely come to the forefront. Perhaps George Croghan would have been the primary interpreter and negotiator. By all accounts, he was not as selfless and skilled as Weiser in this role and it is likely the peace might not have been kept as long. What if, in the time of the Walking Purchase, the natives had risen up and attacked Philadelphia? There certainly would have been a great number of casualties and the settlers coming to the New World would have been less likely to pick the Quaker colony and its vulnerable pacifist government. If Philadelphia is not as attractive a location, it does not become the largest city in England's American colonies and is less likely to be the focal point for the many activities of the American Revolution. Additionally, it is more likely the boundaries of Pennsylvania would be different, with incursions from Maryland in the south, Virginia in the west, Connecticut in the northeast, and the Canadian French from the north. Would Ben Franklin, who traveled with Weiser in the 1750s for some of the treaties, have risen to such importance if there was no peace with the natives and Philadelphia was a backwater town on a violent frontier? Without Franklin's pragmatism, would we have been able to unite thirteen disparate colonies into a new nation? Weiser did his duty on behalf of the colonial proprietors and died five years before the Stamp Act and fifteen before the battles at Lexington and Concord. Thus, we can never know what role an elder Weiser would have played in those times. We do know, however, the roles his progeny played in the next great act in American history.

Henry Melchior Muhlenberg is credited with being the founder of Lutheranism in America. Muhlenberg married Weiser's daughter Anna Maria, and the two had eleven children which were the beginning of a long line of generations involved in the ministry, military, politics, and academia. Son Peter, a minister, became a Major General in the American Revolution and later became a US Congressman. Son Frederick was a Congressman who became the first Speaker of the House. Henry, Jr. became a minister and Henry Ernst, a scientist, became the first president of Franklin (later Franklin & Marshall) College. Daughter Elisabeth married Francis Swaine who later became a general. Maria Salome "Sally" married Matthias Richards, who became a Congressman. Eve married Emmanuel Schulze. Their son, John Andrew Schulze, was elected Governor of Pennsylvania. Weiser's great-grandson, Peter Weiser, was a member of the Lewis and Clark Expedition. Other Weiser descendants served in the Congress, as diplomats, and as prominent architects. In fact, similar to the Lees of Virginia, select few American families have so many accomplished individuals.

Despite his contributions and his successful descendants, Conrad Weiser is a largely forgotten figure in American history, often overlooked and likely misunderstood. His Pennsylvania-German heritage was outside the mainstream of the politics and customs of the time as was his lack of connection to the Quaker faith of his employers. His best advocates were those associated with the colonial governments which were soon overthrown by a younger generation.

Conrad Weiser's homestead near Womelsdorf, Pennsylvania, is a National Historic Landmark administered by the Pennsylvania Historical and Museum Commission. There you can find his original stone house and his grave as well as those of many of his native friends. A monument to Weiser was erected there as well as a statue of his friend Shikellamy.

Nearby, the Conrad Weiser School District is based in Robesonia. Route 422 west of Reading on the way to Lebanon is named the Conrad Weiser Parkway. This road passes the high school and the homestead.

Camp Conrad Weiser is a 500-acre YMCA camp in Berks County. The Conrad Weiser State Forest is a tract of woodlands in upstate Pennsylvania.

If you wish to try to connect with Conrad Weiser, I suggest a visit to his homestead. After spending a few hours understanding the essence of the man, drive the old Shamokin/Tulpehocken path north from Weiser's to Fort Henry, Pilger Ruh, then to Pine Grove, then to Good Spring, then to Klingerstown, passing through Sacramento. Next follow the back roads to Sunbury, the site of the former Indian village of Shamokin. There you can find the rock that contains a plaque memorializing Shikellamy on a busy street corner. Some say you can look across the Susquehanna near that point and see the profile of the Indian chief in the cliff face. While you will be disappointed with the sprawl of Sunbury, Pennsylvania overtaking the once tranquil riverside native community, you will thoroughly enjoy the peaceful ride through the mountains. While in Sunbury, also check out the Northumberland County Historical Society for the native artifacts.

The interior of the Weiser's house at the Conrad Weiser Homestead.

The monument erected in honor of Conrad Weiser at his homestead.

Statue of Shikellamy at the Conrad Weiser Homestead.

AFTERWORD

My Friend Arthur Graeff
by George M. Meiser, IX

Dr. Graeff was born September 23, 1899, in Adamstown, Lancaster County. His dad was a farmer; his mother taught school and was a homemaker. When he was in his early teens, the family moved to a farm near Charming Forge. It was during this period that he was greatly influenced by two outstanding men, Michael A. Gruber and Reverend P. C. Croll. From Womelsdorf High School he matriculated at Franklin and Marshall College, where his interest in Pennsylvania German culture was heightened. Following graduation, he taught locally before beginning, in 1924, a distinguished thirty-five-year career at Overbrook Senior High School in Philadelphia.

In 1926, he married Marie Knorr of Wernersville. This was a union in every sense of the word, as Marie had the inclination and capacity to share Arthur's interests, activities, and responsibilities.

During his time at Overbrook, he authored and co-authored a number of texts that were "standards" for years, and in addition to producing three *Schollas* a week for the *Reading Times*, he spoke extensively and was incredibly active in numerous historical organizations, some of which he founded.

Following his retirement from Overbrook, Berks County, Pennsylvania, became the Graeffs' full-time home once again. But he was not ready to give up as an educator. For a half-dozen or more years he taught at Kutztown and Alvernia Colleges, and at St. Isaac Jogues, near Wernersville . . . until shortly before his demise.

I feel privileged to have known and worked with Dr. Graeff as he was indeed an incredible person. He was at home in the loftiest of academic circumstances or working in his truck patch. He could devote endless hours to concentrated research or be content to enjoy the quietude of some remote fishing hole. When the occasion demanded, he could compose a scholarly dissertation equal to the best—or produce newspaper columns that had great popular appeal. On any level, his writing was both effective and affective. He had a definite way with words.

Dr. Graeff had a great capacity for work, and when he was somewhere in charge, things were accomplished. His leadership qualities and infectious enthusiasm generated both a respect for his ideas and a willingness on the part of others to assist. He could sense potential, and did his best to develop it. This is how I became "involved" in both history and photography (a natural combination). Had our paths never crossed, it is more than likely that my many books would never have come in to existence.

Early *Scholla* columns carried no regular byline; they were signed '*N Ewich Yaeger*, which translates to "the eternal hunter." Those who knew Dr. Graeff could never argue against the validity of that reference. Not only was he an eternal hunter, he was invariably a successful one, thanks to an uncanny sense for ferreting out anything of potential interest. Moreover, he possessed the wherewithal to take his "find" and turn it into an engaging piece of reading.

It has been written that the chronology of *Scholla* may be taken as a running commentary of his life as these columns indicate the depth and breadth of his basic interests. They tell of the personalities that intrigued him and provide us with an insight into the way he associated with other people.

Arthur Dundore Graeff passed away on March 28, 1969, . . . on the same day the last *Scholla* installment appeared in the *Reading Times*. His death created a considerable void. Not only had Southeastern Pennsylvania lost a lecturer, writer, teacher, and leader of singular magnitude—but it lost *Scholla*, the termination of which was deeply felt by his large readership-family, many of whom had never met the "Ewich Yeager" personally but who knew him well, vicariously, through a thrice-weekly communion of interest.

George M. Meiser, IX
December 31, 1976

Dr. Arthur Graeff

INDEX

1732, Treaty of, 24, 29
1740, Treaty of, 65
1744, Treaty of, 141, 151, 165, 190

Acrelius, Israel, 78
Adams, Doctor, 150
Adams, John, 231
Adamstown (Pennsylvania), 392
Aix la-Chapelle, Treaty of, 204, 214, 235, 257
Albany (New York), 6–7, 55, 62–64, 110, 167, 175, 177–182, 184, 186, 188, 190–193, 234, 236–237, 239–240, 243, 248–252, 254–255, 262, 266, 274, 276–286, 288–289, 295–297, 309, 367
Albany (in Berks County, Pennsylvania), 83, 350
Albany Plan of Union, 279
Albany Purchase, 280–281, 289–290, 292, 295–298, 321
Alexandria (Virginia), 322–323
Allegheny County (Pennsylvania), 209
Allegheny Hill, 208
Allegheny Mountains, 19, 131, 155, 159, 199, 221, 228, 230, 232, 248, 255, 258, 260, 265, 267, 282, 380
Allegheny River, 209
Allegheny Road, 203
Allemängel (Pennsylvania), 83, 350
Allen, William, 308–309, 312–313, 350
Allumpees (chief, *see also see Sassoonan*), 29, 31, 61, 68, 121, 123, 133–134, 136, 197, 201, 247
Alsace & Lorraine, 271
Alvernia College, 393
Amboy (New Jersey), 249
American Philosophical Society, 124, 353
Andastes (prehistoric tribe), 46
Annapolis (Maryland), 113, 115, 117, 141, 199, 232
Anne (Queen of England), 2–4, 6–7, 11, 14, 181
Antes, Henry, 81, 311
Antigua, 64
Anton's Wald (Pennsylvania), 86
Appalachian Mountains, 206–207, 255, 272
Aquoyiota (chief), 128
Armstrong, Alexander, 133–134
Armstrong, John (trader), 130–136, 141, 160
Armstrong, John (colonel), 362
Armstrong County, 209
Arndt, Jacob, 75, 351, 353
Arnold, Woodward, 131, 133–134

Assaryquoa (Governor of Virginia), 126–127, 129, 157, 229, 236, 242
Astaet (Germany), 1
Aughwick (Pennsylvania), 199–200, 258, 285–294, 300, 310–311, 335

Backnang (Germany), 99
Baer, John, 310
Bagenkopf (cleric), 77
Bally (Pennsylvania), 324
Baltimore (Maryland), 387
Baltimore, Lord, 30, 158, 229
Bartram, John, 124–126, 137, 172, 224
Beaver (chief), 288
Beaver Creek (Indian village in Pennsylvania), 209, 212
Bedford County (Pennsylvania), 208, 212
Bechtel, John, 81
Beissel, Conrad, 80, 148
Benigna, Countess, 87
Berks County (Pennsylvania), 16, 44, 76, 99, 101, 161, 219, 275, 287, 301, 307–309, 312, 323–325, 328, 338, 350, 352, 374, 378, 382, 386, 389, 392
Berks History Center, 318
Bernard, Francis, 376
Berry, James, 130, 133, 145
Bethel (Pennsylvania), 101, 109, 219, 275, 317, 351
Bethel Township (Pennsylvania), 333
Bethlehem (Pennsylvania), 83–84, 87, 214, 234, 242, 274, 348, 361–362, 366–367, 375
Bethlehem Inn (Pennsylvania), 357, 361
Beverly, William, 141, 144
Bickel, Tobias, 101
Biddle, Edward, 331
Bienville, Celeron de, 228, 255
Big Island (Pennsylvania), 296, 326
Big Spring (Pennsylvania), 208
Bingaman, John, 301
Binghamton (New York), 233
Bird, William, 325
Black, William, 141, 146
Black Log Valley (Pennsylvania), 208
Blackheath Common (London), 3–4, 6–7, 13
Bladen, Thomas, 122, 140, 142, 146
Blair County (Pennsylvania), 208
Blue Mountain(s) (Pennsylvania), 16, 36, 44, 86, 120, 125, 172, 218–219, 275, 283, 295, 308, 326–328, 333, 338, 343, 350–351, 354, 362, 387
Blue Mountain Massacres, 331–334, 343, 350

Blunston, Samuel, 103, 108
Boehler, Peter, 274
Boehme, Jacob, 75
Boone, Daniel, 317
Boone, George, 317
Bordentown (New Jersey), 249, 261
Boss, Konrad, 3
Boston (Massachusetts), 21, 177, 199
Bouquet, Henri, 380
Boyertown (Pennsylvania), 81
Braddock, Edward, 322–325, 354–356
Braddock Expedition, 320, 354, 374
Bradford, William, 119
Brainerd, David, 173, 187
Brant, Joseph (Indian), 237
Brant, Nickus (Indian), 235–237, 252. 376
Bricker (wagoner), 335
Bristol (Pennsylvania), 180
British Board of Trade, 4–5
Broad Mountain (Pennsylvania), 45
Broken Thigh (Indian), 335–336, 343
Brother Enoch (Conrad Weiser at Ephrata), 67, 78, 148
Brown's blockhouse (Pennsylvania), 351
Brunnholz, Peter, 91–92, 305, 313, 338
Brunswick (New Jersey), 278
Bucks County (Pennsylvania), 61, 64, 73, 330, 386
Buettner, Gottlob, 89
Bull, John Joseph, 171
Bull, William, 250–251, 253–255
Burd, James, 352, 362, 369, 373, 384
Burnt Cabins (Pennsylvania), 222–223
Bushkill (Pennsylvania), 310
Busse, Christian, 335, 352, 357, 361
Butler County (Pennsylvania), 209
Butler, Mrs., 68

Cachisdasche (village in New York), 126
Caheshcarowana (Indian), 127
Cahichodo (Indian interpreter), 21
Callowhill, Hannah, 302
Camberwell (England), 3
Cambria County (Pennsylvania), 208
Camp Conrad Weiser (Pennsylvania), 389
Canada, 5, 17, 19, 21–22, 27, 71, 147, 157, 161, 167, 170, 175–176, 179, 183, 185, 190, 193, 202, 229, 234–236, 239, 252, 257, 261–262, 388
Canajoharie (village in New York), 239
Canassatego (chief), 69, 85, 112, 127, 147, 149, 153–154, 157, 160–162, 174–176, 185, 217–218, 240, 242, 247–248
Canataquamy (village in Pennsylvania), 123
Canusorago (Pennsylvania, see also Muncy Creek), 46
Cape Breton (Canada), 192
Carbon County (Pennsylvania), 350

Carlisle (Pennsylvania), 208, 265–267, 270, 272, 293, 329, 335–338, 342
Carlisle, Treaty of, 268, 288
Cartlidge, Edmund, 18
Cast, Jean, 5–6
Catawba (tribe or village), 41, 62–64, 118, 129, 132, 156–157, 165–169, 171, 174–176, 179, 189–191, 232, 236–239, 246, 250–254, 261, 286, 296
Catholicism, 239, 243
Catskill (region in New York), 5, 236
Caxhayan (chief, see also Kackshajim), 56, 66, 68, 82, 116, 127, 240, 247
Cayuga (tribe), 17, 42, 51–52, 55, 68, 82, 129, 157, 175, 182, 195, 202, 212, 219, 224, 235, 237, 241, 252, 282, 298
Cecil County (Maryland), 142
Chambers, Joseph, 133, 145–146, 195, 219
Chandler, Samuel, 309
Chapman, John, 311
Charity Schools (Pennsylvania), 301, 308–313
Charles II (King of England, see also Charles Stuart), 280
Charles XII (King of Sweden), 80
Charles, Robert, 26
Charleston (South Carolina), 177, 199
Charming Forge (Pennsylvania), 333, 392
Chartiers, Peter, 170, 176, 185, 188
Chartier's Old Town (Pennsylvania), 209–210
Chartier's Town (Pennsylvania), 209–210
Chase, Mr., 114
Cheaver, Peter, 26
Cherokee (tribe), 41–42, 62–63, 156, 165, 169, 246, 367, 373–374
Cherry Valley (New York), 237
Chesapeake Bay, 153
Chester County (Pennsylvania), 386
Chickasaw (tribe), 342
Chillisquaque Creek (Pennsylvania), 45
Chinkanning (village in Pennsylvania), 343
Chugnut (tribe), 374
Civility (chief), 36
Clapham, William, 352, 362
Clarke, George, 63, 158
Claus, Daniel, 247, 259, 343
Clearfield Creek (Pennsylvania), 208
Clinton, George, 179, 181–184, 188–189, 191, 193, 202–203, 233–235, 238, 240, 247–253, 255, 257, 262, 264, 276–277
Coat, George, 239
Cocalico Creek (Pennsylvania), 67, 80, 149
Collegeville (Pennsylvania), 219
Conestoga (tribe or village), 23, 25, 36, 59, 153, 280, 342, 369, 373
Conestoga Creek (Pennsylvania), 145
Connecticut, 178, 181–182, 184, 273–277, 281, 283–284, 289, 297–299, 320, 388

Index 397

Conodoguinet Creek (Pennsylvania), 205
Conoy (tribe or village), 18, 59, 373
Conoy Creek (Pennsylvania), 23–24, 170
Conrad Weiser Homestead, 38, 383, 389–391
Conrad Weiser Parkway, 389
Conrad Weiser School District, 389
Conrad Weiser State Forest, 389
Conrad Weiser's Creek, 87
Continental Congress, 151
Cookson, Thomas, 103–104, 134, 157, 162
Cool (interpreter), 250
Coplin, John, 310
Corlear, Governor, 157, 229, 240, 253
Court of St. James (England), 177
Cosby, Colonel William, 42, 56
Creek (tribe), 161
Cresap, Thomas, 122–123, 138, 140, 225, 258–259
Cresap's War, 122
Croghan, George, 196–197, 200, 203–205, 207–209, 211, 212, 223–224, 247–249, 255–260, 266, 285–288, 290–295, 300, 310, 328, 335–337, 343, 367–370, 372, 384, 387
Croll, P.C., 392
Crown Point (New York), 192
Cuba, 118
Cumberland (Maryland), 322
Cumberland County (Pennsylvania), 205, 207–208, 223, 291, 338, 350
Cumberland Valley (Pennsylvania), 221–223, 225, 236, 258, 326
Cut-Fingered-Peter (Indian), 341, 343

Dauphin County (Pennsylvania), 87, 386
David (Indian), 337, 340
Davis, John, 312
Davison, John, 341–342
DeLancey, James, 276–277, 279, 281
Delaware (tribe or nation, see also Lenni Lenape), 16–18, 23–24, 28–32, 35–36, 45, 59–62, 65–66, 68, 71–72, 83, 121, 123, 130–133, 135–136, 197, 201, 212, 217, 223, 228, 245, 247–248, 255, 267, 275–276, 285, 288–290, 292, 297, 327, 329, 336–337, 341–342, 344–350, 356–360, 362–363, 365–367, 369–371, 373, 375–376
Delaware River, 23, 35, 43, 59, 110, 180, 218, 229, 234–235, 342, 349, 370
Denny, William, 362–366, 368–370, 373–374, 376, 381, 384
Deppen, Peter, 334
DeTurck (family), 81, 97
Diadachton (Pennsylvania, see also Lost & Bewildered Creek), 48
Dieffenbach (captain), 331
Diemer, Doctor (and Captain), 189, 193

Dietrich Sixes blockhouse (Pennsylvania), 351
Dinwiddie, Robert, 260–261, 265–266, 270–271
Disononto (chief), 240
Documentary History of New York, Volume III, 11
Donegal (Pennsylvania), 24, 207
Dongan, Thomas, 153, 156
Dove, David, 383
Dreiner, John, 310
Dresden (Germany), 81
Dunbar, Thomas, 320, 324
Dunkards (religious sect), 144, 148
Dunning, Robert, 208
Durham Iron Works (Pennsylvania), 330
Durst, Caspar, 101
Dutchess County (New York), 172

Easton (Pennsylvania), 309, 311, 353–354, 357–364, 366–367, 369–375, 377, 379
Easton Treaty of 1758, 378
Economy (Pennsylvania), 209
Endless Mountains (Pennsylvania), 36
Endt, Theobald, 81
England, 1, 11–13, 41, 64, 68, 102, 107, 110, 116, 138, 140, 143, 151, 153, 156, 162, 177–178, 186, 194, 212, 220, 228–229, 235, 238, 243, 252, 255, 271, 277, 302–303, 362, 375, 382, 388
Engle (Lieutenant), 361
Ephrata Cloisters (Pennsylvania), 59, 67, 77–81, 88–89, 91, 94–96, 109, 144, 148–149, 162
Erdmuth, Countess of, 86
Erdmuth's Spring (Pennsylvania), 86
Erie (region or Indians), 203, 207
Evans, Jabez, 262
Evans, Lewis, 124–126, 172, 224, 284, 296
Ewing, Thomas, 103

Falckner's Swamp (Pennsylvania), 81
Feg, Peter, 12
Finney, Samuel, 301–302
Finney, Widow, 219, 302, 306
Fire Poker (Indian), 343
First Pennsylvania Regiment of Volunteers, 350, 372, 380
Five Nations (Iroquois Confederacy), 17, 20, 30, 212, 234
Flathead (tribe), 30, 42, 49, 63, 118, 157, 165–166, 175, 179, 190, 250, 252–253
Flushing (New York), 250, 262, 264
Flying Hills (Pennsylvania), 301
Forbes, John, 374–375, 377
Forrest County (Pennsylvania), 210
Fort Allen (Pennsylvania), 350–351, 362, 366
Fort Augusta (Pennsylvania), 348, 352, 362

Fort Duquesne (Pennsylvania), 279, 286, 322–324, 329, 371, 373–375, 377
Fort Frederick (Maryland), 367
Fort Granville (Pennsylvania), 362
Fort Henry (Pennsylvania), 351, 357, 361, 369, 389
Fort Hunter (Pennsylvania), 237–238, 351–351
Fort Lebanon (Pennsylvania), 351
Fort Ligonier (Pennsylvania), 375
Fort Manada (Pennsylvania), 351
Fort Necessity (Pennsylvania), 273, 279, 287
Fort Norris (Pennsylvania), 351, 361–362
Fort Northkill (Pennsylvania), 351, 369
Fort Oswego (New York), 342
Fort Shirley (Pennsylvania), 300
Fort Swatara (Pennsylvania), 351
Fort Zeller (Pennsylvania), 351
Fox, Joseph, 336
France, 3, 64, 66, 71, 87, 102, 110, 160, 165, 175, 177–178, 186, 213, 222, 228, 235, 239, 255
Franke, Augustus, 75–76, 88
Frankfort-on-the-Main (Germany), 87
Franklin (Pennsylvania), 271
Franklin, Benjamin, 124, 129, 231, 266, 268, 270, 278–279, 281, 285, 308–309, 311–313, 322, 334, 342, 350–352, 382, 388
Franklin, William, 208
Franklin & Marshall College (Pennsylvania), 388, 392
Frankstown (Pennsylvania), 208, 210, 212
Frederick (Maryland), 191
Fredericksburg (Virginia), 231–232, 242
Freeman (Indian), 65
French and Indian War (*see also* Seven Years' War) 19, 86, 377, 387
Fricker, Anthony, 325
Friendship, Treaty of, 23, 43
Frontenac, Fort (Canada), 177
Fry, Henry, 215

Gabriels, George, 336
Galbreath, James, 207, 219
Gale, Levin, 122, 140–141
Gallick (captain), 254
Galloway (brothers), 223
Galloway, John, 141
Ganawese (tribe), 23–26, 28
Ganonsseracheri (aka David Zeisberger), 174
Gachradoda (chief), 157, 162, 282
Gechdachery (Indian), 240–241
George I (King of England), 11
George II (King of England), 162, 177, 243
Georgia, 59, 89, 161
Gera, Mr., 310
Germantown (Pennsylvania), 29, 40, 68, 81, 83, 180, 218, 313, 320, 328, 383

Germany, 1, 76, 107
Girty, Simon, Sr., 145
Gist, Christopher, 228, 271
Glen, James, 204, 250, 253, 255
Gnadenhutten (village in Pennsylvania), 171, 350
Goldman, Conrad, 101
Gooch, Sir William, 23, 25, 28, 39, 42–43, 62–63, 118, 121, 124, 138–140, 142, 144, 158–159, 167–168, 189–192, 236
Good Spring (Pennsylvania), 389
Gordon, Lewis, 311
Gordon, Patrick, 19–20, 25, 26, 29–30, 39, 64
Goschgoshing (village in Pennsylvania), 209–211
Goshenhoppen (Pennsylvania), 324
Graeff, Arthur Dundore, 392–394
Graeff, Sebastian, 310
Graeme, Thomas, 142–143, 145, 196, 205
Grant, James, 375
Great Island (Pennsylvania), 30
Great Lakes, 59, 177, 188, 197, 207, 255, 381
Great Meadows (New York), 184
Greenwich (England), 3
Greenwich Observatory (England), 4, 13
Greter, Michael, 307
Groningen (Holland), 3
Gross Aspach (Germany), 2, 99
Gruber, Michael A., 392

Hager, John Frederick, 75
Hagingonis (aka Brother John Joseph), 174
Haig (captive), 204
Haines, Adam, 110–111
Halle University (Germany), 76, 81, 88, 90, 314
Hamilton, Andrew, Jr., 149
Hamilton, James, 150, 215–216, 222, 226, 235–236, 243, 247–250, 252, 257, 259–262, 264–266, 272–276, 278–279, 285–286, 288, 290, 293, 306–312, 334–336
Hampden Reservoir (Pennsylvania), 302
Handschuh, John Frederick, 313
Hanover (Pennsylvania), 309
Hardy, Charles, 347
Harmony Society of the Rappites (religious order), 209
Harris, John, 26, 133, 146, 275, 293, 324, 336
Harris' blockhouse (Pennsylvania), 351
Harris Ferry (Pennsylvania), 129, 138–139, 143, 145, 163, 287, 293, 295, 323–324, 326, 335–338, 341, 343, 348, 367–368
Harrisburg (Pennsylvania), 123, 133, 207, 275, 287, 293
Hartley, William, 219, 302, 306
Harvey, Henry, 325
Haycock Mountain (Pennsylvania), 64

Index

Heads of Complaints (pamphlet), 382
Heckewelder, John, 230
Heidelberg (Pennsylvania), 86, 101, 168, 180, 287, 296, 308, 312, 317, 320, 326–327, 330–331, 333, 335–336, 339, 342, 348, 352, 357, 361, 367–368, 383
Heintzelman, J.D.M., 325, 338–339
Hellefoetsluice (Holland), 3
Heller, Jacob, 307
Hendricks (chief), 235–237, 263, 282–284, 297–299, 320
Herrenberg (Germany), 1
Hetequantagechty (chief), 22, 24, 27, 29–30
High, Samuel, 310
Hockley, Richard, 301, 303, 381
Holland, 2–3
Holland, Edward, 250
Hollenbach, John, 101
Hollidaysburg (Pennsylvania), 208
Horsfield, Timothy, 353, 362, 372, 384
Host (Pennsylvania), 180
Hoster, Wilhelm, 101
Howe, William, 151
Hudson River, 4–5, 10, 178, 180–182, 233–234, 236, 278
Huebner, George, 81
Huguenots (religious sect), 3
Huling, Marcus, 219
Hunter, Robert, 5–7, 14, 181
Hunter's Mills (Pennsylvania), 326, 350
Huntingdon (Pennsylvania), 208
Huntingdon County (Pennsylvania), 285

Indian Henry (Indian), 183
Ingoldsby, Colonel Sir Richard, 6
Iroquois (tribe), 9, 17, 25, 28–29, 42–43, 63, 65, 118–120, 128–129, 153, 167, 172, 175, 181, 191, 193–194, 233, 246, 252, 265, 358

Jack's Narrows (Pennsylvania), 133
Jagrea (Indian), 343, 347–349, 357
Jamaica, 4
Jamestown (Virginia), 8
Jarvislawis (chief), 219
Jemmy (Indian), 131–133, 136
Jennings, Edmund, 146, 225
Jenoniowana (Indian), 45
Jersey (region or Indians), 35–36, 61
Jesuits (religious sect), 17, 243
Johnson, William, 191–192, 194, 202–203, 233–239, 241, 244, 247–250, 253, 255, 262–264, 274–275, 277, 289, 297–298, 320, 323, 344, 347, 363, 367–370
Jonathan (Indian), 313, 343, 368
Jonathan the Mohawk (Indian), 313
Joncaire (aka Jean Couer, aka Marquis de la Jonquiere), 233, 241, 248, 255–257
Jonnhaty (Indian), 118, 127–128

Jool (interpreter), 254
Joseph, John, 174
Jumonville, Joseph Coulon de, 295
Juniata County (Pennsylvania), 208
Juniata River, 27, 117, 120, 131, 133, 218, 221, 223, 284, 295
Juniata Valley (Pennsylvania, aka Choniata), 27, 222, 260, 280–281, 283

Kackshajim (chief, see also Caxhayan), 85
Kalm, Peter, 221
Kaloping (captive), 53
Karsnitz, John, 101
Keim, Nicholas, 306
Kentucky, 317
Kepner, Andrew, 311
King George's War (aka The Spanish War), 65, 102, 204, 207, 235
King William's War, 240
Kingston (New York), 236
Kinsey, John, 179, 182–183
Kintzer, Nicholas, 335
Kiskiminetas River (Pennsylvania), 209
Kittanning (Pennsylvania), 209, 362
Kittanning Path (Pennsylvania), 209
Kittatinny Mountain (Pennsylvania), 44
Klinger's Gap (Pennsylvania), 45, 57
Klingerstown (Pennsylvania), 57, 389
Knorr, Marie, 392
Knorr, Peter, 227
Kobel, Barbara, 334
Kobel, Frederick, 333–334
Kobel, Henry, 29
Kraft, Valentine, 90
Krebs, Henry, 311
Kresgeville (Pennsylvania), 351
Kuhn, Adam, 310
Kupingen (Germany), 1, 75
Kurtz, John Nicholas, 91–92, 305, 327
Kuster, Nicholas, 310
Kutztown (Pennsylvania), 357
Kutztown University (Pennsylvania), 393

Lake Champlain, 229
Lake Erie, 71, 196–197, 199–200, 207, 283
Lake Huron, 71
Lake Ontario, 126, 176–177, 233
Lancaster (Town or county in Pennsylvania), 16, 23, 25, 45, 99, 101, 103, 107, 109–110, 134–136, 139–141, 145–154, 157, 162, 164, 166, 170, 190, 197, 203–204, 215, 222–223, 231, 261–262, 308–312, 322, 333, 341, 367–369, 386, 392
Lancaster, Treaty of, 141, 146, 158, 161, 163, 165, 199, 206, 208, 211, 214, 230, 238, 242, 272, 282
Lappawinzo (Indian), 61
Laquis, William (Indian), 347
Lauer, Christopher, 100–101, 215

Lawrence, Thomas, 179, 301
Lebanon County (Pennsylvania), 16, 101, 352, 386
Lee (family), 388
Lee, Thomas, 79, 141, 144, 148, 154, 158–159, 163–164, 190–192, 207, 221, 230–232, 243, 246
Lefevre, John, 311
Lehigh County (Pennsylvania), 353, 386
Lehigh Gap (Pennsylvania), 83
Lehigh River, 218
Lehighton (Pennsylvania), 362
Leidig, John Philip, 311
Lenni Lenape (also see Delaware Nation), 59
Lesh (wagoner), 335
Lesher, John, 335
LeTort, James, 62, 170
Leutbecker, Casper, 77–78
Levan, Daniel, 361
Levan, Isaac, 310
Lewis' Rest (Pennsylvania), 87
Lewis and Clark Expedition, 388
Lexington & Concord (Massachusetts), 388
Lincoln, Abraham, 101
Lincoln Highway (Pennsylvania), 374
Line Mountain (Pennsylvania), 218
Livingston, Philip, 180
Livingston, Robert, 4–5, 7
Livingston Manor (New York), 4, 6–8, 74, 180, 193, 236
Loch, Peter, 101
Lock Haven (Pennsylvania), 30, 119, 296
Logan, Diana (Indian), 342
Logan, James, 19–20, 22, 29–35, 37, 40, 42–43, 60, 62, 63–66, 68, 71, 79, 104, 107, 113–115, 149, 157, 166–167, 184, 189, 194, 196, 198, 200–201, 204, 246, 275, 284, 330, 344, 381
Logan, William, 149, 157, 330, 344–346
Logstown (Pennsylvania), 199, 203, 209–213, 255–256, 258–260, 271
London (England), 2, 4, 7, 74, 231, 243, 261, 323
London Board of Trade (England), 276
London Society for the Propagation of the Gospel (England), 308–310, 383
Long's Church (also Christ Church), 90–97, 100, 327
Loskiel, George Henry, 230
Lost and Bewildered Creek (Pennsylvania, see also Diadachton), 48
Louis 14th (King of France), 1
Louis 15th (King of France), 1, 177, 228
Louse Creek (New York), 8
Lower Rhine valley (Germany), 1
Ludwig's Ruh (Pennsylvania), 87
Lutherans (religious order), 80–81, 88–91, 100, 180, 215, 301, 305, 311–314, 327, 338

Lycoming Creek (Pennsylvania), 173
Lycoming Valley (Pennsylvania), 48
Lycon, Andrew, 223
Lydius, Henry, 194, 274, 297–298
Lykens Valley (Pennsylvania), 45
Lyon (ship), 4

Mahantango Mountain (Pennsylvania), 45, 57, 86
Mahonoy (village in Pennsylvania, aka Mahoni), 22, 36, 125
Maidencreek (Pennsylvania), 302
Manada Gap (Pennsylvania), 350–351
Maqua (tribe, village, or language), 9, 14, 17–18, 21, 55, 182, 233–234, 246, 250, 254, 372
Marienborn (Pennsylvania), 87
Marshall, Edward, 62, 365
Marshe, Witham, 146–150, 158, 162–163
Maryland, 30, 32, 34, 37, 80, 112–114, 121–125, 128–129, 135, 138–142, 144–147, 149–150, 152–159, 162–163, 165, 191, 199, 218, 222, 224–225, 229, 238, 258, 260, 278, 322–324, 350, 367, 373, 387–388
Mason-Dixon Line, 225
Massachusetts, 178, 181–182, 184, 194, 205, 231, 252, 254, 321
Maugridge, William, 311
Maurer, John Philip, 89
Maxatawny Township (Pennsylvania), 161, 234, 357, 361
McGee, Thomas, 197
McKee, Thomas, 119–121, 370, 372
McLaughlin, James, 335
Meginness, J. F., 117
Miami (tribe, see also Twightwee), 232, 246, 255, 260, 265–267, 290–292
Miami River (Ohio), 229
Mill Creek (Pennsylvania), 332
Miller, Peter, 76, 78
Millersburg (Pennsylvania), 145
Milton (Pennsylvania), 45
Mingo (tribe), 280
Minisink (tribe or village), 59, 61, 64, 349–350, 357, 363, 367, 370–371, 373, 375
Minisink Forks (Pennsylvania), 83
Miranda, George, 62
Mississippi River, 71, 188, 198, 257
Mitchell, James, 24
Mohawk (tribe), 7–8, 10, 12, 17, 31, 129, 178, 182–183, 192–195, 212, 233–239, 241, 247, 249–250, 252, 254, 263, 274–275, 277, 281–282–284, 289, 292, 297–299, 312–313, 320, 336–337, 340, 359, 367–368, 372, 376
Mohawk River, 233, 239
Mohawk Trail (New York), 234
Mohawk Valley (New York), 234

Index

401

Mohawk's Castles (New York), 263–264, 277, 282, 367
Mohican, (tribe) 7, 51, 172, 212, 217, 342, 358
Monckatootha (chief, see also Scarroday), 285
Monongahela River, 267
Montgomery County (Pennsylvania), 89, 172, 386
Montour, Andrew, 87, 171, 173, 176–177, 203–204, 210–212, 224, 255, 257–258, 260–261, 264–266, 272, 285, 287, 290, 292–294, 328–329, 340, 342
Montour, Esther (aka Queen Esther), 150
Montour, Henry, 376, 378, 384
Montour, Lewis, 290
Montour, Madame, 27, 40, 46, 87, 116, 143, 150, 171, 203, 247–249, 260
Montour, Margaret (aka French Margaret), 150
Montreal, 21, 177, 179, 185, 190, 241, 261
Moravians (religious order), 79–81, 85–91, 100, 116–118, 171–172, 176, 214, 247, 274, 350–351, 358, 365, 375
Morris (captain), 321–322
Morris, Robert Hunter, 180, 285, 293, 299, 312–313, 320–322, 326–330, 332, 335–336, 340, 342, 344–349, 357–362
Moses (Indian), 343
Mount Airy (Pennsylvania), 309
Mount Johnson (New York), 233–235, 237–238, 263
Mount Penn (Pennsylvania), 301
Muhlenberg (family), 227
Muhlenberg, Elisabeth, 388
Muhlenberg, Eve, 388
Muhlenberg, Frederick, 388
Muhlenberg, Henry Ernst, 388
Muhlenberg, Henry Melchior, 67, 88, 90–92, 98, 100, 118, 250, 305, 310–311, 313–314, 388
Muhlenberg, Henry Melchior Jr., 388
Muhlenberg, Maria Salome "Sally", 388
Muhlenberg, Peter, 388
Muncy (tribe), 358, 373
Muncy Creek (Pennsylvania, see also Canusorago), 46, 173, 177, 296
Murray, Joseph, 182
Mushemeelin (Indian), 130–136, 160
Musser, John, 151
Mystics (religious sect), 77

Nanticoke (tribe), 113–114, 128, 145, 218, 329, 369, 373
Narskeekee (chief), 250–251, 254
Nathanial (Indian), 367
Nazareth (Pennsylvania), 234
Nescopeck (tribe), 18, 59, 280, 329, 336–337, 340–342

Neshellamy (chief), 131–132, 134–136
Neversink Mountain (Pennsylvania), 301
New Born (religious sect), 77
New England, 17, 178–179, 181–184, 192, 274–275, 281, 283–284, 297
New France, 21, 175, 229
New Mooners (religious sect), 77
New Hanover (Pennsylvania), 89, 100, 310–311
New Jersey, 23, 32, 79, 124, 180, 261, 293, 358, 365, 373, 376
New Spain, 178
New York, 4, 7–8, 12, 20, 22, 36, 42, 44, 52, 58, 63, 68, 99, 118, 124–125, 150, 153, 157–158, 161, 165, 171–172, 176, 178–181, 183–184, 189, 191, 194, 199, 207, 212, 229, 232–234, 237–238, 243, 245–253, 255, 261–265, 276–277, 280–281, 297, 299, 323, 340–341, 347–348, 367, 375, 387
New York City, 249–250, 278, 387
Newcastle (Indian), 338, 343, 345, 347–349, 357, 363
Newmanstown (Pennsylvania), 351
Newport (Pennsylvania), 133
Niagara (region in New York), 195, 260
Norland, Henry, 212
Norris, Isaac, 179–180, 182–183, 186, 266, 278, 281, 285
North Carolina, 8
Northampton County (Pennsylvania), 353, 364
Northumberland County (Pennsylvania), 45, 87, 383
Northumberland County Historical Society (Pennsylvania), 389
Nutimus (chief), 35–36, 61
Nyberg, Lawrence, 90

Oehl, John Jacob, 76
Ogle, Samuel, 30, 112–115, 121, 137, 199, 260
Ogilvie, William, 274
Ohio (region or Indians), 17, 19–22, 46, 179, 196–207, 224, 228–229, 233, 236, 241–242, 249, 255–261, 263–264, 266, 271–272, 279, 280, 283, 285, 290–291, 309, 323–324, 329, 341, 349, 367, 375, 380–381
Ohio Company, 221, 230–232, 234, 246, 265
Ohio River, 71, 106, 170, 209, 228–229, 255, 265, 267, 273, 276, 373
Old Belt (Indian, aka The Belt of Wampum), 335–337, 341–344
Old Britain (chief), 265
Oley (Pennsylvania), 77, 81, 97, 161, 335
Olstuago (village in Pennsylvania), 46–47

Onas, Brother (Indian name for the Penns), 21–23, 27, 32, 54, 63, 126–129, 142, 153, 157, 175, 179, 191, 214, 219, 229, 254, 267, 284, 294, 349

Oneida (tribe or village in New York), 16–17, 42, 48, 115–116, 118, 128–129, 168, 182, 192, 194, 204, 212, 216, 235, 237, 239–242, 254, 260, 264, 282, 285, 290, 292, 322, 375

Onondaga (tribe or town in New York), 17, 25, 29, 41–44, 48–49, 52–54, 56, 58–59, 62, 68–69, 75, 82, 85, 110, 114–116, 118, 121–122, 124, 126–129, 138–139, 147, 156–157, 165, 167–174, 179, 182, 190, 194–195, 198–199, 201, 203, 207, 212, 215, 224, 232–243, 246–247, 252, 259–264, 266, 276, 280–282, 286, 291, 298, 322, 330–331, 344, 373, 375

Onontiquoah (name for French King), 238

Onontijo (name for Governor of Canada), 21, 157, 167, 229, 235, 241, 330

Ontelaunee (Pennsylvania), 83

Oquaga (village in New York), 233

Osborne, Danvers, 277

Oscohu (Pennsylvania, see also Sugar Creek), 49–51

Oswego (tribe or village in New York), 167, 175–179, 181, 183, 187, 192, 196, 233, 263

Otatuaky (village in Pennsylvania), 323

Otkon (Evil Spirit), 48, 49

Otsiningo (village in New York), 52–54, 347

Ottawa (tribe), 329

Otterbein, Philip, 310

Otzinachson (see also Susquehanna River), 45, 117

Overbrook Senior High School, 392

Owego (village in New York) 49, 52

Owisgera (Indian), 44, 47, 50, 53, 56

Palatinate (Germany), 4, 181

Palatine Bridge (New York), 239

Palmer, Anthony, 194, 199, 202, 213

Parsons, William, 302, 304–305, 311, 328, 339, 353, 362, 364, 384

Parvin, Francis, 301–303, 306, 310

Patterson, John, 369

Patton, James, 121, 141, 258–259

Pawling, Henry, 310

Paxinosa (chief), 341, 347

Paxtang (Pennsylvania), 23, 45, 120, 130, 133–134, 195, 324

Paxton (Pennsylvania), 327, 351

Paxton Boys, 387

Pemberton, Israel, 346, 370

Penn, John (son of William Penn), 189, 194

Penn, John (grandson of William Penn), 278, 281, 285, 297, 301

Penn, Thomas, 21–23, 26, 30–32, 35, 38, 49, 54–55, 59, 61, 63, 65–66, 107, 116–117, 119, 121, 143, 173, 220, 252, 261, 301, 303–305, 308, 323, 384

Penn, William, 12, 28, 38, 64, 229, 281, 288, 301–302, 386

Penn's Creek (Pennsylvania), 22, 283, 295, 321, 326

Pennsbury Manor (Pennsylvania), 61

Pennsylvania, (and Pennsylvania Assembly), 11–12, 16, 18, 20, 22–25, 27–29, 34–35, 37, 42–43, 46, 55–57, 59–61, 64, 67–68, 81, 85, 87, 90, 99–101, 109, 114, 116–120, 122, 124, 126–127, 129–130, 135–136, 138, 141–145, 149, 151–152, 154, 156, 158, 160–162, 167–169, 171–172, 178–181, 183–186, 189–197, 199–200, 203, 205–207, 209, 212, 215–216, 220, 222, 224–226, 229–230–232, 234–235, 238, 240, 242–243, 245–246, 248–249, 252, 256–269, 272–275, 277–286, 288–289, 294–295, 297–298, 308, 320, 322–325, 328–329, 333–335, 340–341, 343–344, 346–350, 353–354, 357, 359, 361–362, 367–371, 374, 376, 379–380, 382, 386–389, 392, 394

Pennsylvania, Historical Society of, 104, 353

Pennsylvania, University of, 308

Pennsylvania German Society, 352

Perkiomen Creek (Pennsylvania), 219

Perry County (Pennsylvania), 133

Pesquetomen (chief), 36, 61

Petar, Andrew, 183

Peter's Mountain (Pennsylvania), 86–87

Peters, Abraham (chief), 254, 263, 297

Peters, Richard, 64, 66–68, 73, 79, 82, 88, 107–108, 113, 116–117, 121, 138, 140–141, 143–144, 158–159, 166–167, 169, 188, 191–192, 195–196, 198, 200–201, 203–205, 208, 217, 222, 224, 236, 242–243, 246, 258–260, 264, 266, 277–278, 281, 284–285, 294, 296–297, 299, 303–310, 312–313, 321, 334, 336, 339, 358, 360, 363, 368, 370–371, 377–384

Petty, John (Indian), 296, 342

Philadelphia (Pennsylvania), 16, 19–23, 25–26, 29–35, 37, 44, 63, 65–66, 68–69, 71, 82–83, 88, 102, 113, 118–119, 122, 124, 127, 135–136, 139–142, 144, 146, 149, 151, 160–161, 166, 170, 177, 180–181, 184, 189, 194, 196–203, 205, 207, 214–216, 218–219, 222, 231, 236, 240–241, 248–249–250, 255, 260–261, 264, 278, 294–295, 298, 303, 309, 312–313, 320–321, 326, 328, 331, 333–335, 338–344, 348, 350, 352–353, 359, 363–364, 366, 368, 372–374, 386–388, 392

Philadelphia Academy (Pennsylvania), 313, 343, 368, 383

Index

Philadelphia County (Pennsylvania), 307, 386
Philip (Indian), 313
Pickert, John, 239
Pickert, Nicholas, 239
Pilger Ruh (Pennsylvania), 86, 98, 125, 173, 389
Pine Creek (Pennsylvania), 145
Pine Grove (Pennsylvania), 45, 219, 275, 317, 389
Pittsburgh (Pennsylvania), 229, 259, 381
Plymouth (England), 8
Pompton (tribe), 374
Pontiac's War, 387
Port Clinton (Pennsylvania), 351
Post, Christian Frederick, 375, 378, 384
Potomac River, 42, 122, 140, 153, 242, 259, 322
Potts, John, 311
Pottstown (Pennsylvania), 219
Principio Iron Works (Maryland), 142, 144
Proud, Robert, 279
Providence (Pennsylvania), 310–311
Providence Plantations (Rhode Island), 252
Pumpshire (Indian), 370

Quagnant (chief), 10
Quakers (aka Friends), 33–34, 37, 43, 59, 63–65, 69, 99, 101–103, 105–108, 130, 181–183, 186, 229, 259–260, 265, 272, 279, 301, 344–347, 349, 353, 357, 359–360, 370–371, 386–387, 389
Queen Anne's War, 5, 180
Queensbury (New York), 5
Quidahickgunt (chief), 136

Raby, Christopher, 219
Rappahannock River, 232
Ray's Creek (Pennsylvania), 375
Read, Adam, 328
Read, James, 310, 325–326, 384
Reading (Pennsylvania, aka Widow Finney's Town), 215, 219, 227, 260, 301–310, 312, 314, 317–319, 322, 326, 331, 335, 352, 369, 380, 382–383
Reading Times, 392–393
Reed, Peter, 103
Reed's Church (see Rieth's Church)
Rehrersburg (Pennsylvania), 44
Reifsnyder, John, 311
Reynolds (Captain), 362
Richards, Matthias, 388
Rieger, John Bartholomaus, 311
Rieth's Church (Stouchsburg, Pennsylvania), 76–78, 81, 89–90, 93, 100, 180
Rigbie, Nathaniel, 150, 157
Rittenhouse, David, 225
Robesonia (Pennsylvania), 389
Rockingham County (Virginia), 118

Rosebloom, Robert, 252
Rotterdam (Holland), 2–3

Sa Ga Yeath Qua Pieth Tow (chief), 15
Sacramento (Pennsylvania), 389
Saghisdowa (Indian), 121–122, 124
Sahler, Adam, 310
St. Isaac Jogues, 393
St. Katherine Docks (London), 4
St. Lawrence River, 178, 207, 229
Sanders, Robert, 262
Saratoga (New York), 184, 192
Saristaquoah (chief), 240
Sassoonan (chief, *see also Allumpees*), 28, 61, 66
Sattelihu (aka Andrew Montour), 174
Sauer, Christopher, 88, 110, 130, 135, 149, 151, 161, 163, 216, 243, 295, 307, 310, 312–313
Scarroday (chief, *see also Monckatootha*), 204, 285, 290–291, 294, 322–323, 326, 328–330, 337, 340–348, 369
Schellsburg (Pennsylvania), 208
Schenectady (New York), 9
Schlatter, Michael, 309, 311–313, 319
Schlosser, John, 353
Schmauck, Theodore E., 76
Schmidt, Mathias, 101
Schoenbrunn (Ohio), 171
Schoharie (New York), 7–8, 10–12, 16, 52–53, 75, 99, 128, 181, 234–235, 237, 252, 263, 333, 372
Schoharie Creek (New York), 7–8
Scholla (article series), 392–394
Schrack, John, 219, 310
Schubert's Gap (Pennsylvania), 350
Schulze, Emmanuel, 388
Schulze, John Andrew, 388
Schuyler, Pieter, 240
Schuylkill County (Pennsylvania), 45, 101, 145, 219, 275, 383
Schuylkill River, 43, 72, 83, 301, 307, 338
Schuylkill Valley (Pennsylvania), 125
Schwenkfelders (religious sect), 79
Scull, John, 18
Second Mountain (Pennsylvania), 45, 275
Seely, James, 310, 335
Seely, Jonas, 325
Selinsgrove (Pennsylvania), 304, 317
Seneca (tribe), 17, 20, 22, 36, 42, 68–69, 113, 129, 175, 181–182, 195, 212–213, 216, 237, 241, 248, 252, 263, 286, 290–291, 293, 336, 341, 376
Seneca George (Indian), 343, 345, 384
Seth (chief), 237, 263
Seven Years' War (*see also French and Indian War*), 19, 235, 273
Seventh Day Baptists (religious sect), 77–78, 148

Seyfert, Anton, 86
Shamokin (Indian village now Sunbury, Pennsylvania), 16, 19–20, 28, 30–33, 35, 45, 53, 56, 68, 86–87, 114–118, 120–123, 125–126, 130, 133–135, 141, 144–145, 166, 169, 173–174, 191, 194–197, 199–202, 215, 223, 232, 273, 275–276, 280, 283, 295, 298, 304, 321, 323, 326, 328, 332, 336–337, 341–344, 346, 348, 352, 362, 387, 389
Shamokin Trail (Pennsylvania), 44, 219, 275, 351, 389
Shawanese Cabins (village in Pennsylvania), 208–212
Shawnee (tribe), 19, 21, 27–28, 30, 59–60, 62, 65–66, 86, 113–115, 119–121, 126, 170–171, 176, 178–179, 197, 212, 232, 245, 248, 255, 267, 276, 285, 288, 290, 292, 294, 297, 320, 323, 329, 336–337, 341–342, 371, 373, 375
Shebosch (aka John Joseph Bull), 171
Shenandoah Valley (Virginia), 42, 64, 116, 118, 121, 155–156, 166
Sherman's Creek (Pennsylvania), 145, 295, 326
Sherman's Valley (Pennsylvania), 221
Sherwood Forest (England), 4
Shikellamy (chief, see also Swatane), 16–18, 20, 22–26, 34–35, 37, 43, 45–46, 48–50, 53–55, 65–66, 87, 114–116, 118, 121–124, 126–127, 131, 133–134, 137, 144, 155–156, 158, 166–169, 171, 173–174, 176, 190, 195–197, 199–202, 214–215, 221, 224, 226, 240, 247, 296, 337, 340, 354, 387, 389, 391
Shikellamy, James (Indian), 342
Shikellamy, John (Indian), 134, 176, 202, 223, 273, 275, 281–282, 290, 297, 340–343
Shippen, Edward, 18, 166, 170, 310
Shippensburg (Pennsylvania), 224
Shirley, William, 194, 205, 321
Shirleysburg (Pennsylvania), 285
Silver Heels (Indian, aka Aroas), 336–338, 340–341, 343, 345
Silver Spring Township (Pennsylvania), 207
Six Nations (Iroquois Confederacy), 10, 17, 19, 20–22, 24–25, 27–31, 34–37, 42–43, 45–46, 60–66, 68–69, 71–72, 82–85, 110, 112–114, 116–119, 121–123, 126–127–130, 135, 138–139, 141, 144–145, 151–159, 161–162, 165–173, 175–176, 178–179, 181–185, 189, 191–192, 194–196, 198, 201–202, 204, 206–207, 209, 214–215, 217–218, 220, 224–225, 230–234, 236–240, 242–243, 246–257, 260–264, 266–267, 272, 274, 279–286, 288–292, 294–295, 297–298, 331, 336–337, 340, 343–348, 357–358, 360, 366–369, 373–374, 376
Skippack (Pennsylvania), 77, 79, 309–310
Smith (magistrate), 291
Smith, Horace, 104
Smith, James, 103, 108, 130–133, 135
Smith, William, 308–309, 311–312, 319, 383
Smithfield (Pennsylvania), 234
Snyder County (Pennsylvania), 22, 284, 295, 321, 383
Soterwanachty (chief), 241
South Carolina, 49, 167, 199, 204, 213, 238, 250–251, 253–254, 337
South Mountain (Pennsylvania), 16, 313
Spain, 65, 69, 102
Spangenberg, Augustus, 79, 171–174, 176, 186, 348, 384
Spener, Philipp, 75–76, 81, 88
Spring, Cornelius, 72
Spring Church (Pennsylvania), 209
Spyker, Benjamin, 327
Spyker, Peter, 330–332
Stamp Act, 388
Standing Stone (Pennsylvania), 208
Stenton (Pennsylvania), 29, 31–34, 36, 40, 44, 65, 68–69, 104, 167, 200
Stevens, Arent, 253–254
Stevenson, George, 328
Stevenson, James, 281, 283
Stichters (family), 306
Stobo, Robert, 286
Stockbridge Indians, 274
Stoever, John Casper, 76–78, 89–90
Stoke Poges (England), 220
Stouchsburg (Pennsylvania), 76, 90, 100
Stoy, William, 311
Stratford (Virginia), 141, 164, 190, 199, 230–231, 243
Strausstown (Pennsylvania), 351
Stroudsburg (Pennsylvania), 83
Stuart, Charles (King of England), 229
Stump, Christopher (Stoeffel), 44, 47, 49–51, 53, 55–56
Sugar Creek (Pennsylvania, see also Oscohu), 49–50
Sugar Indians (tribe), 49, 51
Sunbury (Pennsylvania), 16, 31, 45, 123, 215, 218, 226, 387, 389
Surrey (England), 3
Susanna (squaw), 262–263, 277
Susquehanna Company, 281, 297
Susquehanna Indians, 28–31, 34, 153, 322
Susquehanna River (see also Otzinachson), 11, 16, 22, 31, 37, 45, 50–51, 53, 59, 62, 66, 117, 119–120, 123, 126, 130, 133, 143, 153, 163, 196–197, 200–201, 206, 215–216, 218–219, 221–223, 233, 248, 273, 275–276, 281–283, 287–288, 295–297, 304, 308, 317, 324, 326–329, 331, 335–336, 338, 340–342, 348–351, 362, 368, 387

Index

Susquehannock (tribe), 59
Swaine, Francis, 388
Swatane (chief, see also Shikellamy), 17
Swatara Creek (Pennsylvania), 11, 109, 380
Swatara Gap (Pennsylvania), 327, 350
Sweden, 4
Syracuse (New York), 44, 280

Tanacharisson (chief), 285, 290
Tarachawagon (Indian name for Conrad Weiser), 72, 84, 127, 143, 145, 156, 159–160, 163, 171, 174–175, 188, 202, 215, 217, 234, 239, 242, 250, 252–253, 373
Tarentum (Pennsylvania), 209
Tawagaret (Indian), 46, 48–50, 52
Teedyuscung (chief), 343, 349, 356–367, 369–374, 376
Ten Mile Lick (Pennsylvania), 209
Tennant, Gilbert, 313
Thick Leg (Indian), 343
Thomas, George, 64, 66–67, 69, 80, 82, 86, 101–102, 110–112, 114–115, 119–124, 135–136, 138–139, 143, 146, 148, 150, 152, 157–158, 160–163, 166–168, 170, 175, 179, 182, 184, 189–190, 194, 221
Thomas, Philip, 146
Thomson, Charles, 371–372
Thurnstein (Pennsylvania), 86
Tigerhitonti (aka Bishop Spangenberg), 174
Tioga (Pennsylvania), 342, 349, 357
Tionesta (village in Pennsylvania), 210
Tocanuntie (chief, aka The Black Prince), 127–129, 147, 154–155, 175–176, 240
Tocarryhogan (Governor of Maryland), 157
Tolheo (village in Pennsylvania), 44, 327
Towamensing (Pennsylvania), 172
Trappe (Pennsylvania), 100, 250, 310
Trent, William, 279, 367
Trenton (New Jersey), 278
Trexler, John, 361
Trexler, Peter, 311
Tri-Colony Indian Treaty (see 1744, Treaty of)
Tribekko, John (pastor), 4, 6, 74
Tulpehocken (Creek or valley in Berks County, Pennsylvania), 11–12, 16–17, 22, 29–33, 35–38, 44, 56, 61, 67–68, 71–72, 76–78, 82–84, 86, 89–90, 99–101, 107, 109, 113–114, 120, 134, 143–145, 163, 166, 168, 173, 180, 188–189, 199–203, 215, 217, 219, 230, 234, 239, 243, 284, 301, 311–312, 323, 326, 327, 329–333, 341
Tulpehocken, Treaty of 1736, 36, 64, 66
Tulpehocken Confusion, 77–78, 90
Tulpehocken Guards, 327–328, 330–333, 340
Turtle Creek (Pennsylvania), 324
Tuscarawas County (Ohio), 171

Tuscarora (tribe or village), 17, 129, 212, 234, 240–241, 264, 282, 292, 376
Tuscarora Path, 208, 224
Tutelo (tribe), 224, 374
Twightwee (tribe, see also Miami), 203–204, 211–212, 246, 255, 265, 267, 291, 329
Twightwees Treaty, 204

Ullaloes (chief), 24–26
Unami (tribe), 374
Unhappy Jake (Indian), 116, 118, 166, 168

Venango (Pennsylvania), 271, 371
Versailles (France), 177–178
Virginia, 23–26, 28, 34, 37, 42–43, 46, 49, 55, 59, 62–63, 80, 101, 115, 118–124, 126–129, 135, 138–142, 144, 146, 148, 154–160, 162–163, 168, 171, 175–176, 189–193, 199, 207, 221, 228–232, 234, 236–239, 242–243, 246, 251, 258–261, 265–267, 271–273, 279–280, 285, 287, 292, 322–323, 387–388

Wabash River, 170, 203
Wagner, Tobias, 313
Walborn, Adam, 101
Walking Purchase, 61–62, 73, 365–366, 387
Wallace, Paul A. W., 60
Walton, Joseph, 60
Walworth (England), 3
War of the Austrian Succession, 64, 110, 171, 193, 204, 235, 257
Warraghiyagey (aka William Johnson), 233–235, 237, 241, 367
Warren, Peter, 233
Washington, George, 19, 271, 273, 279, 285, 287, 300, 329, 335, 384
Washington, Lawrence, 230
Webb, William, 64
Weiser, Anna Barbara, 239
Weiser, Anna Eve (née Feg), 12, 109, 249, 339, 380, 383
Weiser, Anna Madalina, 67, 76, 109
Weiser, Anna Magdalene (née Uebele), 2–3
Weiser, Anna Maria, 90, 100, 109, 388
Weiser, Benjamin, 36, 109
Weiser, Benjamin (younger), 109, 382–383
Weiser, Catherine, 3
Weiser, Elizabeth, 109
Weiser, Frederick, 109, 173, 326, 331, 352, 378
Weiser, Hannah, 109
Weiser, Hans Michael, 2
Weiser, Jabez, 109
Weiser, Jacob (grandfather), 99
Weiser, Jacob (son), 109
Weiser, Johann Conrad (father), 2, 5, 8–9, 11, 99
Weiser, Margaret, 109, 325, 338

Weiser, Maria Madalina, 109
Weiser, Peter, 109
Weiser, Peter (great-grandson), 388
Weiser, Philip, 109, 166, 173, 321, 331, 352, 378
Weiser, Samuel (aka Sammy), 109, 247, 249–250, 252, 254, 259, 262–263, 275, 278, 287, 321, 326, 363, 380–382, 384
Weissport (Pennsylvania), 350
Wernersville (Pennsylvania), 392–393
Wheeler, George, 352
White, Robert, 310
Whitemarsh (Pennsylvania), 218–219
Wiconisco Creek (Pennsylvania), 86
Wiconisco Township (Pennsylvania), 87
Wiegner, Christopher, 79, 172
Williamsburg (Virginia), 42, 55, 62–63, 118, 139, 170, 175–176, 190, 199, 230, 259
Wills Creek (Maryland), 322, 324
Winchester (Virginia), 261, 285, 323
Wissenberg, Catherin, 233
Wolcott, Roger, 181, 275
Womelsdorf (Pennsylvania), 16, 38, 317, 333, 361, 385, 389
Womelsdorf High School (Pennsylvania), 392

Woodbridge & Williams (agents), 284
Worrel, Peter, 146–147, 149
Wright, James, 310
Württemberg (Germany), 1–2, 20, 75, 80, 99
Württemberg Blue Dragoons, 2
Wyandot (tribe), 212, 232, 246, 255, 260, 267, 290, 326
Wyoming (region in Pennsylvania), 86, 115, 117, 172, 199, 216, 273–276, 280–284, 289, 297–298, 340–344, 347–348, 373–374
Wyoming Valley (Pennsylvania), 281
Wyomink (tribe), 59

Yohe, Adam, 370
York (Pennsylvania), 309, 311

Zeisberger, David, 171, 173–174, 186, 215
Zigera (Indian), 328, 337
Ziguras (Indian name for Conrad Weiser), 12, 16, 31–32, 47, 234
Zimmerman, Sebastian, 310
Zinzendorf, Count Nikolaus Ludwig von, 67, 81–87, 89, 97, 100, 113, 115–118, 127, 137, 172–174, 240

www.ingramcontent.com/pod-product-compliance
Lightning Source LLC
Chambersburg PA
CBHW021847230426
43671CB00006B/297